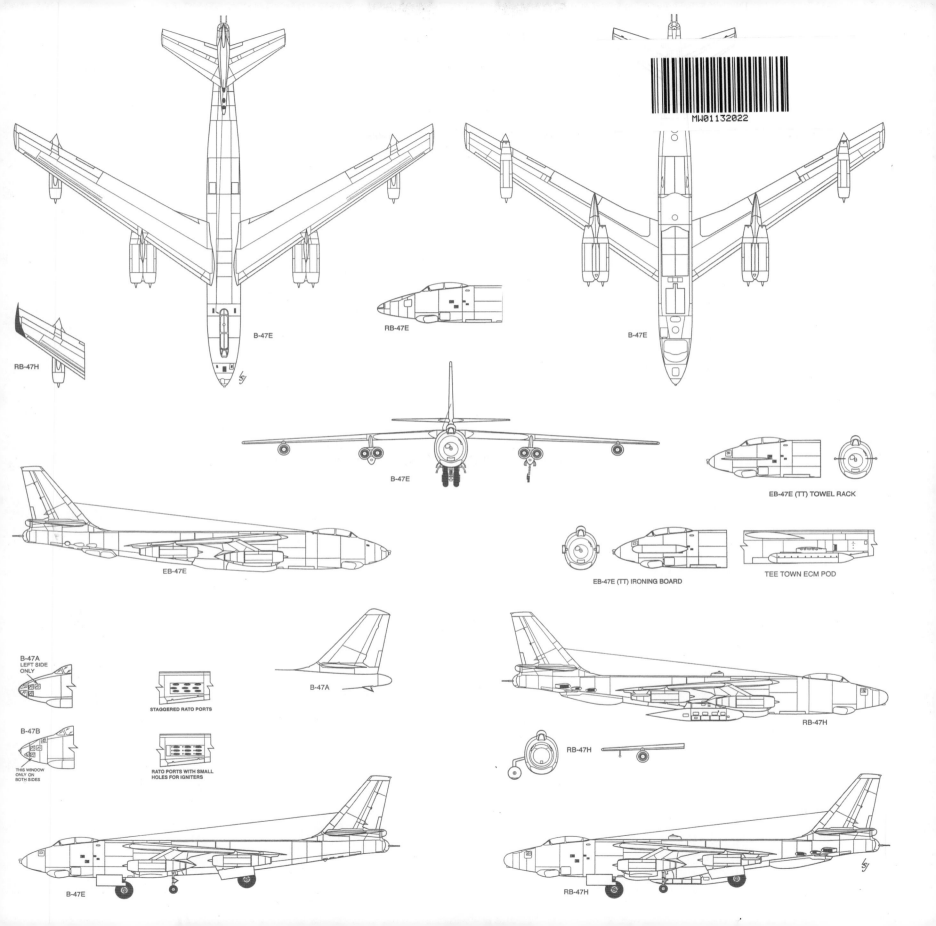

RB-47H

B-47E

RB-47E

B-47E

B-47E

EB-47E (TT) TOWEL RACK

EB-47E

EB-47E (TT) IRONING BOARD

TEE TOWN ECM POD

B-47A
LEFT SIDE
ONLY

STAGGERED RATO PORTS

B-47A

B-47B

THIS WINDOW
ONLY ON
BOTH SIDES

RATO PORTS WITH SMALL
HOLES FOR IGNITERS

RB-47H

RB-47H

B-47E

RB-47H

# Boeing's B-47
# *STRATOJET*

Alwyn T. Lloyd

**specialty**press
PUBLISHERS AND WHOLESALERS

ISBN-13  978-1-58007-071-3
ISBN-10  1-58007-071-X
Item #SP071

**specialty**press
PUBLISHERS AND WHOLESALERS

39966 Grand Avenue
North Branch, MN 55056 USA
(651) 277-1400 or (800) 895-4585
www.specialtypress.com


Printed in China


Distributed in the UK and Europe by:

Midland Publishing
4 Watling Drive
Hinckley LE10 3EY, England
Tel: 01455 233 747 Fax: 01455 233 737
www.midlandcountiessuperstore.com


Library of Congress Cataloging-in-Publication Data

Lloyd, Alwyn T.
   Boeing's B-47 Stratojet / by Alwyn T. Lloyd.
      p. cm.
   Includes bibliographical references and index.
   ISBN 1-58007-071-X (hardcover)
   1. B-47 bomber. I. Title.
   UG1242.B6L57 2004
   623.74'63--dc22

                                        2004013646

**Front Cover, Main:** *B-47E-110-BW, s/n 53-2271, was over 10 years old when photographed as indicated by the 0- in the tail number. The aircraft was painted with a full white anti-radiation finish. The last four digits of the tail number were applied to the nose later in the life of the Stratojet. The external fuel tanks were painted in aluminum paint. Note the chipping of the white paint on the aft fuselage. This was not uncommon due to aerodynamic erosion and runway FOD. (USAF)*

**Front Cover, Left Inset:** *This photograph (circa May 1956) shows a DB-47E with its refueling door open and four Radioplane GAM-67 Crossbow missiles mounted on the wing pylons. (Via Gordon S. Williams)*

**Front Cover, Right Inset:** *This giant thrashing machine was known as the XB-47D. The two inboard Wright YT49-W-1 turboprop engines drove four-bladed Curtiss 15-foot-diameter x 4-foot-chord propellers. (Boeing K76)*

**Back Cover:** *The final RATO system installed on the B-47s was the 32-rocket split rack or 33-bottle horsecollar rack. Here B-47E-90-BW, s/n 52-509, was equipped with the 33-bottle horsecollar rack. Note that the national insignia was still applied to this test aircraft. Camera blisters were located aft of the bottles and heat sensor tape was applied to the fuselage aft of the bottles. Tests showed that the heat from the rockets was absorbed by the national insignia, which caused skin buckling. (SAC Combat Crew Magazine)*

**Front Jacket Flap:** *B-47E-75-BW, s/n 51-7069, spectacularly marked with red and white stripes on the nose, waist, wingtips, and vertical tail. Note the theodolite pattern aft and to the right of the canopy. A camera was mounted in the fairing along the spine. (Via Gordon S. Williams)*

**Front Endsheet:** *On the left are four preliminary designs that led up to the B-47, while the right shows a three-view of the B-47 as built. (Left: Boeing 112505; Right Lloyd S. Jones)*

**Back Endsheet:** *These Stratojets were on the Lockheed-Marietta modification line. The raceway doors on the fuselage spines were open for control system access. Waist cavities (formerly used for the 18-bottle RATO system) were open for work on the ECM equipment that was installed there. The vortex generator guards may be seen on the aircraft in the foreground. B-47E-130-BW, s/n 53-4225, was equipped with a Phase III ECM wingtip. (Lockheed-Marietta RF-1757-4)*

**Title Page:** *The AFFTC also used this B-47B-25-BW (51-2047) for various tests. Note the early AFFTC logo on the forward fuselage. (AFFTC History Office via Tony Landis)*

# TABLE OF CONTENTS

# Brigadier General Guy M. Townsend (USAF, Ret.)

# *FOREWORD*

The beginning of the jet age was probably the largest transition that the aircraft industry has ever experienced. It was revolutionary, quite painful at times, but ultimately, most rewarding. The B-47 was the first heavy aircraft in the jet age that showed promise to replace piston engine aircraft.

With the B-29s we seldom calculated takeoff performance. We took an aircraft designed for a 120,000-pound maximum gross weight and loaded it to 140,000 pounds for the long combat missions. We prayed a lot of aircraft into the air. It was not until the advent of the B-47 that we began calculating takeoff performance. To make it easier for pilots I campaigned for the 1,000-foot markers along the runway that were eventually added for the B-52 program.

Prior to flying the B-47, I flew the Consolidated XB-46 and was very familiar with the North American B-45 that had been put into production from the drawing board. As soon as I flew the B-47, I knew the B-45 we had bought was the wrong aircraft. The B-47 was superior to the rest of the B-4x series. Design of the B-47B began in September 1948, and the first flight occurred in February 1951. Bugs were worked out during Operation SKY TRY and with the aid of the SAC Operational Engineering Squadron stationed at MacDill AFB, Florida. Production was ramped up and accommodated the changes found to be necessary during the evaluation programs in an orderly manner.

Immediately after the B-47 production decision was made in 1949, I was proud to have been part of a unique briefing team that went to SAC Headquarters and the three numbered SAC Air Forces to help usher the command into the jet age.

While the B-47A had a combat radius of 1,350 nautical miles, the B-47B was improved to 1,750 nautical miles; later B-47Es had a combat radius of 2,050 nautical miles. The addition of external fuel tanks provided this range extension. However, it was aerial refueling that increased the endurance, limited only by engine oil and crew capability. Despite the fact that the early B-47s were deficient in range, General Curtis LeMay wanted these aircraft quickly to train his personnel and build a formidable deterrent bomber force.

The early GE J47 engine had a service life commensurate with that of contemporary jet engines, although it only produced 7,200 pounds of static thrust. With the advent of the Pratt & Whitney J57 engine in 1955 came a major increase in thrust to 10,000 pounds. An accelerated service test for the J57 engine was conducted using two B-47Bs. With one J57 engine installed in each outboard position (while retaining the dual J47 inboard pods), the aircraft would outperform a Stratojet equipped with six J47s. The J57 also demonstrated a remarkable service life. The question arose as to why the J57 was not incorporated in B-47 production and retrofitted into the fleet. Bob Kuhn of the B-47 Program Office at Wright-Patterson AFB, Ohio, went to SAC Headquarters to propose a new B-47 with J57 engines. As the presentation started, General LeMay immediately stopped him, retorting: "How deep do you have to bury something before you guys at Wright Field won't dig it up and try to breathe life into it?" The reason was that it was too late in the B-47 program, and it would have jeopardized the B-52 program. The last B-47s were delivered in early 1956, only a year later.

The large numbers of B-47s produced presented a viable deterrent force during the early days of the Cold War. These large numbers also kept the Arsenal of Democracy working through brief periods before later, more capable aircraft, namely the B-52, came into the inventory.

The podded engines and swept wing developed for the B-47 have proven to be extremely successful. The revolutionary B-47 paved the way for future large jet aircraft with its swept wing and podded engines. Most large transport aircraft today have this configuration.

Mr. Lloyd has done an excellent job of telling the whole B-47 story.

*Guy M. Townsend*
*Brigadier General (USAF, Ret.)*

*When he came to the B-47 program, Major Guy M. Townsend had flown 450 combat hours in B-17s and B-29s in the Pacific Theater during World War II. Subsequently, he amassed over 8,000 hours of flying time, with 5,000 hours being in test flying. Townsend was the first military pilot to fly the B-50 Superfortress, B-47 Stratojet, and B-52 Stratofortress. On 1 October 1970 he retired as a brigadier general and came to Boeing in Seattle, where he worked in commercial derivative aircraft for the Defense and Space Group until his retirement in 1987.*

*The sleek fuselage and high aspect ratio wings of the Convair XB-46 are readily apparent in this in-flight shot of the aircraft over the Southern California mountains. Four 3,820-lbf Allison J35A-C3 engines installed in pairs powered the aircraft. This is the first (45-59582) of three prototypes built. Major Guy Townsend flew the XB-46 prior to being introduced to the Stratojet. (Convair)*

*Martin's six-engined XB-48 was a stubby straight-winged aircraft. This is the first (45-59585) of two prototypes. Propulsion was by six 3,820-lbf General Electric J35-GE-B1 engines mounted in a pair of nacelles with separate inlets. Martin adapted their Middle River Stump Jumper XB-26H Marauder bicycle landing gear configuration for the aircraft. (Martin Aircraft)*

Progress continued quickly, and General Electric developed an improved 5,200-lbf TG-190 that was first flight-tested in May 1948. The resulting J47 was produced in at least 17 different series and powered the F-86, XF-91, B-36, B-45, B-47, and XB-51. In February 1949 General Electric reopened a plant in Evendale, near Cincinnati, for J47 production and in just 20 months Evendale grew from 1,200 to 12,000 employees; finally, General Electric was building one of its own engines. Demand for the engine soared during the Korean War and production peaked at 975 engines per month during 1953-54. More than 35,000 J47s were built before production ended in 1956. The J47 was finally retired when the last Boeing KC-97J was dropped from the Air National Guard inventory in 1978, spanning 30 years of service.

### NINE USAAF BOMBERS OF 1945

| Aircraft | Manufacturer | Propulsion | First Flight | Status |
|---|---|---|---|---|
| XB-43 | Douglas | Jet | 17 May 1946 | Test |
| XB-35 Flying Wing | Northrop | Piston | 25 June 1946 | Test |
| B-36 | Convair | Piston | 8 August 1946 | Production |
| B-45 Tornado | North American | Jet | 17 March 1947 | Production |
| XB-46 | Convair | Jet | 1 April 1947 | Test |
| XB-48 | Martin | Jet | 22 June 1947 | Test |
| B-50 Superfortress | Boeing | Piston | 25 June 1947 | Production |
| B-49 Flying Wing | Northrop | Jet | 21 October 1947 | Production Cancelled |
| B-47 Stratojet | Boeing | Jet | 17 December 1947 | Production |

*Northrop produced two XB-35 and one YB-35 Flying Wings. The aircraft were powered by two inboard Pratt & Whitney R-4360-21 and two outboard R-4360-17 Wasp Major engines, each driving contra-rotating propellers, with a top speed of 391 mph. While a total of ten B-35s were ordered, the program was terminated because of problems encountered with the propeller reduction gear and propeller governor systems. This did not spell the end of Jack Northrop's efforts, and development of the flying wing concept was furthered with the jet-powered B-49s. (USAF via L. S. Jones)*

## FIRST FOUR AMERICAN JET BOMBER DESIGNS

| Manufacturer | Model | Number Built | Span (feet) | Length (feet) | MGTOW (pounds) | Ceiling (feet) | Cruise/Max. (knots) | Engines (number) | Thrust (lbf each) | Radius (nm) | Load (pounds) |
|---|---|---|---|---|---|---|---|---|---|---|---|
| North American | B-45 | 149 | 89.0 | 75.3 | 91,775 | 46,400 | 408/496 | J35-A-11 (4) | 3,500 | 463 | 22,000 |
| | | | | | | | or | J47-GE-7/9 (2) | 5,200 | | |
| | | | | | | | and | J47-GE-13/15 (2) | 5,200 | | |
| Convair | XB-46 | 1 | 113.0 | 105.8 | 94,400 | 38,100 | 381/425 | J35-A-C3 (4) | 3,820 | 603 | 22,000 |
| Boeing | B-47 | 2,049 | 116.0 | 106.8 | 162,500 | 38,100 | 502/462 | J47-GE-7 (6) | 3,750 | 1,175 | 22,000 |
| Martin | XB-48 | 2 | 108.3 | 85.8 | 102,600 | 39,400 | 360/454 | J35-GE-B1 (6) | 3,820 | 433 | 22,000 |

The competitors for the 17 November 1944 specification had the characteristics shown in this table. The B-47 had the highest maximum gross takeoff weight (MGTOW) and unrefueled combat radius. In addition, the Stratojet had the largest bomb bay and greatest growth potential.

The Northrop B-49 Flying Wing was ordered into series production (by Convair), but various technical and political issues resulted in the program being terminated before any aircraft found their way into SAC's inventory. Power was provided by eight General Electric J35-GE-B1 engines buried in the wing. (Via Peter M. Bowers)

This is the first (46-685) of two XB-51s built by Martin. The aircraft used bicycle landing gear, with the outrigger gear mounted in the wingtips. The XB-51 was powered by three 5,200-lbf General Electric J47-GE-13 engines, with two nestled in pods mounted low on the fuselage just forward of the wings, and the third buried in the aft fuselage. Note the Air Force Flight Test Center insignia on the forward fuselage. This aircraft first flew on 28 October 1949, just over one year and ten months after the XB-47. (L. S. Jones)

## THE FIRST AMERICAN JET BOMBERS

By late 1945 the United States Army Air Forces began to merge jet engine technology into its bomber designs. Hedging its bets, the USAAF pursued development of nine new bomber designs, three of which were powered by reciprocating engines and the other six by turbojets. While two of the piston-powered aircraft eventually went into production, only two of the six jet bombers were developed beyond the test stage. Three of these bombers were derivative aircraft: the Douglas XB-43 was a jet-powered version of the XB-42 Mixmaster that had first flown on 6 May 1944; the Boeing B-50 was an upgraded version of the B-29 Superfortress; and the Northrop YB-49 was a jet-powered version of the XB-35 Flying Wing. The 19 months between May 1946 and December 1947 witnessed the first flights of the nine new bombers, placing a heavy workload on both the aircraft industry and the Air Materiel Command (AMC) Bomber Division.

Not directly a part of the nine experimental bombers was the Martin XA-45. Martin was awarded a contract on 1 April 1946 for an attack aircraft with a top speed of 505-mph, a cruise speed of 325-mph, and an 800-mile combat radius. In the spring of 1946 the A-for-attack designation was abolished and the design was redesignated XB-51. Three J47 turbojets provided power, one in the tail fed by a top air inlet and two in nacelles underneath the forward fuselage. The wings were swept back 35 degrees, had 6 degrees negative dihedral, and used variable incidence to enhance performance for

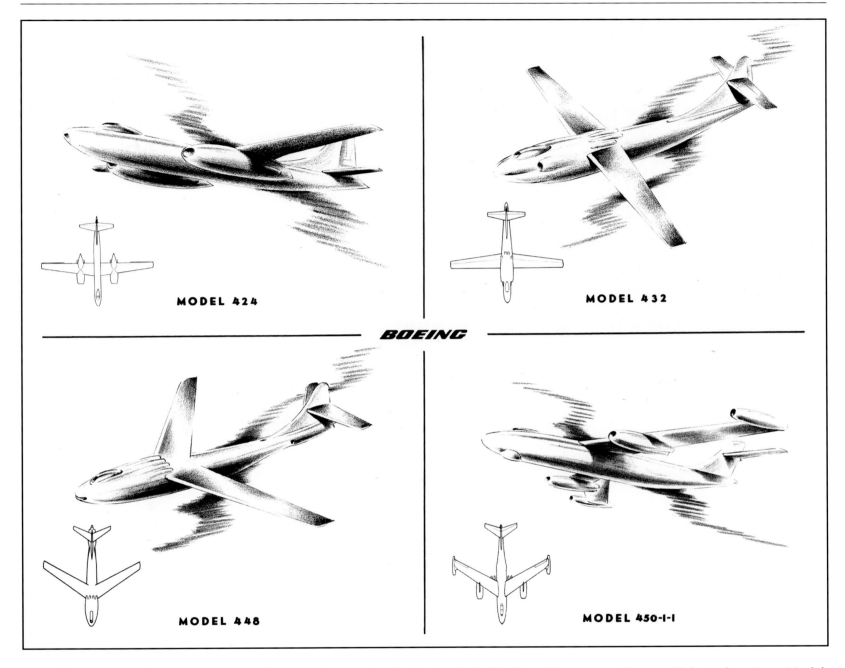

MODEL 424

MODEL 432

*BOEING*

MODEL 448

MODEL 450-1-1

*These illustrations depict four of the preliminary designs that led up to the B-47. Most bizarre were those with buried engines, Models 432 and 448. (Boeing 112505)*

takeoff and landing. The wings were fairly advanced for the day, having spoilers instead of ailerons and sporting leading-edge slats and full-span flaps. The bicycle-style landing gear consisted of a set of tandem dual main wheels that retracted into the fuselage and a set of small outrigger wheels that retracted into the wingtips. An unusual feature was the use of a rotary bomb bay door on which the

bombs were mounted. Two aircraft were ordered under a $9.5 million contract issued on 23 May 1946, and the first prototype made its maiden flight on 28 October 1949. Significant test data was gained on bicycle landing gear and Martin's high-speed bomb release system, but ultimately both prototypes were lost in crashes. The program was cancelled in November 1951.

*Shown are three of the wind tunnel models used in the development of the B-47. To the rear is the Model 424 with paired engines in long nacelles, similar to those on the Convair XB-46, along with a tail reminiscent of the B-29. (Boeing P11997)*

**KEY BOEING PERSONNEL**

| | |
|---|---|
| William M. Allen | Boeing President |
| Wellwood E. Beall | Senior Vice President |
| Edward C. Wells | Vice President, Engineering |
| John O. Yeasting | Vice President, Comptroller |
| J. Earl Schaefer | Vice President, WIBAC |
| C. B. Gracey | Vice President, Manufacturing WIBAC |
| J. Bruce Connelly | Director of Contract Administration |
| George C. Martin | B-47 Chief Engineer |
| Noah D. Showalter | Assistant Chief Engineer |
| George S. Schairer | Chief Aerodynamicist |
| H. W. "Bob" Withington | Aerodynamicist |
| William H. Cook | Aerodynamicist |
| Victor Ganzer | Aerodynamicist |
| Robert "Bob" Jewett | Product Development Chief |
| Charles "Chuck" Davies | Product Development |
| Edward Pfafman | Mechanical Engineering |
| Howard "Bud" Hurst | Structures Engineering |
| E. Z. Gray | Stress Engineering |
| William "Bill" Ramsden | Liaison Engineering |
| Noah D. Showalter | Boeing Chief Test Pilot |
| Robert M. Robbins | XB-47 Chief Test Pilot |
| Scott Osler | XB-47 Test Pilot |

## SAC DESIGN COMPETITION

In June 1943 an informal USAAF request led several aircraft manufacturers to begin studies of jet-powered aircraft for fast photographic reconnaissance or medium bombing missions. Considering that a truly satisfactory jet fighter had yet to fly, it was surprising when the USAAF issued requirements for a jet bomber for use by the Strategic Air Command (SAC) on 17 November 1944. The new aircraft was to have a top speed of 500-mph, an operating altitude of

**KEY AIR FORCE PERSONNEL**

| | |
|---|---|
| Lieutenant General Curtis E. LeMay | Commander, Strategic Air Command |
| Major General Kenneth B. Wolfe | Commander, Air Materiel Command |
| Colonel Albert Boyd | AMC Chief of Flight Test |
| Lieutenant Colonel Henry E. Warden | Chief of Bomber Development, Air Materiel Command |
| Major Guy M. Townsend | Flight Test Pilot, Bomber Development, Air Materiel Command |

35,000 to 40,000 feet, and a range of 2,500 to 3,500 miles. A maximum bomb load of sixteen 500-pound bombs needed to be carried along with a defensive armament consisting of 0.50-caliber machine guns in either a nose or tail turret. The aircraft had to be capable of clearing a 50-foot obstacle after taking off from a 5,000- to 6,500-foot runway.

Four manufacturers – Boeing, Convair, Martin, and North American – took up the challenge. While all four aircraft ultimately flew, only two went into production. The four-engine B-45 Tornado would serve as a light bomber and reconnaissance aircraft with the Tactical Air Command (TAC) for almost a decade. It was the B-47 Stratojet, however, that won the competition as SAC's first medium-range strategic bomber, but not without some major hurdles.

## SETTING THE STAGE

During the 1930s, suitable large wind tunnels were relatively few and were owned and operated by either the National Advisory Committee on Aeronautics (NACA) or a select group of universities. Therefore, aircraft manufacturers had to schedule tests at these facilities. The University of Washington had a low-speed tunnel, with a 20-foot test section, and Lockheed built a similar facility for its use in Southern California. Boeing considered making their own copy of the tunnel, but Dr. Theodore von Karman from the California Institute of Technology (Caltech) advised famed Boeing test pilot and engineer

A Boeing wind tunnel technician was attaching the left inboard strut and nacelle package on this 1/20-scale B-47 model. (Boeing P7555)

A Boeing engineer was checking the landing gear on this wind tunnel model. The photo dates from 25 February 1952. (Boeing P12007)

Edmund T. "Eddie" Allen that Boeing should build a high-speed tunnel instead. Allen took his request to the company and, after appropriate deliberations, Boeing decided to spend approximately $750,000 to design and build the new facility.

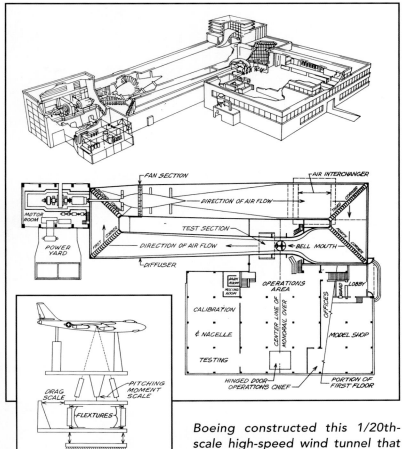

Boeing constructed this 1/20th-scale high-speed wind tunnel that was powered by a 150-hp electric motor attached to a single General Electric 14,000-cfm centrifugal blower. A 20-foot settling duct was located ahead of the transition duct. A bell mouth and an 8 x 12-foot test section followed this. (Boeing)

A team of Boeing engineers designed the tunnel and provided detailed drawings to the Austin Company to build the facility on the western edge of Boeing Field in Seattle. While many tunnels were circular in cross-section, Boeing opted for a 12-foot-wide, 8-foot-high throat with a flat floor that permitted easier access to the model being tested. The facility had a maximum velocity of approximately 0.95 Mach. Completed in the spring of 1944; it became the first privately owned high-speed wind tunnel in the United States.

By the time the wind tunnel was completed, the slowdown in war requirements saw the facility sit virtually idle. Nevertheless, the Army Air Forces in general, and the Air Materiel Command (AMC) in particular, had a high degree of interest in its capabilities. The Army Air Forces provided limited funds to Boeing under what is known as Independent Research and Development or IR&D. These funds are proportional to the amount of business the company is doing with the government – in this case it was considerable. Timing is everything.

Tufts were applied to the upper surface of the right wing on this 1/20th-scale B-47 wind tunnel model. These tufts permitted engineers to observe the airflow over the wing under varying simulated flight conditions. With the tufts turning forward, the wing was approaching the stall. (Boeing P12008)

This display model of the Model 450 bore a strong resemblance to the final B-47 design, although the outboard engines are mounted on the wingtips. (Boeing 94785B)

Von Karman would play another role in the future B-47 when, during late 1944, he was approached by General Henry H. "Hap" Arnold to assemble a team of experts to go to Germany after the surrender and gather vital information on aerodynamics, armament, rocketry, nuclear weapons, and electronics. It was through this group of experts that the USAAF, American universities, and aircraft manufacturers were infused with a plethora of data regarding the technological achievements of the Third Reich.

## Developing the B-47

The early concepts for a post-World War II bomber were usually straight-wing designs. The initial Boeing study was the Model 424, essentially a scaled-down B-29 with four jet engines paired in two nacelles mounted under the wing. However, wind tunnel testing proved this engine arrangement unsatisfactory. In December 1944, Boeing engineers went back to the drawing board and came up with the Model 432 that placed all four engines inside the fuselage in an attempt to improve the efficiency of the wing. The engines were located over the main fuel tank and were fed by bulbous air intakes located beside the cockpit. The engine exhaust was on top of the rear fuselage. The aircraft still resembled a B-29, but with a much thinner wing.

The USAAF was sufficiently impressed to award Boeing a $14,669,459.34 Phase I contract covering preliminary engineering, wind tunnel tests, and structural tests. The contract also covered the construction of a mock-up, three experimental aircraft, a static test article, and spares. At the same time, contracts were awarded for the North American XB-45, Convair XB-46, and Martin XB-48.

Prior to Boeing submitting their proposal for Phase I, the contract award was reduced to $1,319,968 per contract W33-038-ac-8429. Approved on 1 February 1945, this contract covered development of the Boeing Model 432 that would carry the Army Air Forces designation of XB-47.

Despite the apparent success, Boeing was having a hard time designing a jet bomber with truly satisfactory performance. Fortunately, Boeing's George Schairer was part of the American team that went into Germany to study their technology and his findings were reported in a letter dated 10 May 1945. The original letter apparently no longer exists; only a copy is in the Boeing Historical Archives. Schairer reported that the Germans had excellent data on wings with a 29-degree sweep on the leading edge and research had shown that the normal shock wave was delayed proportionate to the cosign of the sweep angle. Delaying the shock wave allowed higher airspeeds without causing the airflow to separate on top of the wing, a phenomenon that caused a loss of lift (i.e., inducing an aerodynamic stall). This was the first breakthrough to designing a high-speed bomber.

Based on this new data, the straight-wing design was quickly discarded for a new concept with a swept wing and four engines nested in the top of the fuselage. This configuration was called the Model 448, while retaining the XB-47 designation. Boeing proposed a contract amendment to include construction of a full-scale mock-up, preliminary design studies, wind tunnel tests, and structural tests of both models at no change to the contracted price. Boeing aerodynamicist Vic Ganzer calculated that a 35-degree sweep (at quarter chord) would allow even higher speeds using the more powerful jet engines then under development. Both Ed Wells and Bob Jewett traveled to

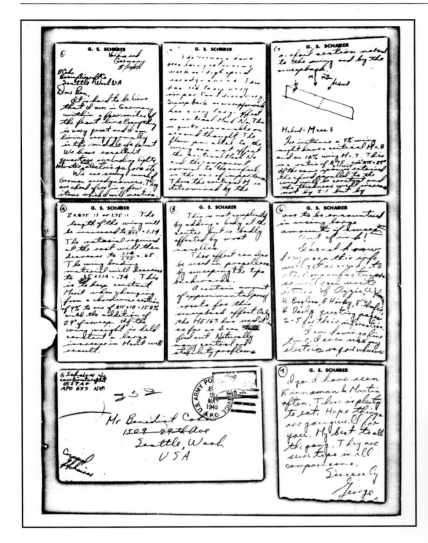

*George Schairer's letter describing German technology.*

ance was achieved. An exception was made when it was found that the stalling characteristics of a swept wing led to severe rolling and pitching that could prove dangerous. This problem appeared so serious that a concentrated wind tunnel program was authorized to find the reason and a cure.

At first, the model experienced severe pitch-up early in the stall. Initially, this was attributed to the wingtips stalling because they were behind the aircraft's center of gravity. Additional investigation, however, surmised that the horizontal tail was being caught in the turbulent wake behind the wing. Tests were conducted with the horizontal tail placed at varying locations up the vertical stabilizer without any significant improvement. By inserting a pole with a string attached to it into the wind tunnel, a probe could be moved aft to check the airflow around the wing. It was quickly discovered that a wake emanating from the wing's inboard leading edge filled a considerable vertical envelope behind the wing. To solve this problem, engineers fell back on knowledge gleaned from biplanes, and the leading edge of the wing was drooped below the wing chord plane. This simple fix cured most of the low-speed pitch-up problem. The residual pitch-up condition was subsequently rectified when the podded engines were introduced.

Confident that they had solved the mysteries of the swept wing, Boeing presented the revised design to the AMC. This design still incorporated four jet engines mounted in the top of the fuselage, and

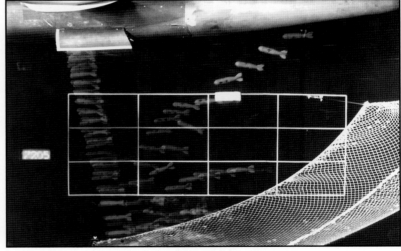

*This cluster of dummy bombs was salvoed from a model of a B-47 during wind tunnel drop tests conducted at the University of Washington laboratory. To obtain this multiple exposure picture and similar ones of drop tests with bombs, missiles, and jettisonable fuel tanks, Boeing used a specially modified 4x5 Speed Graphic camera developed by company personnel. Bomb images to the right of the drop line are bombs that struck the net and bounced up again. The white grid painted on the opposite wall assisted in spotting the tumble and drift of the bombs, while markings on the bombs themselves indicated the rotation and other factors during the fall. (Boeing WT-194592)*

the AMC Project Office at Wright-Patterson AFB, Ohio, to present their case. Members of the AMC Laboratories scoffed at the idea of a 35-degree sweep because there was no evidence substantiating the idea other than some preliminary wind-tunnel data gathered by the Germans on several advanced concepts that had not reached the prototype stage when the war ended. Nevertheless, during a subsequent trip Wells was able to convince AMC that the 35-degree wing sweep would result in a more efficient wing, allowing higher speeds and longer ranges for the new bomber.

The first tests conducted in the Boeing high-speed wind tunnel confirmed the effectiveness of the 35-degree sweep angle, but – not unexpectedly – also uncovered various problems. No attempt was taken to solve each major problem as it arose since this would have required a great deal of time. As it was, some areas of the design were changed two to five times until an acceptable level of perform-it met with disapproval from the AMC Project Office. Much of this disdain was based on the increased drag penalty caused by the large frontal area required to accommodate the engines and the inherent maintenance difficulties with having the engines located inside the fuselage. In addition, tests conducted on a P-80 with simulated 0.50-caliber holes in the engine resulted in blowtorch-like flames – a definite hazard for fuselage-mounted engines. The easiest solution appeared to be to move the engines out onto the wings, as had been done with the earlier piston-engine bombers. Ed Wells had witnessed the ballistic tests at the Armament Laboratory and made the first sketches of engine pods suspended under the wings during his flight home to Seattle. Each pod would contain two engines in a side-by-side arrangement.

Tests in the Boeing wind tunnel revealed that if podded engines were suspended so that the exhaust gases did not impinge on the extended flaps and the engine exhaust was placed just ahead of the wing's trailing edge, there were no unfavorable penalties. These tests showed that podded engines also reduced the potential for the wingtip to stall, eliminating the last of that problem. In addition, the forward-cantilevered engine pods reduced center of gravity concerns and diminished the potential for flutter with the extremely thin wing. Podded engines also reduced the fire hazard to the aircraft and improved maintenance access. Locating the inboard pods at one-third the span resulted in a weight-efficient installation, and the engineers were able to design nacelles that had an extremely low drag coefficient.

However, the aircraft continued to get larger and heavier, and it was soon determined that four engines would not provide sufficient power; two more engines would be required. It was decided to add a single engine near each wingtip, increasing available thrust by 50 percent and actually improving wing performance slightly without an appreciable increase in total drag. This resulted in the Model 450-1 and the USAAF approved the design in October 1945.

The extremely thin wing did present some problems, in particular, finding a place for the landing gear. To solve this, Boeing opted for a bicycle-style main landing gear located forward and aft of the bomb bay. This solution had been prototyped by Martin on a modified B-26 Marauder and had proven satisfactory. Small outrigger gears were placed under the inboard engine nacelles to balance the aircraft.

*This full-size plywood mock-up was employed by Boeing to ensure the location and fit of all components and wiring for the B-47. A technician, in white coveralls, was working in the pilot's station while an engineer, in the suit, was observing the copilot's station. (Boeing P6425)*

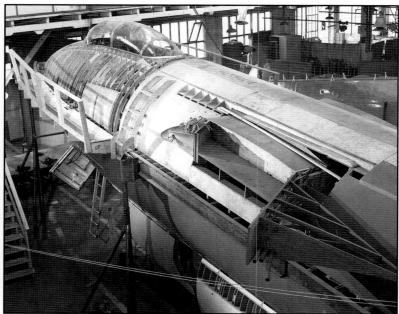

*This view of the B-47 mock-up reveals the wing root area with its wire bundles, fuel lines, and control cables and pulleys. A canopy has been installed. The entryway hatch and crew ladder may be seen to the lower right. (Boeing P7603)*

On 9 November 1945 Boeing proposed the construction of two stripped-down Model 450s with provisions for installation of future tactical equipment. Within a month, Technical Instruction 2247 authorized a fixed-price contract not to exceed $9,357,800, including the amount already allocated for Phase I, for the two aircraft. After reviewing the contractor's proposal for a new price of $9,441,407, the Price Control Branch at AMC concluded that the cost of $95 per airframe pound was fair and equitable since it was lower than the corresponding costs for the XB-45 and XB-48 aircraft.

*This right side view of the B-47 mock-up reveals the blown plexiglass nose, navigator's escape hatch for the upward ejection seat system, and the RATO installation. The pair of horizontal stabilizers may be seen in the foreground. The upper surfaces are facing each other because the stabilizers have the airfoil section on the bottom for negative lift to hold the aircraft's nose up in flight. (Boeing P7602)*

## MOCK-UP INSPECTION

Aircraft designers use mock-ups to evaluate the major structural components, joints, installation of multiple systems components, hydraulic tubing, and wire runs. The basic structure for a Class III mock-up is constructed of plywood and the systems components may either be the actual part or a wooden shape. The mock-up was also used to ensure the components were placed in operationally desirable locations, and that maintenance access was possible. Crew ergonomics were also evaluated in the mock-up.

The mock-up of the XB-47 was inspected during April 1946. Although generally well received, the inspection committee made suggested changes to the nose compartment, pilot and copilot seating, and landing gear arrangement. The Chief of the USAAF Requirements Division cautioned Boeing that any changes should not compromise the high-speed capabilities of the aircraft.

Developing the suggested changes for the landing gear, control surfaces, and engine installations presented major technological challenges for the Boeing engineers. In some cases new components had to be designed, or their mounting provisions had to be changed to meet AMC requirements. In addition, Boeing had made a decision not to authorize overtime pay, and the workforce was not enamored of working additional hours at no additional pay. All factors considered, the B-47 program had already slipped six months.

*On 13 August 1947, General of the Army Dwight D. Eisenhower listened to Wellwood Beall describe the features of the B-47 mock-up. (Boeing P7243)*

Boeing engineers and technicians went over the XB-47 with a fine-tooth comb prior to its first flight. Safety was of utmost importance as denoted by the hand-held fire bottles positioned around the periphery of the aircraft and the reeled hose on a fire truck that may be seen in the foreground. In the background to the left was a pair of North American B-25s, a Douglas C-47, and a Beech C-45; while a C-97 was on the right. (Boeing P7490)

# Chapter 2

# *PROTOTYPES*

At the time of the B-47, the Air Force typically used an "X" prefix for a pair of experimental aircraft and a "Y" prefix for a larger number (typically 13 for some reason) of pre-production service test aircraft. This was not the case for the B-47 that had two experimental XB-47s and ten B-47A (not YB-47A) service evaluation aircraft. Both XB-47s were built in Seattle and flown directly to Moses Lake, Washington, for flight-testing. All subsequent B-47s were produced at other plants.

## CONTRACTUAL ITERATIONS

After conducting two-and-a-half years of negotiations, the definitive fixed-price contract (W33-038-ac-8429) for the B-47 was issued on 10 July 1947. The contract provided for a pair of stripped-down XB-47s, spare parts, mock-ups of the complete aircraft and fuselage, and wind tunnel tests at a total cost of $9,668,483.52. In addition, major contractor-initiated changes from flight-testing were expected to increase the total cost to approximately $10,594,000. By February 1950 the costs had risen to $11,944,043.09, but were approved by the Air Force. The major cost-drivers for the cost increases were:

- Relocating the flight test program from Seattle to Moses Lake and changing the delivery dates.
- Wind tunnel tests of a 1/20-scale flutter model and a full-scale empennage model.
- Installation of 18 x 1,000-lbf rocket-assisted takeoff bottles.
- Installation of J35-GE-7 in lieu of J35-GE-9 engines and an oil heating system on the first aircraft.
- Installation of bomb racks and bomb release mechanism on the second aircraft.
- Contractor maintenance and inspection services during Phase II flight tests on the first aircraft.
- Instrumentation and flight testing the first aircraft beyond Phase I flight testing.
- Incorporation of an inhabited-type gunner's enclosure and simulated Emerson Model 161 turret in the second aircraft plus a full-scale mock-up of the installation.

- Installation of a deceleration parachute in the first aircraft.
- Installation of a deceleration parachute in the second aircraft and modification of the aircraft for checkout of the aircraft for Project HANDBOOK.
- Contractor flight testing, maintenance, and inspection of the second aircraft during the government's Phase II testing.
- Necessary maintenance services associated with flying the first XB-47 from Moses Lake to Andrews AFB.

## XB-47

The basic planform and dimensions established for the XB-47s (Boeing Model 450-3-3) were carried forward for all subsequent variants with the only significant external change being the noses of some reconnaissance series aircraft and a variety of ECM bulges and antennas on most later aircraft. One exception was that only the first XB-47 (46-065) was equipped with leading edge slats along the wing, outboard of the inboard engine nacelle struts. Testing revealed that this feature was not required. For such a radically new design this was a testament to the engineers getting it right in the first place.

As with all Stratojets, the crew of each XB-47 consisted of two pilots and a navigator positioned within the pressurized cockpit. Upward ejection seats were provided for all three crew positions. An escape hatch above the navigator and ahead of the pilot's windscreen would have been separated before the seat was ejected through the opening. A blown clear plexiglass nose was installed on the aircraft. In addition, the navigator was afforded a small window in his upper escape hatch as well as three small trapezoidal windows on the left side of the nose with two more on the right side.

Six General Electric J35-GE-7 (TG-180-B1) axial-flow turbojets powered the first XB-47, while the second aircraft was scheduled to use J35-GE-9 (TG-180-C1) engines. The only externally visible differences were that the -7 engine had a 60-inch tail cone and a stainless steel firewall, whereas the -9 engine had a 30-inch tail cone with an integral firewall. Each engine developed 3,750-lbf of static thrust.

Eighteen Aerojet No. 12 rocket-assisted takeoff (RATO) bottles, each providing 1,000-lbf for 12 to 14 seconds, provided addi-

The long cigar of the first XB-47 was built at Boeing's Plant 1 at the mouth of the Duwamish River in Seattle, Washington. It was loaded on a barge for its journey upstream. (Via Gordon S. Williams)

The tugboat, just visible behind the long cigar, propelled the barge upstream. (Via Gordon S. Williams)

The XB-47 long cigar arrived at Boeing's Plant 2, located across the road from Boeing Field. (Boeing via Gordon S. Williams)

tional power during takeoff. These were mounted in three rows of three within a waist cavity on each side of the fuselage, covered by a corrosion-resistant stainless steel shroud for aerodynamic smoothness. A selector switch allowed the pilot to fire the bottles sequentially or simultaneously.

Oddly, the crew entry ladder on the XB-47 was fraught with developmental problems. When it was pulled down, the lower leg continued its journey until it was lying on the ramp. Hence, a set of steps was always rolled up to the aircraft. Bob Robbins assessed the situation and did not feel comfortable if an emergency egress on the ground was required. His solution was to rig a rope ladder in the entryway. A standing joke with the pilots was why Boeing was able to design such a magnificent aircraft and yet not be able to make a reliable entry ladder.

## BUILDING THE XB-47S

As with the three XB-29s, Boeing built the two XB-47 fuselages in Plant 1 at the mouth of the Duwamish River on Harbor Island, along the south shore of Lake Union in Seattle. At the time, the company's original building, the Red Barn, was still in operation at this location. Subsequently, the building was relocated to Boeing Field

*A Boeing technician making some adjustments on the No. 2 engine of the first XB-47. Note the stepladders surrounding the aircraft. A stepladder was required for entry into the aircraft because an effective integral ladder was yet to be designed. The Boeing XB-47 lettering was applied to the first aircraft only. (Boeing P7494)*

*The main wing box for the No. 1 XB-47 was resting on jacks just prior to being lowered into position on the long cigar. This photo dates from 3 March 1947. (Boeing 99490-B)*

Right and Above: *The first XB-47-BO (46-065) was rolled out of the factory at Boeing's Plant 2 in Seattle and towed across East Marginal Way to Boeing Field for final checkout and its first flight. This was the same plant that had turned out B-17s during World War II at a peak rate of 16 per day. (Boeing P7376; Boeing P7395 via William E. Collins)*

*The east gate at Seattle's Plant 2 was opened to tow the first XB-47 across East Marginal Way to Boeing Field. (Boeing P7391)*

where it became the cornerstone of the Museum of Flight, a privately owned institution with heavy company funding.

The XB-47s were essentially hand-built without the aid of sophisticated factory tooling. The fuselages were floated upstream to Boeing's Plant 2 located on the west side of Boeing Field south of Seattle. Final assembly was completed in the building previously used to assemble B-17s. The XB-47 design and manufacturing teams worked in concert to produce an incredible aircraft in the shortest possible time. While some in the shop balked at the myriad of continuous design changes, there were others who made things happen. Bill Ramsden, a liaison engineer, would have discussions with key factory managers, make copies of blueprints, and leave them on the appropriate desks. The shop built each piece per drawing. Such an operation permitted rapid resolution to some monumental engineering challenges.

## Preparing the Test Pilots

Boeing selected Bob Robbins to be the XB-47 project pilot and Scott Osler as the copilot. For a year before the first flight, Robbins and Osler roamed freely throughout the company talking with management, engineering, manufacturing, and quality control personnel. It was during these walkabouts that the pilots asked questions, gained insightful answers, and became thoroughly familiar with the XB-47. They considered the experience truly confidence building.

Boeing installed a TG-180 in the bomb bay of the XB-29G-BA (44-84043), attached to a trapeze that could be lowered into the airstream, and numerous air starts and acceleration runs were conducted by Robbins to gain jet engine operating experience.

Briefings by Bill Cook familiarized the pilots with the expected approach and landing characteristics of the XB-47. Because of the bicycle-style landing gear, the aircraft would have to make long, shallow approaches. Both Robbins and Osler gained experience while making touch-and-go landings in an XB-29. The pilots also went to Martin Field outside Baltimore to fly the Martin XB-26H Marauder that had been retrofitted with tandem landing gear. The XB-26H was known as the *Middle River Stump Jumper* (the Martin plant was at Middle River, Maryland) and was part of a project to test the bicycle landing gear being developed for the XB-47, XB-48, and XA-45 (XB-51). Flight tests were carried out during May and June 1945. In addition, Robbins and Osler each logged seven hours in a Lockheed P-80 and made one rocket-assisted takeoff at Muroc Army Air Field, California.

To learn more about the handling characteristics of the XB-47, Robbins and Osler "flew" the B-47 wind tunnel model and the flutter test model under the watchful eye of aerodynamicist Bill Cook. Witnessing the flailing engine pods and flapping wings gave the two pilots a better appreciation of what to expect during real flights.

Safety for the pilots was paramount, and exposure to various conditions made them better prepared for their first flight. Part of this introduction involved Robbins and Osler going to Wright Field to experience an ejection seat ride. The seat was mounted to a 60-foot-high set of rails attached to the outside of one of the structural test laboratory buildings. Robbins and Osler flipped a coin to see who would go first. Robbins lost and was summarily escorted to the seat where he was strapped in by the technicians. Three blasts of a horn sounded inside of the building to alert workers that a loud noise was coming, and workers scrambled out of the building to look at their next victim. The rides gave the two pilots confidence in the ejection seats.

The National Advisory Committee on Aeronautics (NACA), the forerunner of the National Aeronautics and Space Administration (NASA), was very active in supporting the aircraft industry and military services. The NACA operated several large wind tunnel complexes, and performed a variety of wind tunnel tests for the B-47 program.

For example, at the Ames Aeronautical Laboratory (now the Ames Research Center) in Mountain View, California, the entire empennage of the second XB-47 was placed in the Full Scale Aerodynamic Complex (NFAC), the world's largest wind tunnel. The unit had to be

*In the wind tunnel, Boeing engineers employed this model to assess the flight characteristics of the B-47 with control forces induced by their inputs. Supported only by a single rod, articulated from the bottom, control inputs were induced into the model so that they could evaluate the behavior of the extremely flexible swept-back wings, tail, and body during conditions of high-speed flight. Both Bob Robbins and Scott Osler got to witness first hand the effects of control inputs prior to their first flight while under the tutelage of Bill Cook. (Boeing P10924)*

*Prior to flying the XB-47, Boeing test pilot Bob Robbins learned the operating idiosyncrasies of the General Electric J47 turbojet that was suspended from the bomb bay of the XB-29G-BA (44-84043). (General Electric Flight Test)*

mounted seven feet below the tunnel centerline to obtain the desired angle-of-attack range due to the height of the vertical tail. This required a special set of support struts, despite the fact that the NFAC had a test section that measured 40 by 80 feet. Electric actuators drove the control surfaces instead of the hydraulic systems that would be used on the real aircraft. The wind tunnel tests were used to gain data on the pitch and yaw characteristics of the empennage.

After the basic aerodynamic tests were completed, the pilots were given a unique opportunity to "fly" the empennage. Bill Cook designed a reinforced steel bullet-shaped shell that was attached to the forward end of the empennage. Within the shell was a rudimentary cockpit for Robbins and Osler. It was there that the pilots got to experience flying the elevators and rudder with and without the aid of hydraulic power boost. The force tests were run at a dynamic pressure of 30 pounds per square foot, corresponding to a speed of about 110-mph at standard sea-level conditions. This gave the pilots the feel of approach and landing conditions.

## Flight Pay

Because it was a radically different aircraft, Boeing instituted a new first-flight pay schedule for the pilots. Robbins would be paid $10,000, while Osler received half that amount. The pilots would earn 30-percent of the money for the first flight, an additional 30-percent after 10 flight hours, 20-percent for the completion of the structural demonstration, and the final 20-percent upon the completion of the Phase I flight test program.

Since the test program took the Boeing pilots further into the unknown areas of the flight envelope, Edward Wells recommended to Bill Allen that additional compensation be authorized. Concerns had arisen about flying at high speeds beyond the capabilities of the early

ejection seats. Additionally it was believed that safety margins would be reduced when flying above 45,000 feet. A 26 December 1950 memo recommended a supplemental payment of $100 per flight during which either condition was exceeded. These supplemental fees were not expected to exceed $3,000 for the contract period.

There were other concerns as well. Lateral control spoiler tests were scheduled to begin around 10 January 1951, and the test plan required high-speed flight beyond the capabilities of the ejection seats. Because reliability and performance data were not available for the spoiler system, testing would require exceptional skill and involve

*The empennage from the second XB-47 was transported to NACA's Ames Facility at Moffett Field, California, where it was mounted on three plinths. An aerodynamic dome was added to the nose. Hydraulic jacks moved the structure within the wind tunnel. A rudimentary crew seat, controls, and instruments were installed so that the pilots could get a feel for flying the aircraft at slow speeds for approach and landing. (Via Bob Robbins)*

hazards not normally encountered in test flying. In a second 26 December 1950 memo Wells recommended an additional $5,000 compensation for these flights to be divided at 60 percent for the pilot and 40 percent for the copilot.

## XB-47 FIRST FLIGHT

The first XB-47 (46-065) rolled out of the factory on 12 September 1947 and was towed across East Marginal Way to the Boeing Flight Test Center in the northwest corner of Boeing Field. The Air Force and Boeing decided to conduct flight testing of the XB-47 at Moses Lake in the eastern part of Washington State. This former World War II airfield was sufficiently remote to draw little attention to the activities surrounding this radical new aircraft, and offered a sparse population in case of an accident.

Inclement weather postponed the first flight of the XB-47 until 17 December 1947 – 44 years to the day after the Wright Brothers performed the first controlled powered flight at Kitty Hawk. The weather was still poor, so a P-80 was dispatched from Boeing Field to evaluate the weather along the flight path to Moses Lake. It was overcast, but there was a hole in the clouds over the field that would allow the XB-47 pilots to safely descend and land.

As the XB-47 trundled to the north end of Runway 31-13 at Boeing Field, a crowd of Boeing workers and their families lined the airfield. A southeasterly heading was chosen because of the lighter population in that direction. As the aircraft roared down the runway, a fire warning light for one of the engines illuminated. Robbins opted to abort the takeoff and taxi back to the north end of the field. It was believed that it was a false warning due to the temperature sensor locations; this was subsequently verified and a second takeoff was made.

Once again the XB-47 roared down the runway belching six plumes of black smoke. The warning light returned, but the pilots

*Bob Robbins was climbing out of the cockpit of the Lockheed P-80 Shooting Star powered by a single 3,850-lbf J33-GE-9 axial-flow turbojet. (USAF via Bob Robbins)*

opted to continue with the takeoff. Once airborne, Robbins proceeded to clean up the aircraft and retracted the landing gear. He then attempted to retract the flaps, but they were jammed and the aircraft was rapidly approaching its flap limit speed. Robbins still

*Bob Robbins (cockpit) and Scott Osler received their first jet orientation in a Lockheed P-80A-1-LO (44-85085). This photo dates from 17 July 1947. (USAF via Bob Robbins)*

*Bob Robbins (left) and Scott Osler (center) discuss the Aerojet General rocket-assisted takeoff installation on the P-80. (USAF via Bob Robbins)*

*Ed Wells observed his creation – a model of the XB-47. Note the old-style USAAF national insignia (sans red bar) on the aft fuselage. (Boeing P6247)*

Bob Robbins and Scott Osler made history on 17 December 1947 when they made the first flight in the XB-47. Note the tail skid that was a carryover from the B-29s and was only on the two XB-47s. (Boeing P7805 via William E. Collins)

Major Guy Townsend (left) was introduced to the B-47 by Boeing test pilot Bob Robbins on 14 July 1948. These two happy flyers knew they had something special in this aircraft. (Boeing P8336)

had a lot of trepidation about the performance of the early jet engines and swore he would not reduce the power until he was at a safe altitude. He had but one option, and that was to pull the nose up. Mrs. Robbins gasped, knowing full well that her husband had hit the RATO bottles and, if things did not go well, the next step would be an ejection. Fortunately, this was not necessary. Robbins smoothly took the aircraft to altitude and headed for Moses Lake. En route he and Osler performed rudimentary flight control checks and practiced landing on clouds. They had sufficient fuel reserves to return to Boeing Field if necessary.

A flat approach was made into Moses Lake although at times the pilots experienced a high roll rate of 1.5-degrees per second due to yaw. If he were forced to execute a missed approach, the early jet engines would need a prolonged spool-up time and would not have generated sufficient thrust to execute a go-around, so Robbins carried a lot of additional power that was not really necessary. While the higher thrust increased the lift on the wings, the pilot held the airspeed critically close to stall. The net result was a long landing roll.

The second XB-47 (46-066) was fitted with more powerful 5,200-lbf J47-GE-3 engines prior to its first flight on 21 July 1948. The new engines raised the top speed past the 600-mph mark. The Air Force formally accepted the first XB-47 on 29 November 1948; the second XB-47 was accepted a month later. The first XB-47 was later retrofitted with J47s, and first flew with the new engines on 7 October 1949.

## XB-47 Flight Testing

Initial flight testing for the XB-47s consisted of Boeing performing several phases of basic airworthiness tests, while the Air Force flew more definitive, operationally-based tests. Because the Stratojet was designed around radically new concepts, the program appeared to languish for a bit as the bugs were worked out. Unlike many programs where the design is frozen prior to the flight test program, the B-47 engineers had essentially an open-ended schedule and many issues uncovered during the initial flights were resolved through innovative solutions.

### Boeing Flight Testing

Boeing's pilots, Bob Robbins and Scott Osler, flew the Phase I flight demonstrations from Moses Lake. This program lasted 40 flight hours during which the pilots gradually flew at increased speeds. Nevertheless, because of the newness of the technology, Phase I testing was not to exceed 60 percent of the aircraft's calculated performance. Tests included an evaluation of takeoff and landing speeds, asymmetrical power performance at various altitudes, and airspeed calibrations.

During one of the flights the pilots experienced an unusual flight characteristic known as Dutch roll. As the aircraft began to roll in one direction, Robbins countered with opposite wheel. He overshot and the aircraft continued its opposite roll. After several attempts to counter the wallowing aircraft, Robbins reduced the airspeed and the

*After only six flights in the XB-47, Major Townsend took Major General K. B. Wolfe for the famous 19 July 1948 flight that sold the aircraft to the Air Force. This post-flight photo captures (left to right): Wolfe; Wellwood Beall; Captain Jack Ridley, copilot; George Martin; Lieutenant General Joseph McNarney, AMC Commander; Townsend; and William E. Allen, Boeing President. The aircraft was s/n 46-065 and had the B-47 Stratojet markings painted over with a fresh coat of gray paint. (Boeing H6777)*

Dutch roll abated. Robbins radioed Bill Cook on the ground at Moses Lake and advised him of the situation. Cook's reply was to the effect, "I wondered when you'd find that characteristic." The usually mild-mannered Robbins broke radio protocol and uttered a few expletives.

Airspeed calibration is conducted with another aircraft with known airspeed calibration pacing the test aircraft. For these tests the Air Force dispatched Captain Charles "Chuck" Yeager from Muroc AFB with a Lockheed P-80. Robbins and Osler took off with Yeager right behind them and the formation made several calibration runs at ever-increasing speeds. Not too long after takeoff, however, Yeager asked the B-47 to perform a 180-degree turn back toward Moses Lake. This sounded reasonable since the P-80 had less fuel and Yeager most likely did not want to get too far from the field. The XB-47 turned back towards Moses Lake but the P-80 could not be found. Robbins called Yeager and asked him what was up? Yeager had to admit that his P-80 could not keep up with the bomber. This must have been very humbling for a fighter pilot that had no love for pilots of large aircraft.

The maiden flight of the second XB-47 on 21 July 1948 brought some unexpected excitement. Although the flight plan called for a simple ferry flight, Robbins decided to perform some stalls prior to landing and found a 4-knot difference in stall speed. This seemingly small difference was actually fairly critical for landing, and it was a good thing that Robbins had decided to run some tests prior to approaching

the runway. On the ground Robbins asked Cook about the change and was informed that the static pressure ports on the aircraft had been moved. Because the static port was in a different flow field, it reported different data than the one on the first airplane. In itself this is not unusual – static ports and pitot probes are routiNely moved during a flight test program to ensure that the cockpit instruments provide accurate readings – but normally the pilot is warned beforehand.

James A. Frazier, another Boeing test pilot, arrived at Moses Lake to serve as a backup to Robbins and Osler. Between 20 November 1948 and 23 June 1949, Osler and Frazier performed initial work on aerial refueling and demonstrated the landing deceleration parachutes. In early 1949 they were performing fuel system tests when Frazier took control of the aircraft while Osler worked with the myriad of fuel system switches. Suddenly they were in a 120,000-pound glider when all six engines flamed out. Fortunately Osler restored the fuel flow to all six engines and they returned to base.

Tragedy would strike the program on 11 May 1949 during a test flight using the first XB-47. John Fornasero, then Boeing Chief of Flight Test, was making his first B-47 flight as an observer, with Osler and Frazier at the controls. Also aboard was a technical representative from the autopilot manufacturer, Sperry Gyroscope. Fornasero asked if he could spend a few minutes flying the airplane, and Osler relinquished his seat for his boss. Fornasero flew the aircraft with Osler standing in the crawlway and the aircraft performed flawlessly. The two then traded positions again. Suddenly, the canopy unlatched and there was a thunderous on-rush of air. The canopy lifted, then slammed down hard to its partially open taxiing position. The blast of air ripped Osler's helmet from his head, and when the canopy slammed down, it broke his neck, killing him instantly. Fornasero lifted Osler out of his seat and placed him on the crawlway floor. Then Frazier told Fornasero to get into the front seat. Fornasero wanted to swap seats; however, Frazier felt more comfortable landing the aircraft from the seat he was used to flying. Fornasero operated the radio

*While at Moses Lake, Washington, for SEBAC flight tests during 1948-1949, the first XB-47 (46-065) sported white wall main and outrigger gear tires. The tires were used for scuff tests during taxiing and high-speed turn-offs during landings. Note the solid sheet metal covering for the RATO bay. (Gordon S. Williams)*

*Photographed at Boeing Field in Seattle on 13 May 1953, a camera was mounted to the top of the vertical fin of the first XB-47 (46-065). The approach and drag chute doors were open. In the background was a Curtiss C-46 Commando, bailed to Boeing, undergoing some engine work. (Boeing P13330)*

ward latch fittings had failed; the grasshopper actuating arms failed in tension. With all four canopy connections failed, the aft end of the canopy lifted due to air loads, then nosed down considerably, and the frame impacted Osler's head. Further investigation revealed that tolerance build-up in the various canopy mechanical components stacked up to almost disengagement, allowing the forward rollers to fail first. As a result, engineers took another look at how they controlled tolerance build-up, and all future designs used much tighter tolerances. This accident deeply shook Robbins and he would never fly a B-47 again. Robbins returned to his engineering job.

### Air Force Flight Testing

When Boeing completed its Phase I flight tests in July 1948, the aircraft was turned over to the Air Force and Major Guy Townsend became the principal test pilot. Captain Jack Ridley was the Air Force copilot and Robbins checked them out in the XB-47. After his first flight in the XB-47, Townsend opined: "It's a mighty fine airplane. Boeing Company pilots have demonstrated what it will do and we're here to confirm these tests for the Air Force. The Stratojet is a definite step into the future of bombardment aviation."

Unlike the Boeing series, the Air Force tests were intended to evaluate the military operational suitability and the limits of the operational envelope for the aircraft. Early on it was noted that the XB-47 had extremely poor landing and braking characteristics, and it was difficult to make glide path corrections. The long, slender wing offered little drag to assist in an approach and landing and, although they greatly enhanced takeoff performance, the flaps did little to help the pitch angle for landing. Like all jets, engine spool-up was extremely slow and could take up to 30 seconds to produce any acceleration.

During an Air Force Phase II flight in the first XB-47, a catastrophic failure and subsequent fire occurred on the No. 4 engine. The incident proved that the podded engine concept was correct – a similar failure of an imbedded engine would have resulted in loss of the aircraft. To prevent such a failure from causing a mission abort, the Air Materiel Command recommended that Boeing develop a method of blocking air entry into the nacelle to prevent unwanted rotation of a damaged or shutdown engine. The effects of such rotation were increased drag and increased engine wear. Boeing responded by developing a set of inlet close-off doors that would be installed on early B-47s. (Later J47s had built-in brakes that eliminated the need for the doors.)

One day Guy Townsend and Lieutenant Colonel Henry E. "Pete" Warden, Chief of the Bombardment Branch at Wright-Patterson, were talking about the performance of the XB-47. Townsend commented that slowing the aircraft for landing was a real problem – it wanted to fly. He remembered parachutes being used the year before to stop a B-17 during winter operations on the ice in Greenland. The crew had deployed personnel chutes from the waist windows, the same as combat crews returning from missions did during World War II when their hydraulics were shot out. The problem was that conventional solid parachutes could not stand the aerodynamic load imposed by the high

and called for emergency vehicles. On the ground, Ben Werner was in his usual place in the radio trailer and asked for their position. Fornasero replied that he had no idea where they were. The idea passed through Werner's mind that if the aircraft were lost, the B-47 program would have been doomed. Soon afterward, Frazier successfully landed at Moses Lake.

Upon landing it was determined that the canopy was held in place only by its forward lip that had engaged the pilot's headrest. The aircraft was grounded for several months so that a thorough engineering investigation could be conducted. Earlier, a set of grasshopper actuating arms had been installed so that the aircraft could be depressurized and the aft end of the canopy raised to afford clearance for a proposed gun sight for the tail turret. The investigation determined that the for-

speeds seen by the B-47 without ripping. Then the light went on in Warden's head – they had some German ribbon parachutes in storage at Wright-Patterson. In addition they had the man, Theodor W. Knacke, who had developed the parachutes in Germany during the 1930s, working for them. Subsequently Knacke designed the ring slot parachute that was later used on the B-47s, and that was subsequently adopted by many high-speed military aircraft.

At one point, Major Russell Schleeh, flying the first XB-47, complained to Townsend that his parachutes kept experiencing a myriad of problems and asked how Townsend's were doing. The response was, very well since Air Force maintenance personnel were packing the parachutes. When Townsend asked Schleeh who was packing the ones he was using, Schleeh replied that it was Knacke. The German later admitted that he considered every packing to be a test for new methods – on an aircraft that was routinely operating off 6,000-foot runways!

## SELLING THE AIRCRAFT

By July 1948 there was still no production contract for the B-47 in sight. The Air Materiel Command was having issues with the B-50 Superfortresses being built in Seattle and were reluctant to give Boeing another contract until the issue was rectified. To review the situation, Director of Procurement & Industrial Planning Major General Kenneth B. Wolfe, along with AMC Commander General Joseph T. McNarney and Pete Warden, had flown to Seattle from Wright-Patterson in a VB-17 Flying Fortress. Upon finishing their discussions, the generals wished to depart for their long journey back to Ohio.

Warden had earlier told Guy Townsend that he would try to get the generals to have a look at the XB-47 and then he would propose a flight. Warden told Townsend, "You know, K. B. Wolfe has been seeing airplanes go faster and faster but it has always been true airspeed by going to higher altitude. He has never seen 460 mph on the airspeed indicator." Boeing offered to fly the entourage over in a much faster B-50 with the VB-17 following at its own pace. Accompanying the Air Force officers were Boeing President Bill Allen, Boeing Executive Vice President Wellwood Beall, and XB-47 Project Engineer George Martin.

On 19 July 1948 the aircraft was cocked and ready on the ramp at Moses Lake. Townsend escorted the generals through a walk-around of the aircraft and then suggested a short hop. Major General Wolfe retorted to the effect that it was neither a medium nor a heavy bomber and would have no place in the force structure. Finally Wolfe stated to Warden, "Damn you, I'll go ride in the airplane just to get rid of you." The general took the copilot's seat and Jack Ridley situated himself in the walkway to brief the general as required. Townsend fired up the aircraft and took off. Once airborne he put the XB-47 through its paces and let Wolfe get some stick time. When they returned to Earth, Wolfe was visibly elated. When asked if the aircraft was operationally ready, Townsend replied, "Yes." He went on to say, "General, the Air Force and the Nation needs this airplane." This propitious flight apparently changed Wolfe's mind. Discussions on the way back to Wright-Patterson centered on procurement of this vital new weapon system, and adjustments to the existing procurement plans were soon made to accommodate the Stratojet.

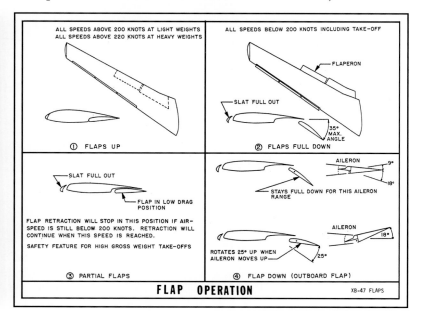

Only the first XB-47 (46-065) was equipped with leading edge slats that may be seen from the inboard nacelle struts to almost the wingtips on each wing. The vortex generators were yet to be installed on the wings. The aircraft was on approach to Moses Lake, Washington. Although the slats were deleted from subsequent B-47s, the flaps retained these operating characteristics. (Boeing P9789)

Decked out in their winter flying gear, Majors Russell Schleeh and Joe Howell prior to climbing aboard the first XB-47 for their transcontinental flight. Note that by February 1949 Boeing engineers were able to design an effective integral ladder. (Boeing P8838)

Brigadier General Y. H. Taylor (center) was on hand to greet Majors Schleeh (left) and Howell (right) upon their arrival at Andrews AFB, Maryland. Note that Major Howell was wearing non-regulation loafers. (Boeing P8973)

As part of selling the aircraft, an unofficial speed record was set between Moses Lake and Andrews AFB, Maryland, on 8 February 1949. An AMC Flight Test Division crew consisting of Major Russell Schleeh and Major Joe Howell was given a one-hour orientation flight in the first XB-47 that included a couple of landings. Unfortunately, the weather at Andrews was not predicted to be the best, especially for a new crew. However, the pilots were not deterred and wanted to make a good impression with this sleek new bomber. The crew developed a how-goes-it chart to predict zero fuel at their destination, and then factored in a reserve. To maximize the load, the fuel trucks sat out overnight to cold soak the fuel, thereby increasing its density.

The pilots kept the engines set at 100 percent for the entire flight except for a point mid-flight when they fell behind their how-goes-it chart. Speed was kept below the critical Mach number to prevent buffeting because the aircraft had no vortex generators to reduce airflow separation over the wings. Navigation was accomplished solely by a low-frequency radio compass that required a lot of tuning. The letdown was initiated about 100 miles out of Andrews. There was a crosswind and the approach chute failed to deploy, presumably due to Herr Knacke's packing. As a result, two main gear tires were blown during the hot, long rollout. With the help of a tailwind, the 2,289-mile flight had been accomplished in 3 hours and 46 minutes, at an average speed of 607.8 mph – an unofficial transcontinental speed record.

While in Washington, the aircraft was shown to members of the House Armed Services Committee in the hope of obtaining sizeable production orders. The aircraft was also placed on display for Pentagon officials and other members of Congress and the Administration. Its record-breaking flight further enhanced the selling of the aircraft to those with the influence and the dollars that could ensure its success.

The Air Force tested the first XB-47 for about 83 hours, including 38 hours of Phase II flight tests carried out between 8 July and 15

*Both XB-47s were nestled into a hangar at Moses Lake. The second prototype (46-066) is at left. The wing of the first aircraft (46-065) reveals its leading edge wing slat in the extended position. Note that no vortex generators were installed. (Boeing P8767)*

These are the nose windows that were installed on the first B-47A-BW, s/n 49-1900. Note the anti-icing tube and spray ring on the blown nose. While the same as that installed on the XB-47, the nose glazing would change with later B-47As and B-47Bs. (Boeing P29946)

Two rows of vortex generators were installed just aft of the front spar to control the boundary layer over the top of the wing at high speeds. Dean Barber, from WIBAC's Flight Test Department, was inspecting the various angles at which the vortex were set. Each vortex generator was precisely located then screwed into the wing upper surface. (Boeing BW90409)

August 1948. All of the pilots that flew the XB-47 during its 330 flight hours were enthusiastic. In 1954, after having been stripped of its wings and engines, the first XB-47 was cut in half and exhibited at Palm Beach AFB, Florida. The second XB-47 is displayed at the Octave Chanute Aerospace Museum in Rantoul, Illinois.

## MORE CONTRACT ITERATIONS

Test flights at Muroc that summer demonstrated that the XB-47 was 74 mph faster than the competing XB-46 and XB-48, not surprising given the straight wings on the other aircraft. However, the XB-47's performance was lower than expected; the service ceiling was 2,500 feet below that promised by Boeing, and 7,500 feet lower than originally required by the Air Force, and top speed was lower than predicted.

Nevertheless, the first production order would be placed for the B-47 in late 1948. The Seattle facility was already heavily committed to the KC-97 tanker and the B-50 bomber, as well as to the conversion of obsolescent B-29 bombers to aerial tankers, so it was decided that B-47s would be built at a government facility in Wichita, Kansas.

As early as December 1947 AMC had been developing plans for the procurement of production B-47s and asked Boeing to present a production breakdown, tentative schedule (if a contract were let by 30 June 1948), Government-furnished property list, flow time of critical Government-furnished property, and a critical materials list. Over the following eight months planning continued while AMC promised to provide a production go-ahead as soon as Boeing presented an acceptable proposal for 13 B-47As and 41 B-47Bs. In September 1948 AMC authorized Boeing-Wichita (WIBAC) to proceed with the engineering, planning, tool design, procurement of tooling materials, and subcontracting for 10 B-47s in an amount not to exceed $35,000,000.

However, a misunderstanding arose during these negotiations. Headquarters USAF was under the impression that the Air Force could get 10 aircraft, plus tooling for 54 B-47s, for the $35,817,000 allocated from supplemental 1948 funds. However, Boeing had estimated that tooling and related costs for producing 54 aircraft would amount to $31,000,000. Therefore, only a single B-47, plus tooling for the 54 aircraft, could be provided for the available funds. The Air Materiel Command had expected to apply the entire $35,817,000 for procurement of 10 aircraft and the requisite tooling for them, and as a result, had to approach Washington for additional funds for the remaining 44 aircraft.

On 2 November 1948 the Air Materiel Command provided letter contract W33-038-ac-224113 for the procurement of 10 B-47As and a follow-on procurement of three additional B-47As and 41 B-47Bs with deliveries scheduled for January 1950 through March 1951. The price for the 10 B-47As was $28,500,000. A 28 February 1949 amendment trimmed the B-47A procurement to just the original 10 aircraft, increased the B-47Bs from 41 to 55, and delayed completion until 30 September 1951. This amendment also provided for the design and construction of a ground test rig for testing the prototype external RATO system.

At the time of the production order, the weapon system concept had not yet been adopted by the Air Force, but when it was, the B-47 became the first aircraft to receive a Weapon System designation, the bomber and photo-reconnaissance versions being WS-100A and WS-100L, respectively.

Despite the good news of a production contract, Boeing's Bill Cook immediately recognized a major problem arising for SAC – namely, how to deal with this vastly new aircraft. The command's existing policies, procedures, and infrastructure would not be able to cope with the quantum leap in technology. Cook proposed that a command briefing be prepared for SAC that explained the challenges they would be facing.

To better understand SAC's requirements, six Boeing engineers and two Air Force officers made a two-week tour of SAC bases beginning on 18 March 1950. These individuals visited five SAC bases and AMC headquarters at Wright-Patterson where they discussed the design, operating, and maintenance features of the B-47. A massive effort was put forth to develop a presentation that resulted in a seven-hour briefing that included an aircraft description, a summary of aircraft performance, aircrew training requirements, maintenance training requirements, logistics and spares issues, and facility and runway requirements.

The Boeing briefing team for the B-47 was composed of Herb Clayman, soon to be Boeing representative at SAC Headquarters, aerodynamicists Bill Cook, Ken Holtby, and Hank Richmond, and Chief Engineer Lysle Wood. The Air Force briefing team consisted of Major S. Fowler, SAC Headquarters, Captain John S. Schaffer, B-47 Program Director, and Major Guy Townsend, AMC flight test pilot.

So complex was the briefing that it was planned for seven hours without questions and answers. Nevertheless, a SAC lieutenant colonel informed the team that they would have only 45 minutes with General LeMay. The team protested to no avail and at 09:00 all personnel assembled into the briefing room. Ken Holtby and Herb Clayman opened the briefing and Guy Townsend was up next. He was unaccustomed to such a large-scale program; after all, he was a test pilot, not a briefer. When LeMay began asking questions, he was informed that these details were in the formal briefing and others on the team began scrambling for the proper 35-mm slide. Eventually LeMay gave up and asked for the complete briefing. The formal briefing was followed by a four-hour question and answer period. This briefing was so well received that it was then taken to the three numbered SAC air forces and MacDill AFB, Florida, where the first B-47 wing would be stationed.

## B-47A

The 10 B-47As (49-1900 through 49-1909) were not considered combat ready and were used mainly for testing and training. The first B-47A (Boeing Model 450-10-9) flew on 25 June 1950 and was essentially identical to the XB-47 prototypes, differing externally only in having a framed Perspex nose cone in place of the fully transparent nose cone of the prototypes. The B-47A was powered by six 5,200-lbf

*This B-47B-10-BW (50-014) shows the deceleration chute during a test flight at Edwards AFB. (AFFTC History Office via Tony Landis)*

J47-GE-11 turbojets and retained the built-in RATO feature of the prototypes, although the bottles were changed to Aerojet 15KS-1000 units that developed 1,000-lbf each. These early production aircraft had their takeoff weight increased from 121,080 pounds to 151,324 pounds. The same ejection seat system incorporated in the XB-47s was carried over into the B-47As.

In order to reduce the length of the landing run, a 32-foot deceleration parachute was provided that was stowed underneath the vertical stabilizer just forward of the tail cone. Deployed immediately after touchdown, this chute helped slow down the aircraft and shorten the landing roll. However, it soon became customary to deploy the drag

*The B-47 wing contained a fair amount of negative dihedral under static conditions; however, almost all of the negative dihedral was eliminated due to lift while in flight. (Gordon S. Williams)*

chute while the B-47 was still a few feet in the air just before touchdown. This led to the addition of a smaller 16-foot deceleration parachute that acted as an in-flight air brake that made it possible to make landing approaches at relatively high engine power. If a go-around became necessary, the drogue chute could be jettisoned and the aircraft could accelerate quickly. If the landing was normal, the drogue chute could be left attached while the main braking chute was deployed. Following the end of the landing roll, both the landing and braking chutes were jettisoned at the end of the runway before the B-47 taxied in. The chutes were recovered and repacked by the ground crews.

Unlike the two prototypes, a modified Honeywell E-6 autopilot known as the MH-7 was installed on the B-47As. Bombing and navigation equipment varied widely on each aircraft according to their test function. A horizontal bombsight and bombsight stabilizer were incorporated in the nose. A radar indicator, bombardier's instrument panel, and bombing control equipment were located on the right side of the navigator's station. Four of the six B-47As equipped with the K-2 bombing and navigation system were assigned to the 306th Bombardment Wing at MacDill for service evaluation, while the remaining two were assigned to the Air Force Special Weapons Command at Kirtland AFB, New Mexico, for spesial weapons compatibility tests.

The bomb bay could accommodate a single 10,000-pound bomb. In addition, space and structural provisions were provided for 1,000-, 2,000-, 4,000-, and 12,000-pound general-purpose bombs and their associated racks. No provisions were included for special (nuclear) weapons.

While a gunnery station was provided for the copilot, the B-47As were delivered with a tail cone in lieu of a tail turret. After delivery, a single B-47A was retrofitted with a tail turret with two 0.50-caliber machine guns and an A-1 fire control system for evaluation.

## THRUST AUGMENTATION

Getting a loaded B-47 off the ground represented a major problem since the six turbojet engines did not have the power to use the short 5,000- to 6,000-foot-long runways at the bases the B-47s were assigned to. For liftoff without assistance, the B-47 required 9,400 feet of runway, and 14,100 feet to clear a 50-foot obstacle at the end of the field.

Boeing suggested several rocket systems to the Air Force. Most acceptable was the installation of nine Aerojet 1,000-lbf solid rocket motors with a 12-second burn time in each side of the aft fuselage. The rockets achieved 80 percent of their thrust within 0.5 second of ignition. Propellants for these motors were a mixture of potassium perchlorate and asphalt-based fuel. The exhaust gasses formed a white cloud of non-corrosive and non-toxic smoke that blew clear of the aircraft.

Four major drawbacks to the solid rocket system were identified during testing. The most notable was that the motors only provided 15 seconds of thrust and the aircraft could not initiate an aborted takeoff until the rockets were expended. The expended rocket units also had to be carried throughout the flight; at 120-pounds each, they reduced the payload by 2,160 pounds. From an operational perspective, during a still-air day, the smoke from the rockets would not dissipate quickly enough, obscuring the vision of following aircraft.

As an alternative, liquid rockets were investigated. In 1948, the Air Materiel Command awarded contracts to both Aerojet and W. M. Kellogg to develop a liquid system using fuming nitric acid and JP-3 as propellants. Use of the non-hypergolic (non-self-igniting) propellants in both the Aerojet and Kellogg systems resulted in a number of explosions early in the program. Kellogg's program was terminated in 1951, most likely because of severe damage inflicted on their test cell during one of these explosions. The Aerojet system continued through its flight test program at Edwards AFB, California.

*This B-47B-15-BW (50-027) is being lifted off the runway at Edwards AFB with a huge plume of white smoke trailing from the solid-fuel RATO bottles. An Air Force Flight Test Center insignia was applied to the nose. The bottles dissipated as the gear was being retracted. (L. S. Jones)*

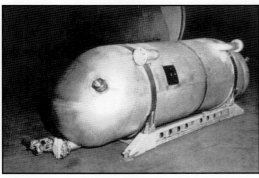

The cockpit (top) of the B-47B-1-BW (49-2644) was modified to accommodate the ATO control panel for the liquid-fueled Aerojet RATO system. The photo above shows one of the oxidizer tanks that was installed in the fuselage above the rocket compartments. (Aerojet via Prof. Charles Ehresman)

Suited-up technicians service the oxidizer tanks. The two rocket engines installed on the left side were rotated outwards for testing. After a 60-second firing on 12 October 1953, the aft fuselage was wrinkled from the thermal abuse. (top: Aerojet via Prof. Charles Ehresman; bottom: USAF)

Two test firings of the YLR45-AJ-1 rocket engines at Edwards AFB. The national insignia served as a heat sink and was later removed (see bottom photo at center). Unlike the solids, the exhaust from the liquids was not smokey, but very toxic. (Aerojet General via Prof. Charles Ehresman)

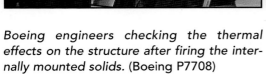

Boeing engineers checking the thermal effects on the structure after firing the internally mounted solids. (Boeing P7708)

Boeing engineers conducted a ground test on the internally mounted RATO solid-fuel bottles on the first XB-47 (46-065) at Boeing Field. Only the aft row of three was being fired when this photo was taken. (Boeing P7703)

*In this view of a B-47A (49-1900) the bomb bay spoiler was deployed. This picture dates from 5 May 1951. (Boeing P11221)*

With the Aerojet system, the oxidizer was supplied to the combustion chamber under pressure from a pair of 200-gallon bleed air tanks while fuel used a turbopump. Initial ignition was accomplished with a glow plug located in a secondary chamber, and then ignition began in the 5,000-lbf main thrust chamber that operated at 365-pounds-per-square-inch ambient pressures. During one test at Aerojet's Azusa facility in 1952, a thrust chamber in the B-47 mock-up ruptured during ignition and shrapnel punctured one of the oxidizer tanks. Coupled with a fuel line rupture, this resulted in an intense fire that destroyed the test stand. This incident caused a temporary halt to testing until the conditions could be eliminated.

Four Aerojet YLR45-AJ-1 rocket engines were installed (two per side) in a B-47B-1-BW (49-2644) for testing at Edwards. This system included a JP-4 tank mounted in the fuselage immediately aft of the rockets and two oxidizer tanks installed in the rocket compartments. The rocket engines were extended to 20 degrees outboard of the aircraft centerline for takeoff and retracted to fair into the fuselage and reduce drag during flight.

Testing of the Aerojet system was conducted over 59 flights with gross takeoff weights ranging between 130,000 and 181,000 pounds. Takeoff rolls ranged between 2,425 and 5,445 feet compared to 9,400 feet without augmentation. The final test with this system was conducted on 25 August 1954. Despite this apparent success, the disadvantages of the liquid system worried everybody. No further liquid rocket ATO tests were conducted on the B-47 and the external rack Aerojet solid-propellant systems were employed on operational Stratojets.

Boeing engineers were confident that a horsecollar or split rack RATO installation would have no adverse effect on the aircraft and wanted to have it placed immediately into production. Bob Robbins, then B-47 Assistant Chief Project Engineer, believed a flight test would be prudent. During the first test, the belly skins were burnt through and the tail cone and horizontal tail surfaces were scorched. The engineers immediately went back to the drawing boards to develop a solution – this being an articulating rack to deflect the rocket exhaust. Noah D. Showalter, then Chief of Flight Test, commented: "One test is worth a hundred expert opinions."

# NACA Flight Testing

Given the significant advances in numerous technologies introduced with the B-47, it is not surprising that the NACA wanted to test the aircraft as soon as possible. The first B-47A (49-1900) was delivered to the NACA Langley Aeronautical Laboratory on 11 July 1952 for a series of studies into the aeroelastic effects on structural loads. The aircraft was then flown to the NACA High Speed Flight Station at Edwards AFB on 17 March 1953 to study the aeroelastic effects on dynamic stability. Unfortunately, the aircraft was out of commission for two months due to a cracked canopy.

The first stability and control test was flown at Edwards on 18 May 1953 with Joseph A. Walker and Stanley P. Butchart at the controls. After this flight, an optigraph was installed and the RATO panels were replaced with solid sheet metal because high gross weight takeoffs were not part of the test program.

During 1953, a dozen flights were conducted. Handling qualities, loads, and dynamic stability data were obtained at four center-of-gravity locations over a Mach range of between 0.55 to 0.80 at altitudes around 35,000 feet. For the initial testing, the aircraft was restricted to 310 knots. Subsequent tests were conducted at 425 knots, the aileron reversal speed, or an indicated Mach number of 0.815; whichever was lower. This initial longitudinal stability testing included speed runs, turns, push-down-pull-up maneuvers, and landing configuration stalls. For the lateral stability tests, one-quarter and one-half deflection aileron rolls and sideslips to two and five degrees were performed at 35,000 feet at Mach numbers up to 0.73. During this early testing, maneuvers would be terminated at the onset of buffet due to a technical order requiring extensive inspections after every flight in the buffet region. Such excursions would have introduced excessive delays into the test program.

During 1954, the aircraft was officially taken into the NACA inventory and was assigned the NACA 150 tail number. Flights 13 and 14 were rather unusual. Conducted on 8 January 1954, they were designed to collect landing data statistics, landing loads data, and to assess the control systems and feel devices. Walker and Butchart conducted a series of touch-and-go landings on the dry lakebed at Edwards. A total of 10 landings were recorded from approximately 15 seconds before touchdown to 15 seconds after touchdown. The aircraft gross weights ranged between 122,000 and 106,000 pounds, and the speed range for the landings was 134 knots at the heaviest weight to 123 knots at the lowest gross weight. A five-knot crosswind was blowing during each of the landings. It was learned that as the aircraft gross weight decreased, there was an increasing tendency for the aircraft to bounce if the shock strut pressure was not serviced to the recommended levels. The drag chute gave improved directional stability on rollout in addition to performing its primary function of deceleration.

Stanley Butchart and John B. "Jack" McKay obtained loads data during Flight No. 28 on 5 November 1954, but a post-flight inspection showed that the wing drag angles were cracked. All of the specialized NACA test instrumentation in the bomb bay was removed

*This NACA technician was removing the protective covers from the angle-of-attack and angle-of-yaw sensors mounted on the airspeed boom on a B-47A (49-1900). In flight, these sensors provided data that was continuously recorded on oscillographs to provide a real-time record of the aircraft's attitude throughout the flight. (NACA E-1344 via Boeing)*

and the aircraft ferried to Tinker AFB, Oklahoma, on 1 December 1954 for repairs. These were completed and the aircraft was returned to Edwards on 6 March 1955.

Another interesting flight took place on 2 October 1956 when Butchart and Neil A. Armstrong flew Flight No. 53. A Convair JF-102A Delta Dagger made two Mach 1.2 passes within 200 feet of the B-47A so that the effect of the shock wave on the vertical stabilizer of the Stratojet could be measured.

During June and July 1957, the B-47A made 10 flights at the Ames Aeronautical Laboratory to measure the effects of aircraft flexibility on wing bending strains in rough air. Henry A. Cole, Jr. and Stuart Brown flew all of the flights. For these tests an instrumented B-29 was also used. Strain gauges were mounted along the rear spar of the B-29 and a pair of accelerometers was installed midchord on the wings between the engines. Eight strain gauges were

The first B-47A (49-1900) reveals its long bomb bay doors, lack of tail armament, internal RATO installation, and the fiberglass radome under the forward fuselage. National insignia and USAF were carried on the underside of the wings. (Boeing P10238)

The first B-47A (49-1900) was assigned to NACA for a number of flight tests. Its USAF markings were retained and the black NACA wings were added to the black-edged yellow tail stripe. The photo is dated 10 August 1953. (NASA Dryden Collection via Tony Landis)

A little-known series of tests were conducted by the NACA Lewis Flight Propulsion Laboratory into silencing jet exhuasts. This B-47B-25-BW (51-2075) was used for the tests that featured a modified outboard nacelle. (NASA Glenn Research Center)

*Later in its life, this B-47A (49-1900) had its USAF markings removed and was redesignated NACA 150. A gust probe was faired into the nose of the aircraft. Note that the inboard wing panels and inboard engine struts were painted white. A camera box was mounted on top of the fuselage behind the cockpit to photograph shock waves and wing bending while in flight. The photo is dated 26 October 1954, and an unrelated Douglas D-558-II Skyrocket is in the foreground. (NASA Dryden Collection via Tony Landis)*

mounted along the front and rear spars of the left wing and one on each spar at the root of the right wing. An accelerometer was installed in the fuselage just aft of the wings. In addition, a gust probe was mounted to the nose of the B-47 that recorded a time history of the vertical gust velocity. Both aircraft had control position recorders and attitude and rate gyros.

For these tests, the B-29 was flown at a gross weight of 105,900 pounds, whereas the B-47 was at 113,200 pounds. These weights gave relative equivalency to the aircraft. However, the B-29 had about 80 percent of its weight in the wings due to the fuel. The B-47 carried all of its fuel in the fuselage, and the ratio of wing weight to total weight was about 36 percent. Weight distribution across the span of the B-29 was relatively uniform, while the B-47 had large mass concentrations at the engines. The wing stiffness of the B-29 was about twice that of the B-47. Because of the swept wing, the lower stiffness, and the concentrated masses, the B-47 had rather large static aeroelastic effects associated with wing twist. In contrast, the aeroelastic effects on the B-29 were negligible or absent.

NACA pilots flew both the B-29 and B-47 in clear air turbulence at an altitude of around 2,000 feet. The flight test speeds were 250-mph for the B-29 and 479-mph for the B-47. In addition to the rough air tests, slow maneuver pull-ups were flown in smooth air at various test conditions to determine quasi-static reference strains (i.e., for reference points).

This testing revealed some serious deficiencies resulting in buffeting at higher speeds, and the B-47 was subsequently restricted to Mach 0.8. These tests showed that the flying in rough air resulted in moderate strain amplification all along the span. For the B-47, the effects of flexibility were complicated by the importance of static aeroelasticity effects in addition to dynamic responses. The dynamic amplifications appeared to be quite large in the midspan region where the inboard engine mass was concentrated.

During late 1957, the research program for the B-47A was expanded to include investigation into the problems associated with blind approaches and landings. For these tests, the Air Force Flight Test Center Electronics Installation Group installed a Very High

*Fuel is drained from a J47 at the NACA High Speed Flight Station. (NASA Dryden Collection via Tony Landis)*

*NASA 150 on 10 February 1958 showing the unique paint scheme on the top of the wings. (NASA Dryden Collection via Tony Landis)*

*The first B-47A after its transfer to the NACA. (NASA Dryden Collection via Tony Landis)*

Frequency Omnidirectional Radio (VOR) system in the bomber. Two flights during September 1957 consisted of a series of approaches with a subsequent touch-and-go landing, alternating between visual, ILS, and GCA approaches, using various initial deviations from the ideal flight path. Unfortunately, a possible malfunction of the ILS instrumentation brought into question the validity of the data obtained during these tests. Four more approach and

landing tests were conducted during October and November with satisfactory results.

After completing 79 flights, the B-47A was flown to Davis-Monthan AFB, Arizona, on 28 February 1958 with Butchart and Armstrong at the controls. The only surviving portion of a B-47A is the nose section of the second aircraft, which is in storage at the Pima Air & Space Museum outside Tucson.

## B-47A DISPOSITIONS

| Aircraft | Serial No. | Disposition |
|---|---|---|
| 1 | 49-1900 | Equipped with solid rocket propellant ATO and bailed to Boeing for flight tests. Transferred to NACA (as NACA 150) for stability and control evaluations and aeroelasticity flight tests. |
| 2 | 49-1901 | Equipped with solid rocket propellant ATO and assigned to AMC for accelerated service evaluation tests. Currently dismantled and in storage at the Pima Air & Space Museum. |
| 3 | 49-1902 | Equipped with liquid-type ATO, air-to-air refueling, and complete tactical equipment and assigned to AMC as a production prototype for the B-47Bs. |
| 4 | 49-1903 | Equipped with solid rocket propellant ATO and K-2 bombing system, and used in bombsight development in the armament testing programs. Permanently assigned to Special Weapons Command. |
| 5 | 49-1904 | Equipped with solid rocket propellant ATO and K-2 bombing system, and assigned to the 306th BMW (SAC), MacDill AFB, Florida, for the transition school and later its tactical squadrons. |
| 6 | 49-1905 | Equipped with solid rocket propellant ATO and K-2 bombing system, and assigned to the 306th BMW (SAC), MacDill AFB, Florida, for the transition school and later its tactical squadrons. |
| 7 | 49-1906 | Equipped with solid rocket propellant ATO and K-2 bombing system, and assigned to the 306th BMW (SAC), MacDill AFB, Florida, for the transition school and later its tactical squadrons. |
| 8 | 49-1907 | Equipped with solid rocket propellant ATO and K-2 bombing system, and permanently assigned to Special Weapons Command. |
| 9 | 49-1908 | Equipped with solid rocket propellant ATO and K-2 bombing system, and assigned to the 306th BMW (SAC), MacDill AFB, Florida, for the transition school and later its tactical squadrons. |
| 10 | 49-1909 | Equipped with solid rocket propellant ATO and modified A-1 fire control system for use in the armament development program. |

These seven B-47As (four in nose docks) were undergoing completion at WIBAC. To the rear were s/n 49-1903, 49-1907, and 49-1908. Note the ramp control tower on top of the hangar. (Boeing 45583A)

# Chapter 3

# PRODUCTION AND PREPARATION

While Boeing President Bill Allen and his staff vigorously petitioned the Air Force to build the Stratojet in Seattle, their efforts were overridden. During World War II, the Japanese had dispatched submarines to the West Coast of the United States and launched balloons with firebombs and infected rats from mainland Japan. In addition, one submarine, the I-17, managed to lob a few rounds from its deck gun onto the oil derricks at Ellwood, north of Los Angeles. With these events in mind, the Air Force recognized the emerging threat from the Soviet Union and directed that B-47 production be moved to Boeing-Wichita (WIBAC) in Wichita, Kansas.

As with the B-17, B-24, and B-29, the requirement for bombers exceeded the capacity of the prime contractor and secondary sources had to be found. In the case of the B-47, both Douglas-Tulsa (DT) and Lockheed-Marietta (LM) were tasked with building additional aircraft.

Early on, WIBAC made some appraisals of the B-47 program and shared the data with the Air Force. By mid-1951, SAC observers were pleased with the B-47, but noted that while the airframe and engines were quantum leaps over previous designs, the overall aircraft program was hampered by many of its piece-parts. The designers and manufacturers of the components and subsystems such as boost pumps, selector valves, and relays, were not in tune with the sophisticated design necessary for such a high-performance aircraft. Consequently, many early B-47s were equipped with the same components that were installed on B-29s and B-50s.

On 28 April 1950 Bill Allen announced an integration of the Seattle and Wichita engineering divisions into a single unit. Assistant Chief Engineer Noah D. Showalter was placed in charge of the Wichita engineering unit, while retaining his former position as Boeing Chief Test Pilot. Showalter moved to Wichita, but reported to the chief engineer in Seattle. Allen opined, "The two primary objectives of this organization revision are to provide a more direct channel for engineering decisions on the B-47 project, and to more completely integrate the engineering effort with Wichita manufacturing requirements." However, Seattle Boeing Aircraft Company (SEBAC) retained overall engineering control and performed all experimental projects relative to the aircraft.

In Wichita, Harold W. Zipp became the Executive Engineer under Showalter and would direct all engineering and administrative activities for WIBAC. George C. Martin became chief of the combined B-47 engineering projects under both Seattle and Wichita, and John J. Clark of the Wichita Division became B-47 Senior Project Engineer in Wichita.

*Key personnel for the B-47 program were assembled at WIBAC on 19 April 1951, to establish preliminary planning for production of the Stratojet by Boeing, Douglas, and Lockheed. Seated at the table (l-r) were Harry Woodhead, VP and General Manager, Douglas-Tulsa; J. E. Schaefer, Boeing VP and General Manager, WIBAC; Colonel Harley S. Jones, B-47 Field Project Officer, headquartered at WIBAC; Brigadier General Phillips W. Smith, Chief of the Procurement Division, AMC; F. W. Conant, Sr. VP Douglas; Wellwood E. Beall, VP and General Manager, SEBAC; J. V. Carmichael, VP and General Manager, Lockheed-Marietta; and R. R. Kearton, Master Scheduling Manager, Lockheed-Marietta. Brigadier General O. F. Carlson, newly appointed Special Assistant to the Chief of Staff for the B-47 Program, was not available for the photograph. (Boeing BW45731)*

## MANUFACTURING PLANTS

Both XB-47s had been essentially handmade in Seattle. When the design and manufacturing functions were moved to Wichita a myriad of tooling had to be designed, fabricated, and certified before any new aircraft could be built. During World War II, Boeing developed a multi-line manufacturing system in which several parallel rows of B-17s and B-29s moved down the assembly where common work was performed. This system was again used for the production of the B-47. With this system, aircraft with a common completion status moved forward in the lines, while components were delivered from the sides to the various assembly areas.

The government had built Air Force Plant 2 in Wichita during World War II specifically to produce the B-29s. After VJ-Day, many government aircraft plants were closed and most of the workers were furloughed; only a skeleton crew remained at WIBAC. With the advent of the Korean War the plant was reactivated to refurbish B-29s destined for their second round of combat.

In 1941 the U.S. Army Corps of Engineers built Air Force Plant 3 in Tulsa, Oklahoma. During World War II, Douglas used the plant to produce 964 Consolidated B-24 Liberators, along with a plethora of their own aircraft types such as the A-24/SBD Dauntless and A-26

*Boeing production engineers and planners worked to assemble this factory floor plan for production of the Stratojet. Receiving areas and subassembly shops were on the periphery. Major subassemblies were in the foreground. The wing laydown area was behind the person at lower left. Next came the fuselage long cigar. Four final assembly lines may also be seen. (Boeing BW40288)*

Invader (redesignated B-26 after the war). The Air Force reactivated the plant, with its 2.8 million square feet of floor space, in 1951 to build B-47s and Douglas received an $11.5 million contract to tool up for the program. Eventually 274 B-47s were produced at this location. In addition, a large number of programmed inspections and special modifications were made there.

The government also built Air Force Plant 6 at Marietta, Georgia. It was operated by Bell Aircraft during World War II and produced 668 B-29 Superfortresses. The plant was turned over to Lockheed late in 1950 to refurbish B-29s for the Korean War. Within a year the facility employed 10,000 people, including 275 engineers and managers who moved from Burbank, California. Being in a prime position with an established and skilled workforce, Lockheed-Marietta was also tasked to produce the B-47s. Lockheed produced a total of 386 Stratojets, and numerous programmed inspections and modifications were accomplished at this plant. Lockheed also did the WB-47E conversion for the Air Weather Service in Marietta.

## PRODUCTION PLANNING

Boeing industrial engineers, production engineers, manufacturing planners, and procurement specialists worked long hours to define a viable production plan that would meet the Air Force delivery requirements for the B-47. There was an 18-month lead-time to produce the aircraft. Not only were plans laid for the actual production pipeline, but also for the factory layout and tooling requirements. New construction and factory renovation was required to accommodate each new product line.

With the official go-ahead for production of the B-47s, the first one-and-a-quarter months were allocated for administrative work and the defining of subcontracts. Six-and-a-half months were required for long-lead-time aluminum forgings, while an additional month was necessary for steel forgings. Concurrently, four-and-three-quarter months were used to procure magnesium sheet stock and aluminum extrusions. Two months were required to sort out the incoming shipments, perform receiving inspections, inventory them, and allocate them to the proper storage areas. Another month was used to cut and form the raw stock material into individual parts. The following four-and-a-half months were allocated to component fabrication and subassembly.

The aircraft began to take shape with the build-up of the center and forward fuselage that then formed what was known as the short cigar. With the addition of the aft fuselage, the assembly was known as the long cigar. After this the wings were installed and the aircraft sat on its main landing gear as it proceeded down the final assembly line. Almost six months were required from the start of fuselage assembly to the end of final assembly. Two weeks were required to install the myriad of electronics components, and then preflight and system checkout took another three weeks. During the last three weeks of the 18-month production cycle each B-47 underwent Boeing flight tests, Air Force flight tests, acceptance, and flyaway.

*This aerial view of the Lockheed-Marietta plant reveals the compass rose in the foreground, and the preflight ramp and hangar. Five C-130s shared the ramp with no less than 34 B-47s. (Lockheed-Marietta RF0704-2)*

Boeing used this 18-month cycle for every subsequent aircraft type, both military and commercial, until the year 2000 when there was a concerted effort to reduce the cycle time by 33.3 percent.

As any production program matures, the factory personnel become more familiar with their duties and there is first a gradual, then a dramatic, reduction in factory flow times. Within two years of the initiation of production at WIBAC, the production learning curve resulted in an 88-man-hour reduction in fabrication time. By October 1952 the plant was turning out more than one aircraft per day.

## SUPPLIER BASE

Excluding engines, rivets, and bolts, some 52,000 parts went into building each B-47. Each wing required 14,698 bolts and rivets. Of the bolts, 4,297 were of the close-tolerance variety. One type of these bolts had a 0.1- to 0.5-inch tolerance range, while another type

had a 0.004-inch tolerance. There were 415 different aluminum forgings in each B-47. In terms of raw stock, 64,000 pounds of aluminum, 2,000 pounds of copper, brass, and bronze, 20,000 pounds of steel (mostly for forgings), and 1,000 pounds of magnesium were used in each aircraft.

Not only was an enormous quantity of aluminum required for the B-47 program, but also new plastics, high temperature-resistant tubing, and a plethora of newer materials were required for the aircraft's components and subsystems. In many instances it was the lack of suitable materials or knowledge of how to employ them that kept subcontractors from providing reliable components for the program.

More than 27 miles of Boeing-assembled electrical wiring and 1,000 vacuum tubes were installed in each bomber. The tubes ranged in price from 56 cents to $681 each. The periscopic bombsight for the B-47 cost $250,000 as opposed to $8,000 for a Norden bombsight used on the B-17s and B-29s.

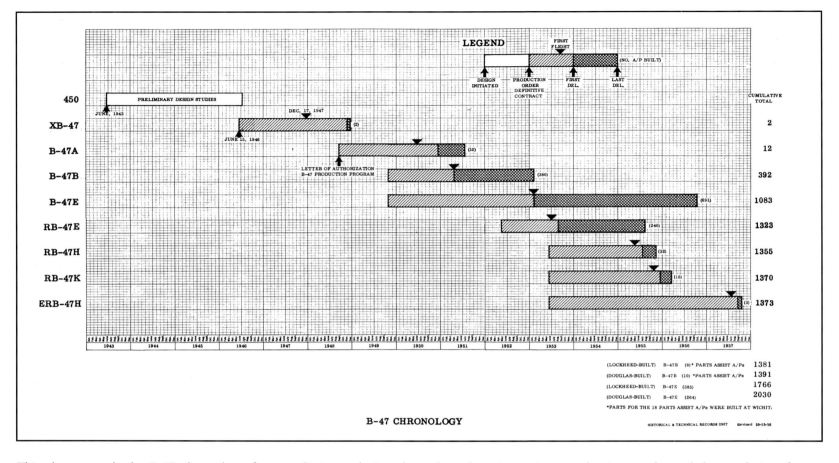

*This chart reveals the B-47 chronology from preliminary design through each major series, production totals, and the total aircraft produced by Boeing, Douglas, and Lockheed. (Boeing)*

As of 22 September 1950, a variety of subcontractors had been approved for the B-47 production program. These included Bell Aircraft in Buffalo, New York, for the inboard engine nacelles; Cleveland Pneumatic Tool Company for the aft landing gear; Bendix in South Bend, Indiana, for the forward and outrigger landing gear; San Diego's Ryan Aeronautical for the 1,700-gallon drop tanks used on the B-47E; Dixon Manufacturing Company in Coffeyville, Kansas, for the drop tank struts, tank deck doors, bomb racks, and landing gear doors; Swallow Airplane Company manufactured the bomb bay doors; and Cessna Aircraft provided the elevators and stabilizers. Subcontracted work on the B-47 accounted for 45 percent of its dollar value.

In July 1951 the Air Force issued three contracts, AF33(038)-21407, -21030, and -18564, directing Boeing to subcontract with the Ford Motor Company for the manufacture of B-47B wing box sets. As a result of a conference held at Air Materiel Command Headquarters on 27 June 1951, it was determined that Boeing would negotiate the terms (except for schedules and price) with Ford. As the prime technical contractor, Boeing would issue purchase orders for all of the tooling required to support Boeing, Douglas, and Lockheed

production. Future Secretary of Defense Robert Strange McNamara was the president of the Ford Motor Company at the time.

But Ford did not prove to be up to the task. A survey conducted at the Ford Plant in Kansas City, Missouri, on 21 October 1953 revealed that Ford was behind schedule and was unable to provide a firm plan to catch up. Since Ford was providing the wing sets for all three manufacturers, this was seriously hampering production of the B-47. The Boeing team advised that WIBAC should immediately start to build wings to use at Wichita, freeing up the limited supply from Ford for use by Douglas and Lockheed. It appeared to the Boeing team that things would begin to improve by February 1954 and that Ford might be back on schedule by March 1954 at which time WIBAC would begin using Ford wings again.

Ford's major problem was a lack of personnel experienced in aircraft production. While Ford had extensive experience mass-producing Consolidated B-24 Liberators at their Willow Run, Michigan, plant during World War II, the B-47's wings were far more advanced and difficult to manufacture. When the first shipsets of Ford wings arrived at WIBAC, they underwent routine receiving

This center fuselage section was supported in its assembly jig. As various installations were completed, the sections moved on rollers along the tracks straddling the work area. The life raft compartment was located in the top foreground. Aft, were the open raceway doors. (Douglas-Tulsa via Harry S. Gann)

Engineers and shop personnel observed the moving of this Section 41 forward fuselage for joining with the forward fuselage. This right side view reveals the circular decompression port, radar compartment, and electronics compartments. (Douglas-Tulsa T2427 via Harry S. Gann)

Here, WIBAC technicians were mating these three fuselage sections to form the short cigar. The man to the right was using a jack to align the forward fuselage, Section 44, with Section 41 and the center section, Section 42. To the left, personnel were joining Sections 41 and 42. (Boeing 55167)

inspection. Boeing determined that the parts were not built to design specification and rejected them. McNamara offered to send a team to fix the discrepant parts, but Boeing stated that they were beyond salvage. The wings had to be scrapped and a protracted battle of words ensued. In the end, Ford had to refund $5 million to Boeing for failure to produce acceptable parts. It would be a while before Ford began producing useable parts.

Besides Ford, several other companies had exclusive supplier arrangements with Boeing or the Air Force. Normally these were for sensitive systems such as engines and avionics, although a few other items were represented also. Aerojet provided the RATO rocket motors; Chance-Vought fabricated the entire structural portion of the navigator's compartment; Emerson Electric produced the A-2 fire control system employed on the early B-47s; Crosley and General Electric provided the A-5 fire control system that was installed starting in August 1953; General Electric manufactured the engines at a unit cost of approximately $50,000; International Business Machines (IBM) produced the improved MA-2 bombing and navigation system designed for the future B-52 Stratofortress and used on later versions of the B-47; Sperry Gyroscope had responsibility for monitoring the K-system on the B-47Bs and B-47Es, and also provided the autopilot system that coupled into the K-system.

A few subcontractors deserve special mention, either because they worked extremely well, or very poorly.

**Revere Copper and Brass –** It would be unusual to single out a company such as Revere Copper and Brass of New York as a subcontractor for the B-47 program, however, their contribution was significant. Balance weights for rudders and elevators were usually made from steel, but this material would have interfered with the fluxgate compass installed in the aft fuselage. Revere worked with Boeing to develop bronze balance weights. Revere Architectural Bronze Alloy 283 was selected for the parts. By using extrusions, the weight billets were cut closely approximating the final shape thereby reducing the machining requirements. The reduction in machining requirements more than offset the cost of the bronze.

**Hudson Motor Car –** In July 1951, the Hudson Motor Car Company in Detroit was contracted with to produce 176 units of the fuselage Section 44 for use by both WIBAC and Douglas-Tulsa. Nearly $15 million had been spent on the program by early 1953 with little to show. In April a Boeing team visited the Hudson facility and determined that either an all-out assistance program should be established, or the contract terminated; the Air Force opted for the assistance program. Some 200 Boeing personnel were loaned to Hudson to help ramp-up production, but quantities again fell off when the Boeing team left in August. At this point the Air Materiel Command opted to terminate the Hudson contract in support of WIBAC. However, Douglas-Tulsa also received Section 44s from Hudson and the AMC asked if any program savings could be realized if Douglas terminated some of the 176 units Hudson was scheduled to produce. On 11 August 1953 Douglas requested the Air Force to allow them to cancel procurement of the Hudson-built Section 44s at 110 units and obtain the balance from Chance-Vought. The B-47 Project Office concurred.

Boeing had also contracted with Hudson to build fuselage Section 49 for the RB-47E. After the 67th unit was obtained from Hudson, the procurement contract was terminated by the Air Force on 19 October 1953. The primary reason was that Hudson was behind schedule, but the Air Materiel Command also felt that the

*In an obviously posed photograph, this pretty young lady was simulating an NDT inspection on one of these B-47 wings. The 12 bolts on each wing root inboard rib were employed to attach each main wing assembly to the wing center section. Four bottle pins then attached the completed wing to the fuselage. The upper portion of the wing assembly on the left reveals the supporting structure within the flap well. (Boeing BW55971)*

quality of the components would be improved and there would be an estimated $4.3 million savings if Boeing brought the production in-house. The Air Force told Boeing that: "In the event publicity is unavoidable, you will be specific in stating that this work was removed from Hudson by Boeing to assure delivery of the RB-47E aircraft to and as required by the Air Force."

**A.O. Smith –** Boeing-built B-47s used main and outrigger landing gears procured from either Cleveland Pneumatic or Bendix. When additional landing gear sets were required to support the Douglas-Tulsa operation, A.O. Smith was contracted with to produce them. In September 1951 the Air Force authorized the expansion of the A.O.

*Engineers were inspecting one of these two Section 43 aft fuselage sections. (Douglas-Tulsa via Harry S. Gann)*

Smith facilities to meet the new requirements. However, by December 1953, A.O. Smith was encountering production problems.

At a 7 December 1953 Production Committee meeting, Douglas reported that they had received 10 sets of forward main gear assemblies with questionable outer cylinders. At the same meeting Lockheed reported that nine questionable outer cylinders had been delivered. Boeing forecasted that A.O. Smith would be behind by six forward gears, two aft gears, and three outrigger gears by 31 December 1953. The Production Committee decided that 10 sets of A.O. Smith gears would be diverted from Lockheed to Douglas to compensate for the defective gears. In addition, the A.O. Smith contract would be terminated and Lockheed would obtain landing gear from Cleveland Pneumatic and Bendix.

In addition to the normal large- and medium-sized suppliers, a variety of small businesses provided parts for the B-47 program. A small business was classified as a firm employing 500 persons or less. For the B-47 program, Boeing contracted with 983 of these sources, or 40 percent of the total program supplier base. These contracts were for bolts, screws, tools, valves, electrical appliances, wire, plastics, automobile parts, tents, and a multitude of other products.

## PRODUCTION CONTRACTS

With the National Security Act of 1947, the Army Air Forces were superseded by the United States Air Force (USAF) as a coequal to the Army and Navy, effective 18 September 1947.

*The long cigar for this B-47B was now resting on its main landing gear at the WIBAC plant. The entire empennage along with the windscreen and canopy were installed at this point. A factory access ladder, not the crew entry ladder, was installed in the crew entryway.* (Boeing BW55977)

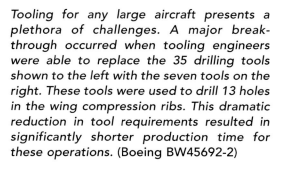

Tooling for any large aircraft presents a plethora of challenges. A major break-through occurred when tooling engineers were able to replace the 35 drilling tools shown to the left with the seven tools on the right. These tools were used to drill 13 holes in the wing compression ribs. This dramatic reduction in tool requirements resulted in significantly shorter production time for these operations. (Boeing BW45692-2)

These factory workers were using large form-boards to assemble the myriad of wire bundles that went into the B-47s. The geometry of the layout on the board does not matter so long as the wires come out the proper lengths. The formboards show the precise length of each wire, and splice and connector locations. Each formboard was for a specific wire bundle. This same method of manual wire bundle build-up is used in aircraft factories today. (Boeing)

Douglas-Tulsa technicians were sling-loading this B-47 aileron. Note the complicated articulating jig that permitted vertical lifting of the component. When in position for installation, the left hoist was lowered and the articulating arm permitted the aileron to assume a horizontal position for mating with the wing. (Douglas-Tulsa via Harry S. Gann)

It should be noted that the federal government operates on two separate calendars. A standard January through December calendar year was (and still is) employed for the recording of events. Hence, history programs are generally based on the calendar year. The second calendar is the fiscal year (FY) that is based on the federal budget year. For decades the fiscal year ran from 1 July through 30 June and was identified as FY54 for 1 July 1953 through 30 June 1954. During the late 1970s the fiscal year was changed to 1 October through 30 September.

On 22 November 1948, contract W33-038-ac-22413 had been approved for the procurement of 10 B-47As plus a follow-on procurement of three B-47As and 41 B-47Bs. In February 1949 the contract was amended to increase the number of B-47Bs from 41 to 55 and to cancel the three additional B-47As. As a result of the cancellation of the Boeing's B-54 (a derivative of the B-50) and savings made in the B-50D and C-119B programs, funds became available for five additional B-47Bs.

Boeing had planned deliveries of the B-47As to begin in January 1950, however, there were critical labor shortages, material procurement difficulties, engine changes, engineering changes, and procurement delays that resulted in deliveries slipping until April 1950. Despite this setback, the Air Force continued to order additional B-47s from all three manufacturers.

By September 1953 the Air Materiel Command had a total of 714 B-47Es and RB-47s on order from the three manufacturers for FY53. However, there was a looming Federal budget crisis, and during the same month the Air Force announced a reduction of 151 B-47s and a stretch-out in the delivery schedule for the remaining aircraft.

Four Boeing mechanics were attaching the wing to the long cigar of the XB-47. Aside from walking, the main mode of transportation within the factory was by bicycle – which continues to this day. (Boeing H6079)

*Both B-47Es and C-130s shared the factory floor at the Lockheed plant in Marietta, Georgia. In the foreground was a B-47E-45-LM (52-385). (Lockheed-Marietta C4997)*

On 8 September 1953, Acting Secretary of the Air Force James H. Douglas announced that there would be an overall cut of 965 aircraft of all types from existing production orders. He went on to state that the $750 million savings were not an economy measure, but a revised estimate of the requirements for the Eisenhower Administration's goal of a 120-wing Air Force. Further, Secretary of Defense Charles Wilson commented, "the Air Force is now operating efficiently." It was so-much propaganda.

WIBAC General Manager J. E. Schaefer moved quickly to place the blow into perspective for his employees. He advised that predic-

tions of long-term procurement had always been difficult because of the government's fiscal and procurement policies. Schaefer added that it was "one of the problems to which Secretary Wilson is now giving particular attention. To the extent possible, he wants to level out the peaks and valleys in aircraft production and eliminate stop-and-go methods of procurement." Typically, production would be truncated at the end. However, in this instance, production would continue through December 1956 with fewer aircraft being delivered each month. With this plan, there was less disruption to the factory and the workforce, while still retaining the surge capacity if conditions warranted its use.

## FISCAL YEAR 1951-53 PRODUCTION CONTRACTS

| Contract | Year | Requirements |
|---|---|---|
| AF33(038)-21407 | FY51 | Initial order for production B-47s. |
| AF33(038)-22284 | FY52 | Boeing was to deliver 195 B-47Es and 77 RB-47Es, plus spares, special tools, ground support equipment, technical data, and engineering changes for a price of $397,391,170.60. The average unit price for the B-47Es was $1,166,390.40 while that of the RB-47Es was $1,506.317.80. |
| AF33(038)-22284 | FY53 | Called for an increase in the total number of aircraft from 195 to 257. This supplemental agreement cost $72,062,333, but the unit price for the aircraft was reduced to $1,151,730; for a $14,550.40 reduction per aircraft. |
| AF33(038)-21030 | FY53 | Authorized Lockheed to produce 290 B-47Es. With a total allocation of $268,628,626, deliveries were scheduled for November 1954 through November 1955. |
| AF33(038)-18564 | FY53 | Supplemental authorization for Douglas to add 158 B-47Es to the existing order for 193 aircraft. The contract, approved on 8 July 1953, totaled $204,762,924. |

### B-47E PROGRAM REDUCTIONS

| Series | Facility | Original Quantity | Reduced Quantity | Terminated Quantity | Percent Reduction |
|---|---|---|---|---|---|
| B-47E | WIBAC | 257 | 252 | 5 | 2 |
| B-47E | Marietta | 209 | 154 | 55 | 26 |
| B-47E | Tulsa | 171 | 94 | 77 | 45 |
| RB-47E | WIBAC | 77 | 65 | 12 | 16 |

The Air Force envisioned that the reduction of B-47 procurement from 714 to 565 aircraft would realize savings of $347,651,122. But, when considering the stretch-out and terminations costs, the net savings was only $241,289,805. Further, factoring in the stretch-out and termination costs associated with engine spares, the total net savings was actually $167,536,631.

*This B-47B, assembled from WIBAC parts, was being fueled prior to an engine run at the Lockheed-Marietta plant. Accompanying the fuel truck was the ever-present fire truck. (Lockheed-Marietta B6003)*

*Lockheed-Marietta had been restoring B-29s for the Korean War effort when it was tasked with building B-47s. A B-47B-20-BW (50-055) was sent to Lockheed for a demonstration. A cleat track was used to tow the aircraft. (Lockheed-Marietta A7521)*

When still further cuts were proposed, the Air Force's B-47 buyer, Lieutenant Colonel J. H. Schaeffer, informed the Aircraft and Weapons Board that such cuts would do several things, "none of them good." He stated that further reductions would "cut the throat" of the B-47 program before its re-order date, and during a period when no successor program could be mobilized. Any such reductions would dispose of a trained workforce before they could be used for another program.

Subsequently, during informal discussions between Undersecretary of the Air Force James Douglas and Assistant Secretary of Defense Roger Lewis they agreed with the Air Materiel Command assessment and believed that the Aircraft and Weapons Board would recommend procurement of the last 200 B-47s.

As late as November 1953, Headquarters USAF was still considering termination of the last 200 B-47s while AMC continued to oppose this action. The alternative was to modernize the B-47B fleet to provide them with capabilities similar to the B-47E. To support AMC's position, Major General David H. Baker, director of Procurement and Production, stated that WIBAC's labor force would be seriously affected by such a cut. Because the B-52 was not scheduled for acceptance until October 1956, there would be a nine-month gap in production. The result would be a cut in WIBAC employment during this hiatus. This same condition existed at Douglas-Tulsa and Lockheed-Marietta where the RB-66 Destroyer and the C-130 Hercules programs, respectively, were coming to fruition.

*This Air Force crew accepted the last Lockheed-built B-47E-75-LM (53-1972). Major Wendell L. Stultz (r), aircraft commander; 2nd Lieutenant Robert R. Alexander (l), navigator; and Captain Hobart D. Kanatzar (c), copilot, accepted the aircraft for the Air Force. In October 1950, Major Stultz accepted the first B-47A from WIBAC. (Lockheed-Marietta RE3822-2)*

*This B-47E-55-DT (53-2137) was the 241st Stratojet produced by Douglas-Tulsa. Note the unusual towing arrangement. A Clark tug and tow bar were employed for the forward gear, but the aft gear was mounted on a multi-bogied dolly towed by a pair of Clark tugs. (Douglas-Tulsa via Harry S. Gann)*

## CAPEHART AND WHERRY HOUSING

The end of World War II saw 15 million American service men and women returning home. This exacerbated an already existing housing shortage in the United States. In 1946, fully 9 percent of American families lived two or three couples to a single family home.

The beginning of the Cold War in the years immediately following World War II resulted in a need to maintain a large, peacetime military. In 1949, Secretary of Defense Louis A. Johnson observed that, "Rather than be separated from their families because of lack of Government quarters and scarcity of adequate rental housing at their places of assignment, many of the service personnel have accepted disgraceful living conditions in shacks, trailer camps, and overcrowded buildings, many at extortionate rents. It cannot be expected that competent individuals will long endure such conditions. There is nothing more vital or pressing in the interest of morale and the security of America than proper housing for our Armed Forces."

On 5 March 1949 Senator Kenneth Wherry of Nebraska introduced a bill to provide for construction of family housing "on or around military installations." Wherry "sponsors," were able to obtain low-interest loans insured by the Federal Housing Administration to construct, own, and maintain the houses and rent them to military families. At the end of a 40-year period, each sponsor was to turn the project over to the Government.

The Wherry bill did not require specific designs, so sponsors took designs from existing "off the shelf" plans that were being built in the civilian market at the time. Therefore, there were no specific Wherry-style homes that were built for the military. A number of problems existed with the Wherry houses, ranging from their small size to shoddy construction. Nevertheless, in the end, 264 Wherry projects were built totaling 83,742 units.

While housing construction nationwide continued at a breakneck pace, by 1957 there was still a shortfall for the military, with the Army estimating a deficit of 100,000 housing units. On 11 August 1955 Congress passed the Capehart Housing Act. Similar to Wherry, Senator Homer E. Capehart of Indiana asked private developers to build housing units for the military, but unlike Wherry, once the houses were completed they came under military control. Capehart houses were also larger, reducing the complaints about the smaller Wherry homes. Privacy, preservation of the natural environment, and integration of the neighborhood into existing facilities were also key issues in Capehart housing, as well as a move toward more single-family and duplex-style housing.

Because of the disparity between the larger Capehart homes and the Wherry homes, many of the Wherry developments were at less than full occupancy and some projects had defaulted. By the end of the 1950s, Congress mandated the acquisition of Wherry housing at all installations that were to receive Capehart units. The primary objective of acquiring the Wherry houses was for the military to bring these homes up to the standards of other assigned housing in size and design of living spaces, so kitchen upgrades and additional bathrooms and utility rooms were authorized.

When the Capehart program came to an end in 1964, nearly 250,000 units of Wherry and Capehart had been built. At the end of 1994, about 175,000 of these homes were still in existence.

*These B-47Bs were at the fuel pit at Douglas-Tulsa. The censor literally scratched the aircraft tail number off the film.* (Douglas-Tulsa)

Headquarters USAF took no further action on the cancellation of the additional 200 B-47s and the issue was dropped. As a result, the three aircraft manufacturers retained their skilled labor force until their next major program could be established.

## BASE AND FACILITY MODIFICATIONS

The introduction of the B-47 required a vast expenditure of funds for both new and upgraded facilities to support operation of the aircraft, and for proving the operational viability of the aircraft against the ever-changing Soviet air defense system. The requirement for a powerful nuclear deterrent force caused the Joint Chiefs of Staff to work with Congress for adequate funding. New bases were constructed; existing bases were upgraded with enhanced ramps, runways, and facilities; and diplomatic negotiations secured sufficient forward operating locations.

## STATIC TESTING

A complete B-47B structural airframe was produced for the static tests. The airframe was built ahead of its normal schedule and rolled out without engines, flight equipment, controls, and accessories. The airframe was loaded into a massive jig with a cable and pulley system actuated by remotely controlled hydraulic jacks within a huge structural frame. External weights were added to the wings to simulate the engines. Incremental loads were applied to the airframe so engineers could measure the deflections at critical areas.

Unlike most aircraft of the era, which were tested at Wright-Patterson, the B-47 static test facility was housed in a hangar in Wichita. More than 700,000 pounds of structural steel was used in fabricating the scaffolding and jigs that supported the aircraft.

Ultimately, the wings were deflected upward for 13 feet and downward for 6 feet. During these tests the loads and cycles applied to the airframe far exceeded that of several combat lives for a

## BASE AND FACILITY UPGRADES TO SUPPORT THE B-47

| Base | Years | Facilities |
|---|---|---|
| Barksdale AFB, Louisiana | 1951-1959 | Assigned to SAC on 1 November 1949. Expanded concrete areas and new runway. |
| Castle AFB, California | 1954 | Assigned to SAC on 21 March 1946. New maintenance hangar in 1954. |
| Davis-Monthan AFB, Arizona | 1953-1954 | Assigned to SAC on 31 March 1946. Extended runways. |
| Dyess AFB, Texas | 1955-1956 | Abilene AFB was renamed Dyess AFB on 1 December 1956. Rehabilitated runway and taxiway system, added aviation and jet fuel storage facilities, new airmens' dormitories, and 1,000 Capehart housing units. |
| Eielson AFB, Alaska | 1952-1955 | SAC was a tenant on this Alaskan Air Command base beginning on 17 May 1955. Facilities were expanded to permit SAC to use Eielson as a staging base for its bombers and tankers. |
| Bunker Hill AFB, Indiana | 1959 | Assigned to SAC on 1 September 1957. Extended runway to 12,000 feet, added two 1,000-foot overruns, expanded ramp space, new maintenance docks, and expanded operations building. |
| Homestead AFB, Florida | 1954-1957 | Assigned to SAC on 5 January 1953. Upgraded to accommodate two B-47 wings in June 1956. |
| Hunter AFB, Georgia | 1952-1957 | Used a tar-rubber runway material that was less costly than concrete for accelerated tests. Became a two-wing base. |
| Lincoln AFB, Nebraska | 1952-1956 | Activated under SAC at a cost of $80 million. Had a 12,900-foot-long by 200-foot-wide runway built. Became a two-wing base. |
| Little Rock AFB, Arkansas | 1953-1958 | Assigned to SAC on 1 February 1955. Completed new construction for two B-47 wings, including runways, ILS, GCA, alert facilities, and 1,535 Wherry housing units. |
| Lockbourne AFB, Ohio | 1951-1958 | Assigned to SAC in September 1951. Expanded to accommodate two wings in January 1955. Served solely in reconnaissance and ECM roles. |
| MacDill AFB, Florida | 1951-1960 | Assigned to SAC on 21 March 1946. Converted facilities, extended runway and ramp area, new hospital, and added 550 Wherry housing units. Accommodated two B-47 wings. |
| March AFB, California | 1952-1955 | Assigned to SAC on 1 May 1949. Strengthened concrete areas, added new hangars and armament and electronics buildings, other new buildings, alternate communications facility built, new alert facility added, and 633 Wherry housing units. |
| McConnell AFB, Kansas | 1951-1963 | Named Wichita AFB on 7 June 1951. Renamed McConnell AFB on 12 April 1954. Assigned to SAC 1 July 1958. Served as an ATC then SAC-operated B-47 training base. RAPCON completed in May 1955, but not operational until September 1959. |
| Mountain Home AFB, Idaho | 1954-1959 | Assigned to SAC on 21 March 1946, then MATS. Returned to SAC on 24 January 1951. Extended the main runway to 12,000 feet, added housing and a hospital. |
| Pinecastle AFB, Florida (later McCoy AFB) | 1951-1963 | The World War II Pinecastle AAF on a 2,216-acre site was reactivated. Expanded to 4,426.40 acres, lengthened runways, strengthened concrete areas, expanded ramp areas, and increased base housing. Established for ATC 31 January 1951. Transferred to SAC on 1 January 1954. First B-47s for ATC arrived on 6 November 1952. Renamed McCoy AFB on 7 May 1958 in memory of Colonel Michael Norman Wright McCoy who had been killed in a B-47 crash. |
| Portsmouth AFB, New Hampshire | 1952-1957 | Construction began on 8 December 1952 at Portsmouth Municipal Airport. Named Portsmouth AFB on 1 February 1955, and assigned to SAC. Base rebuilt to accommodate two B-47 wings. Rehabilitated the runway, taxiways, and ramp. Built new Capehart housing. Renamed Pease AFB on 7 September 1957. Became a two-wing base. Later renamed Pease AFB. |
| Plattsburgh AFB, New York | 1953-1955 | Assigned to SAC on 1 February 1955. New construction to support a B-47 wing and air division headquarters, including runway and 1,685 Capehart housing units. |
| Whiteman AFB, Missouri | 1951-1963 | Assigned to SAC on 1 August 1951. Reopened for B-47 and KC-97 operations in October 1951. Added a hospital and 904 housing units. |

This model was constructed to better visualize the full-scale steel towers and scaffolding that would be built to the B-47 structural test program. Staff engineer George Snyder (left) and Ed Wells, VP Engineering discussed the device when photographed on 24 January 1951. The actual test rig was built in Wichita. (Boeing P10777)

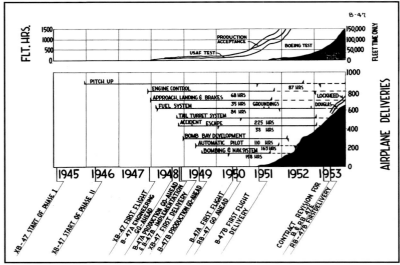

The upper chart shows the B-47 fleet flight hours from first flight through 1953, and reveals flight hours dedicated to USAF tests, production tests, Boeing tests, and cumulative fleet time. The lower chart is a timeline for the B-47 program from the beginning of the XB-47 Phase I in 1945 through the 1953 RB-47 program start. (Boeing)

This composite photograph reveals the full wing deflection of the B-47 structural test wing in the test rig. The wing deflected through an arc of almost 20 ft. A system of hydraulic jacks and cables pulled the wing panel through the test range. (Boeing)

bomber. As a result of these static tests, engineers were able to predict areas that would require structural strengthening to ensure the aircraft met its anticipated service life and was safe for operation by operational crews.

## BOEING PRODUCT SUPPORT

Over the years, Boeing has been recognized around the world for its product support organization. The product support organizations are generally divided between the on-site field service engineer, and the in-house technical department including service engineering and reliability engineering.

The most direct link between the customer (the Air Force, in this case) and the Boeing Airplane Company is the field service engineer. Their primary function is to assist the customer in obtaining maximum safe and efficient utilization from all aircraft of Boeing design. To the customer personnel who operate and maintain the aircraft, the field service engineer is the personification of the Boeing Airplane Company, for through them they have access to the entire technical skill and knowledge of every department within the company. Several field service engineers were stationed at every Strategic Air Command B-47 base and Air Materiel Command test base.

Observations of the field service engineer often resulted in design improvements to ensure safety and efficient operation. Routine reliability reports were fed into the Reliability Department where system and component assessments are made for design engineers to consider for improvements.

This WIBAC engineer was inspecting the clearances between the aileron and articulating engine strut fairing. With the left aileron deflected down, a rolling moment to the right was induced into the aircraft. Note that the aileron tab moved in the opposite direction of the aileron. Such movement allowed airloads to assist the pilot in moving the ailerons. In the background was a B-29 assigned to the Air Research and Development Command. (Boeing BW92892)

The 1,000th WIBAC Stratojet was a B-47E-105-BW (52-609) seen here escorted by an RB-47E-35-BW (52-811). The SAC insignia on the right side was for public relations purposes. When the aircraft was delivered to Forbes AFB, Kansas, on 14 October 1954, it would have the wing insignia applied. (Boeing BW92320)

Section 41 of the forward fuselage was being removed from its circular jig where it had been assembled. Such a jig permitted rotating the fuselage section to ease the working conditions. (Douglas-Tulsa T2425 via Harry S. Gann)

The rollout celebration for the 1,000th B-47 was a major event at WIBAC. Various shops had applied signs to the aircraft, while the Transportation Department went one better and mounted a model of a tractor-trailer rig on top of the canopy. (Boeing P14899)

This striking photograph of an B-47E-115-BW (53-2311) was shot near WIBAC. The aircraft was painted with a full white anti-radiation finish. Note the deflected left aileron that induced this roll, and the extended wingtip. G-loads resulted in wrinkling of the bomb bay door skin. (Boeing BW92850)

# *BOMBERS*

Of the 2,049 Stratojets manufactured by Boeing, Douglas, and Lockheed, 1,990 were either B-47Bs or B-47Es developed specifically for the strategic bombardment mission. The others were RB-47s of various types. The first 87 B-47Bs had been contracted for by the Air Force in November 1949, but the outbreak of the Korean War in 1950 brought increased demands for Stratojets and the Stratojet program was destined to become the largest bomber production program since the end of the Second World War. By December 1950, the Air Force envisioned B-47s rolling off the assembly lines at the rate of 149 aircraft per month.

The Douglas company was awarded a production letter contract in December 1950, and Lockheed soon afterwards. However, neither the Douglas nor the Lockheed plants commenced production before 1953. The first Stratojets built by these two additional plants were actually assembled from components supplied by Boeing-Wichita. Only 10 B-47Bs were completed by Douglas-Tulsa and eight by Lockheed-Marietta – all of them built from Boeing-supplied components – before production switched over to the more advanced B-47E version.

## B-47B

The first combat-capable Stratojets were B-47Bs (Boeing Model 450-11-10), albeit after considerable upgrades to the first 254 aircraft under Project HIGH NOON and Project EBB TIDE. The B-47B was generally similar to the B-47A, although it was 3 inches taller and 8 inches shorter in length. The top of the vertical stabilizer was squared-off instead of rounded. The initial B-47Bs were powered by six General Electric J47-GE-11 engines and had structural modifications that allowed takeoff weights as high as 200,000 pounds.

The B-47B had a Nesa glass windshield with special rain-repellent that replaced the earlier windshield wipers. The glass was also coated with transparent electrical heating elements for deicing. A single-point ground-refueling receptacle was fitted, and the ability to refuel in-flight was included.

A major external difference between the B-47B and earlier versions was the elimination of the glazed nose. The B-47B carried a K-2 bombing and navigation system with a periscopic sight in a modi-fied nose that replaced the transparent nose cone of the B-47A with solid sheet metal, although the side windows remained the same. In any case, navigators preferred to work in the dark without bright sun flashes and reflections.

The K-2 bombing and navigation system (in the interest of brevity, the various bombing and navigation systems are normally referred to as K-systems, omitting reference to their specific designations) initially fitted to the B-47B was unreliable and hard to maintain. It had 370 vacuum tubes and nearly 20,000 separate parts, with components scattered all throughout the aircraft. In-flight maintenance was impossible and failures were frequent. By mid-1952, the K-2 had been made to work better, but it still needed improvement even after additional modifications had resulted in its redesignation as the K-4.

*This B-47B-10-BW (50-014) is being refueled by a KB-29P-45-BW tanker that had been converted from an old bomber. Like the KC-97s that would follow, the KB-29 was too slow to make a truly adequate tanker for the jet-powered bombers. (AFFTC History Office via Tony Landis)*

*This rocket sled was developed to evaluate ejection seat configurations for the B-47. For Test #6 the sled was equipped with four 1,000-lbf rocket motors. This test was conducted at Edwards AFB on 28 September 1953. (Boeing BW77340)*

In the interest of saving weight, the troublesome ejection seats that had been fitted to the B-47A were deleted on all B-47Bs. Instead, an escape hatch was provided for emergency crew egress, with a spoiler door at the aircraft's main entrance to make in-flight escapes safer.

The omission of ejection seats from the B-47B turned out to be a serious mistake. SAC believed that ejection seats were the safest way to escape from a high-speed aircraft. Even under controlled flight conditions, escape from a B-47 via the escape hatch was hazardous, and it was for all practical purposes impossible to escape from an uncontrolled B-47 using such a system. In mid-1950, a request was made to immediately reinstate the ejection seats, but it was clear that they could not be incorporated in production B-47s for quite a while. This left as many as 400 B-47s flying without ejection seats.

The tail defense system originally earmarked for the B-47 was the Emerson A-2, but continual problems forced its cancellation in late 1951 and many early B-47Bs did not have any defensive armament. The General Electric A-5 system was eventually selected to replace the A-2, but it would not be ready until the end of 1953. As a stopgap measure it was decided to retrofit early B-47Bs with a pair of 0.50-caliber machine guns and an N-6 optical sight. The A-5 fire control system would eventually be installed in most B-47s as part of Project BABY GRAND.

The 89th and later B-47Bs were equipped with more-powerful J47-GE-23 engines rated at 5,800-lbf. The first 88 B-47Bs were subsequently retrofitted with these more powerful engines. Beginning at Line Number 298 (51-2255) the –23 engines were replaced by the J47-GE-25 version that would ultimately power all B-47s.

The first B-47B was accepted by the Air Force in March 1951, and 87 similar planes were delivered within a year. The 306th Bomb Wing (Medium) was the first to receive the type. However, these B-47s were almost immediately deemed unsuitable for the Strategic Air Command, and the Air Force recommended no less than 2,000 changes. A program began in January 1952 to correct some of the problems and this effort eventually involved the modification of 310 B-47Bs. At first, this work was to be done at the Grand Central Aircraft facility in Tucson, but it soon became apparent that the job was much too large for them and both Boeing and Douglas were enlisted to assist. Initially, SAC had expected to receive the first modified aircraft in July 1952, but this ultimately slipped until October 1952.

The last of 339 B-47Bs was manufactured in June 1953, with the Air Force taking delivery the next month. Production was immediately shifted to the B-47E version, which was destined to become the major production version of the Stratojet.

## B-47B SERVICE EVALUATION

Establishing the B-47 as a weapon system in SAC's arsenal was no small task. A myriad of systems integration and logistical problems required identification, resolution, and implementation at Boeing, within SAC, and at a number of other operating and support commands. The B-47 pioneered the operational concepts of a large multi-engine jet aircraft that would carry forth to future bomber programs, military transport programs, and commercial jetliners.

The B-47 was a quantum leap in technology over the jet fighters of the day. Debugging the aircraft took 3,096 hours of wind tunnel tests and five years of flying. Colonel Michael N. W. McCoy, commander of the 306th Bombardment Wing, flew the first B-47B (50-008) from the Boeing plant in Wichita to MacDill AFB on 23 October 1951. Another six B-47Bs were scheduled for delivery to the 306th that month, but serious deficiencies delayed subsequent deliveries. Nevertheless, 12 of the aircraft arrived before the end of the year. While the XB-47 first flew on 17 December 1947, it would take until June 1953 to accumulate 5,000 hours of test flying, along with 50,000 hours of operational flying before the Stratojet was ready for integration into SAC's war plan. The Strategic Air Command found more than 50 deficiencies with the new aircraft and an all-out effort to rectify them was undertaken. The Air Materiel Command asked Grand Central Aircraft to reopen its modification facility in Tucson to correct the most critical problems.

The B-47 offered numerous technical challenges. As funding became available, the aircraft were literally thrown into production at a prodigious rate. As a result of the service evaluation program, a number of projects were initiated to make the B-47 service ready.

**Project WIBAC** was instituted at Boeing-Wichita (WIBAC) during July 1950 to operate the experimental and production test fleets as if they were part of a combat unit. An organizational structure was established to provide overall surveillance (command and control), ramp operations, and flight line maintenance. This was a combined task

In this plan view of the B-47, the flaps and flaperons are extended. A flat black anti-glare panel surrounds the cockpit. This photograph also reveals the walkway stripes along the spine of the aircraft and on the wings. The sawtooth forward stripe was joggled to afford clearance for the vortex generators. This aircraft appears to be B-47B-25-BW, s/n 51-2057, which was not equipped with tail armament. The aircraft was parked on the ramp at Eglin AFB, Florida. (USAF 153003AC)

## PROJECT WIBAC B-47s

| Series | Serial Number | Delivery Dates | Assigned Command | Remarks |
|---|---|---|---|---|
| B-47B-1-BW | 49-2645 | 31 July 1951 | APG | Burned at Eielson AFB, Alaska, during refueling on 20 September 1951 |
| B-47B-10-BW | 50-018 | 2 November 1951 | APG | N-1 compass tests |
| B-47B-10-BW | 50-019 | 2 November 1952 | APG | CCTS equipment |
| B-47B-10-BW | 50-023 | 15 October 1951 | APG | Crashed on 2 November 1951 |
| B-47B-15-BW | 50-028 | 26 November 1951 | APG | Transferred to ARDC, Davis-Monthan AFB, Arizona |
| B-47B-15-BW | 50-034 | 18 December 1951 | APG | Full-up SAC equipment |
| B-47B-15-BW | 50-036 | 20 November 1951 | SAC | Full-up SAC equipment |
| B-47B-15-BW | 50-037 | 21 November 1951 | SAC | Full-up SAC equipment |

force with representatives from SAC, the Air Materiel Command, and the Air Proving Ground Command. With this joint operation testing could be consolidated in a single location thereby providing quicker and unified results. In addition, costs were significantly reduced.

Colonel Paul W. Tibbets, Jr., who had commanded the 509th Composite Group during World War II, commanded the unit between July 1950 and February 1952. Lieutenant Colonel O. F. "Dick" Lassiter, formerly SAC Chief of Requirements, served as deputy commander under Tibbets.

One of the more interesting flights during Project WIBAC was on 20 September 1951. Colonel Richard C. Neeley was assigned to Project WIBAC from 10 December 1950 until late 1951. Along with copilot Lieutenant Colonel John G. Foster, and navigator Captain D. J. Haney, Neeley flew the first jet aircraft over the North Pole. The B-47B-1-BW (49-2645) had been deployed to Eielson, Alaska, earlier in September for routine cold weather testing. The aircraft took off from Eielson at 08:37 hours, crossed Point Barrow, and then headed out over the Arctic Ocean toward the Pole. After circling the Pole, they turned back toward Alaska via the normal weather reconnaissance route. The flight was flown at the altitudes normally used by Air Weather Service WB-29 weather reconnaissance aircraft.

**Project SUITCASE** – Orders came down from SAC

Headquarters for Colonel Neeley to use the same aircraft that had flown over the Pole to conduct the first jet overflight of the Soviet Union under Project SUITCASE. For this mission a camera pod was installed in the bomb bay. Unfortunately, the aircraft would be destroyed prior to the mission during a refueling accident on 20 September 1951, and Neeley notified SAC of the event as the B-47B smoldered on the ramp. He remembered General LeMay's comment in a return telegraphic message: "Fix responsibility and court-marshal!" The ensuing investigation revealed that a stuck check valve had caused fuel to be directed out of a vent onto a C-22 power cart. No court-marshal ensued because it was a Boeing crew that had been refueling on the aircraft as a test of the new single-point refueling system. It would be another year before the overflight actually happened.

**Project EAGER BEAVER** – The first B-47s were delivered without defensive tail armament. Under this project, the B-36 tail armament was evaluated on the B-47 to no avail.

**Project RELIABLE** was initiated to improve the performance of the computerized K-system, make components more accessible for maintenance, and locate them conveniently for the navigator. Similar projects were undertaken for the B-36 fleet. Modifications included a mount that permitted the navigator to move the AN/APS-23 radar indicator fore and aft to suit his requirements, providing adequate cooling for the radar indicator, and providing a retractable cover for the Y-4 bombsight optics dome. Other changes included the installation of bomb bay spoilers and vortex generators on the wings.

*This band of seasoned aviators comprised the USAF pilot team for Project WIBAC on 17 August 1951. From l-r were: Major Robert O. Celotto, Captain David M. Hines, Lieutenant Colonel Patrick Fleming, Colonel O. F. "Dick" Lassiter, Colonel Paul W. Tibbets, Jr., Lieutenant Colonel Robert Robinson, Major Eugene Crahen, Lieutenant Colonel Richard Neeley, and Captain John Whitehead, instructor pilot. (Boeing P11637)*

Project RELIABLE also provided the necessary changes to permit the so-called "Sharkey" method of bombing. SAC bombardment crews flew profile missions to gain confidence in their aircraft and mission requirements. In addition, SAC wings tested new bombing radars and electronic countermeasures (ECM) equipment with their B-50s and B-36s. The aircraft would take off from their home base, flying long navigation legs across the United States and performing several electronic bombing runs on targets at radar bomb scoring (RBS) sites located at various places around the country. They would also drop a load of live bombs on a bombing range before heading back to base. The crews practiced evasive action, chaff and ECM jamming, and offset bombing techniques. An interesting bit of history was the evolution of the offset bombing technique that was developed by Ed Sharkey, an electronics engineer who had been with Bell Laboratories and the RAND Corporation. During World War II he was in the South Pacific with Section 22, one of the first units to employ radar for bombing. This technique was called a Sharkey, in his honor. The Sharkey employed fixes on known reference points from which a bomb run on a blind target (small or obscured on a radarscope) could be established. With the Sharkey, came the philosophy for SAC's offset radar bombing program.

**Project HORNET** – The prototype A-2 fire control system was tested on both a B-29 and a B-47A (49-1906) under this project and then fitted to a B-47B-5-BW (50-002) in 1952.

Also a carry-over from World War II tradition was the application of a squadron insignia on the nose. Early SAC B-47Bs had the squadron insignia on the left side of the nose and the World War II group insignia on the right side. Here SA-GUA, a B-47B-46-BW (51-2291), displayed its 369th Bombardment Squadron insignia. Records indicate that the tail stripe would have been blue. (Colonel George A. Johnson)

Initially B-47s from the 306th BMW carried a large Square P on the vertical tail to identify the wing the airplane was assigned to. This was a carry-over from the large geometric markings used during World War II. Here, a pair of armament technicians was working on the 0.50-caliber guns in the tail turret of a B-47B. In the background was another B-47B (51-2074) from the 368th BS with its yellow tail band. (USAF 47119AC)

**Project SNOW TIME** – This was a special storage program to ensure complete logistical support for units receiving the B-47 that was developed in June 1953. The Rome Air Materiel Area at Griffiss AFB, New York, was selected as the single location for the storage of all parts and equipment that would be required at SAC's B-47 Zone of Interior (ZI) bases at the time of conversion. Continental United States (CONUS) replaced the term ZI during the late 1960s.

Alterations were also made to the B-47s to permit them to carry spare parts. Because the aircraft were not carrying heavy nuclear weapons, their gross takeoff weight was well within limits, and consequently RATO was not required. Mechanics removed the RATO compartment fairings and then removed the RATO rocket support structure. These compartments now became available to carry engine nose cones, tail pipes, spare parts, personal luggage, and anything else that would fit. The fairings were then reinstalled. Spare engines were carried in the bomb bay. As a test, one Ryan

*This inboard profile of the B-47B reveals the various compartments within the fuselage. Note the long bomb bay that was capable of carrying the outsized weapons of the day.*

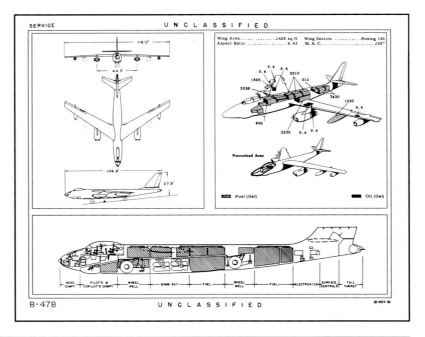

Aeronautical-built external fuel tank was modified as a blivet. A door was cut into the side of the tank and a plywood floor, replete with tie-down rings, was installed. While not used operationally, this innovative design proved that the tanks could be used for additional cargo space.

**Project SEA WEED** – Similar to Project SNOW TIME, this was a depot program to support SAC's B-47 bases overseas.

**Operation SKY TRY** – Between 23 January and 20 February 1953, the 306th Bombardment Wing flew its B-47Bs in Operation SKY TRY in full-scale simulated combat tests. This was followed by a 90-day deployment of 15 B-47Bs, supported by KC-97Es, to RAF Fairford on 3 June 1953. The aircraft staged through Limestone AFB, Maine, where they remained overnight. Colonel McCoy broke the existing trans-Atlantic crossing record by making the 3,120-mile flight in 5 hours 38 minutes. Before the deployment was over, this record would be broken nine times, with 5 hours and 22 minutes

*This B-47B (51-2077) was equipped with the short bomb bay. Note that the eyeball for the Y-4 bombsight was in the closed position. (Boeing BW60174)*

*A B-47B-10-BW (50-014) from the Air Force Flight Test Center at Edwards AFB shows the approach chute (top) and braking parachute (bottom) used to slow the bomber down when it used the short runways that equipped most of its bases. (AFFTC History Office via Tony Landis)*

being the best. By way of note, some of the first aircraft arrived at RAF Mildenhall before heading to RAF Fairford.

The 306th Bombardment Wing deployed to RAF Brize-Norton between September and December. Next was the 22nd Bombardment Wing that deployed to RAF Upper Heyford between December 1953 and March 1954. These deployments by entire wings continued until 1958. When an entire wing deployed for 90 days it placed an extreme burden on the families. As a consequence, SAC changed its policy in 1958 to rotate several aircraft from each wing to these bases in what became known as a REFLEX operation that lasted only a few weeks per aircraft and crew.

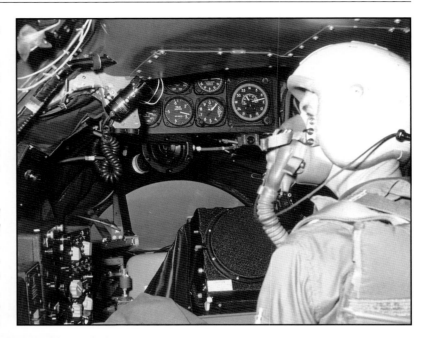

*The man in the nose was a triple-threat – navigator, observer, and radar bombardier. The clear nose of a B-47B permitted forward visibility. A cover protected the radarscope when not in use. Primary navigation instruments were located on the upper instrument panel. An oxygen blinker was installed just below the radio compass. The map light was stowed to the left of the instruments. As indicated by the flight bag, this individual was part of the Boeing flight test organization. (Boeing P15250)*

*The AFFTC also used this B-47B-25-BW (51-2047) for various tests. Note the early AFFTC logo on the forward fuselage. (AFFTC History Office via Tony Landis)*

Mechanics at MacDill AFB used a crane and an engine hoist to remove the J47 from a dolly and maneuver it into the No. 1 position on the bomber's wing. Note the large arc in the hook that was designed to allow the engine to slip under the wing while the crane's block and tackle remained above the wing. The left side view shows the crane, its boom arm, block and tackle hoist system, and the engine hoist holding the No. 2 engine in place until the mechanics could attach the engine to the strut. (Above: SAC Combat Crew Magazine; left: USAF 43707AC)

# B-47E

The B-47E (Boeing Model 450-157-35) was the major production version of the Stratojet. It was the only version that was mass-produced by all three members of the production pool. Iterations of the B-47E were such that Roman Numerals were employed to differentiate the various sub-series of aircraft. The basic B-47E-I included a water-alcohol injection system for the engines, Phase II ECM systems, provisions for a 33-bottle RATO rack, an aft auxiliary fuel tank, and the Cycle I bombing/navigation system. The B-47E-II aircraft included all of those changes, and added the Phase XI modifications and Phase III ECM systems. The addition of constant-speed alternators to provide 3-phase AC electrical power resulted in the B-47E-III. The ultimate B-47E-IV configuration included all the earlier changes plus increased structural provisions for a 230,000-pound gross weight capability, the Cycle I CP bombing/navigation system with the MA-1 radar, and the short bomb bay configuration (only).

The B-47E-IV also introduced a series of electronics upgrades including the MA-7A bombing radar, the AN/ASP-54 warning radar, and the AN/APG-39 gun-laying radar. The B-47E-IV had a takeoff weight of 230,000 pounds, which was 28,000 pounds more than previously permissible. This extra weight was largely devoted to extra fuel, enabling the combat radius to increase to 2,050 nautical miles, almost twice the distance demonstrated five years earlier by the first B-47A. The maximum warload was 25,000 pounds. The Air Force received its first B-47E-IV in February 1955 and by

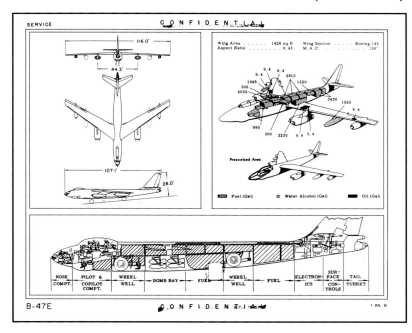

This inboard profile of the B-47E reveals the various compartments within the fuselage. Note the short bomb bay and the additional fuel tank at the aft end of the bomb bay.

This B-47E-50-DT (53-2128) displayed its partial white anti-radiation finish. The red squadron color was applied to the engine nose cones, fuel tank tip, and tail. The tail band was bordered in white. Stowed anti-radiation curtains may be seen along the upper part of the canopy. To the rear was a 1956 Chevy and part of the base flight ramp with a pair of B-25s and a venerable C-47 Gooney Bird. (SAC Combat Crew Magazine)

March 1955 it had been decided that all active B-47s would be brought up to the IV standard.

The B-47E incorporated an in-flight refueling receptacle on the starboard side of the nose. The use of in-flight refueling capability enabled the total fuel capacity to be reduced to 14,610 gallons, including two 1,700-gallon drop tanks carried underneath the wings between the engine nacelles.

The crew was finally provided with ejection seats as standard equipment, with the pilot and copilot ejecting upward over the tail and the bombardier/navigator ejecting downward through a hatch in the lower nose. During production, a clamshell cockpit canopy was introduced, hinged on the right side.

The first B-47E flew on 30 January 1953, and was accepted by the Air Force in February. The first B-47Es went to the 303rd Medium Bomb Wing at Davis-Monthan AFB, Arizona. The next recipient was the 22nd Wing at March AFB, California, retiring their B-47Bs to the Air Training Command. By mid-year, 127 similar examples had been delivered.

During mid-1953, B-47 procurement was expected to reach almost 2,200 aircraft, but was cut by 140 in September 1953. A further production cut of 200 aircraft considered in October was prevented in favor of a 20-month production stretch-out during the period in which the B-52 production line was getting up to speed.

The B-47E rapidly became the dominant component of the Air Force strategic deterrent during the mid- and late-1950s. In December 1953, SAC had eight B-47 wings and a year later the SAC inventory counted 17 fully equipped B-47 wings. By the beginning of 1956, 22 wings had received the B-47. In December 1956, SAC had 27 combat-ready B-47 wings, with 1,204 combat-ready B-47 crews and 1,306 B-47 aircraft assigned.

*Various views of a B-47E-120-BW (53-2343) reveal the sleek aerodynamic lines of the aircraft and the application of the full anti-radiation white paint on the forward fuselage, nacelles, and pylons. The left rear view reveals the full anti-radiation paint on the aft fuselage and the absence of national insignia on the waist. The 90-degree set of the horizontal stabilizers to the vertical stabilizer is readily apparent. Also note that the engine nacelle struts are perpendicular to the wing chord plane. A careful examination shows that the Phase II ECM antenna wingtip extensions are visible and the built-in 6-degree angle of attack that assisted the pilots to achieve the most efficient lift for takeoff. (Boeing)*

*Boeing assigned this B-47E-75-BW (51-7069) resplendently marked with red and white stripes on the nose, waist, wingtips, and vertical tail for the toss-bombing tests. A black and white stripe was painted along the bomb bay and a camera was mounted in the fin cap. Boeing test pilot Richard W. "Dick" Taylor was the prime pilot on these tests. To the right was Jack Funk, another Boeing test pilot. (Boeing BW93215 and BW93206)*

Spurred by the Suez crisis of 1956, SAC demonstrated its ability to launch a large striking force on short notice when in December more than 1,000 B-47s flew nonstop, simulated combat missions, averaging 8,000 miles each over the American continent and Arctic regions.

Early in 1955, the Strategic Air Command requested the B-47 be adapted for low-level bombing, with the aircraft delivering its bomb via the toss-bomb technique. In a toss-bombing attack, the aircraft enters the run at low altitude, pulls up sharply into a half loop with a half roll on top, and releases the bomb at a predetermined point in the climb. The bomb continues upward in a high arc, falling on the target at a considerable distance from its release point. In the meantime, the maneuver allows the airplane to reverse its direction and gives it more time to get a safe distance from the blast. This technique was adopted because it was thought that high-speed B-47s flying at low level would be less vulnerable to enemy defenses. The existence of low-level capable B-47s would mean that a potential enemy would now be faced with threats from both high- and low-level attacks.

**Operation HAIRCLIPPER** – Special crew training for low-level bombing began in December 1955. However, adverse weather, excessive maintenance requirements, serious deficiencies in the Low-Altitude Bombing System (LABS), and several accidents caused HAIRCLIPPER to be discontinued in March 1958. However, the end of HAIRCLIPPER did not signify the end of low-level flying.

**Operation POP UP** – A related training program that took advantage of recent advances in weapons development fared better than HAIRCLIPPER. In the POP UP maneuver, the aircraft came in at low level, pulled up to high altitude, released its weapon, and then dove steeply to escape being spotted by enemy radars.

The discovery of fatigue cracks in the wings of several B-47s during April 1958 triggered an immense inspection and repair program

*The LABS tests used a B-47B-1-BW (49-2642) flown by Boeing test pilot Richard W. "Dick" Taylor. This series of six photographs shows the aircraft in various portions of the LABS maneuver as the aircraft was flown through an Immelmann profile (pull-up, half loop, and half roll). The weapon would have been released just prior to entering the half loop. (Via Gordon S. Williams)*

Above: *Boeing test pilot Richard W. "Dick" Taylor and S. L. "Lew" Wallick conducted a final briefing in front of the B-47B-1-BW (49-2642), prior to a 5 August 1954 LABS test.* (Boeing BW91890)

Top Right: *The entire engineering, flight test, and maintenance crews for the LABS test aircraft.* (Richard W. Taylor via Boeing HS-657)

Middle Right: *This black and white checkered instrumentation boom was used for the LABS test. This photograph was taken at WIBAC on 20 February 1954, hence the parkas.* (Boeing BW219200)

Bottom Right: *Note the camera mounted on top of the aircraft's midsection for recording the structural deformations during the LABS maneuver. The Plexiglas cover for the camera had been removed. Reflectors at the wing end caps provided a reference point for the camera. This photograph dates from August 1954.* (Richard W. Taylor via Boeing HS-656)

These B-47s were a mixture of B-47Es, all of which had the full white anti-radiation finish applied. Note how the white paint was eroding from the leading edge of the wing. Thermal reflecting boots were draped over the noses to reduce the effects of the sun on the ramp at Dyess AFB, Texas. The aircraft in the foreground was a B-47E-40-LM (52-1296) equipped with a sliding canopy and the earlier UNITED STATES AIR FORCE lettering on the forward fuselage. The second aircraft had a clamshell canopy and the later U.S. AIR FORCE fuselage lettering. (SAC Combat Crew Magazine)

This B-47B-40-BW (51-2198) was updated to the B-47E standard and sported a partial white anti-radiation finish. The red arrow high on the vertical fin indicates that the aircraft was assigned to the 2nd BS, 22nd BMW. (Gordon S. Williams)

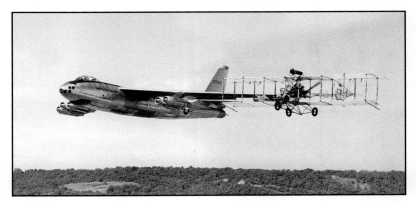

Famed aviation historian Peter M. Bowers designed this replica of a Curtiss Pusher. The USAF flew it to various airshows around the country for static display and flying. Here, Billy Parker flew the biplane as he was passed by a B-47E-75-BW (51-7375), but it looks like a classic formation shot. (Boeing BW90588)

This B-47E-70-LM (53-1915) was just coming in over the fence with its approach chute retarding its forward speed. Note the partial white anti-radiation paint on the lower fuselage and the lack of external fuel tanks under the wings. (Via SAC Combat Crew Magazine)

known as Project MILK BOTTLE by all three B-47 manufacturers as well as the Air Materiel Command. The low-level B-47s of the 306th and 22nd Bomb Wings were the first to enter the program, since they were most in danger of fatigue cracking. The program ended in July of 1959. Although MILK BOTTLE did not solve all the problems, it did go a long way in making operations with the B-47 a lot safer. Operation POP UP was resumed in September 1959, and by the end of the year had finally been completed.

SAC initially wanted 1,000 B-47s modified for low-level flying, which meant fitting virtually the entire fleet with absolute altimeters, terrain-avoidance equipment, and Doppler radar. Because of the MILK BOTTLE repairs, testing delays, and the phase-out of some B-47 wings due to a lack of funds, SAC was forced to scale down its low-altitude requirements to only 500 Stratojets. This program was given a new sense of urgency by the belief that by 1963 all B-47s would be hopelessly obsolete if they were not equipped for low-level

The Wright Air Development Center used this JB-47E-55-BW (51-2359) for a variety of tests at Wright-Patterson AFB. Note the short bomb bay doors and ARDC logo on the nose. (Peter M. Bowers)

A total of 691 B-47Es were built by Boeing-Wichita, 264 by Douglas-Tulsa, and 386 by Lockheed-Marietta. The final B-47E (53-6244) was delivered on 18 February 1957 to the 100th Bomb Wing at Pease AFB, New Hampshire. This was the 29th and last SAC bomb wing to be equipped with B-47s.

The beginning of the phaseout of the B-47E coincided with the delivery of the last example. In 1957, the 93rd Bomb Wing started exchanging its B-47s for B-52s. In March of 1961, President John F. Kennedy directed that the phaseout of the B-47 be accelerated, however, this was delayed by the onset of the Berlin crisis of 1961-62. In the following years, B-47s were gradually delivered to storage at Davis-Monthan AFB. The last two B-47s from the Strategic Air Command went to storage on 11 February 1966.

## SPECIAL WEAPONS

In early 1949, an inspector from Headquarters USAF reviewed the B-47 mock-up and reported that the bomb bay would not accommodate the Mk. III special (atomic) weapon and possibly not even the Mk. IV weapon. The Atomic Energy Commission and USAF Special Weapons Command held all of the design and performance data on the atomic bombs. Some data was afforded to special staffs within Headquarters Air Force, while the Air Materiel Command and SAC were given minimal information. Almost none was given to the contractors. This situation resulted in a major bomb bay configuration dilemma for the B-36 and B-47. While major turf battles and infighting occurred at the higher levels, personnel at the working level generally interacted quite well. It was the lack of official technical data that impeded requisite development for the aircraft interfaces.

Without data on the size and shape of the weapons, problems surrounding aircraft structural and fuel tank interference could not be resolved. This data was also required to develop a loading plan with considerations for maneuvering room. Would the bomb be placed in

*This E-model, converted from a B-47B-10-LM (51-15811), still had the internal RATO system. Note the protective boot on the tail turret, and the guards for the vortex generators on the left wing. (Lockheed-Martin B6002)*

flight. However, funding shortfalls ultimately dictated that SAC scale down its low-altitude requirements to only 350 aircraft.

In the meantime, the Stratojet continued to demonstrate its performance. On 25 January 1957, a B-47 flew from March AFB to Hanscom Field, Massachusetts, in 3 hours 47 minutes, at an average speed of 710 mph (assisted by strong tailwinds). On 14 August 1957 a 321st Bomb Wing B-47 made a record nonstop flight from Andersen AFB, Guam, to Sidi Slimane Air Base in French Morocco, a distance of 11,450 miles in 22 hours and 50 minutes using four midair refuelings. In November 1959 a B-47 assigned to the Wright Air Development Center stayed in the air for 3 days 8 hours 36 minutes, covering 39,000 miles, breaking all previous time-and-distance records.

*This B-47A-BW (49-1907) was assigned to the AFSWC at Kirtland AFB. The aircraft was equipped with the 18-bottle RATO system and K-2 bombing system. (Air Force Research Laboratory Historian)*

*This AFSWC JB-47B-40-BW (51-2222) was undergoing maintenance in one of the base hangars to escape the effects of the heat. (Air Force Research Laboratory Historian)*

a pit and have the aircraft rolled over it or be jacked, as did the B-29s and B-50s? Of major concern were the airframe structural loads. The center of gravity of the bomb dictated where the bomb shackles and the sway braces would be placed.

To further address these concerns, the Air Force Special Weapons Command (AFSWC) Development Group loaded a completely assembled Mk. IV bomb and assorted requisite equipment in the mock-up to ensure the adequacy of the bomb bay and equipment for carrying and releasing the weapon. The tests also included verifying that the in-flight insertion (IFI) techniques that provided the manual arming of the weapon in flight would work. It was concluded that the B-47 would accommodate the weapon and its ancillary equipment with the following changes:

- Eliminate the right forward auxiliary bomb bay tank that interfered with the hoisting procedure.
- Adjust and tighten the sway braces.
- Install bomb fin guide rails inboard of the left and right rear auxiliary bomb bay fuel tanks to protect the tanks during hoisting.
- Relocate the bomb bay lights to assure adequate lighting.
- Incorporate a mechanical release system to open the bomb bay doors and salvo the bombs in one operation, then close the doors.
- Provide a 10-degree fall clearance at both ends of the bomb bay.
- Extend the catwalk 20 inches further aft on the left side of the bomb bay.
- Modify the left rear auxiliary fuel tank to carry 15 gallons less fuel for improved access during the in-flight insertion process.
- Incorporate six indicator lights that showed the status of the bomb on the copilot's panel duplicating those on the flight test box for visual checks by crewmen facing away from the flight test box.

On 17 March 1950 the Air Materiel Command authorized the engineering required for the B-47 to carry either the Mk. IV or Mk. VI special weapon, despite the fact that the center-of-gravity locations for these weapons were at Body Station 45 and Body Station 40, respectively.

Most critical to the B-47's bomb bay design was the bomb suspension system. This consisted of a bomb rack, moveable shackles, sway braces, arming control, and release unit. In 1949 it was decided that the Air Force should design a universal suspension system to load, carry, and release all atomic weapons. During a conference in December 1949, where aircraft modification for carriage of atomic bombs was discussed, it was concluded that some organization, other than the Air Materiel Command, needed to develop the universal suspension system. North American Aircraft was selected to develop the prototype.

*This late-model JB-47E-110-BW (53-2276) sports the new AFSWC insignia on the nose. In March 1968, the B-47 was transferred to the Eighth Air Force Museum at Barksdale AFB, Louisiana. (Air Force Research Laboratory Historian)*

The Mk. IV and Mk. VI weapons did not present much of a problem, but the Mk. V raised considerable concern. Its pneumatically operated U-1 rack had release criteria of 0.033-second to ensure placement of the bomb precisely on the target. A lighter hydraulically operated system took 0.095-second to release the bomb. The slower release was installed on the first four B-47As and the faster unit on all subsequent aircraft. Tests showed that when a Mk. V weapon was dropped from a B-47, moving at 550 mph at an altitude of 10,000 feet, violent pitch oscillations occurred. The low-density Mk. V with its low moment of inertia was subject to high initial acceleration forces within the confines of the bomb bay. These oscillations were due to high velocity circulating air currents striking the bomb tail. After a series of tests, Boeing developed a special adapter for lowering the Mk. V weapon more than 10 inches inside the bomb bay, thereby reducing the time the bomb was in the disturbed airflow.

## Project HANDBOOK

Late in 1950, the Air Materiel Command directed Boeing to modify the second XB-47 (46-066) for Project HANDBOOK, a test to ensure a nuclear weapon could be released from the aircraft. The crew of four consisted of a pilot, copilot, telemetry operator, and bombardier. Modifications at the pilot's station added a position display indicator (PDI) and a smoke signal switch. The new telemetry operator's station was located in the navigator's position.

The bombardier's station was modified with numerous components, including an M9B Norden bombsight, kneeling pads straddling the bombsight, and an SCR-718 radar altimeter. For landing and take-off, the bombardier was afforded a seat cushion, seat belt, oxygen provisions, and an audio select panel in the walkway below the copilot's position. The bomb bay was modified with a U-1 bomb rack and supports, revised bomb bay doors, three Jerome B-2 cameras, and ten floodlights for the cameras.

Lieutenant Colonel Ed Nabell conceived Project HANDBOOK for two purposes. First was to check for safe separation of the weapon and have a photo chase aircraft to document the event. Second was to obtain the necessary ballistics on the weapon's descent: hence the instrumented range at the southern end of the Salton Sea, located along the California-Nevada border, was chosen.

Major Guy Townsend flew the aircraft to Kirtland AFB, New Mexico, for the tests. During a preflight briefing with members of the Atomic Energy Commission and Sandia it was determined that the aircraft was to return to Kirtland if possible, but could divert to Davis-Monthan AFB in the event of an emergency. Townsend advised that if he had an emergency he did not plan on returning to Kirtland because of his anticipated fuel state, and that Davis-Monthan was too far away. He preferred Edwards AFB, with its long runways and dry lakebeds. At Kirtland, Nabell told Townsend to negotiate a secure place at Edwards to park the B-47, just in case. Using a Beech C-45 Expeditor, Townsend went to Edwards and made arrangements with Colonel Robert L. Cardenas, then B-47 Program Chief, who was TDY from Wright-Patterson. He would park on a remote taxiway. From there, Townsend could walk or have a vehicle retrieve him.

It was arranged for Captain Chuck Yeager to fly chase in an F-86 from Edwards. To keep up with the B-47, the F-86 was flown without external fuel tanks. Townsend provided Yeager with his ETA at the range so that an intercept could be achieved within the last three to four minutes of the bomb run.

This was the first time a B-47 had been at Kirtland. It was towed to the end of the runway and fueled for the mission, and dozens of on-lookers were on hand for the first mission. Townsend lined up on the runway and made his takeoff roll. At the appropriate time he fired the RATO bottles and enveloped the field behind him in smoke. The base fire department started to run, but the fire marshal ordered them to go save the aircraft and crew. Then there was a silver glimmer above the mountain range as the Stratojet climbed out in the distance. An air of relief came over those on the ground.

Townsend was joined by Yeager and headed towards the range. Climbing to the requisite 40,000-foot altitude, they set up for the drop. Then, when the shape was released, it hung up in the bomb bay. A second run was made, and once again the shape failed to drop. Townsend issued his preplanned emergency code and headed toward Edwards.

En route, Yeager advised he was running low on fuel and Townsend suggested he land at Blythe, California. Yeager's response was to the effect that he wanted a good meal and would press on towards Edwards. When about 75 miles out, Yeager advised that the engine was showing the effects of fuel starvation and eventually it flamed out. Yeager declared an emergency and asked if he could land on the dry lakebed. The request was denied because a Douglas D-558-2 Skyrocket was using the lakebed. Yeager landed the silent fighter on the active runway and taxied to the ramp where he stopped a few slots from his assigned space.

*When the XB-47 arrived at Kirtland AFB, the crew was met by a crowd. To the left in the winter flight suit was Major Townsend. Lieutenant Colonel Ed Labell stood in the center with his hand in his pocket. Immediately to the right rear of Labell were Captain Thompson and Lieutenant Ryan next to him in the leather flight jacket. It was obviously cold at the mile-high air base. (Via Brigadier General Guy M. Townsend)*

*The crew for Project HANDBOOK consisted of (l-r): Major Guy M. Townsend in the winter flight suit, aircraft commander; Captain Allan W. Thompson, copilot; and 1st Lieutenant Pat Ryan, navigator/bombardier. (Via Brigadier General Guy M. Townsend)*

Meanwhile, Townsend was coping with his overweight B-47. He landed the Stratojet and parked midway along the taxiway near a gun butt. The plan called for 1st Lieutenant Pat Ryan, the bombardier, to guard the rear of the aircraft and have Townsend walk about three-quarters of a mile to a waiting jeep that was directed into position by Cardenas who was observing the operation. Next, the base commander, Colonel Signa A. Gilkey, arrived, approaching the aircraft from the rear. The colonel wanted to see the new aircraft parked on his airplane patch. Ryan challenged the colonel and pulled his gun on him. Gilkey's eyes widened – "You guys act as if you have an atomic bomb on the plane," he exclaimed. The incident was over and nothing more was said about it. Meanwhile, Cardenas and Townsend went to a building where the personnel were asked to leave so that Townsend could make an urgent call on a secure line.

Inspection revealed that the U-1 bomb shackle had frozen at altitude and prevented the weapon from releasing. The solution was simple – add an electric heater.

### Project ON TOP

The highest priority program within the Air Materiel Command was Project ON TOP – the modification of most SAC bombers, including all B-47s, to have special weapons capability. Project ON TOP was divided into at least 10 phases, but only three had direct relation to the B-47. Phase I added the capability to carry the Mk. IV and Mk. VI weapons to 58 B-47Bs; Phase III added the ability to carry the Mk. V weapon to the same aircraft; and Phase IV added the Mk. VIII.

The two XB-47s, ten B-47As, and first 87 B-47Bs were delivered without any special weapons capability. Contract W33-038-ac-22413 authorized incorporating a special weapon capability into the 88th B-47B, and the first 87 B-47Bs would be retrofitted beginning in August 1951. Because of installation difficulties, the first 87 B-47Bs were eventually limited to carrying only the Mk. IV and Mk. VI weapons.

The first aircraft B-47B-15-BW (50-026) to be modified as part of

*This front quarter view shows a Mk. IV riveted case atomic bomb that was based on the Mk. III Fat Man used at Nagasaki and during Operation CROSSROADS at Bikini Island. Note the nose door through which the navigator performed IFI and IFE operations. (Sandia Corporation)*

ON TOP arrived in Seattle in January 1952. While at SEBAC, the bomb bays were modified, bomb bay spoilers installed, and a revised bomb-arming panel was installed.

Unfortunately, this aircraft crashed on takeoff from Kirtland AFB on 26 March 1952, killing all four aboard. The accident investigation revealed that the aircraft became airborne prematurely in an extremely nose-high attitude during a crosswind takeoff. The pilot

*The Mk. V was an improved Mk. IV and was used in large numbers. The arming doors are shown in the open position. (National Atomic Museum)*

*The Mk. 28, known as the building block bomb, was the standard atomic bomb in SAC's inventory for many years. (National Atomic Museum)*

*This Mk. 39 thermonuclear bomb weighed 6,230 to 6,400 pounds. A pair of parachutes slowed its descent. It was in the inventory between 1957 and 1966. (A. T. Lloyd)*

over-controlled at RATO ignition with the aircraft at a low gross weight. Aileron power control was off. A recommendation was made for a design change to add a control wheel-mounted trim control system, and flight testing at gross weights between 100,000 and 125,000 pounds with RATO.

Along with the ability to carry nuclear weapons, the Air Force needed to understand the potential effects of flying a B-47 near a nuclear blast. The Air Force Special Weapons Command was also responsible for electromagnetic pulse (EMP) testing of various combat aircraft. A B-47B-5-BW (50-016) was selected as the first Stratojet EMP test vehicle, and the aircraft was flown from Kirtland to NAS China Lake, California, for testing. There it was suspended above the ground by an elaborate system of cranes and hoists. High-intensity electromagnetic pulse energy was directed at the aircraft to determine if the equipment and systems onboard would survive a nuclear blast. From these tests, system hardening was developed individually for each aircraft type. In March 1958 another B-47B-35-BW (51-2155) began EMP testing at Kirtland AFB. The Air Force Special Weapons Command was so concerned about the effects that they requested that the aircraft be permanently assigned to the tests and that the command would not be responsible if it was irreparably damaged.

This aircraft was subsequently redesignated JB-47B-35-BW and retained at Kirtland AFB for use in non-flying development of specialized EMP instrumentation. The program was known as Project 3763, "Survivability Evaluation of Aeronautical Systems." The objective of the tests involving the JB-47 was to determine the survivability and vulnerability of operational aeronautical systems to the effects of EMP.

Between January 1963 and March 1968 the Air Force Special Weapons Command also operated a JB-47E-110-BW (53-2276) for a variety of tests. This aircraft was declared excess in March 1968, and was flown to Barksdale AFB, Louisiana, for display in the Eighth Air Force Museum.

## NUCLEAR WEAPONS TESTING

Several B-47s participated in various U.S. atmospheric nuclear weapons tests between 1953 and 1962. SAC B-47s flew a profile known as Initial Bomb Damage Assessment (IBDA) for a number of these tests using special equipment to measure blast effects on both the aircraft and the crew. The mission profile called for the B-47 to be flying away from the blast to simulate departing an area after dropping a weapon.

### Operation GREENHOUSE

The first atomic testing involving the Stratojet was conducted in 1951 during Operation GREENHOUSE, at Eniwetok Atoll. Just less than 9,000 Army, Air Force, Navy, Atomic Energy Commission, subcontractors, and universities personnel participated in the operation. The objectives were to test new and improved weapon designs, conduct experiments contributing to research on thermonuclear weapons, expand knowledge of the fundamentals of atomic blasts, and to study the direct effects of atomic weapons. A total of 110 aircraft, of 15 types, were used in this test including F-80s, B-50s, DB-17s, and DT-33s. The aircraft were instrumented to record stresses and pressures. While drone aircraft flew close to ground zero, manned aircraft remained at safe distances from the blast. The second XB-47 (46-066) participated in this test.

### Project IVY

During the fall of 1952, a series of atmospheric thermonuclear tests was conducted out of Kwajalein Atoll under Project IVY. Initially, the B-47 portion of the test was assigned to SAC, but delays at WIBAC precluded crew training. A short-notice request was placed within the

*A single B-47B-10-BW (50-0016) was flown from Kirtland AFB to NAS China Lake for EMP testing. At left the aircraft was being hoisted into its inverted test position (shown at right). (Air Force Research Laboratory Historian)*

Air Research and Development Command for a volunteer Stratojet crew to support the tests – pilot Major James E. Bauer, copilot Major George Mathis, and navigator Captain Charles J. Gilmore were selected. Bauer and Gilmore had participated in Operation GREENHOUSE along with a SAC copilot and maintenance crew.

An ETB-47B-25-BW (51-2046) was instrumented for Project IVY. B-47Bs had been delivered without ejection seats and the crew was concerned about the short field from which they would operate. A compromise was made with the installation of an experimental tail-cone type drag chute. While en route from Wright-Patterson AFB to Travis AFB, California, the aircraft was cruising at 25,000 feet near Omaha, Nebraska, when it experienced severe turbulence. The tail cone departed and the parachute deployed. The crew notified Air Traffic Control and jettisoned the chute. After landing at Travis they discovered that when the tail cone departed, the ensuing turbulence ripped a canvas flap causing the chute to deploy. Repairs were made at Travis prior to heading across the Pacific. Fortunately, the crew had brought additional drag chutes.

The detonations included Shot MIKE on Eluklab Island and Shot KING over Runit Island. The nearest alternate to the base at Kwajalein was Eniwetok, some 360 miles to the northwest. The ETB-47 was returning to Kwajalein on 18 October 1952 when a tropical rainstorm covered the base. After three landing attempts, the crew elected to go to an alternate on Roi Island, 30 miles away, due to their low fuel state. The runway at Roi was just above sea level and made of crushed coral. The strip was 4,000 feet long and 400 feet wide, with a 200-foot overrun at each end dumping into the ocean. Capitalizing on prior experience, Bauer made his approach using the drag chute, then, when they were 20 feet above the water, he ordered Mathis to shut down the outboard four engines (No. 1, 2, 5, and 6), thereby only using No. 3 and 4 for the landing. The ETB-47 touched down, rear gear first, about 100 feet down the runway. Major Bauer eased the careening aircraft to a stop just 350 feet short of the water on the far end of the strip.

Several days later, Major General Thomas S. Power, SAC Vice Commander, visited Kwajalein where he learned about the short landing distance of the ETB-47. This was at a time when SAC was spending millions of dollars to extend their 8,000-foot-long runways to 10,000 to 12,000 feet. After General Power had learned of the ordeal, he was satisfied that SAC's pursuit of longer runways was in order.

### Operation UPSHOT-KNOTHOLE

The UPSHOT-KNOTHOLE series of atomic tests were conducted between 17 March and 11 April 1953. Two of these tests, Shot DIXIE and Shot SIMON involved B-47s.

**Shot DIXIE** was conducted on 6 April 1953 with an 11-kiloton weapon dropped from a B-50 that exploded at an altitude of 6,020 feet. The Atomic Energy Commission objective of the test was to evaluate nuclear yield, blast, thermal, and radiological phenomenon produced by this experimental device. The Department of Defense

*In this profile view of this JB-47B-35-BW (51-2155) from the AFSWC, the Day-Glo Orange nose and waistband are readily apparent. (Air Force Research Laboratory Historian)*

*These views of the JB-47B-40-BW (51-2222) reveal its partial white anti-radiation finish, Day-Glo Orange nose, and ARDC insignia. The inscription beneath the insignia reads AIR FORCE SPECIAL WEAPONS CENTER. (Air Force Research Laboratory Historian)*

(DoD) objective was to evaluate military equipment, tactics, and doctrine; to measure the effects characteristics and evaluate the military applications of the device; and to indoctrinate DoD personnel in the use of nuclear weapons.

As part of the test, crews from the 4925th Test Group flew a B-50 and a B-47 that each dropped five instrumented canisters. While the B-50 flew at 35,000 feet and dropped the canisters at 500-foot intervals, the B-47 flew at 45,000 feet and dropped the canisters at 650-foot intervals. The telemetry-equipped canisters passed through the atomic cloud relaying radiological information to a ground station. In addition, SAC provided 11 B-47s from MacDill AFB that orbited the test site at 37,000 feet for 50 minutes.

**Shot SIMON** was conducted on 25 April 1953. While the expected weapon yield was 35 kilotons, the actual yield was 43 kilotons – an increase of almost 23 percent. For this test SAC provided eight B-50s from the 2nd Bombardment Wing at Hunter AFB, Georgia, and seven B-47s from the 305th Bombardment Wing at MacDill AFB. These aircraft flew at altitudes of 25,000 and 37,000 feet for the IBDA profile.

## Operation TEAPOT

Operation TEAPOT was conducted at the Nevada Test Site between 18 February and 15 May 1955. This series consisted of 14 nuclear events and one non-nuclear detonation intended to evaluate nuclear devices for possible inclusion into the weapons arsenal, improve military tactics, equipment, and training, and study civil defense requirements. Only the tests involving B-47s are listed here.

**Shot TURK** was planned for 15 February 1955, but the test date slipped until 7 March and consisted of a 43-kiloton tower burst in Area 2. In what was known as Project 9.4, this atomic cloud study was conducted using elements from the Air Force Cambridge Research Center, SAC, and the U.S. Weather Bureau. SAC provided one RB-47 each from Lockbourne AFB and Forbes AFB to photograph the nuclear cloud. The aircraft flew directly over ground zero, one at 43,000 feet and the other at 47,000 feet. Two pilots and a radiological safety monitor manned each aircraft.

**Shot APPLE 2** was planned for 26 April 1955, but was delayed until 5 May. This was a 29-kiloton tower blast conducted in Area 1. SAC provided two RB-47s that flew over the Nevada Test Site at the time of detonation on an IBDA profile. One aircraft flew at an altitude of 42,000 feet, 1.86 miles northwest of ground zero: while the other flew at 43,000 feet, 13.98 miles northwest of the detonation.

**Shot HA** was planned for 4 March 1955, but was conducted on 6 April. An airdrop from an Air Force Special Weapons Command B-36 at an altitude of 36,620 feet was accomplished over Area 1. A flight of seven F-86s and one B-47 laid a smoke trail below the B-36 just prior to bomb release and moved out of range while the 3-kiloton device dropped. The smoke trails assisted in blast photography. SAC provided a pair of RB-47s assigned to the 55th SRW from Forbes AFB. The aircraft flew directly over ground zero, one at 47,000 feet and the other at 43,000 feet, conducting photography of the area. SAC also provided

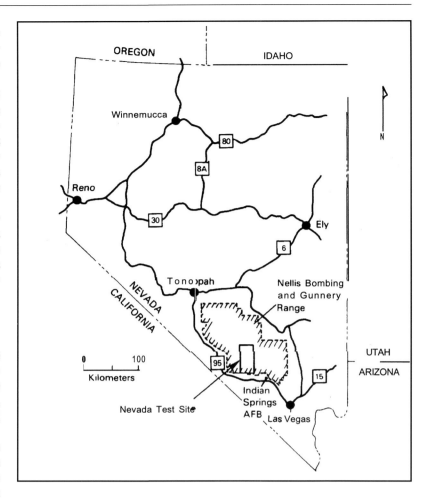

The Nevada Test Site was located along Highway 95 near the California-Nevada border north of Las Vegas, within the Nellis Bombing Range that extended north to Tonopah.

four B-47s from Davis-Monthan AFB to pass over ground zero at altitudes ranging between 34,000 and 39,000 feet some three minutes prior to the blast to train the crews in simulated nuclear weapons delivery.

**Shot ZUCCHINI**, originally scheduled for 1 April 1955, was conducted on 15 May and marked the end of Operation TEAPOT. The 28-kiloton tower blast in Area 7 occurred at an elevation of 500 feet. SAC provided three B-47s from Davis-Monthan AFB to train aircrews in nuclear delivery tactics while flying an IBDA profile. These aircraft flew over ground zero three minutes prior to detonation at altitudes of 34,500, 39,000, and 40,000 feet.

## Operation PLUMBBOB

The United Nations Disarmament Commission was dealing with growing international sentiment to ban nuclear testing; however, irreconcilable differences between the United States and the Soviet

Union kept the issue at bay. Between May and October 1957, the DoD performed 29 nuclear weapons tests at the Nevada Test Site, three without aircraft. It was against this international political backdrop that Lewis Strauss, chairman of the Atomic Energy Commission, requested presidential approval for a new test series on 21 December 1956. These tests became Operation PLUMBBOB.

**Shot JOHN** was a 2-kiloton blast conducted on 19 July 1957. It was an airburst at 20,000 feet from an MB-1 Genie rocket fired by a Northrop F-89J Scorpion. The rocket traveled 13,780 feet before det-onating. As part of this test, SAC provided a pair of RB-47s that flew in formation in a 35-nautical-mile left-hand holding pattern at an altitude of 25,000 feet, five nautical miles to the left and behind the F-89.

**Shot WHITNEY** on 23 September 1957 was a 19-kiloton blast tower shot with a 500-foot burst altitude. Two SAC B-47s performed an IBDA as part of the test. The aircraft orbited at 11,000 and 16,000 feet and were 35 nautical miles east of ground zero on a northerly heading just before the detonation. At the time of the blast, the B-47s executed a breakaway maneuver.

*The B-47E-75-BW (51-7069) used for the toss-bombing trials was spectacularly marked with red and white stripes on the nose, waist, wingtips, and vertical tail. Note the theodolite pattern aft and to the right of the canopy. A camera was mounted in the fairing along the spine. (Via Gordon S. Williams)*

**Shot SMOKY** was a 44-kiloton device detonated from a 700-foot-tall tower on 31 August 1957. During this test, two SAC B-47s performed an IBDA survey. At the time of detonation, the aircraft were at a heading of 360 degrees, 35 nautical miles short of ground zero. They did not fly through the visible cloud.

**Shot NEWTON** was a 12-kiloton weapon suspended from a balloon at 1,500 feet detonated on 16 September 1957. SAC had a pair of B-47s orbit at altitudes between 12,000 and 14,000 feet, 17 nautical miles east of ground zero on a northerly heading. At the time of detonation, the two aircraft executed a breakaway maneuver as part of an IBDA test.

### Operation DOMINIC I

Atmospheric testing in the Pacific resumed in 1962 as part of Operation DOMINIC I. These tests consisted of five high-altitude shots at Johnston Island, 29 airdrop airbursts near Johnston and Christmas Islands, one Polaris submarine-launched airburst in the Christmas Island area, and one underwater test in the Pacific Ocean off the coast of the western United States. SAC B-52s from the 4245th Strategic Wing at Sheppard AFB conducted the airdrops. SAC also provided two EB-47Ls for UHF radio relay support during the three FISHBOWL shots.

### Operation REDWING

B-47s were known to have supported at least two Operation REDWING nuclear tests in the Marshall Islands during 1956.

**Shot LACROSSE** was a 40-kiloton surface blast at Eniwetok Atoll conducted on 4 May 1956. The 301st Bombardment Wing at Barksdale AFB provided three B-47s flown by their combat crews to perform an IBDA. The 5,000-foot-long runway at Eniwetok presented quite a challenge after operating from the 12,000-foot runway at their home base. For this mission, two of the aircraft orbited the target area with a 2,000-foot separation and flew in left and right patterns, respectively. The third B-47 served as a backup for the other two aircraft and circled some 25 miles away from ground zero.

**Shot CHEROKEE** was a 3.8-megaton airdrop blast conducted at Bikini Atoll on 20 May 1956. A B-52 from Kirtland AFB dropped the weapon. B-47s again flew IBDA profiles.

## NUCLEAR WEAPONS FLIGHTS

Loading a nuclear weapon in the bomb bay of a B-47 was no easy task. The weapon, loaded on a dolly and covered with a tarp, was maneuvered beneath the bomber until it was precisely positioned. Then, with only inches to spare, the bomb was hoisted into position. The entire operation took 45 minutes to an hour.

SAC B-47s routinely carried nuclear weapons on training flights. Before the days of automatic arming, the navigator-bombardier had to crawl into the bomb bay to arm the weapon after takeoff and disarm

*This SAC B-47E was performing a low-level iron bomb drop over the Eglin range in June 1964. A destroyed ADC T-33A also served as a target. (USAF)*

the bomb prior to landing. It should be noted that such flights were only conducted over the continental United States.

During January 1955 the 2nd Bombardment Wing provided aircraft and crews for Project BUSY BEAVER II to practice in-flight-insertions (IFI) simultaneously with heavy weight refueling, and to determine the maximum practical altitude at which this operation could be performed. It is extremely difficult to fly a heavily loaded aircraft at the edge of the envelope (lines on an aircraft performance chart that define its limitations for maneuvering, approach to stall, resilience to turbulence, etc.). Five crews flew one day and one night mission to prove the concept.

When SAC bombers deployed on REFLEX operations, they were armed only while standing alert. For the deployment and return flights, the aircraft were unarmed. In addition, B-47s never carried nuclear weapons on training flights that approached the Soviet Union.

### A Broken Arrow (?)

On 22 October 1957 Crew L-06 from the 340th Bomb Squadron, 97th Bombardment Wing, stationed at Biggs AFB took off on a routine training mission with a training version of the Mk. 15 weapon. The crew consisted of aircraft commander Captain Clement M. Latimer, copilot Captain Herbert R. Dahl, and navigator Captain George M. Bopp.

The aircraft weighed 190,000 pounds at takeoff, including some 80,000 pounds of JP-4 and the 7,500-pound weapon. Immediately after taking off, the cockpit began filling with smoke and Latimer declared an emergency when the aircraft was over the desert area near Fort Bliss. In order to get down to landing weight, the weapon was jettisoned.

Latimer set up an approach speed of 210 knots and touched down at 180 knots. He ordered Dahl to deploy the brake chute – it operated exactly as advertised and separated from the aircraft because the maximum deployment speed was 165 knots. Using maximum breaking, only the antiskid prevented the tires from blowing. All 13,000 feet of the runway and some of an adjoining taxiway were used to stop the aircraft. The base fire department met the aircraft and began putting out the brake and tire fires.

Both the squadron commander and the air division commander met the crew, with the former congratulating the crew for getting the aircraft back on the ground. Shortly thereafter it was learned that SAC had declared a Broken Arrow (codeword for a nuclear incident).

The crew boarded an Army half-track and went out to look for the weapon. While Fort Bliss had mobilized several hundred personnel to help in the search, the crew found it in less than an hour, embedded in four feet of the indigenous calcite rock. The weapon appeared to be fairly intact, but further investigation revealed that most of the internal components had migrated towards the weapon's nose.

Captain Latimer's Air Force career flashed through his mind – the end was near. A few days later the crew was ordered to appear before the wing commander, Colonel Salvatore E. Manzo. Much to their surprise, the crew was presented the Crew of the Month Award. Later investigation revealed that the pressurization and air conditioning system had burned.

### A Real Broken Arrow

On 5 February 1958 a B-47E-50-BW (51-2349) from the 19th Bombardment Wing at Homestead AFB, Florida, was on a routine training flight with a Mk. 15 Mod 0 training weapon without a nuclear capsule onboard. The bomber experienced a midair collision with an F-86L Sabre near Sylvania, Georgia, around 02:00 hours. The fighter pilot ejected successfully, but the bomber suffered extensive damage to its empennage, No. 6 engine nacelle, and outboard right wing.

The crew of the bomber headed for the nearest B-47 base, which happened to be Hunter AFB. Several attempts to land were made, but the high gross weight due to the weapon made a successful landing extremely improbable. Radio communications with the command post resulted in the recommendation to jettison the weapon in the ocean off the coast of Georgia. The weapon carried a 400-pound conventional charge as well as uranium. After dropping the 7,600-pound weapon, the crew was able to land the considerably lighter aircraft. Despite being classified as an incident (instead of a more-serious accident), the B-47 was subsequently scrapped.

The weapon was dropped several miles from Savannah, in the Wassaw Sound area of the Atlantic Ocean. When released, the bomber was flying around 7,200 feet and at an airspeed near 200 knots. The crew did not see an explosion on impact. The Air Force's 2700th Explosive Ordnance Disposal Squadron, supported by nearly 100 Navy personnel equipped with hand-held sonar and galvanic drag, searched a three-square-mile area. The water depth in the

This B-47B-25-BW (51-2068) was employed in conventional bomb drop tests. (Boeing BW93239)

These Boeing technicians were loading 1,000-pound bombs into the B-47 bomb bay. (Boeing BW65583)

search area ranged between 8 and 40 feet. The 12-foot-long weapon was believed to be nose down in a vertical position, with its tail buried 5 to 15 feet into the silt layer beneath the water. Attempts to salvage the weapon between 6 February and 16 April 1958 were fruitless. After duly considering the economic, environmental, and potential recovery costs, the Air Force declared the weapon irre-

trievable. Based on the facts that there was no possibility of a nuclear explosion, no public risk, and that the weapon avoided unacceptable environmental impact, the Air Force recommended leaving the weapon in its resting place.

On 20 March 1958 all SAC training flights with nuclear weapons were terminated.

*In early 1953, this dedicated Boeing flight test crew consisting of: Ed Brashear (center) and Ed Harts (right), alternate aircraft command-ers, and Gerald Simons who performed the navigator's duties flew this B-47B-55-BW (51-2137) for the conventional weapons drop test program. During this 1,000-hour test program, the aircraft and crew covered 432,066 miles and performed 92 bomb runs, including 12 actual drops. All flights were based out of WIBAC. (Boeing BW61578)*

The YB-52 Stratofortress (49-231) flies with a B-47B-20-BW (50-056). The B-47 pioneered many of the concepts that would ultimately be used on the B-52 and every successful commercial jet transport. (AFFTC History Office via Tony Landis)

## CONVENTIONAL WEAPONS TESTING

One day while General LeMay was still CINCSAC, he called in his Chief of Plans and asked him how many B-47s it would take to destroy the runways on an airfield halfway around the world. The Director of Operations, Major General Archie Olds, went into the bowels of Building 500 and asked one of his planners, Lieutenant Colonel Rudolph Koller, who had been the lead navigator with the 2nd Bombardment Group, a B-17 unit in North Africa during the early stages of World War II. Koller's comment was: "Think B-17." How many B-17s did it take to do the job in World War II? The answer was usually two bomb groups with four squadrons each with 10 to 12 aircraft per squadron dropping 6,000 pounds of bombs each! That was a total of 480,000 to 576,000 pounds. Olds took Koller up to see LeMay. The general knew this planner well – he was the one who was always summoned when LeMay was reviewing the EWO Plan and found a Soviet target he did not recognize. When Koller came to his office, LeMay would say: "Where's ___?" The answer was usually an obscure place on the map that was half an alphabet long and had more consonants than vowels. Koller would point to a spot on the map and he was excused. Olds entered with Koller and stated, "General, think B-17" and turned the floor over to Koller who ran through the numbers. Koller was excused and Olds and LeMay ruminated over their problem. From this meeting sprang the genesis of SAC's conventional bomber capability, using conventional bombs in lieu of nuclear weapons.

As with anything of this magnitude, a myriad of man-hours had to be spent analyzing the situation. This was essentially a problem for the SAC operational analysts (Ops Annies). A plan was developed, and between March and June 1964 SAC completed a series of bombing tests to verify and improve the conventional munitions capability of the B-47 and B-52 fleets. The tests were conducted at the bombing ranges adjacent to Eglin AFB, Edwards AFB, Wendover Field, and Matagorda Island in the Gulf of Mexico off the coast of Texas. During these tests approximately 150 sorties were flown and more than 2,200 tons of conventional bombs were dropped to provide confidence in dropping these type weapons.

CHAPTER 4

## EARLY B-47 ACCIDENTS

| Date | Model | Serial | Unit | Remarks |
|---|---|---|---|---|
| 18 Aug. 1951 | XB-47-BO | 46-065 | SEBAC | Stalled on landing with major structural damage sustained. No injuries. |
| 1 Sept. 1951 | B-47B-5-BW | 50-006 | SAC | Mid-air collision near Wichita AFB with 50-024. Destroyed with 2 fatalities. |
| 1 Sept. 1951 | B-47B-10-BW | 50-024 | ATC | Mid-air collision near Wichita AFB with 50-006. Destroyed with 2 fatalities. |
| 20 Sept. 1951 | B-47B-1-BW | 49-2645 | APG | Burned at Eielson AFB during refueling. Fire destroyed aircraft. No injuries. |
| 2 Nov. 1951 | B-47B-10-BW | 50-023 | APG | Crashed while flying a Project WIBAC mission. Chute failed on landing. Major damage, no injuries. |
| 19 Nov. 1951 | B-47B-5-BW | 50-006 | ARDC | Crashed after takeoff from Edwards AFB. Destroyed with 3 fatalities. |
| 25 Jan. 1952 | B-47B-15-BW | 50-041 | SAC | Engine failed. Minor damage, no injuries. |
| 26 Feb. 1952 | B-47B-25-BW | 51-2067 | WIBAC | While on a ferry flight from WIBAC to OCAMA, the No. 1 engine tore loose from its mounting and departed over the top of the wing. The aircraft went into a violent skid. Control was regained and an uneventful landing was made at Tulsa. Major damage, no injuries. Investigation revealed that a No. 2 bearing failure resulted in a sudden stoppage of the engine. This bearing also served as a thrust bearing and its failure permitted the compressor section to shift aft causing the sudden engine stoppage. The ensuing skid resulted in major damage to the fuselage and vertical stabilizer. Recommendation – redesign the engine attachment supports to withstand torque loads resulting from a sudden stoppage. Technical orders were revised to require non-destructive testing of all engine mount bolts and attach fittings after each instance of an engine change due to sudden stoppage. |
| 28 Feb. 1952 | B-47B-25-BW | 51-2073 | WIBAC | While on a ferry flight from WIBAC to OCAMA, the outboard cowling of the No. 2 engine departed the aircraft. It was determined that inadequate securing was designed into the cowling. Minor damage, no injuries. Recommendation – redesign the cowl to provide an adequate and positive protective fastening device and retrofit the entire fleet. |
| 26 Mar. 1952 | B-47B-15-BW | 50-026 | 4925th TG | Crashed on takeoff. Destroyed with 4 fatalities. Project ON TOP aircraft. Aircraft became airborne prematurely in an extremely nose-high attitude during a crosswind takeoff. Pilot inadvertently over-controlled at RATO ignition with aircraft at low gross weight. Aileron power control was OFF. Recommendation – a design change to add a control wheel-mounted trim control system, and flight testing at gross weights between 100,000 and 125,000 pounds with RATO. |
| 11 Apr. 1952 | B-47B-15-BW | 50-038 | 306th BMW | Ditched in Tampa Bay during approach. Destroyed with no injuries. Cause was complete power loss due to fuel management. Fuel warning lights were not seen by the student pilot and cannot be seen from the instructors' station. Recommendation – retrofit master fuel warning light for both pilot's stations, and modify fuel selectors with a safety devise to preclude inadvertent selection of the manifold to engine fuel selector position. No crew injuries. |
| 11 Apr. 1952 | B-47B-20-BW | 50-064 | 3520th FTW | After landing, the aircraft turned left onto a cross strip, stopped and dropped the approach chute, then continued to the taxiway that paralleled the runway. The left outrigger gear went off the concrete into soft mud. As the airplane continued to taxi, the inboard side of the wheel contacted the edge of the concrete. The aircraft was steered to the right in an effort to pull the wheel back onto the concrete surface. The outrigger gear was deflected outboard about 30 inches before it slipped back onto the concrete. The sudden release of the side load resulted in a compression failure on the inboard side of the nacelle strut. The complete outrigger and nacelle strut were replaced. No crew injuries. |
| 24 June 1952 | B-47B-25-BW | 51-2048 | ARDC | Stalled during landing. Destroyed with no injuries. |
| 3 July 1952 | B-47B-20-BW | 50-065 | 306th BMW | Canopy struck crew. Destroyed with 3 fatalities. |
| 22 July 1952 | B-47B-15-BW | 50-035 | 3520th FTW | Aircraft landed short at Wichita AFB breaking the wheel and twisting the axle on the right outrigger gear. Minor damage also occurred to the flap and flaperon due to flying debris. No crew injuries. |

88                                                                                       BOEING'S B-47 STRATOJET

## EARLY B-47 ACCIDENTS (CONTINUED)

| Date | Model | Serial | Unit | Remarks |
|---|---|---|---|---|
| 22 July 1952 | B-47B-20-BW | 50-081 | 306th BMW | While 1 hour and 29 minutes into a routine practice-bombing mission, the aircraft apparently exploded. Forward portion of fuselage forward of forward wheel well fell free with no evidence of fire. Wing departed in one piece with evidence of severe fire in wing center section. All engines separated from the wings. Destroyed, 3 crew and 2 civilians on ground killed, and 3 civilians seriously injured. Recommendation – expedite review for satisfactory fuel system, determine if a malfunctioning autopilot could place aircraft in a dangerous attitude, consider center section sealing and baffles, consider fuel fume detection system, review fireproof qualities of flight control system components, install a reliable fuselage fire warning system, provide a satisfactory cover for electrical terminals in center fuselage to preclude contact by elevator cables, pressurize battery compartment, and improve fuel cell manufacturing/quality control procedures. |
| 24 Sept. 1952 | B-47B-15-BW | 50-027 | WADC | Prior to brake release for takeoff, the No. 2 engine exploded and burst into flames. Investigation revealed that the cause was FOD damage to the compressor. The FOD was determined to be a bolt attaching the engine nose dome assembly. No crew injuries. Recommendation – replace the self-locking nuts with safety-wired castellated nuts. Modify the instrument panel light shield so that the fire button switch is not obscured from the pilot's vision, and revise pilot handbook instructions to include a compressor failure. |
| 1 Oct. 1952 | B-47B-45-BW | 51-2266 | WIBAC | During a Boeing test flight at WIBAC to check in-flight canopy opening, the canopy was opened at an altitude of approximately 13,000 feet and an indicated airspeed of 130 knots. The cockpit was not pressurized. Apparently the canopy opened several inches before departing the aircraft. The canopy struck the right wing leading edge near the root creating a large hole in the leading edge. No crew injuries. Recommendations – after extensive engineering evaluations, the canopy system was redesigned and all aircraft were retrofitted with an improved latching system. |
| 22 Oct. 1952 | B-47B-20-BW | 50-068 | 305th BMW | While on a routine training mission from MacDill AFB the aircraft descended from 31,000 feet and the crew could not get an aft gear down and locked indication. A decision was made to continue the approach and landing with a diversion to Eglin AFB. During the landing rollout at 30 knots, the aft main landing gear collapsed. Landing weight was 85,000 pounds. Maintenance had to replace the aft gear doors and fuselage skin section aft of Station 1166. Fairing around horizontal stabilizer was also damaged. No crew injuries. |
| 4 Dec. 1952 | B-47B-20-BW | 50-060 | 3520th FTW | During a touch-and-go landing considerable damage was incurred on the right inboard engine nacelle strut while landing at Wichita AFB. The IP noticed that the aircraft was about 10 knots above the best approach speed for the 105,000-pound gross weight and that the round-out was late. He applied some backpressure to the elevator. The student pilot applied full power for a go-around, but the aircraft settled back onto the runway. The crew felt a jolt and noticed that the right inboard strut and nacelle had dropped about 3 feet. The go-around and landing were successfully accomplished. It was determined that the right outrigger gear struck a pile of snow along the right side of the runway resulting in high drag on the wheel and strut. No crew injuries. |

NOTES: 1. Unit Designators – APG = Air Proving Ground Command; ARDC = Air Research and Development Command; ATC = Air Training Command; BMW = Bombardment Wing (Medium); FTW = Flying Training Wing; SAC = Strategic Air Command; SEBAC = Boeing-Seattle; TG = Test Group; WADC – Wright Air Development Center; WIBAC = Boeing-Wichita. 2. FOD = Foreign Object Damage. 3. Remarks: Crew fatalities may have been reduced if ejection seats had been available for the 1 September 1951, 3 August 1952, and 22 August 1952 accidents.

In the foreground is an RB-47E-30-BW (52-0765) undergoing a fiscal year modification program with other Stratojets at the Douglas-Tulsa facility. Note the Phase III ECM antennas on the aft fuselages. (Douglas-Tulsa via Harry S. Gann)

# Chapter 5

# *CONTINUAL CHANGES*

After completion of the service evaluation, a series of major design changes was made for follow-on production aircraft. A major modification program was instituted to retrofit the existing fleet to the new standard that had been established at Line Number 731 (B-47E-95-BW, 52-508). In addition, tactical operational changes for the B-47 resulted in huge structural problems that had to be resolved.

By October 1951 it became readily apparent that a major impasse had developed relative to upgrades required to make the B-47 operational. A conference was held at WIBAC to come to grips with the situation. Major General Bryan L. Boatner, commander of the Air Proving Ground Command, believed that better results could have been achieved if both the Air Materiel Command and Air Research and Development Command had personnel assigned to WIBAC to more closely monitor the program. Lieutenant General Earle E. Partridge, commander of the ARDC, believed that concentration of B-47 testing at Wichita had been a mistake. Both generals agreed that the B-47 was an extremely complicated aircraft and that the production problems were of a magnitude heretofore unseen. General Nathan F. Twining, USAF Vice Chief of Staff, stated that the B-47 problem fell to the Air Staff and that it would be solved. To meet this new requirement, the Air Force directed that B-47s be sent to Grand Central Aircraft in Tucson beginning in early 1952 where minimum modifications would be accomplished to make the aircraft combat-capable. Grand Central, and its workforce of nearly 4,000 people, had previously been used to bring B-29s out of storage and refurbish them for the Korean War effort.

Starting in January 1952, 310 B-47Bs were to undergo modification. Unfortunately Grand Central Aircraft was ill prepared for the modification program. The company did not have the facilities, the funds to upgrade the facilities, or the requisite personnel to accomplish the task. A meeting was held in Tucson between personnel from Boeing and Grand Central on 21 July 1952, where Boeing presented its observations. These included that Grand Central did not realize the complexity of the electronics job involved with the program and were short 275 experienced electronics technicians. Boeing also believed that Grand Central lacked skilled supervisory personnel in specific areas.

Boeing offered to provide 10 to 12 supervisory personnel to meet the near-term urgent requirement. These individuals would be terminated from Boeing and reassigned to the Grand Central payroll. As such, these people would have no allegiance whatsoever to Boeing. At the end of the service, Boeing, making the lack of allegiance somewhat questionable, would rehire the individuals.

Boeing also agreed to modify 90 of the aircraft at a cost of $10 million. In addition, Douglas-Tulsa was asked to provide assistance for another 49 aircraft. Difficulties in providing sufficient retrofit kits caused a slippage in the program, and further slips occurred in September 1952 when inspections for fuel tank leaks were added.

*On 19 April 1957, these Douglas-Tulsa technicians were boresighting this GE A-5 tail turret utilizing a mobile tracking device. In the background were Douglas B-66 Destroyers. (Douglas T-2867PR)*

*This GE technician was boresighting the A-5 tail turret on an RB-47E on 27 December 1954. The dish antenna was being calibrated to account for the parallax between the antenna line of sight and the gun line of fire. (GE A164 202)*

## MAJOR MODIFICATIONS

A basic safety deficiency had been identified early on when it was determined that the B-47 ejection seats were unreliable. SAC eventually took delivery of 400 B-47Bs with inactivated ejection seats. An estimated 26,000 engineering man-hours were required to develop a viable ejection seat system and the modifications caused the relocation of numerous pieces of critical equipment.

Range also severely hampered the early B-47s and General LeMay directed that an in-flight refueling capability and external fuel tanks be retrofitted to the delivered aircraft under Project TURN-AROUND and Project HIGH NOON, respectively.

Another major deficiency involved the K-2 bombing and navigation system that consisted of 41 major components with some 370 vacuum tubes and approximately 20,000 separate parts that were scattered throughout the aircraft. The total system weighed 1,600 pounds. Some components, by necessity, had to be located outside of the pressurized cabin, precluding any in-flight maintenance. On the ground, system checkout took up to eight hours versus one hour on the B-36 (which was a much larger aircraft with many of the components locat-

ed near each other). Because of the size constraints within the B-47, many of these issues could not be resolved. One change incorporated in 1954 was a voltmeter and frequency meter to reduce the probability of overloading the K-system inverters. A second change installed an A.C. current amplitude modulation suppressor to reduce control system jitter when the A-12D autopilot system was operating.

Development of the defensive armament was also fraught with difficulties. The initial Emerson A-2 was cancelled in 1951 in favor of the General Electric A-5 fire control system. However, it would take until 1953 before the A-5 system became available; therefore, SAC opted for an interim installation of the B-4 system with a pair of 0.50-caliber machine guns and tail warning radar that offered a modicum of harassing fire for defense. The definitive A-5 system incorporated a pair of 20-mm cannon coupled to gun-laying radar that was incorporated under Project HIGH NOON. In August 1953 the 938th B-47 (B-47E-120-BW, 53-2355) was delivered with an improved A-5 known as the MD-4. The MD-4 was installed on all subsequent production B-47s and was also retrofitted into the last 14 B-47s going through Project HIGH NOON.

**Project BABY GRAND** was initiated at WIBAC during January 1953 to install the A-5 fire control system. This system was also incorporated on new production aircraft between Line Numbers 400 and 454 (B-47E-55-BWs, 51-2357 through 51-2411).

**Project FIELD GOAL** – In January 1953 Douglas-Tulsa was contracted to convert B-47Bs (49-2642 through 49-2646 and 50-001 through 50-082) into TB-47Bs for the Air Training Command. These changes were accomplished under contract AF33(600)-23716 to Douglas-Tulsa; the total cost was $12.1 million.

*This trainload of collapsed fuel cells was being transported for storage/preservation at the Douglas-Tulsa plant during one of the modification programs. (Douglas-Tulsa D-382)*

*Douglas engineers and mechanics were building up the interior of the new Section 41 that resulted from Project HIGH NOON. A completely new Section 41 was installed on the B-47Bs, including a window arrangement identical to the B-47Es. (Douglas-Tulsa via Harry S. Gann)*

*Douglas-Tulsa held an open house commemorating the first B-47 Mod Program. A B-47B-25-BW (51-2078) was in the foreground while a B-47B-25-BW (51-2073) was in the background. The aircraft in the left foreground appears to have been a B-47B-25-BW, (51-2067). (Douglas-Tulsa via Harry S. Gann)*

**Project TURNAROUND** took completed aircraft between Line Number 617 and 730 (B-47Es, 52-394 through 52-507) and modified them to the same standard as Line Number 731 (B-47E-95-BW, 52-508) prior to delivery. The modifications included ejection seats, installing the 33-unit external RATO system, reworking the K-system, reinforcing the landing gear, installing the in-flight refueling system, and incorporating the approach parachute system. This program cost over $23 million.

**Project HIGH NOON** brought 165 in-service B-47Bs up to the TURNAROUND standard. The first aircraft entered the line in June 1954 and was completed in February 1955. Over time the learning curve improved and the last aircraft was begun in September 1955 and delivered in January 1956. Aircraft retrofits included the installation of Weber upward ejection seats for the pilots and Stanley downward ejection seats for the navigator, structural strengthening, increased fuel capacity, and replacing the J47-GE-24 engines with J47-GE-25s with water-alcohol injection. The internal 18-bottle RATO system was deleted and replaced by solid skins, and provisions for an external RATO rack were added. The bomb bay capacity was increased for general-purpose bombs, and provisions were added to carry a single nuclear weapon. Phase III ECM equipment was added, and the AN/ARC-21X long-range radio system developed under Project BIRDCALL was installed. The A-5 fire control system was installed on all but the last 14 aircraft, which received the MD-4 system. The K-system was also upgraded to the Project RELIABLE standard. To accommodate these changes, the entire

Section 44 and Section 41 were replaced with new sections that incorporated the latest structural and systems design changes.

**Project PEACH STATE** was an IRAN program conducted by Lockheed-Marietta. This project called for the upgrade of B-47Es WIBAC Line Number 400 through 616 (51-2357 through 51-17386) and Lockheed Line Numbers 9 through 127 (51-15812 through 52-319). The first aircraft arrived on 13 July 1954. Initial estimated cost for preproduction planning and manufacture of the kits was $4,124,941.

*At least 12 B-47Bs were on the outside mod line at the Douglas-Tulsa plant. (Douglas-Tulsa via Harry S. Gann)*

This B-47B-46-BW (51-2240) was resting on jacks for this landing gear swing test. The -46 block number indicated that this was a -45 aircraft that had undergone a mod program. (Boeing 60825)

**Project OIL TOWN** was an IRAN program conducted by Douglas-Tulsa during 1954 on 275 aircraft. Douglas-Tulsa was awarded $68 million under contract AF34(601)-1315 to upgrade a number of B-47Es: WIBAC Line Number 400 through 616 (51-2357 through 51-17386), Douglas Line Numbers 11 through 124 (52-029 through 52-166), and WIBAC RB-47E Line Numbers 1 through 123 (51-5258 through 52-756).

**Project EBB TIDE** upgraded Line Numbers 1 through 234 (B-47Bs 49-2642 through 51-2211) to various standards. The first aircraft entered the Boeing line in January 1956 and the last was delivered in June 1957. Between November 1956 and June 1957, 30 aircraft were converted into DB-47s. A 40-kVA alternator system was added to these aircraft to support operation of the RASCAL missile. All of these aircraft had their J47-GE-23 engines replaced by the more powerful J47-GE-25s.

**Project BIRDCALL** developed a worldwide SAC communications network. When the B-50A *Lucky Lady* flew around the world, the Soviets took notice. However, General LeMay knew that the logistics for this operation were horrendous and a worldwide communications network would be needed to conduct global operations. Collins Radio Company developed a complete single-sideband air-ground and point-to-point communications system for SAC. Prototype equipment was installed in a VC-97 assigned to SAC Headquarters. Over the next two years extensive tests were conducted with SAC aircraft flying long-range missions in the North Polar Region, the Far East, Europe, and Africa. Ham radio operators, of whom LeMay was one, also supported these tests. In 1958, the program was expanded under Project SHORT ORDER. Most B-47s would be equipped with the AN/ARC-21 long-range liaison radios that evolved from these tests under Project BIG EVA.

**Project TEE TOWN** was carried out between 24 February 1958 and 17 February 1959 when Douglas-Tulsa modified 99 B-47s under contract AF34(601)-4742. This $2.5 million program installed a pair of large ECM pods on the waist of the B-47s just above the bomb bay doors. Each pod was about 14 feet long and carried four AN/ALT-6B jammers each. Antennas were located beneath each jammer. Ram air was ducted around the jammers for cooling and larger generators were installed on these aircraft to provide the requisite electrical power for the additional ECM equipment. The TEE TOWN pods were hinged upward to permit loading of the bomb bay. The 303rd and 509th Bombardment Wings at Davis-Monthan AFB and Pease AFB initially operated the aircraft. Subsequently they were dispersed throughout a number of B-47 wings.

**Project MILK BOTTLE** added a low-level attack capability to the B-47. Initially the B-47s were able to fully utilize their high altitude capabilities to penetrate Soviet airspace with impunity. As Soviet defensive capabilities increased through new radars and surface-to-air missiles, tactics for the B-47 had to change accordingly. While flying at low-level, the bombers would be more difficult to track by radar and therefore be less likely to be intercepted by fighter aircraft, ground fire, or SAMs. The use of this tactic would force the Soviets to

prepare to counter both high-level and low-level attacks. SAC had previous experience with the Low-Level Bombing System (LABS) employed on their Republic F-84 Thunderjet fighter-bombers. The Air Staff quickly approved the new tactics.

Initial LABS tests with the B-47 indicated that the aircraft could successfully accomplish the requisite escape maneuver after dropping a thermonuclear weapon. With the advent of the heavyweight B-47E-IV in January 1955 came the confidence that the LABS could

*A line of 13 B-47s, with Phase III ECM, shared this modification line with Douglas B-66s. Note how the last four digits of the tail number were applied low on the forward fuselage, and the last two digits were painted in large numerals below the FY (indicating the aircraft were part of a fiscal year Mod Program). The third and fourth aircraft retained their SAC bands. (Douglas-Tulsa T79877 and T79872)*

*At least 12 B-47Bs were on the outside mod line at the Douglas-Tulsa plant. (Douglas-Tulsa via Harry S. Gann)*

be incorporated into the aircraft on the production line without awaiting the results of concurrent flight tests. It was envisioned that 1,100 B-47s would be mission-capable by the end of April 1956.

For the pop-up maneuver, the crew brought the B-47 in at low level and climbed rapidly to 18,000 feet. At the apex of the zoom climb the weapon was released and the aircraft was placed into a steep dive so as to not only escape enemy radar, but to place the aircraft as far away from, and tail-on, to the blast.

Shortly into the test program, however, a B-47 flying at low-level was lost over Bermuda. Such flights were halted until Boeing and the

Air Research and Development Command provided assurances to the Air Proving Ground Command that the structural integrity of the aircraft was not an issue. During June 1955, an instrumented B-47 successfully released a 6,000-pound dummy bomb during a 2.6-g pull-up. On a subsequent flight an 8,850-pound dummy bomb was released during a 2.6-g pull-up. In each of these flights, the weapon was released in the initial portion of an Immelmann. In December 1955 the Air Staff directed that 150 B-47s be modified by Boeing to accomplish this mission.

While neither the LABS nor the pop-up maneuvers were difficult to perform, pilots could easily exceed the aircraft's g limitations during their execution. Between 13 March and 15 April 1958, SAC experienced six flying accidents that were attributed to fatigue cracks in the B-47 wings. The Stratojets were grounded until a cause could be found. Project MILK BOTTLE was initiated in May 1958 and was conducted in two phases. Because of the extensive low-level flying training being conducted by the 22nd Bombardment Wing at March AFB and the 306th Bombardment Wing at MacDill AFB these aircraft were placed at the head of the list for Phase 1 of the modification program.

Inspections revealed that stress corrosion in the bottle pins holding the wing to the fuselage at Body Stations 525 and 515 had caused the structural failures. Cracks in other fasteners were also noted. Boeing's concern that pilots were exceeding the g-limits of the aircraft led to an article entitled *Structural Load Factors and Service Life* in the August 1958 *Boeing Field Service News* magazine. The article served both as a refresher course for pilots and provided details on the basic design of the aircraft.

**Phase 1** of Project MILK BOTTLE was an interim program where the wings were removed and a series of non-destructive tests

*Three B-47Bs and a pair of RB-47Es at the Douglas-Tulsa facility. In the foreground is a B-47E with the SAC Milky Way band applied to the nose. To the right was an RB-47E. Directly across from the RB-47E was an RB-47E-5-BW (51-5265) from the 90th SRW, as denoted by the lightning bolt on the fin. (Douglas-Tulsa via Harry S. Gann)*

*These aircraft in the nose docks were undergoing a Mod Program at the Douglas-Tulsa plant. At this location the aircraft were undergoing bomb/nav system checkouts. From front to rear were B-47B-30-BW, s/n 51-2176, 51-2177, 51-2181, 51-2172, and 51-2189. (Douglas-Tulsa via Harry S. Gann)*

*These brightly painted external fuel tanks were installed on this B-47B-1-BW (49-2642) as part of the drop tank tests conducted at WIBAC during 1951. Ryan Aeronautical in San Diego, California, built these 1,695-gallon tanks to Boeing specifications. (Boeing P11968)*

were accomplished using borescope and dye penetrant inspections. In the suspect areas, fasteners were removed, the holes were inspected and reamed to the next oversize, and new larger-diameter fasteners were installed. The same procedures were used on the bottle pins. Boeing believed that these interim measures would give the aircraft an additional 400 hours of service life before Phase 2 had to be accomplished. A total of 457 B-47s underwent the Phase 1 inspection program, requiring about 1,700 man-hours per aircraft.

**Phase 2** was a permanent fix carried out at all three manufacturing locations, plus the Sacramento and Oklahoma City Air Materiel Areas. Project MILK BOTTLE cost more than $15 million by the end of July 1958 but it ultimately restored 1,230 B-47s to service, with 895 of them completed during 1958. Project MILK BOTTLE was completed in June 1959 with only a few aircraft requiring follow-on work that was easily accomplished at the next scheduled IRAN visits.

## MODIFICATION MAYHEM

Beginning with Project HIGH NOON in 1953, Boeing had been instrumental in developing the first major B-47 modification program upon which all subsequent modification programs were modeled. Each successive program was based upon joint Boeing and Air Force program planning, statements of work being prepared by Boeing, program engineering accomplished by Boeing, and the technical assistance furnished by Boeing to other modification contractors and Air Materiel Areas.

Second source procurement of B-47 major modification work began in FY56, and by early 1958, Boeing had noticed a major shift in the allocation of modification work to other companies. For instance, during FY57 Boeing had initially been allocated 165 Project BOW STRING modifications. This quantity was subsequently reduced to 136 aircraft and later to 105. The Air Force stated that this reduction was intended to permit WIBAC to accept part of Project SHORT CYCLE that installed ECM equipment and safety of flight changes on the B-52s, in lieu of having the work allocated to Oklahoma City Air Materiel Area.

Boeing responded to an Air Force request for a proposal for the modification of B-47s during FY58 under Project JAY HAWK and was awarded a contract to produce kits for 182 aircraft. Prior to the arrival of the first aircraft, however, the quantity was progressively reduced until none of the work was allocated to Boeing. With the exception of the 36 aircraft removed from the FY58 modification

*B-47E-55-BW, s/n 51-2388, was being towed to a parking spot on the Lockheed-Marietta ramp next to a C-130 during March 1957. U.S. AIR FORCE had replaced the UNITED STATES AIR FORCE on the forward fuselage. The numbers aft of the SAC Milky Way band related to the fiscal year modification program. For safety, the aircraft was surrounded by a number of wing walkers to warn if the aircraft was about to be towed into an object on the ramp. The last three digits of the tail number were applied ahead of the anti-glare panel to assist boom operators in identifying the aircraft during in-flight refueling. (Lockheed-Marietta)*

*These Douglas-Tulsa technicians were applying stencil markings to this B-47 with its pristine full white anti-radiation belly paint. There was no OSHA in those days, hence no safety goggles and masks. (Douglas-Tulsa via Harry S. Gann)*

*This 68th BMW B-47E, with Phase III ECM, was tucked into a hangar at the OCAMA for its Programmed Depot Maintenance. (Oklahoma Air Materiel Area Historian)*

These B-47E-65-BWs (51-7050 and 51-7041), B-47E-95-BW (52-517), and B-47E-65-LM (53-1848) all had the aft attachment for the AN/ARC-21 long-range low frequency radio antennas, visible in this picture. Note that the antenna had been removed from the aircraft in the foreground. If damaged in flight, the antenna could break away at this attachment, preventing the wire from getting entangled in the empennage flight control surfaces. (Lockheed-Marietta RD-4450)

cycle, this entire work package was allocated to Douglas-Tulsa. Boeing's bid for Project TEE TOWN modifications was rejected and the work was given to Douglas-Tulsa. In April 1957 the Air Force informed Boeing that they were to be phased out of the B-47 modification programs entirely. This resulted in a cutback in trained personnel, tools, and materials, and placed Boeing at a disadvantage in subsequent competitive bids for in-plant business at WIBAC. When Boeing presented their case to the Air Force and requested a portion of the field team FY59 work, they did not get a response from the government.

Though it was the prime contractor for the B-47, by 1958 Boeing had slipped to being a provider of services to other companies and Air Force organizations. Under separate contracts, totaling approximately $2,750,000, Boeing provided technical assistance to Oklahoma City and Sacramento Air Materiel Areas, Douglas, and Lockheed consisting of engineering drawings and data, consultation services at WIBAC, and limited liaison engineering services. Other functions performed by Boeing included B-47 fleet surveillance engineering, including design studies, processing and coordination of Air Force unsatisfactory reports, preparation and submittal of engineering change proposals and technical orders, and assistance to the Air Force in modification programming. The company also provided technical indoctrination at Air Force request, accident and incident investiga-

| Year | Boeing | Douglas | Lockheed | Total | Boeing Participation |
|------|--------|---------|----------|-------|----------------------|
| FY55 | 161 | 0 | 0 | 161 | 100 percent |
| FY56 | 201 | 266 | 266 | 733 | 27 percent |
| FY57 | 105 | 204 | 216 | 525 | 20 percent |
| FY58 | 0 | 278 | 281 | 559 | 0 |
| FY59 | 0 | 142 | 203 | 343 | 0 |

**B-47S THROUGH IRAN IN FY55 THROUGH FY59**

tions, field support and necessary reports, surveillance and preliminary designs for special tools, and general surveillance of engineering data for maintenance training unit (MTU) applicability. Boeing also revised technical orders and flight handbooks to reflect the changes from the modification programs.

By the end of 1956 the B-47 program had reached its zenith. Production was 90 percent complete by February and of the 2,029 aircraft then on order, 1,823 had been accepted by the Air Force. After undergoing a tenuous growth process, the B-47 had finally emerged as a viable weapon system. As such its tether to the Air Materiel Command would be severed and the program was transferred to the Oklahoma City Air Materiel Area.

A blast fence divided the ramp areas at OCAMA. At least 20 B-47Bs, B-47Es, and RB-47Es may be seen on the ramp and in the hangars. RB-47E-45-BW (53-4257) is in the foreground. A 22nd BMW B-47E-120-BW (53-2354) is at the left end of the first row of aircraft. (Oklahoma Air Materiel Area Historian)

This B-47B-35-BW (51-2140) was undergoing an engine run while undergoing a modification program at the Douglas-Tulsa plant. All of the engine cowls were removed. Note the guards for the vortex generators on the wing. (William A. Austin/Douglas-Tulsa)

These B-47Bs were moving through the Douglas-Tulsa modification line in this 4,600-foot-long building. (Douglas-Tulsa via Harry S. Gann)

This B-47E-90-BW (52-0480) from the 393rd BS, 509th BMW, was equipped with TEE TOWN ECM pods hanging from the waist. Note the partial white anti-radiation finish. The 509th BMW carried the arrow midway between the vertical fin cap and the tail number. A wing insignia was applied on the SAC Milky Way band. Note the last four digits of the tail number on the nose. The aircraft had just lifted off and the main gear doors were just retracting when the photograph was taken. (SAC Combat Crew Magazine)

An B-47E-50-LM (52-0377) equipped with Phase III ECM and the TEE TOWN ECM pods. The aircraft was assigned to the 303rd BMW and was photographed while deployed to Elmendorf AFB, Alaska, in May 1960. The aircraft had a full white anti-radiation finish that was also applied to the bottom three-quarters of the TEE TOWN pods. The last four digits of the tail number were applied to the nose. Note how the SAC insignia was placed over the anti-radiation paint. "Remove before flight" streamers hung from the engine inlet covers, Pitot probe, landing gear, and air conditioning inlet and exhaust ports. (USAF Museum A1 B-47E/Pho 2)

This front view of the TEE TOWN ECM pod shows the device being installed. The pod came complete with the pylon that was attached to hinge points on the fuselage. A chain fall device was used to lower the pod into position. The pod dolly was parked to the rear. Also of interest is the RATO rack that was also hinged outward awaiting attachment. (Fifteenth Air Force Historian)

The RB-47E was capable of carrying any of this array of cameras to meet mission requirements. The 10 ordnance pieces were flash bombs for night photography. (Boeing 90762)

# Chapter 6

# *RECONNAISSANCE*

Revisionist historians state that General Curtis E. LeMay, Commander-in-Chief Strategic Air Command (CINCSAC), conducted overflights of the Soviet Union at will. These allegations are blatantly untrue. Such overflights were under the purview of the Central Intelligence Agency. On occasion SAC did fly these penetration missions, but they were always at the direction of the White House.

The post-World War II Soviet Union was a great unknown. In 1949 they exploded their first atomic bomb and by October 1951 they had employed a Tupolev Tu-4 Bull (B-29 copy) to test such a weapon in an airburst. By 1953 they were known to have a thermonuclear weapon several years ahead of most intelligence estimates. It was believed that the Soviets had around 600 Tu-4s in service and built a stockpile of as many as 100 nuclear weapons. There were genuine fears of a Soviet first strike.

The Americans and their British allies had developed the Peacetime Airborne Reconnaissance Program (PARPRO) in 1946. Through this program, local theater commanders were authorized to fly intelligence-gathering flights along the periphery of the Soviet Union – direct overflights were absolutely forbidden. Even these flights were dangerous because of interpretations of coastal sovereignty limits, or the blatant disregard of them. While these peripheral flights garnered limited information, it would take daring overflights to achieve truly meaningful results.

Several new reconnaissance aircraft came into the SAC inventory toward the end of LeMay's tenure as CINCSAC. These new aircraft in the B-47 series included the Convair RB-36, Boeing RB-47, Martin RB-57D, Lockheed U-2, and the unusual Convair GRB-36 and Republic RF-84K FICON parasite.

The RB-47s were produced under Weapons System 100L.

## RB-47B

The design of a reconnaissance version of the B-47B began in March 1951. Shortly before October 1952, it was decided that the aircraft would feature the A-5 fire control system and more-powerful J47-GE-25 engines. Since it was projected that this aircraft would not

## RECONNAISSANCE STRATOJET UNITS

| Wing | Base | Squadrons |
|------|------|-----------|
| 26th SRW | Lockbourne AFB | 3rd, 4th, and 10th SRS |
| YRB-47B | 1953 – 1955 | |
| B-47 | 1953 – 1954 | |
| RB-47E | 1954 – 1958 | |
| | | |
| 55th SRW | Forbes AFB | 38th, 338th, and 343rd SRS |
| RB-47E | 1954 | |
| RB-47E | 1954 | |
| RB-47K | 1955 | |
| RB-47H | 1955 – 1967 | |
| ERB-47H | 1957 – 1967 | |
| EB-47E (TT) | 1958 | |
| | | |
| 70th SRW | Little Rock AFB | 6th, 26th, and 61st SRS |
| RB-47E | 1955 – 1962 | |
| | | |
| 90th SRW | Forbes AFB | 319th, 320th, and 321st SRS |
| RB-47E | 1954 – 1960 | |
| RB-47K | 1954 – 1960 | |
| | | |
| 91st SRW | Lockbourne AFB | 323rd, and 324th SRS |
| YRB-47B | 1953 | |
| RB-47E | 1953 – 1957 | |
| RB-47K | 1955 | |
| | | |
| 301st BMW | Lockbourne AFB | |
| RB-47 | 1958 | |
| EB-47E | 1961 – 1965 | |
| | | |
| 305th BMW | MacDill AFB | |
| RB-47B | 1958 | |

be ready before 1954, and by that time it would more closely resemble the B-47E than a B-47B, the definitive reconnaissance version of the Stratojet was redesignated RB-47E.

However, there were RB-47Bs also, although oddly, the first reconnaissance versions to reach SAC were the RB-47Bs, followed by YRB-47Bs. The former were basically bombers that could be readily converted into reconnaissance aircraft through the installation of a reconnaissance pod while the latter were intended specifically for the reconnaissance role.

Twenty-four B-47Bs were modified into RB-47Bs that carried a Boeing-designed bomb bay pod housing eight cameras. Both Grand Central Aircraft and Douglas-Tulsa performed modifications to the bomb bay structure, added special wiring between the bomb bay and the cockpit, and provided hot air ducting for a camera pod that was only capable of performing daylight photoreconnaissance. Aeronca Manufacturing in Middletown, Pennsylvania, built the camera pods to Boeing specifications. Most of the 90 RB-47Bs were used as train-

This pod was carried aboard the YRB-47s. All cameras were installed and then the shroud supporting ribs were installed. (SAC Historian)

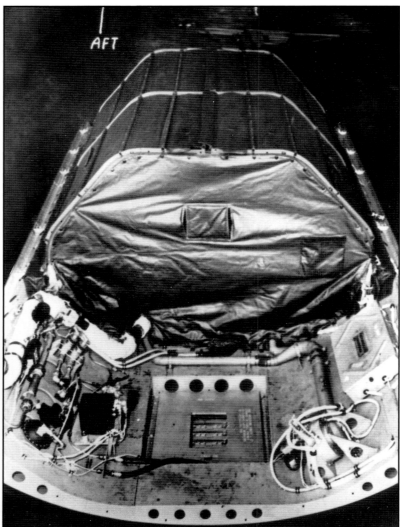

With the shroud installed, this camera pod was ready for installation in a YRB-47. This pod was carried in the bomb bay of 320th BMW aircraft. (SAC Historian)

ers until the RB-47Es became operational. These aircraft were also employed as trainers within SAC's bombardment wings.

The YRB-47B was a later conversion of the B-47B specifically intended to train crews for the forthcoming RB-47E, but any number of these aircraft flew operational reconnaissance missions. Douglas-Tulsa delivered the first YRB-47B to the 91st Strategic Reconnaissance Wing (Medium) in April 1953. Later in 1953 a decision was made to also equip the 320th Bombardment Wing at March AFB with YRB-47Bs. However, by the end of the year the wing began to restore the aircraft back to a bomber configuration, completing all re-conversions by March 1954. Eventually, the aircraft were exchanged through HIGH NOON and other programs.

*This ERB-47B-5-BW (50-005) operated by the ARDC was photographed at the Dayton Air Show in 1954. (Olson via Victor D. Seeley)*

*The ARDC also operated this ERB-47B-46-BW (51-2379), photographed at Dayton in 1954. (Olson via Victor D. Seeley)*

The graceful lines of the standard B-47 were enhanced with the 32.5-inch nose extension housing the camera operator and his specialized equipment controls in the RB-47E. (Boeing BW93540)

## RB-47E

As compared with the standard B-47E, the nose of the RB-47E was 32.5 inches longer so that it could house a special air-conditioned compartment for cameras and other sensitive equipment. Eleven cameras could be carried, along with ten photoflash bombs and supplementary photoflash cartridges for night photography. The bombing equipment was deleted, but the 20-mm tail armament and the A-5 fire control system were retained. Oddly, there was a return to the built-in RATO units that had been used on the B-47B. Although the RB-47E could be refueled in flight, the fuel tankage was increased to 18,405 gallons. A photographer/navigator replaced the normal bombardier/navigator in the three-man crew.

The Air Force Photographic Reconnaissance Laboratory-designed Universal Camera Control System permitted simultaneous automatic operation of the cameras. This system included an optical viewfinder, photocell-operated shutters actuated by flash lighting for night photography, and intervalometers for shooting photographs of large areas at regularly spaced intervals. Developmental problems resulted in a two-year delay before the final product was incorporated into the 136th RB-47E and retrofitted to earlier examples. The Air Force accepted a total of 255 RB-47Es; Boeing knew the first 52 examples as Model 450-216-29, with the remainder being Model 450-158-36.

The first RB-47E (51-5258) made its maiden flight on 3 July 1953 and the last of the type was delivered in August 1955. The final 15 RB-47Es were completed as RB-47K weather reconnaissance aircraft. When the RB-47E was introduced into the inventory, the piston-engined RB-50s continued with electronic intelligence (ELINT) missions until the RB-47H evolved.

Interestingly, for a while the Air Force apparently designated these aircraft as R-47Es (no "B"), or at least that is what the Flight Manual and other technical orders called them. The same was true of the electronic warfare versions, which were E-47Es (again, no "B").

This RB-47E-25-BW (52-731) from the 90th SRW was on the compass rose at the Douglas-Tulsa plant after having undergone programmed depot maintenance. The aircraft carried the wing's distinctive lightning bolt on the tail. (Douglas-Tulsa via Harry S. Gann)

This RB-47E was on the assembly line at WIBAC. The refueling slipway doors were open. (Boeing BW90176)

This Boeing mechanic was adjusting an A9B film magazine for a K-17C camera in the trimetrogon camera station on an RB-47E. The three K-17Cs were charting cameras arranged in a battery to provide horizon-to-horizon low-altitude photographs. Alternatively, this station could carry three T-11 precision cameras or three K-46 night reconnaissance cameras. The A9B magazine held 390 feet of 9-inch-wide film, and also had image motion compensation equipment and a vacuum system to insure flatness of the film when the photographs were taken. The film provided excellent resolution for contact prints for recce tech personnel to make an initial assessment, then chose individual frames for enlargement to make a more detailed analysis. (Boeing BW65921)

This RB-47E-30-BW (52-756) was assigned to the 91st SRW at Lockbourne AFB. The last three digits of the tail number were applied to the forward nose main landing gear doors. This aircraft employed external RATO bottles for high gross weight takeoffs and carried the external fuel tanks. (SAC Combat Crew Magazine)

This nose-to-nose view of a B-47E and RB-47E-1-BW (51-2560) reveals the 32.5-inch nose extension on the recce aircraft. A Boeing flight line mechanic was polishing the nose glazing. (Boeing 90302)

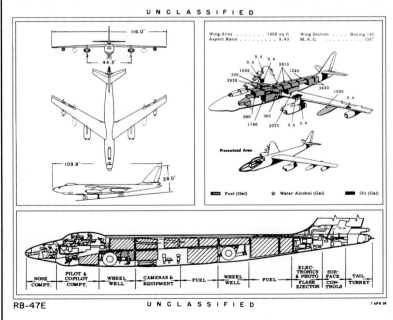

The RB-47E inboard profile shows the general arrangement for each compartment of the fuselage.

This RB-47E-15-BW (51-15838) used the internal RATO system and was not carrying external fuel tanks. (SAC Combat Crew Magazine)

Photographed later in its career, this RB-47E-15-BW (51-15838) carried the SAC Milky Way band on the nose and U.S. AIR FORCE lettering on the forward fuselage. Seen here, the aircraft was assigned to the 26th SRW at Lockbourne AFB and was being refueled by a KC-97G-140-BO (52-2790). It was such a refueling that permitted Captain Hal Austin to get his aircraft safely back to RAF Fairford on 8 May 1954. (Via Colonel Hal Austin)

THE RAZORBACK was the first RB-47E assigned to the 70th SRW, Little Rock AFB, Arkansas. The motto on the wing insignia said WE WATCH OUT FOR YOU. (USAF)

This long-nosed RB-47E was assigned to the 91st SRW when it was based at Lockbourne AFB, Ohio. It was TDY at Barksdale AFB, Louisiana. The ground power cart was courtesy of the 301st CSG also stationed at the base. In the background was a transient C-119. (SAC Combat Crew Magazine)

Doing it by the book was SAC's policy. Here a maintenance technician from the 324th SRS, 91st SRW, Lockbourne AFB, Ohio consulted with his flight chief to obtain the correct information from an engineering technical order before commencing work on the aircraft. (SAC Combat Crew Magazine)

*This EB-47E-50-DT (53-2126) from the 301st BMW, 32nd BS, reveals its Phase V ECM capsule installed in the bomb bay. Two ravens occupied the capsule. Only the aircraft to the right carried its squadron color on the tail. This was during the transition from squadron-level maintenance to the wing consolidated maintenance plan. Note that 15 RATO bottles and the rack remained on the aircraft. The wing used 33 bottles for EWO missions and 15 bottles for the yearly training missions. "Gus" Letto recalls that the 26th SRW had one aircraft drop its expended rack on an uninhabited island in Lake Erie, all the rest returned to base with their spent RATO load. (Augustine "Gus" Letto)*

## EB-47E

The EB-47E designation was applied to a number of electronics countermeasure conversions of the standard B-47E. Initially these were equipped with the Phase IV (Blue Cradle) ECM package but later Phase V aircraft carried a pressurized capsule inside the bomb bay that carried two electronics warfare officers.

*An EB-47E-65-DT (53-2169) from the 301st BMW, 32nd BS, being towed on the ramp. The engine inlets were covered with canvas boots to prevent FOD. Note that the four-digit nose number was not applied at this time. (Augustine "Gus" Letto)*

The EB-47E Phase IV system was operated by the copilot. The Blue Cradle system included 16 AN/ALT-16 jammers in the bomb bay cradle, a pair of AN/ALT-6B jammers in the aft fuselage, two AN/ALE-2 chaff dispensers in the aft fuselage, and an AN/APS-54 radar warning receiver. These aircraft were assigned to the 376th Bombardment Wing at Lockbourne AFB, and subsequently to the 801st Air Division.

There were known limitations to the Phase IV Blue Cradle system; an exercise conducted in 1957 showed that the ECM equipment could draw away the defensive effort expended against the penetrating bombers. During this exercise, a force of 30 to 40 B-47s was flown up to Canada for a night penetration of the northeastern United States. The bombers came down the eastern seaboard at altitudes ranging from 25,000 to 30,000 feet to conduct simulated bombing runs against Boston, New York, Washington, and other cities along the coast. Fourteen Blue Cradle EB-47Es spread out and flew at various altitudes where they performed their jamming. As they approached the targets, the bombers ceased their own jamming, stopped all radio communications, and silently dropped to an altitude of 1,000 feet to penetrate the target areas beneath the radar defenses. Then the bombers would fly their pop-up maneuver, drop their bombs, and exit the area at low altitude. NORAD later claimed that the bombers had successfully attacked not only Boston, New York, and Washington, but had also bombed cities as far away as Buffalo and Chicago.

EB-47Es equipped with the Phase V ECM suite carried two ravens (electronic warfare specialists) in a pressurized capsule installed in the bomb bay. The ravens sat side-by-side in rearward facing ejection seats. The capsule was suspended from the bomb shackles and had its own pressurization, lighting, electrical power, and oxygen systems. The ravens had a remote compass repeater indicator, altimeter, airspeed indicator, clock, and cabin pressure altitude gauge. An intercom system for communications between the capsule and the cockpit was also provided. For takeoff and landing, the ravens sat in the walkway below the pilots. After takeoff, the ravens wended their way through the cockpit pressure floor hatch, along the crawlway, and through the hellhole into their capsule. Ingress and egress of the ravens was accomplished while flying below an altitude of 10,000 feet to preclude physiological hazards.

At first, the ravens were delighted to know that they had ejection seats sitting on top of the fiberglass fairing that had a giant cookie-cutter to cut a hole for them as part of the ejection cycle. Then one crewmember found a copy of a test film that revealed that a successful ejection would be doubtful. Consequently the ravens were willing to crawl back through the hellhole and bail out through the entry hatch.

Initially, the Phase V EB-47E carried nine AN/ALT-6B jammers tuned to E/F band, a single ALT-6B tuned to G/H/I bands, another ALT-6B tuned to D band, an AN/ALT-7 jammer, and a single AN/ALT8B E/F band jammer.

Intelligence information gathered from CIA overflights and early satellite reconnaissance soon revealed that the Soviets were fielding

This EB-47E-70-LM (53-1930) was assigned to the 301st BMW. The nose number was not painted along a waterline. Note the bulged belly denoting the Phase V pod for the ravens. The aircraft was photographed at an airshow at the Philadelphia International Airport in September 1955. (Gordon S. Williams)

An EB-47E-65-DT (53-2169) from the 301st BMW, 32nd BS, being towed on the ramp. The engine inlets were covered with canvas boots to prevent FOD. Note that the four-digit nose number was not applied at this time. (Augustine "Gus" Letto)

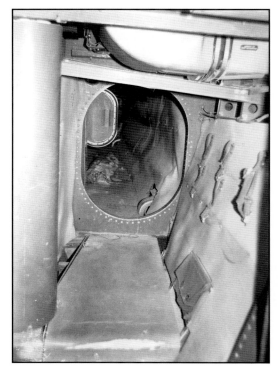

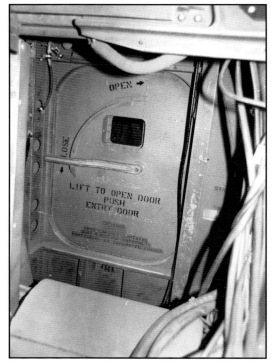

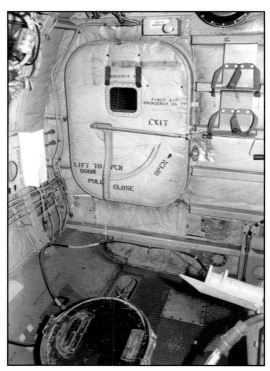

This was the hellhole at the aft end of the passageway from the entry hatchway through which bombardiers crawled to perform IFI and IFE operations on the early atomic bombs, and through which the ravens passed into their Phase V ECM pod. (Bruce M. Bailey)

Looking aft from the crawlway, this was a closed Phase V hatch with a slightly larger cross section. A simple lever engaged the door lock. Note the kneepad below the door. (Bruce M. Bailey)

Looking forward from within the Phase V pod shows the acoustic lining on the bulkheads and the aft face of the access hatch. Note the simple over-center lock for the hatch. The knob above the door was pulled to depressurize the pod prior to opening the hatch. (Bruce M. Bailey)

*This view shows the external details of the Phase V pod and the degree of extension from the lower fuselage contour. (Bruce M. Bailey)*

their then-new SA-2 Guideline SAMs for both point and area defense of potential targets. SAC targeting planners then determined that both the B-47s and B-52s could not survive high-altitude target penetrations, and new low-level tactics were developed for these aircraft. Only the B-58 could hold its own at altitudes around 50,000 feet and Mach 2 airspeeds. Should the B-58s run low on fuel, they too would be forced to penetrate at lower altitudes. A disturbing fact was that the end of 1963 would relegate all of SAC's bomber force to low-altitude penetration of Soviet targets. Meanwhile, the EB-47Es were to fly at high altitudes and provide jamming for the bomber force. The 301st BMW used Phase V Blue Cradle EB-47Es between 1957 and 1964. Their mission was to jam, drop chaff, and draw off the Soviet defenders. One raven, Lieutenant Anton Brees, stated that their mission was to fly out of England and support up to three penetration waves. They were to orbit between Moscow and Leningrad for as long as they had fuel. In essence, they were Kamikaze Sorties 1 through 12 – they had no doubt that they could get there but their return was doubtful.

## EB-47E (TELL TWO)

The Air Force wanted a method of monitoring telemetry that was broadcast during Soviet space launches from the missile facility at Kapustin Yar and the space center at Tyuratam. One solution was to

*An EB-47E-35-BW (52-814) being refueled at Torrejon AB, Spain. Note the ECM sensors on the aft fuselage. The single-point ground refueling port was plumbed into the air refueling system. Also visible are the aft attach points for the AN/ARC-21 single sideband radio long-wire antenna and the Q-spring inlet at the base of the fin leading edge. (Via SAC Combat Crew Magazine)*

*While deployed to RAF Brize Norton between 20 December 1962 and 6 January 1963, innovative maintenance crews protected the engine inlets of their EB-47Es with these inner tubes. If the klaxon sounded, they would simply pull on the nylon tapes to extract the inner tubes. Apparently this system was employed only once during this snowstorm for this deployment. (Augustine "Gus" Letto)*

have an aircraft packed with electronic sensors to fly at a high altitude near these facilities during these Soviet launches, intercepting and recording the electronic telemetry for later analysis by U.S. experts.

Three B-47Es were converted into the Tell Two configuration with the addition of a pressurized bomb bay capsule that housed two operators who gathered Soviet missile telemetry data. The EB-47E(TT) was a unique-looking aircraft that carried long antennas along the forward fuselage. At times these were long towel rack antennas; other times they were large, flat ironing boards protruding from the fuselage. The first EB-47E(TT) was delivered to the 55th Strategic Reconnaissance Wing in December 1958.

At any one time, two of the EB-47E(TT) aircraft would stand alert at Incirlik AB in Turkey, ready to scramble at a moment's notice as soon as an impending Soviet launch was detected. For launches out of Kasputin Yar, missions were flown over the Black Sea, and for launches out of Tyuratam the missions were flown over northeastern Iran. During the missile flights, the missions were flown at high altitude to obtain the clearest reception of the telemetry.

This right side view of The Playmate reveals the full size and shape of the antenna on the EB-47E(TT). The fairing for the belly ECM pod is also visible. This crew (from left to right) consisted of: Captain L. W. Hall, Captain P. E. Fortin, Captain D. J. Birmingham, Jr., Captain D. D. Brockel, and Captain Regis F. A. Urschler. Captain Urschler was wearing the insignia of the 343rd SRS. He went on to command the 55th SRW between May 1978 and August 1980 and later became the first vice commander of the Air Force Electronic Security Command. (Bruce M. Bailey)

The Playmate was an EB-47E(TT) aircraft equipped with the ironing board-style forward-mounted sensors. Above the entry hatch were the names of the proud maintainers – B. L. Brown, Crew Chief, and H. L. Carr, Assistant Crew Chief. A raven mission marker was applied above the crew chiefs' named. The flight crew consisted of Major Johnny Drost, Aircraft Commander; Captain Dwight Lindley, Pilot; Captain Woody Spritzer, Navigator; Captain Dick Paquin, EWO; and 1st Lieutenant Wes DeLoach, EWO. The latter two rode in the ECM pod in the bomb bay. (Bruce M. Bailey)

*Another EB-47E-24-BW-IV Tell Two (53-2326), this time with a tooth-pick-like towel rack antenna mounted on the forward fuselage. Note the scars from an earlier configuration. This was one of the three Tell Two EB-47Es. (Bruce M. Bailey)*

*Towel rack antennas were carried on both sides of EB-47E Tell Twos. Scars from an earlier antenna configuration are visible on the fuse-lage. (Bruce M. Bailey)*

## RB-47H

The RB-47H (Boeing Model 450-171-51) was an electronic reconnaissance and countermeasures version of the B-47 built in response to a mid-1951 requirement or an aircraft capable of counter-ing enemy air defense systems. General Nathan B. Twining, USAF Vice Chief of Staff, personally wrote Boeing President William M. Allen emphasizing the urgency.

Initial plans had called for a two-man ECM capsule to be installed in the short bomb bay of the B-47, but this was amended to a three-man capsule; thus raising the total crew complement to six – pilot, copilot, radar-navigator, and three ECM operators. Up to 845 pounds of chaff could be carried. The first RB-47H entered service with the 55th Strategic Reconnaissance Wing at Forbes AFB in August 1955. The last RB-47H was delivered in January of 1957 and a total of 35 RB-47Hs were built, although three of these were deliv-ered as ERB-47H electronic ferret aircraft.

A wide variety of equipment was added in the form of various mission-related antennas, including the AN/ALD-4 Silver King pod mounted on the right waist of the aircraft in 1961. Studies for a wide-spectrum ferret device began as early as 1948 with both the Federal Telephone Laboratories in Naulty, New Jersey, and the Airborne Instrument Laboratory in conjunction with the Wright Air Development Center. This early equipment was tested on SAC RB-50s. A still newer system was envisioned for the anticipated Convair RB-58 Hustler. The Wright Air Development Center award-ed a contract to Melpar for the AN/APD-4 system. This system was

*This view of the aft antenna array shows the large belly fairing hous-ing (front to rear), the AN/ALD-6 DF (low-band), AN/ALA-6 DF (high-band), and QRC-91 antennas. Above were the (front to rear) two side-facing AN/AN/APD-4, and AN/APR-17 RL1 antennas. Between (front to rear) were the AN/APR-17 RC-1 and RX-1 anten-nas. (Via Bruce M. Bailey)*

*This blunt-nosed bird was the first RB-47H-1-BW (53-6245). Subsequently it was converted into an ERB-47H. Note the skin wrinkles below the wing leading edge that were the result of the different loads applied to the airframe because of the ECM pod installed in the bomb bay. A number of ECM blade antennas may be seen from beneath the nose, along the belly, and around the aft lower fuselage. This aircraft was not yet equipped with an astrocompass system. (SAC Historian)*

extremely complex and consisted of around 200 crystal video receivers providing complete coverage of the 100 to 16,000 MHz frequency range, along with three scanning superheterodyne receivers for searching weaker signals. A spherical Luneberg lens antenna was mounted in each end of the pod where their 15 pick-offs automatically provided bearing data on incoming signals. This equipment essentially doubled the intelligence gathering capability of the RB-47H.

Melpar also developed the Ground Installed Reconnaissance Data Handling System (GIRDHS) for retrieving the data after flight. Subsequently the GIRDHS was identified as an AN/GSQ-17 finder. By using the GIRDHS, recorded data could be fed automatically into SAC's computer database on the Soviet radar order of battle. SAC constructed a separate building at Offutt AFB to accommodate the GSQ-17 system.

*This RB-47H-BW (53-4296) was photographed later in its career. The under-wing pylon and astrocompass antenna may be seen. Also, heat-seeking sensors were mounted to the aft portion of the outboard engine pylon. (SAC Combat Crew Magazine)*

This flight crew and crew chief close the drag chute compartment. Note the door hinge linkage forward. (USAF)

Looking forward into the interior of the raven pod of an RB-47H. The hatch to the crawlway may be seen on the left. (Bruce M. Bailey)

This left three-quarter view of an RB-47H-BW (53-4296) shows the aircraft taxiing out for a mission. Note the turned forward main gear and castered outrigger gear. The left under-wing sensor is visible outboard of the No. 1 engine. To prevent reflections, the interiors of the engine inlets were painted flat black. (SAC Combat Crew Magazine)

The first RB-47H (53-4280) also served as the test aircraft for the 25-foot-long, 5-foot-diameter ALD-4 Silver King pod. Initially the pod was mounted to a waist-mounted pylon with a 90-degree crank in it, but this arrangement resulted in a significant increase in the forces required to control the aircraft. Subsequently a pylon that was attached to the fuselage at a 45-degree angle eliminated the adverse loads.

All 35 RB-47Hs were assigned to the 55th SRW at Forbes AFB with the first aircraft delivered on 9 August 1955. The RB-47H had the distinction of being the last version of the Stratojet that was operational with the Air Force, and the last aircraft (53-4296) was ferried to Davis-Monthan AFB on 29 December 1967.

*RB-47H-1-BW, s/n 53-4299, had been assigned to the 55th SRW at Forbes AFB, Kansas, until August 1966. The aircraft was parked in an unobtrusive place on the base and fenced in to keep out intruders. Note the "0-" in the tail number, indicating that the aircraft was over 10 years old. The black bulge on top of the center of the fuselage behind the inboard nacelle was for the astrotracker. Eventually this aircraft suffered from vandalism, but was rescued. It underwent extensive restoration at the Air Force Museum at Wright-Patterson AFB to become the centerpiece of the new Cold War exhibit. (SAC Combat Crew Magazine)*

*This is a typical view of the buildings along the flight line access road at Forbes AFB, Kansas, when the first RB-47s for the 55th SRW began arriving in September 1954. These were T-buildings erected during World War II – with the T standing for temporary. Many of the buildings were heated with pot-bellied stoves – great for barracks during a Kansas blizzard! This photo dates from August 1953. (SAC Combat Crew Magazine)*

*This view of Forbes AFB reveals the flight line with nine RB-47Hs. A T-33 and a set of mobile airstairs were located near base operations (to the left of center). (Via Bruce M. Bailey)*

THE JOY BOYS *was an RB-47H assigned to the 55th SRW. An MD-3 ground power cart was standing by to provide electrical power to the aircraft. (Bruce M. Bailey)*

The first AN/ALD-4 ECM pod was mounted on a cranked pylon, which resulted in excessive buffeting. Note the boots on the tires to protect them from leaking MIL-H-5606 hydraulic fluid. An air conditioning hose was attached to the aircraft's air conditioning system. (Boeing A21391)

This waist view reveals the aft end of the ALD-4 pod mounted on the cranked pylon. Additional sensors were carried in the ventral pod on the aft fuselage and blisters above. (Boeing A21392)

## ERB-47H

Three RB-47Hs (53-6245, 53-6246, and 53-6249) were modified to detect and locate electromagnetic radio frequency emissions. While similar to the RB-47H, these ERB-47Hs were modified to eliminate one raven position and install passive ECM receivers and extra-wide band recording equipment to gather fine-grained information on Soviet radar and air defense emissions.

*This was the maintenance crew for the 55th SRW's ERB-47-BW (53-6246) on deployment to RAF Sculthorpe. (Via Bruce M. Bailey)*

## RB-47K

Fifteen RB-47Es were modified into RB-47Ks (Boeing Model 450-158-36) during production in Wichita. These aircraft carried equipment to perform the photoreconnaissance mission and a weather reconnaissance mission at both high and low altitudes. The RB-47K also carried the high-resolution and side-looking radars. All of these aircraft were delivered to the 55th SRW. The first was delivered in December 1955, but it would not be until the latter half of 1956 that the aircraft were mission-capable. SAC sent a number of crewmembers to Air Weather

*This right profile view of the first RB-47H-BW (53-4280) shows the aircraft later in its career with the 0- tail number indicating that it was at least 10 years old. An ALD-4 pod was retrofitted on the aircraft and has the newer straight pylon that reduced the turbulence. An astrocompass sensor was mounted on top of the mid-fuselage. (SAC Combat Crew Magazine)*

*This RB-47H-BW (53-4296) was photographed later in its career. The under-wing pylon and astrocompass antenna may be seen. Also, heat-seeking sensors were mounted to the aft portion of the outboard engine pylon. (SAC Combat Crew Magazine)*

*This RB-47K-45-BW (53-4264) came to rest with the right inboard pylon ripped away and settling on the No. 6 nacelle. Note that the crew had blown the canopy after the aircraft came to rest, hence it landed directly below the cockpit. (USAF)*

Service to learn the mission. These aircraft flew worldwide to provide weather data for SAC and to sample radiation fallout from foreign nuclear blasts. The aircraft were phased out in the early 1960s.

The USAF inventory ledgers do not identify the RB-47K as a delivered configuration, because they were conditionally accepted by SAC as RB-47Es and modified prior to delivery. The modifications took five months and cost less than $5 million.

## EB-47L

While the EB-47Es were electronic jamming aircraft that would afford ECM protection to the bomber stream, the EB-47Ls served as radio relay aircraft to transmit messages from SAC Headquarters to the bombers. In 1963, 36 obsolescent B-47Es were modified to serve as relay stations between other aircraft (such as the USAF "Looking Glass" EC-135 command post or the Navy's EC-130Q) or between aircraft and ground stations during and after a nuclear attack.

Temco Aircraft in Dallas accomplished the EB-47L conversions under Project PIPECLEANER. Special radios provided an Ultra High Frequency (UHF) relay (line of slight) that would be less susceptible to interference during periods of sunspot activity, interference from nuclear detonations, long-range interference, and/or jamming.

The Project PIPECLEANER system consisted of an ARC-89 radio relay system with ART-42 transmitters. The entire package was installed in the forward end of the bomb bay. Three pressurized containers, each housing a complete ARC-89 system, were suspended from a rack system. A regulator sensed pressure and controlled an outflow valve to maintain ambient pressure up to an altitude of 8,000 feet. For altitudes between 8,000 and 43,000 feet, the system maintained a pressure altitude of 8,000 feet within each pressure container. Above 43,000 feet, the system maintained an 8.8-pounds-per-square-inch pressure differential (not unlike today's jetliners). Integral with the pressurization system was an air conditioning system. Engine bleed air was cooled and maintained a maximum airflow of 64 pounds of air per minute to the system. Aircraft equipped with the ARC-89 radio relay system could be identified by a ram air scoop located on the right bomb bay door just below the hinge line and a cooling air inlet near the door centerline. In the event of an air conditioning system failure, ram air could be used for transmitter cooling for altitudes above 10,000 feet.

The ARC-89 radio relay system exhibited very poor reliability, with extremely high component failure rates. Probably the most pernicious problem was equipment cooling resulting from inadequate airflow and system freezing. To circumvent the conditions

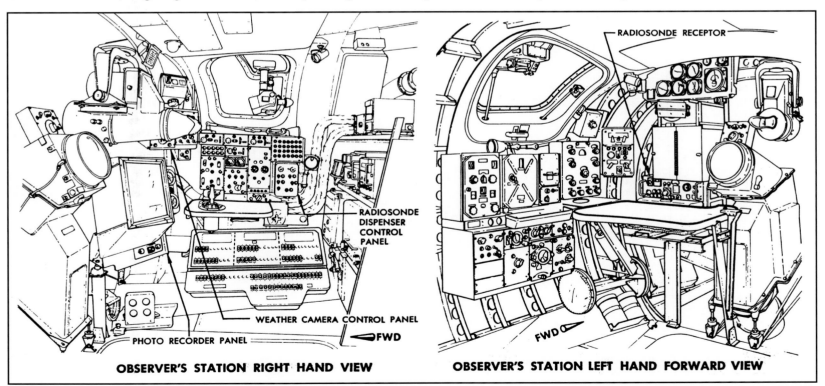

In addition to the normal RB-47E mission equipment, the RB-47Ks had a weather reconnaissance suite added. This equipment consisted of a radiosonde dispenser, radiosonde receptor, radio altimeter, cloud formation camera, and a weather data monitoring camera that recorded the indications of the various instruments located within the observer's station. These two views show the added equipment within the compartment.

resulting in these failures, improvements were made to the airflow. Heaters were installed in the system to prevent ice build-up in the air conditioning lines and the ram air scoop. A water separator with a 35-degree Fahrenheit switch ensured heating to prevent ice build-up in the system.

A pair of B-47Es was allocated to Temco in September 1961 for test purposes. The initial cost for system development on these two aircraft was $2,626,000. This phase was completed in January 1962 and proved that the concept was operationally feasible. Hence, 34 additional aircraft were scheduled for modification in May of that year.

Initially SAC had planned on two radio relay squadrons to be activated at two undefined locations in July 1962. SAC continued to refine its concept and decided to place the aircraft in four squadrons, each equipped with nine aircraft, at bases closest to the nearest required orbital areas. These squadrons were to be designated as Airborne Communications Relay Squadrons (ACRS). Headquarters USAF approved the request, but stipulated that these squadrons be attached to the wings rather than assigned to them. Headquarters Fifteenth Air Force questioned the advisability of such a relationship because of its potential for complicating organization, equipment, and staffing of the squadrons. However, SAC concurred with the Headquarters USAF position stating that the squadrons would be retained longer than the wings and it was necessary to maintain separate identity for the units.

The 4362nd ACRS was attached to the 98th BMW at Lincoln AFB, Nebraska; the 4363rd ACRS was attached to the 376th BMW at Lockbourne AFB, Ohio; the 4364th ACRS was attached to the 9th BMW at Mountain Home AFB, Idaho; and the 4365th ACRS was

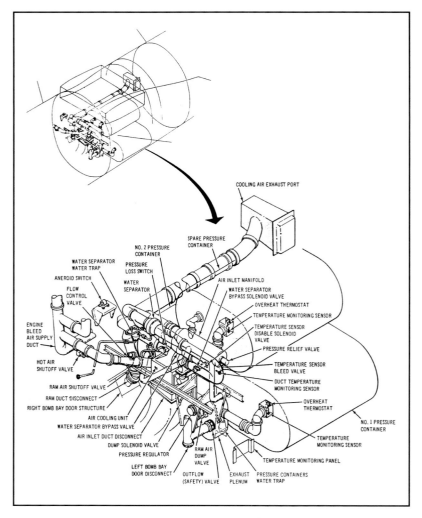

*The AN/ARC-89 radio relay system was mounted in these three pressure containers located in the forward end of the bomb bay of the EB-47L aircraft. There were two primary systems and a spare. (USAF)*

*Conditioned air was provided for the AN/ARC-89 radio relay system aboard the EB-47Ls via this plumbing system that controlled pressure, temperature, and humidity. (USAF)*

attached to the 380th BMW at Plattsburgh AFB, New York. The four support squadrons were subsequently redesignated Post Attack Command and Control Squadrons (PACCS).

At the sounding of the klaxon, the EB-47Ls were the first aircraft airborne and flew predetermined tracks to place them out ahead of the bomber stream that would follow. Their mission was to relay messages from the various SAC command posts to the bombers. The copilot/radio operator was truly like the proverbial one-armed paperhanger on these missions – monitoring the flight, and coordinating radio messages from the SAC Command Post to the bomber stream. Fortunately their mission kept them out of hostile territory, thereby relieving him of his gunnery duties. The EB-47Ls were phased out during 1965-66.

## WB-47B

While balloon-borne radiosondes work quite well over large landmasses, they are not feasible for use over large areas of water. For eight years, the Air Weather Service employed propeller-driven WB-50s to gather data over the vast oceans where violent storms brew. Older WB-29s were flown for an even longer period. A crew of eight manned these aircraft.

With the advent of the WB-47, the crew size was reduced to three since automated airborne meteorological equipment aboard

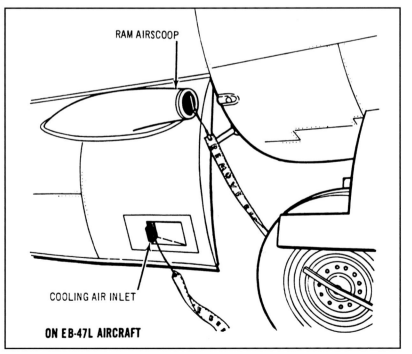

The two photographs above show an EB-47L being used by the U.S. Navy. A chaff drum was mounted in the tail turret, and a large transmitter under the rear fuselage (Terry Panopalis)

The EB-47L PIPECLEANER aircraft could be identified by this ram air scoop and cooling air inlet mounted on the forward end of the right bomb bay door. (USAF)

*The Air Weather Service WB-47B (51-2115) was photographed at McClellan AFB, circa 1962. This was one of the most dazzling paint schemes on a B-47. It had a full white anti-radiation belly with black-edged Day-Glo Orange trim running along the fuselage, up the vertical fin, and on each engine nacelle. An Insignia Yellow-edged Insignia Blue band with white WEATHER lettering was applied to the vertical tail. All national insignia were retained, despite the white undersurfaces. The aircraft was acquired for the National Hurricane Research Project. (USAF)*

the WB-47s reduced the crew workload, thereby eliminating the weather specialists from the aircraft. With the WB-50s, the weather was observed and encoded manually, then transmitted by Morse code, received aurally, and decoded manually. The automated equipment not only reduced the processing time, but also almost eliminated human errors. In addition to performing the weather reconnaissance mission, the WB-47s were also equipped for atmospheric sampling for the Atomic Energy Commission and other governmental agencies.

A disastrous hurricane season in 1954 provided the impetus for Congress to authorize funding for a new weather reconnaissance program that eventually resulted in procedures to better forecast the phenomenon. The U.S. Weather Bureau developed plans in 1955 for con-

ducting investigations during the 1956 hurricane season. Basic research would be conducted in the hurricane breeding grounds – the Atlantic Ocean just south of Bermuda, the Caribbean, and the Gulf of Mexico. The Weather Bureau did not have the requisite weather reconnaissance capability and turned to the Navy and Air Force. To gather the requisite data a flotilla of ships, a number of ground weather stations, and three heavily instrumented aircraft would be used. For these studies, the 55th Weather Reconnaissance Squadron (WRS) provided a pair of WB-50s and a B-47B. While the 55th, 58th, and 59th Weather Reconnaissance Squadrons provided maintenance and aircrews for the WB-50s, the B-47B was flown and maintained by Air Training Command personnel while the Air Weather Service awaited the delivery of a dedicated aircraft.

At the beginning of the 1956 hurricane season, only one WB-50 was available for the strongest of the year's blasts – Hurricane Betsy. A lack of equipment from the Weather Bureau caused the delay in having the second WB-50 and the B-47B available. When all three aircraft arrived on station, it was then possible to provide the requisite weather reconnaissance support for the remainder of the hurricane season. While the WB-50s staged out of Palm Beach, Florida, the WB-47s operated from Homestead AFB, Florida, where the unit was able to use the resources of the 376th Bombardment Wing stationed there. Procedures called for each of the three aircraft to make two penetrations of the storm at altitudes varying between 1,200 and 40,000 feet. The same pair of WB-50s and the B-47B were used for the 1957 hurricane season.

In 1956, General Precision Laboratories modified a single B-47B-30-BW (51-2115) as a weather reconnaissance aircraft under the designation WB-47B. This first Stratojet in the Air Weather Service was resplendently painted and was assigned to the 55th WRS stationed at McClellan AFB during November 1957. The aircraft participated in the Hurricane Research Project, and performed research work in conjunction with the Trios II weather satellite program. The aircraft was retired in 1963 after accruing 126.5 hours of flying in the weather reconnaissance role.

As the 1958 hurricane season approached, the B-47 fleet came under a Time Compliance Technical Order (TCTO) that prevented rough air penetration, except where necessary, until a structural inspection could be accomplished. Major T. A. Aldrich, AWS Air Operations Directorate, telephoned Mr. Bob Simpson, National Hurricane Research Project Director, to advise him of the situation. The response was that the mission was of far greater importance than the TCTO; if the WB-47B could not be provided then a WB-66 should be substituted. Orders were cut that directed the WB-47B be sent to the Oklahoma City Air Materiel Center on 5 May 1958 for inspections.

Prior to the structural evaluations, the WB-47B was restricted to 1.5-g and could not fly into areas of known moderate to severe turbulence. The restrictions kept the aircraft from making actual hurricane penetrations. The Air Force-directed operational limits for the WB-47B included:

- Based on a 35,000-foot constant level cruise, missions could not exceed 5.5 hours, including time from destination to alternate airport. This restricted the effective tracks to approximately 2,100 nautical miles.
- All flights had to be conducted during daylight hours while maintaining visual flight rules (VFR) in all areas of tropical storm activity.
- Flights could not be made into any areas where moderate or severe turbulence was reported or forecast to exist.

In view of these restrictions, the Air Weather Service asked the Weather Bureau if they still desired to use the WB-47B for the 1958 season. The Weather Bureau was concerned that meaningful data could not be collected and compared to the WB-50 data taken at lower altitudes. As a result, negotiations between the Department of Commerce and the Department of Defense began to find a suitable alternative aircraft. The result of these talks was inconclusive and the Weather Bureau was advised to make what use of the WB-47B they could under the circumstances.

*This WB-47E (51-7049) was operated by the 55th WRS at McClellan AFB. This photo was taken in early 1964 as the aircraft was preparing for takeoff. A U-1 foil was mounted to the right bomb bay door. Standard USAF markings were applied. In addition, the typical MATS identification block was applied to the forward gear doors. A MATS insignia was applied to the fuselage aft of the national insignia, and the AWS insignia was placed beneath the tail number. The aircraft crashed while TDY at Eielson AFB, Alaska, in April 1964. (USAF)*

*These seven WB-47Es shared the McClellan AFB ramp with a WB-57. For safety reasons, the ground power carts were placed at 45 degrees between the forward fuselage and wing. (USAF)*

*This belly shot of a WB-47E (51-2415) shows a single U-1 foil mounted in the right side of the bomb bay. (Boeing BW175495 via Military Airlift Command Historian)*

*This 53rd WRS crew included (left to right): Captain Robert Bailey, Major Dale Sutherland, and Captain David McGrath. They were briefing prior to taking off to observe Hurricane Dora that struck the coasts of Florida and Georgia in 1964. An Air Force Outstanding Unit Award was applied to the forward fuselage. (USAF)*

There were 10 named storms during the 1958 hurricane season, only the first of which was not supported by the Air Weather Service. For the remaining nine storms, the Air Weather Service flew twelve one-plane missions, six two-plane missions, and five three-plane missions. Greater use was made of photography during these missions with some 3,000 frames being shot per mission. Data gathered during these flights was placed on IBM punch-cards and a single three-plane mission required the use of 40,000 punch-cards. Robert Simpson, Director of the National Hurricane Research Project, was satisfied with the quantity and quality of the data gathered by the Air Weather Service, particularly from the three-plane missions. During the 1958 season, the two WB-50s flew 133:30 and 95:35 hours in direct support of hurricane research missions. The single WB-47B flew 99:55 hours on research flights, and a total 168:20 hours including ferry and training flights.

After the 1958 season the WB-47B was relegated to prototyping equipment for the WB-47Es that would follow.

## WB-47E

WB-47E was the designation assigned to converted B-47Es used for weather reconnaissance. They had nose-mounted cameras that recorded cloud formations, and carried air-sampling and data recording equipment inside the bomb bay.

Because the aircraft did not require a bombing capability, all bombing and gunnery equipment was removed. In addition, high gross weight takeoffs were no longer a concern and the RATO and air refueling systems were also deleted. While the external fuel tanks were generally not required, the capability for reinstallation was retained.

The crew duties on the WB-47 were redistributed to suit the new mission. While the aircraft commander retained his duties, the copilot no longer had to concern himself with the ECM and gunnery functions, and the navigator was not required to be a bombardier. The copilot became the meteorological observer and system operator. The navigator operated the air sampling equipment and assisted in the operation of the meteorological system equipment.

Typically the contractor is tasked with acceptance flights for a new aircraft, however, because of the highly specialized nature of the equipment and mission, it was decided to perform these tests at McClellan AFB, California. The 9th Weather Reconnaissance Group (WRG), Scientific Applications Section was tasked with evaluating the WB-47E. Engineering and technical personnel from both Lockheed and Bendix supported these tests.

The Air Weather Service received the first of 34 Lockheed-Marietta-modified WB-47Es on 20 March 1963. The 53rd and 55th Weather Reconnaissance Squadrons operated them. The WB-47Es began to be replaced by WC-130 and WC-135 aircraft in 1965, but total phaseout took another three years. The last WB-47E – actual-

ly the last operational B-47 in the Air Force inventory – was delivered to Davis-Monthan AFB on 31 October 1969.

The WB-47E was the first aircraft to incorporate a completely automatic weather collection system. This system constantly recorded the weather horizontally along the synoptic track. At predetermined times a meteorological sensing and telemetry device known as a dropsonde was ejected from the tail of the aircraft. As the dropsonde descended, it measured pressure, temperature, and humidity. This data was transmitted back to the aircraft where it was stored on tape. The recorder held that data until it could be transmitted to a ground station. Personnel at AWS ground stations used high-speed computers to reduce the data into a useable format for onward transmittal to the worldwide weather network via teletype.

The AN/AMQ-19 Meteorological System used on the WB-47Es

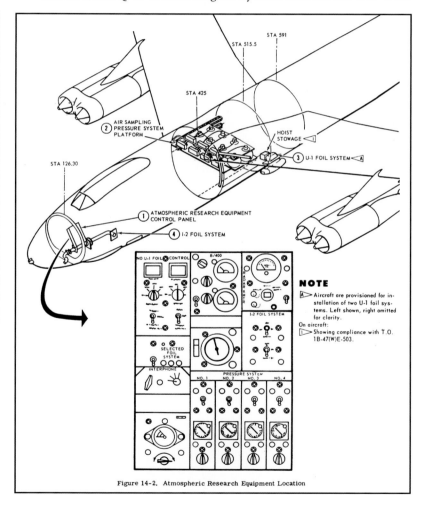

Figure 14-1. AN/AMQ-19 Meteorological System Equipment Location

Figure 14-2. Atmospheric Research Equipment Location

*This illustration shows the AN/AMQ-19 meteorological equipment installed on the WB-47E.*

*WB-47Es carried the I-1 and U-2 foil systems to conduct atmospheric research. The I-1 system was installed in the nose, while the U-2 systems were carried in the bomb bay. A control panel was located at the observer's station.*

While making an emergency landing at Lajes AB, Azores, on 10 November 1963, this WB-47E (51-2420) skidded into the ramp area striking a C-97C (50-0690). The right outboard wingtip and No. 6 engine of the WB-47 was ripped off. The upper skin covering the flap wells was burnt away leaving just the stringers and ribs. A piece was knocked out of the leading edge of the left wing. Scorch marks are visible on the waist and left wing leading edge, as is the flap well damage on the left wing. The left inboard nacelles were torn from the aircraft. Note that the navigator's upper hatch and pilots' canopy had been blown. (USAF)

was designed and manufactured by the Bendix-Friez Instrument Division. The AN/AMQ-29 Dropsonde Data Recording System used an off-the-shelf Hewlett-Packard 9206A to record and quantify signals captured by the AMQ-19. A General Precision AN/APN-102 Doppler Radar and a Bendix AN/APN-42 Radar Altimeter were also carried. The pencil-beam afforded obstacle detection: whereas the fan-shaped beam was employed as a navigation aid providing terrain features. In combination, this system provided warnings for terrain, another aircraft, and severe weather. A Rosemount AN/AMQ-28 Total Temperature System was installed to measure outside air temperature. Monmouth Electric manufactured the AN/AMT-13 dropsondes that were carried in the aft fuselage; the company was awarded a contract to produce 81,000 dropsondes over a five-year period. A single U-1 foil collector was installed near the forward edge of each bomb bay door. Each foil was approximately six feet long by two feet in diameter. Air samples were drawn in through these foils and ducted into a self-contained box where samples of any particulate matter

were deposited on 18-inch paper filters. A filter changing mechanism resembling a jukebox record changer removed clean filters from a storage unit, placed it within the airstream, removed the contaminated filter, and placed the contaminated filter in the storage unit.

The automated weather data collection system on the WB-47Es was fraught with problems during the first half of 1963. Because of poor performance of the AMQ-19 system, production aircraft were delivered without the system being fully operational. Consequently, aircrews had to manually encode and transmit the data, much like the WB-50s before them. No dropsonde capability existed and operation of the WB-47s was further hampered by delays in the delivery of the APN-42 radar altimeters. This equipment would not be available until late August.

Eventually, the WB-47Es were excellent for high altitude work, but were restricted to a rough weather penetration speed that made them unsuitable to fly into the centers of the storms. Consequently these aircraft were limited to checking the periphery of the intense storms.

*This WB-47E (51-7066) arrived at Boeing Field in October 1969, marking the last flight for a weather Stratojet. The aircraft was turned over to the Museum of Flight. (Vern Manion via Gordon S. Williams)*

This TB-47-10-BW (50-015) was assigned to the 3520th FTW at McConnell AFB, Kansas. No identifying squadron tail color had been applied at the time the picture was taken. (Boeing BW60479)

# Chapter 7

# *TRAINING*

With the Stratojet's introduction into SAC inventory came a requirement for a new, intensive transition-training program for both flight crews and maintainers. Not only did the pilots have to thoroughly know the aircraft systems and performance, they had to learn to stay ahead of the aircraft with their thinking. In addition, all of this knowledge had to be known by three instead of ten crewmen and everything was happening at least twice as fast as it did with reciprocating engine-powered aircraft. Not possessing the ability to react quickly was almost a sure ticket for a student washing out of the program.

Older aircraft required the maintainers to have a thorough knowledge of sheet metal repair, rudimentary cable flight control systems, and powerplants. The B-47's maintainers needed these skills, but also added pressurization, air conditioning, and electronics knowledge to their résumés. Needless to say, SAC ensured that only high-scoring personnel were sent to the various schools and only those with top grades were assigned to the command's units.

## TB-47B

The TB-47B was a conversion of the standard B-47B as a transition trainer for pilots and navigators. It was basically similar to the B-47B but had a fourth crew position added for an instructor. This rudimentary position incorporated cushions in the crawlway to form a semblance of a seat, an interphone box, and an oxygen regulator. The instructor was free to move about the cockpit to observe and instruct the student. The copilot's instrument panel was modified to incorporate more of the instruments found in the forward crew position. All armament and ECM equipment was removed. The TB-47 had a maximum takeoff and landing weight of 179,292 pounds and was powered by J47-GE-23 engines.

## FLIGHT TRAINING

Learning to fly the B-47 was a challenge, especially for a crew without jet experience. While the handling characteristics in flight were relatively easy to master, it was the critical takeoff and landing performance that presented the real challenge. Reciprocating engines with propellers have an almost instant response to power changes, whereas the early jet engines had an inherent spool-up lag time. Learning to properly judge this spool-up time was no easy task since it varied due to aircraft gross weight, temperature, and density altitude (due to a combination of field elevation and temperature).

*Like all jet aircrews, B-47 flight crewmembers received training in an altitude chamber to learn the effects of hypoxia. First was a long ascent with the masks off to learn one's individual symptoms of hypoxia – your top three were to be remembered for life. In this large chamber, one learned to identify symptoms and learned how to properly use the oxygen mask. In a smaller chamber, smaller groups underwent rapid decompression training. Note the wings on the instructor – the lieutenant was a bombardier. (Boeing P13497)*

*Formation flying was part of the syllabus at the ATC Stratojet transition school of the 3520th FTW, ATC at McConnell AFB, Kansas. Here is a trio of B-47B-5-BWs (50-010, 50-021, and 50-013). The pilots in the two outboard aircraft positioned themselves on the middle aircraft. Note the early unstaggered RATO ports. Aircraft 50-013 was launched on 13 March 1958 with a student in the front seat and an instructor in back. The student was practicing unusual attitude recovery. While recovering from the second maneuver, the aircraft was in a 30-degree right wing low descent when the crew heard a thump or crack. While establishing a 45-degree bank, the student heard another unusual noise. As the control column was pushed forward, the student pilot noted flames and ordered a bailout. His ejection was successful, however, the instructor had not completed his ejection sequence. When the aircraft was inverted, they managed to bail out. Both crewmen survived. This was believed to be the first event that led to Project MILK BOTTLE. On 17 November 1959, aircraft 50-021, then assigned to SAC's 4327th CCTW at McConnell, had deployed to Whiteman AFB, Missouri, during a training flight. The aircraft crashed on takeoff, killing all four crewmen. (Boeing BW60758)*

To augment engine thrust, the assisted takeoff (ATO) system – water-alcohol injection for the engines – could be activated at a specific point during the takeoff roll. For higher gross weight takeoffs, the rocket assisted takeoff (RATO) system could also be used. Care had to be taken, however, since activating the system too early could result in them depleting their propellants before the aircraft could benefit from their added thrust. Conversely, should the systems be activated too late during the takeoff roll, the aircraft would not achieve flying speed, possibly resulting in a runway overrun.

The B-47 was designed to fly. Its speed and lift characteristics made landing particularly critical, especially while carrying a nuclear weapon on a round-trip training mission. Making a jet penetration to an air base required a rapid letdown. To achieve minimum time in the descent, lowering the outrigger gear and the aft main gear dirtied the aircraft up. Although a routine procedure, there was no special switch in the cockpit. Instead, the crew pulled the circuit breaker associated with the forward main gear thereby precluding it from getting a gear-down electrical signal.

At the high speeds necessary to maintain flight, it was difficult to get the aircraft to stop, even on a 10,000-foot-long runway. The approach chute allowed the pilot to carry extra power to keep the aircraft airborne and be able to initiate a go-around without worrying about slow engine spool-up. If the landing was aborted, the approach chute was generally jettisoned to allow the aircraft to accelerate. If this happened, the subsequent approach became more critical.

Once on the ground, the pilot deployed the large deceleration chute to slow the aircraft on the runway. Pilots had to learn to plant the aircraft on the aft set of main landing gear wheels. Failure to do so would result in the aircraft porpoising. Because of the relatively short-couple design of the main gear, the oscillation amplitude would increase with each forward and aft gear contact with the runway. The only viable corrective action was to apply full power and execute a go-around.

A number of unusual flight control problems were experienced with the B-47 – among the most serious were frozen rudders and binding ailerons. In a few instances, the aircraft became uncontrollable. Following the loss of a B-47 in January 1961 due to an uncontrollable roll, data from all flight control malfunctions from the past three-and-a-half years were analyzed. Aircraft having experienced flight control problems between January and March 1961 were isolated and underwent a thorough inspection by flight control and autopilot experts to determine the root cause of these problems.

*This TB-47B-20-BW (50-066) assigned to the 3520th CCTW at McConnell AFB experienced fire damage to the No. 2 engine and outrigger landing gear. The photo dates from 5 April 1955. (USAF)*

By the spring of 1964, it was learned that icing in the Q-spring inlet could contribute to directional flight control problems. The result was to install an electrically heated Q-spring ram air inlet. A low-heat circuit was employed on the ground. High heat was energized through the main landing gear squat switch thereby permitting its use only in flight.

### Boeing Training School

For years, Boeing ran two successful schools in Seattle known as the Fortress School and the Stratofreighter School. Capitalizing on these programs, Boeing instituted a B-47 training school at Wichita that provided classes in both operations and maintenance. This school was operated by the Service Department.

Initial classes were limited to a cadre of personnel from SAC, Air Materiel Command, Air Proving Ground Command, and Air Force Special Weapons Command. Subsequently these classes were opened up for personnel from a large number of commands and were operated on a two-shift schedule.

All students received a one- to two-week general familiarization class, followed by two to six weeks of intensive training in specific subjects. There were a number of hands-on classes, including operation of the engine test stand. Factory tours included detailed parts fabrication with hydropresses, contour skin forming, the wing line, and fuselage assembly. Safety around an operating B-47 was paramount and special instruction was provided. The pilot classes on performance included fuel management, mission planning, takeoff procedure, and landing procedure. The maintenance classes provided coverage of powerplant, electrical systems, hydraulic systems, and electronics. Between April 1950 and August 1951, Boeing conducted 25 Model B-47A and B-47B Factory Familiarization Training Classes under Contract W33-038-ac-22413. The Boeing instructors kept current on the latest engineering changes. They were able to provide the latest data to the students. The instructors also ensured that the maintenance and operations manuals contained the most current information.

### Strategic Air Command

The Strategic Air Command began training B-47 crews at the 306th Bombardment Wing at MacDill AFB under the command of Colonel Michael N. M. McCoy. An initial cadre of SAC B-29 and B-50 crews transitioned into the Stratojet along with former TAC fighter pilots with jet time. The SAC pilots loved their new aircraft's performance and spectacular view from the canopy. However, the fighter pilots believed they were downgraded to an aircraft that was less agile than their former mounts.

After the 306th Bombardment Wing completed its transition and service evaluation of the B-47, SAC established a training wing at McConnell AFB across the field from the Boeing plant. This new unit, the 3520th Combat Crew Training Wing (CCTW), was established on 5 July 1951 and continued operation until 1 March 1962.

A pair of TB-47B-15-BWs (50-030 and 50-050) undergoing Project FIELD GOAL modifications at Douglas-Tulsa. The aircraft were in nose docks. Aircraft 50-030 had a shelter erected above the vertical tail so that technicians on the ground would be out of the inclement weather. The cylindrical chute on the shelter permitted workmen to dump trash into a bin that would have been placed on the ground below. Note the open RATO bays on the aircraft. (Douglas-Tulsa T-16970)

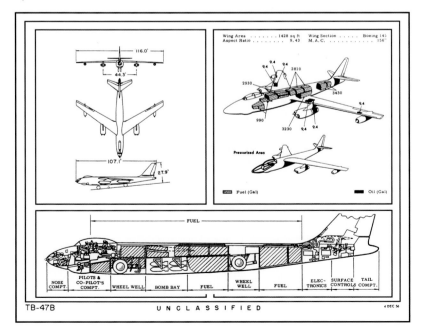

TB-47B inboard profile.

This TB-47B-20-BW (50-057) was assigned to the 3520th FTW at Wichita AFB. The nacelle close-off doors were closed to protect the engine inlets. In the background was an air policeman armed with an M-1 Garrand rifle posted for security. (William Balogh via MSgt. David W. Menard)

This TB-47B-15-BW (50-042) was assigned to the 3520th FTW at Wichita AFB and carried the ATC insignia on the nose. Note the lettering McCONNELL around the ATC insignia. The broad Insignia Yellow band identified the squadron. While the RATO bottle compartment had been faired over, the red warning outline remained. A tow bar was stowed between the forward gear. (William Balogh via MSgt. David W. Menard)

### Air Training Command

The Air Training Command was established on 1 July 1946, and was responsible for developing training courses for both officer and enlisted personnel to meet the ever-changing technological advances of the modern Air Force.

Initial plans called for a four-phase, 15-week course of instruction for the B-47. The first three weeks encompassed jet transition training in the Lockheed T-33, three weeks with the B-47 Mobile Training Detachment, three weeks in B-47 transition, and six weeks that included 89 flying hours in combat crew training. A subsequent plan called for six weeks of T-33 transition training that included 36 hours of flying; three weeks of B-47 transition that included 25 flying hours, 64 simulator missions, and 513 academic hours; and six weeks of combat crew training in 132 hours.

On 31 January 1951 Headquarters USAF directed SAC to transfer B-47 combat crew training to the Air Training Command so that SAC could concentrate on developing its combat potential. At the same time, Headquarters USAF allocated $100 million for new construction at Pinecastle AFB and Wichita AFB, allotted 84 B-47Bs equipped with the K-systems, and transferred 30 experienced crews to serve as the initial instructor pilot cadre. Twelve simulators were provided during the first quarter of FY52. The schedule called for 33 B-47s to be delivered to the ATC from SAC by the end of November 1951; however, only four aircraft were actually transferred.

The ATC established the 3520th Combat Crew Training Wing at Wichita AFB on 5 June 1951, although it was redesignated as the 3520th Flying Training Wing (Medium) on 11 June 1952. The first instructor pilot class began with eight students on this date. The first three B-47s arrived at the base in July and another two classes were started in August, but mechanical problems with the aircraft brought training to a halt. The aircraft problems were resolved but training continued to fall behind schedule because the Air Training Command had only seven B-47s and none were equipped with the K-system. Transition training was transferred to SAC at MacDill until mid-February 1952, when that phase of training resumed at Wichita and later began at Pinecastle.

Pinecastle AFB was established on 10 September 1951, and the Air Training Command activated the 3540th Combat Crew Training Wing at the base on 10 January 1952. The wing was redesignated the 3540th Flying Training Wing (Fighter) on 27 June 1952, and again as the 3540th Flying Training Wing (Medium) on 8

October 1952. The first B-47 combat crew training class commenced at Pinecastle on 22 December 1952.

There was an increase in the B-47 training program between July and December 1953, when 548 crewmembers were trained at Wichita and another 567 went through the school at Pinecastle. The latter also produced 131 instructor pilots.

On 1 January 1954 Headquarters USAF directed that the Air Training Command relinquish the B-47 combat crew-training role and the mission reverted to SAC. Pinecastle was transferred from the Air Training Command to SAC on the same date, and the 3540th FTW(M) was redesignated the 4240th CCTW.

Wichita AFB was renamed McConnell AFB on 12 April 1954, in honor of Second Lieutenant Thomas L. McConnell and his brother Captain Fred McConnell, Jr. The brothers had been assigned to the 307th Bombardment Group serving in the Pacific Theater during World War II.

In December 1954 Headquarters USAF indicated that it wanted the Air Training Command to resume B-47 combat crew training at McConnell. During February 1955 the Air Training Command was directed to resume this training in May 1956, but on

*Caught during its landing rollout, this TB-47B-30-BW (51-2120) was assigned to 3520th FTW and carried the ATC insignia on the nose. The large 20 under the tail number assisted maintenance personnel in locating their aircraft on the ramp. The broad Insignia Blue band on the tail denoted the squadron. (Air Training and Education Command Historian)*

Jet engine mechanics from the 340th BMW, Whiteman AFB, Missouri, received instruction on the finer points of the J47 ignition system. The instructor was using a cutaway model of the engine as a training aid. (SAC Combat Crew Magazine)

1 July 1958 the responsibility for B-47 combat crew training was again returned to SAC. The 3520th wing at McConnell was redesignated the 4347th CCTW.

A new transition-training program went into effect on 30 June 1954, and included a 13-week course with an increase in aircraft commander flying hours from 40 to 50 hours. At the same time, copilot time decreased from 40 to 36 hours, and for the first time the course offered a 9-week training program for observers.

Maintenance personnel received their initial training through the Air Training Command at Chanute AFB, Illinois, or at Sheppard AFB. Chanute mainly taught sheet metal and systems classes, while Sheppard offered mostly engine courses. Many went to specialized technical schools at various bases, at Boeing, and at other contractors. Keesler AFB provided classes in avionics.

### Mobile Training Detachments (MTD)

To provide training at the various SAC bases, Mobile Training Detachments (MTD) were employed. A cadre of highly skilled Air Force instructors accompanied the shipment of freestanding training devices that were generally constructed by Boeing. These detachments were replete with instructors, handbooks, wall charts, movies, and freestanding training mock-ups. Specialized training devices were constructed for powerplant, hydraulics, flight controls, pneumatics, pressurization, electrical, and other systems.

The ETB-47B-15-BW (50-040) was photographed at the 1955 Dayton Air Show. The leading "E" in the designation denoted "special tests" and this aircraft became the sole KB-47G tanker. (Ewie Feist via Victor D. Seeley)

## Multi-Talented Aircrews

Initially SAC operated World War II-vintage bombers with 10- to 11-man crews. With the advent of the B-47 the crews were reduced to three, and all of that skill and expertise had to be concentrated in these individuals. Lieutenant General Ray B. Sitton related how a transport pilot became *SACimcized*:

He returned from Korea in July 1955, and was assigned to B-47s. Sitton had no previous involvement with heavy bombers or SAC; he had been on the operations staff for the 314th Air Division that flew C-46s, C-47s, C-54s, C-119s, and C-124s. His first assignment was to James B. Connelly AFB, just outside Waco, Texas, for an intensive six-month Aircraft Observer Bombardier (AOB) course. The program included advanced navigation (mostly celestial), radar operation for both navigation and bombing, and limited exposure to visual bombing. Upon completion of the course he was awarded a navigator rating to go with his pilot's wings. Sitton was then assigned to McConnell AFB where he had an intensive ground school on all aircraft systems and 43 hours of flying time.

The next stop was Stead AFB, Nevada, where he received five days of survival training. There the country boys fared much better than the city slickers. In August 1956 Sitton was reassigned to the 524th Bomb Squadron, 379th Bombardment Wing, at Homestead AFB, Florida. After two years with the wing he learned several SAC slogans.

- If at first you don't succeed, you're fired.
- To err is human; to forgive is not SAC policy.
- I have neither the time nor the inclination to differentiate between the unfortunate and the incompetent.
- Once accepted, you can never get out of SAC, not even by dying. They will bury you on base, in a kneeling position, facing Omaha.

## Gunnery Training

In order to provide an inexpensive target for bomber crews, Radioplane in Van Nuys, California, designed and built the 350-pound OQ-19D Aerial Gunnery Drone Aircraft. The unmanned aircraft were built from aluminum, had an 8-foot wingspan, were powered by an air-cooled McCullough O-100-1 2-cycle, 4-cylinder engine, and could fly at speeds up to 200 mph at sea level. This device was employed for gunnery practice by B-29, B-47, B-52, and B-58 aircrews. An enlisted technician flew the OQ-19 much like a standard radio controlled model airplane.

These drones were operated on gunnery ranges at a number of SAC bases. A row of tail turrets was installed outside of a building housing a simulated aircraft gunnery station. Shooting down the drones was an extremely difficult task. For those lucky enough to succeed, a Certified Dead Eye certificate was developed. Later, radar reflectors were added to the drones and too many aces resulted, causing the government great expense. The fix was to incorporate radar offset into the system.

*These mechanics were being trained in the B-47B electrical power system. Boeing developed these training devices for use at ATC schools and with Mobile Training Detachments. (Boeing P13495)*

*Here, a mechanic at Whiteman AFB employed a hand-actuated hydraulic jack to raise the wheels off of the ramp. Note the erosion of the white anti-radiation belly paint. (SAC Combat Crew Magazine)*

This view reveals the open slipway door, refueling receptacle, and the connected air refueling boom. The Stratojet was a B-47B as denoted by its nose windows and lack of external fuel tanks. The circular cabin depressurization door was located below the cockpit. Note the early UNITED STATES AIR FORCE markings on the forward fuselage. (USAF)

# Chapter 8

# *OPERATIONS*

Since 1947, SAC had operated under the Hobson Plan that placed the operational combat group under the control of the base commander who may not have been a rated officer. In January 1951 General Curtis LeMay reorganized SAC under the Wing-Base Plan that was governed by SAC Regulation 20-15. In this scheme, the base commander owned the real estate and buildings, but not the aircraft; those belonged to the wing commander. A combat wing consisted of a combat group with two to five tactical squadrons and three maintenance squadrons. An air base group consisted of seven housekeeping squadrons. At stations with two combat wings, an air division was also created.

During 1951 a bombardment group became a bombardment wing and a reconnaissance group became a reconnaissance wing. The combat group-level as such disappeared.

**Wing Headquarters** – The wing headquarters consisted of staffs directly related to combat operations of the unit. A wing commander and deputy wing commander headed the organization.

**Combat Group** – Led by a group commander, the combat group supervised the operations of three or four bomb squadrons and oftentimes an air refueling squadron. The combat group had staffs for operations, maintenance, intelligence, and administration.

**Tactical Maintenance Squadrons** – These three squadrons divided the maintenance workload according to level of work:

Field Maintenance Squadron was responsible for all maintenance activities performed on the flight line. These activities consisted of refueling and servicing, pre-flight and post-flight inspections, engine runs, and any minor maintenance that would not jeopardize the mission readiness of the aircraft. The aircraft crew chiefs belonged to this squadron.

Periodic Maintenance Squadron performed regularly scheduled maintenance inspections and any unscheduled maintenance that would take an aircraft out of service for an extended period.

Armament & Electronics Maintenance Squadron – Because the avionics associated with the bomb/nav and fire control systems were so complex, a separate unit with sophisticated shop capabilities was established within each wing. While members of the field maintenance squadron identified a problem with the armament and elec-

tronics on the B-47s that could not be resolved by minor adjustments, the defective components were removed and sent to the Armament & Electronics Maintenance Squadron for corrective action. Newly bench-certified components were installed on the aircraft to maintain its combat readiness.

Typical B-47 wing manning was based on 1.5 crews per aircraft (three crews per two aircraft) and 15 bombers per squadron – for a total of 45 bombers per wing. In 1958, a fourth squadron was added to each wing to meet SAC's alert requirements; this additional

*The status boards were cleaned up for the photographer so as not to reveal any sensitive information. This was the SAC command post at Offutt AFB, Nebraska, that statused aircraft movements across the CONUS, Pacific, and Atlantic. REFLEX bomber and tanker status was also shown. These lighted screens replaced the former hand-marked maps. The projected data included weather conditions, force deployment, aircraft and missile status, and a host of other operational data. Computers in the building updated the data within 30 seconds. (SAC Combat Crew Magazine)*

*This B-47E-105-BW (52-609) was the 1,000th Stratojet produced by Boeing. It is shown here with its appropriate markings; however, the SAC insignia on the right side of the nose was for public relations purposes only. The 40th BMW insignia would soon replace it. The aircraft was delivered on 17 December 1954 and flown to Smoky Hill AFB, Kansas, by Captain Paul R. Houser. An Insignia Red stripe was applied to the fin denoting the 44th BS. (Boeing P14926)*

squadron may have been solely a training unit, or it may have actually added another 15 aircraft.

Maintenance manning requirements for a typical bomb wing were a function of the maintenance man-hours per flight hour required to maintain an aircraft. This figure, multiplied by the wing's average monthly flying hour commitment and divided by 84 (productive direct man-hours per man per month) provided a basic manning figure, to which 10 percent was added for supervisory personnel. Added to this basic manning figure was the manpower not reflected directly by aircraft maintenance man-hour-per-flight-hour figures or flying hours. These included the precision measuring equipment laboratory, aerospace ground equipment maintenance, and survival equipment. While manning authorizations were based on about 140 hours per man per month, over a 32-hour workweek, it was not uncommon for workweeks in SAC to exceed 70 hours.

Until 1958, aircraft maintenance was an integral part of each individual bomb squadron – each taking great pride in displaying a specific color stripe on their aircraft. However, during October 1958, SAC reorganized its wings under the Deputy Commander concept

*The 1,000th Stratojet was named CITY OF SALINA shortly after its arrival at Smoky Hill AFB. The inappropriate SAC insignia on the right side of the nose would be replaced with a 40th BMW insignia. At the ceremony were (l-r): Bob Robbins, then Senior B-47 Project Engineer; Brigadier General J. R. Sutherland, 802nd AD Commander; Major General Walter C. Sweeney, Fifteenth Air Force Commander; and Colonel Berton H. Burns, 40th BMW Commander. Bob Robbins had presented Sutherland a duplicate of the commemorative plaque installed inside the aircraft. (Boeing BW92375)*

where the aircraft were reassigned from individual bomb squadrons to the wing's new Deputy Commander of Maintenance. Bombers were now *loaned* to the tactical squadrons and all squadron colors were removed from the aircraft.

Under the Deputy Commander Concept, the typical SAC wing had a combat support group commander and two deputy wing commanders – Deputy Commander for Operations (DCO) and Deputy Commander for Maintenance (DCM). The combat support group had a headquarters and five squadrons. Under the DCO were seven divisions and four flying squadrons, with the fourth squadron generally serving as a training unit. The DCM had six divisions and five squadrons. As with the wing commander, each of these deputy commanders held the grade of colonel. Under this new scheme, a typical SAC bombardment wing consisted of:

**Combat Support Group (CSG)** was permanently assigned to manage SAC installations and was subordinate to the combat wing. Generally this unit remained at the home station, but had the capability of forward deploying personnel and equipment to support wing operations.

**Operations Group** was responsible for managing the operational activities of the unit. The commanders of the bombardment and air refueling squadrons reported to the DCO for administration and operation of their respective units.

**Aircraft Maintenance Group** was responsible for all aircraft maintenance activities within the wing and reported to the DCM. As required, personnel and equipment from this organization could forward deploy in support of operational squadrons.

## KOREAN WAR

While SAC's newer bombers – B-36, B-47, and B-50 – were operational during the Korean War, they were not employed for two reasons. First, the major targets were capable of being destroyed with the existing B-29 Superfortresses. Secondly, and most importantly, was the chance of losing one of the newer bombers over enemy territory. If recovered, the aircraft would reveal much of America's advanced technology and, if the crews were captured, the Soviets could potentially extract vital data on operations and tactics. Navigator/bombardiers, especially, were highly desired by the Soviets for interrogation.

## BUILDING THE FORCE

SAC had waited more than five years to obtain combat-ready Stratojets for its strategic bombardment force. While Headquarters USAF wrestled with the performance of the B-47 during 1951 as part of its expansion to 143 wings, SAC developed plans for the deployment of 25 B-47-equipped wings. The delays delivering operational aircraft were costly; SAC sent crews through transition training only to have their skill wane away due to a lack of aircraft. The best that could be done was to place the navigators in B-50 wings for the interim. Only pilots would be assigned to the emerging B-47 wings. A

| B-47 BASE AND WING ACTIVATION | | |
|---|---|---|
| Date | Wing/Squadron | Base |
| 25 Oct 51 | 306th BMW | MacDill AFB, Fla. |
| 15 Apr 52 | 305th BMW | MacDill AFB, Fla. |
| 1 Dec 52 | 320th BMW | March AFB, Calif. |
| 20 Jan 53 | 303rd BMW | Davis-Monthan AFB, Ariz. |
| Jan 53 | 22nd BMW | March AFB, Calif. |
| 16 Jun 53 | 68th BMW | Lake Charles AFB, La. |
| 6 Feb 54 | 40th BMW | Smoky Hill AFB, Kans. |
| 23 Mar 53 | 321st BMW | Pinecastle AFB, Fla. |
| Jun 53 | 44th BMW | Lake Charles AFB, La. |
| Jul 53 | 301st BMW | Barksdale AFB, La. |
| Oct 53 | 68th BMW | Lake Charles AFB, La. |
| 18 Nov 53 | 96th BMW | Altus AFB, Okla. |
| Jan 54 | 43rd BMW | Davis-Monthan AFB, Ariz. |
| Jan 54 | 308th BMW | Hunter AFB, Ga. |
| Feb 54 | 2nd BMW | Hunter AFB, Ga. |
| Mar 54 | 93rd BMW | Castle AFB, Calif. |
| Apr 54 | 340th BMW | Sedalia AFB, Mo. |
| Aug 54 | 310th BMW | Smoky Hill AFB, Kans. |
| Sep 54 | 9th BMW | Mountain Home AFB, Idaho. |
| Oct 54 | 19th BMW | Pinecastle AFB, Fla. |
| Dec 54 | 98th BMW | Lincoln AFB, Neb. |
| 11 Jan 54 | 380th BMW | Plattsburgh AFB, N.Y. |
| Aug 55 | Det. 1, 380th BMW | Pinecastle AFB, Fla. |
| 27 Jan 56 | 329th BS | Pinecastle AFB, Fla. |
| Mar 55 | 307th BMW | Lincoln AFB, Neb. |
| Jun 55 | 509th BMW | Roswell AFB, N. Mex. |
| Jul 55 | 97th BMW | Biggs AFB, Tex. |

If all of the wings were fully operational, this would represent a force of 1,125 aircraft.

pilot without observer training would be relegated to the back seat. While SAC had excesses of flight crews, maintenance personnel were in extremely short supply.

By way of example, Major Clyde R. Denniston, Jr., had been a rated pilot in both B-29s and B-50s. Between June 1950 and September 1951 he underwent navigator training at Ellington AFB, Texas, and Mather AFB, California, in preparation for his assignment to the 367th Bomb Squadron, 306th Bombardment Wing at MacDill AFB. There he was assigned as a dual-rated aircraft commander and navigator.

Base readiness was another major problem facing SAC. In some instances an entire wing could move into a base. Other units were only able to establish a headquarters and one or two squadrons at their new home. In this case another squadron would be remotely stationed until the facilities were completed.

## BOMBER OPERATIONS

SAC was unique in its early days by having aviation field depot squadrons (shortened to just aviation depot squadrons) assigned to the various bombardment wings. Their purpose was the assembly, maintenance, and loading of the nuclear weapons. In addition, these personnel were tasked with ensuring the weapons training level of key flight crew personnel within the combat units.

There were 23 bases with aviation depot squadrons that supported SAC's B-47 operations between 1950 and 1966. Subsequently this function was integrated into the armament and electronics squadrons for the B-52s, B-58s, and FB-111s.

### B-47 Profile Missions

The combat radius for the non-refuelable B-47B was 1,704 nautical miles, while the unrefueled radius for the B-47E-VI with a pair of 1,700-gallon external fuel tanks was 2,050 nautical miles. Aerial refueling greatly extended the range of the B-47Es and the B-47Bs that were modified under Project TURNAROUND. With the refueling capability, crew endurance and engine oil capacity became the limiting factors to the B-47's range.

A typical profile mission for the non-in-flight-refuelable B-47B was:

- Take off and climb on course to optimum cruise altitude for the given aircraft weight, at normal power.
- Climb to 10,000 feet and arm the nuclear weapon.
- Cruise at long-range speeds, increasing altitude with decreasing fuel weight.
- Climb to reach cruise ceiling 15 minutes from the target.
- Run in to the target at normal power, drop bombs, and conduct 2 minutes of evasive action and an 8-minute escape run from the target at normal power.
- Cruise back to base at long-range cruise speeds, increasing altitude with decreasing fuel weight.
- Descend to 10,000 feet and disarm the nuclear weapon.

Allowances were included in 5-minute normal-power fuel consumption for starting engines and takeoff, 2-minute normal-power fuel consumption at combat altitude for evasive action, and 30 minutes of maximum endurance (on four engines) fuel consumption at sea level plus 5 percent of initial fuel load for landing reserve.

A typical profile mission for the in-flight-refuelable B-47E-IV was the same as the B-47B, except:

- Cruise at long-range speeds, increasing altitudes, dropping external fuel tanks when empty.
- Dropped bomb load and chaff, and conduct 2 minutes of evasive action, and an 8-minute escape run from the target at normal power.

*Note the partially extended flaps on the B-47 that were required for slow-flying the bomber behind the lumbering KC-97G with external tanks. The wings of the B-47 were bending due to the increased weight resulting from taking on fuel. Phase III ECM gear was installed on the bomber as indicated by the wingtip extensions and the blisters on the aft fuselage. Note that the external tanks on the bomber were missing. (USAF)*

### B-47/KC-97 Refueling Operations

Jet aircraft operate more efficiently at higher altitudes, whereas reciprocating engine-powered aircraft operate better at lower altitudes. Even with turbosupercharging, a KC-97 tanker could not match a B-47's altitude performance. As a consequence, jet bombers – B-47 or B-52 – had to descend from their optimum operating altitudes around 30,000 feet to the KC-97 refueling altitude of 17,000 to 19,000 feet. The tanker was prepositioned ahead of the bomber and a radio beacon onboard the tanker served as a homing device. Refueling sometimes took place in a shallow formation dive (known as tobogganing) with the two aircraft connected via the refueling boom. As the bomber became heavier with more fuel, it had to fly faster to preclude stalling so the tanker would accelerate as it descended to keep from being undershot by the bomber. The refueling usually terminated at an altitude of about 12,000 feet with both aircraft climbing back to their optimum cruise altitudes. The performance mismatch between the piston-powered KC-97 and the jet bombers resulted in many nervous refuelings, including some with mid-air contacts that were not intended.

For example, on 9 August 1955 a KC-97G (53-128) from the 9th Air Refueling Squadron (AREFS), 9th Bombardment Wing at Mountain Home AFB, was refueling a B-47E (52-586) from the 1st Bomb Squadron, 9th Bombardment Wing. The tanker took off at 08:27 hours MST, followed by the B-47 three minutes later. At 10:14 hours the aircraft were engaged in refueling approximately 46 nautical miles north of Winnemucca, Nevada, at 15,200 feet with unlimited visibility.

92592

"SAC Snack"

© Hank Caruso 1993

Titled SAC Snack, this Hank Caruso caricature depicts the mood of a KC-97/B-47 refueling. He has captured the feeling of the lumbering gas bag and the wary Stratojet in this 1993 illustration. (Courtesy – Hank Caruso)

*This B-47B was in the far forward range of the refueling envelope. The receiver held position, while the boom operator flew the boom into the receptacle. (Gordon S. Williams)*

The B-47 had completed the last of five scheduled hook-ups and dropped approximately 200 feet below and to the right of the tanker. As the receiver pilot looked down to check the Master Refuel Switch position, the bomber began to climb under the tanker. The vertical stabilizer of the B-47 struck the right side of the KC-97's fuselage directly behind the right flap, and then proceeded to cross under the fuselage of the tanker striking the inboard side of the No. 2 engine nacelle and the No. 1 engine propeller. Both aircraft remained under control and proceeded back to Mountain Home. The aircraft landed without incident and there were no injuries.

The damage to the B-47E was mainly that 10 feet of the rudder and vertical stabilizer had been sheared off, although several small holes were noted in the upper surface of the left horizontal stabilizer and elevator. The KC-97G did not fair nearly as well. The pilot director assembly and inboard end of the right wing flap were damaged, the skin on the lower fuselage lobe between Body Stations 576 and 742 was ruptured and buckled, and 6 to 18 inches of all four propeller blades on the No. 1 engine were bent or missing. In addition, there was minor damage to the inboard side of the No. 2 nacelle and wheel

*Refueling was generally initiated at altitudes between 17,000 and 19,000 feet; hence the contrails from the KC-97. (Boeing BW60145)*

*This KC-97 boom operator from the 340th ARS was refueling a B-47B. While the bomber pilot held his aircraft in position, the boom operator literally flew the boom to direct its nozzle into the bomber's refueling receptacle. This picture dates from January 1964. (SAC Combat Crew Magazine)*

well doors, small dents on the inboard side of the left drop tank, and small tears in the fabric covering the left aileron. There was no visible damage to any of the engine mounts.

While an error in pilot procedures for formation flying was found on the part of the B-47 pilot, there was inadequate guidance in the aircraft flight manual for disconnect procedures. As a result, SAC directed that the B-47 flight manual be revised to specifically state, "Drop back and down 500 feet and make a 45-degree left or right turn to get well clear of tanker before proceeding on course."

### B-47/KC-135 Refueling Operations

The introduction of the all-jet Boeing KC-135A Stratotanker made aerial refueling much easier, simpler, and safer. Because both aircraft were jets, their performance was much closer. However, when the B-47 was in the downwash of the tanker, the bomber was power-limited.

Refueling altitudes were dictated by the available performance of the bomber. The recommended formation speeds were Mach 0.72 above 28,600 feet and 280 knots indicated airspeed below 28,600 feet. (A constant Mach number may be flown at altitude at a given airspeed. As the altitude increases, the air becomes less dense, and the same Mach number will read a lower airspeed as the altitude increases. Mach is used for speed at higher altitudes to permit pilots of all aircraft to operate to an equivalent baseline.) This speed schedule was applicable to all receiver weights, and for both level flight and descending refueling.

As the tanker offloaded fuel it became lighter and the pilots had to reduce power to maintain the recommended speed schedule. During refueling, the KC-135 was normally operated at 96 percent power. Mission and safety requirements permitted a B-47 to refuel with one engine out. For such conditions the B-47's thrust was set at 98 percent on the remaining engines and the altitude was reduced by 4,000 feet from that which was published in the flight manual. With ample margin above stall speed the B-47s did not require flaps as they did with the KC-97.

A visual rendezvous would be accomplished, and then the tanker would set the course and contact speed. The receiver would formate on the tanker then move up into the refueling envelope. With both aircraft stable, the boom operator would fly the boom into the receiver's receptacle. When contact was established, the pilots of the tanker controlled the refueling rate.

If required, the rate of descent would be established at 300-feet-per-minute, thereby allowing the B-47 to receive fuel with a minimum deviation from cruise altitude. Once again, the tanker initiated the descent on a predetermined heading and accelerated to the desired speed schedule. The receiver would close slowly on the tanker because it would have been impossible to decelerate by throttle changes. In an emergency, the receiver could lower one or both of its main landing gear to provide rapid deceleration.

Using basic formation rules the receiver pilots used gentle control changes to remain in the contact position. With this technique, gentle turns could be accomplished without disconnecting from the tanker.

Until September 1957 Dyess AFB was home to the 341st BMW. The flight line was filled with the wing's B-47s and KC-97s. In the center background were two C-124s from SAC's 4th Strategic Support Squadron, also based there. (SAC Combat Crew Magazine)

The 341st BMW was joined at Dyess AFB by the 96th BMW in September 1957. Here two B-47s were nosed into the hangar for maintenance – note the technicians working on the tail turret of the nearest aircraft. (SAC Combat Crew Magazine)

The crew of this 341st BMW B-47E-75-LM (53-1956) popped the canopy to get some fresh air after returning from a mission. Note the open approach and brake chute doors under the tail. The aircraft was equipped with the Phase III ECM upgrades. Always ready were members of the bases' fire and crash rescue organization. (SAC Combat Crew Magazine)

## SAC Wing Deployments

As early as 1947, SAC began deploying B-29 units to England and Europe to assess potential bases. With the advent of trained B-47 units, such wing rotations were a normal part of the command's operations. Integral SAC airlift (provided by C-124s from strategic support squadrons and KC-97s from tanker squadrons), Military Air Transport Service aircraft, and contract civilian carriers also supported the B-47 wings. SAC units moved everything including the kitchen sink on these 90-day deployments.

In addition to using established bases in England, Spain, and the Pacific, new bases were built in North Africa, thereby shortening the distances to potential targets in the Soviet Union.

American relationships in French Morocco extend back to the 1787 Treaty of Marrakech, when the Moroccans were one of the signers of this document of peace and friendship. During World War II, Allied forces operated from bases in French Morocco against German forces. In January 1943 leaders from the Allied nations met for the Casablanca Conference to discuss plans for the war effort. During the last few days of this conference, both President Franklin Delano Roosevelt and Prime Minister Winston S. Churchill met with Sultan Sidi Mohammed Ben Youssef without the French being present. The Sultan believed that the United States and Britain would support the Moroccan desires for independence after World War II came to a conclusion.

In 1947, President Harry S. Truman presented the U.S. Congress a policy that would become known as the Truman Doctrine. In essence, this doctrine called for the support of free people resisting attempted takeover by internal minority factions or outside pressures (i.e., Soviet-supported insurrection). The American strategy of containing Soviet expansionism came through this doctrine, and became the springboard for American bases in French Morocco. Negotiations

*This B-47B-25-BW (51-2058) was assigned to the 547th BS, 384th BMW, at Little Rock AFB, Arkansas. The squadron markings consisted of a black & white checkerboard tail stripe. Note the large 058 on the forward gear door. The aircraft was being serviced on the ramp at Lockbourne AFB, Ohio. This photo was used in advertising the Caterpillar D364 diesel engine that powered the Marathon Electric Manufacturing Company's ground power cart. (USAF)*

for these bases were made between the United States and France without, in retrospect, proper Moroccan representation.

SAC first came to visit these bases in Morocco in 1951. Initially there were problems in the command structure at the bases in French Morocco. The infrastructure and war assets placed at these bases came

from the Air Materiel Command and they wanted control of the bases. Because SAC operated the alert aircraft from these bases, they wanted control through their 5th Air Division, headquartered at Rabat, the capitol of French Morocco. In addition to the three bomber and tanker bases at Ben Guerir, Nouasseur, and Sidi Slimane, SAC opened up Nouasseur to two of its fighter wings to provide air defense for their assets. Nouasseur was also the logistics center for the entire Southern Air Materiel Area that extended from Morocco to Greece, Italy, Turkey, Iran, and Pakistan. Further complicating the issue was the United States Air Forces Europe (USAFE) that believed these bases were an extension of their operations.

On 1 July 1957 the Sixteenth Air Force, headquartered at Torrejon AB, Spain, was transferred to SAC and this unit assumed command of the 5th Air Division at Rabat. Because the Sixteenth Air Force was not yet capable of taking control of the North African operations, the Second Air Force retained responsibility of these functions until 15 January 1958. At that time the 5th Air Division was inactivated and the Sixteenth Air Force assumed full control of SAC operations in Morocco.

Operation LEAPFROG was a new post-strike operational concept developed by SAC and placed into operation in August 1954. Missions would launch from the United States, fly non-stop on a simulated bombing mission to targets in the Mediterranean, refuel and rearm at Sidi Slimane, and either fly a second strike mission or return to their home base.

As a proof-of-concept, a pair of B-47s from the 2nd Bombardment Wing, under the command of Colonel Austin J. Russell, and the 308th

*Abilene AFB was renamed Dyess AFB on 1 December 1956. An open house celebrating the event was held on 8 December. With three of the wing's B-47s parked in the background, crowds gathered for the celebration, replete with a pass in review by base personnel. Honored guests at the Dyess open house included Judge Richard T. Dyess and his grandson, William Edwin Denman. (SAC Combat Crew Magazine)*

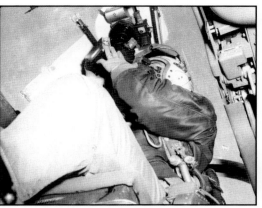

The crew entry hatch was difficult to manage when boarding with a backpack parachute, flight bag, and brain bucket. (SAC Combat Crew Magazine)

Either the copilot or navigator would use the sextant to shoot the sun or stars for celestial navigation. (SAC Combat Crew Magazine)

This Strato-Sack was erected in the crawlway for long endurance flights. One would hope that no turbulence was encountered when occupied. (USAF 159538AC)

Bombardment Wing, led by Colonel John F. Batjier, made a round-trip, non-stop flight from Hunter AFB. The 2nd AREFS was already at Ben Guerir provided refueling support. The first aircraft made the trip in 24 hours 4 minutes, while the other took 25 hours 23 minutes, and each made four refuelings with the KC-97s. The 2nd AREFS had arrived at Ben Guerir on 7 August 1954, marking the first 45-day deployment of the 2nd Bombardment Wing to Morocco.

The first mass deployment as part of Operation LEAPFROG began when the 38th Air Division ordered the 2nd and 308th Bombardment Wings to launch 90 B-47s in two waves – 60 aircraft on the first day and the remaining 30 the following day. One of the squadrons that participated was the 49th Bomb Squadron, which was successful in launching 14 of its scheduled 15 aircraft the first day; one B-47 was delayed because of a last minute fuel leak. The 14 aircraft in the wave made successful bomb runs on a strange target in North Africa where the crews scored a 4,030-foot circular error actual (CEA).

These were the type of barracks used by SAC crews deployed to Ben Guerir, French Morocco. (Via Bruce M. Bailey)

On 16 August 1954 the 49th Bomb Squadron began operations on the Marrakech Bomb Plot (a bombing range in Morocco), scoring a 1,452-foot CEA. This was a record within the 2nd Bombardment Wing, and the 49th Bomb Squadron received a personal commendation from Colonel Russell. The maintenance personnel of the 49th Bomb Squadron also distinguished themselves during August when the unit flew 600:30 hours without an abort. Major George H. McKee was commander of the 49th Bomb Squadron during this period.

Perhaps the most unusual flight from French Morocco occurred on 17 November 1954 when Colonel David A. Burchinal, Commander of the 43rd Bombardment Wing, took off from Sidi Slimane on a routine flight to RAF Fairford where his B-47 wing was deployed on a 90-day rotation. Foul weather prevented his landing at RAF Fairford. Undeterred, he returned to Sidi Slimane only to be weathered out again. The weather finally cleared at RAF Fairford on 19 November, and Colonel Burchinal was able to land there, but not until after making the nine aerial refuelings required to stay aloft for 47 hours 35 minutes and logging 21,163 air miles. The KC-97s flew much slower and were able to takeoff and land in the foul weather that prohibited the much faster B-47 from landing.

## Three Capitals Air Race

As part of the Paris Air Show held at Le Bourget Airport in 1957, General Electric sponsored what was known as the Three Capitals Air Race. It was flown on 28 May 1957 by three B-47s from the 380th Bombardment Wing. The aircraft departed RAF Brize Norton, where they had been deployed, and flew over Le Bourget to begin the race. Then they flew over Madrid, Rome, and back to Paris covering a route of 2,346 statute miles. A B-47E from the 529th Bomb Squadron won the race by completing the route in 4 hours 12 minutes and 7 seconds, at an average speed of 558 mph. The crew of the Stratojet was Captain Robert E. Sheridan, aircraft commander; First Lieutenant J. L. Mombrea, copilot; and Captain Frank R. Beadle, navigator.

## SAC Exercises

When not standing alert or undergoing ground training, SAC crews participated in highly orchestrated exercises. Many of the exercises were conceived, developed, and planned by the staff at SAC Headquarters at Offutt AFB. For others, individual SAC wings were tasked with developing their own training missions known as Unit Simulated Combat Mission (USCM). Such missions further honed the combat crews' abilities. Two are described here as examples.

## Exercise POOR SHOT

The 38th Air Division ordered both the 2nd and 308th Bombardment Wings to perform Exercise POOR SHOT, an overseas USCM that was flown between 31 March and 16 April 1955. While deployed, the two wings were under the operational control of the 5th Air Division in Morocco. A total of 70 bombers from Hunter AFB were scheduled to participate, but one bomber aborted on the runway and a second aborted in the air and returned to base. Sixty-eight B-47s entered the refueling area over Lajes; with one aircraft aborting after it

| FORWARD OPERATING BASES DURING MOROCCO CIVIL UNREST | | |
|---|---|---|
| **Wing** | **Forward Operating Location** | **Dates** |
| 2nd BMW | Sidi Slimane AB | Aug-Sept 54 |
| | French Morocco | Mar-Apr 55 |
| 9th BMW | RAF Fairford, England | May-July 55 |
| | Kadena AB, Okinawa | 3-22 Oct 55 |
| 40th BMW | French Morocco | 1955 |
| | RAF Lakenheath, England | 9 June-9 Sept 55 |
| 68th BMW | RAF Fairford, England | 14 June-17 Aug 54 |
| 98th BMW | RAF Lakenheath, England | 11 Nov 55-29 Jan 56 |
| 301st BMW | French Morocco | Feb-Apr 54 |
| 303rd BMW | RAF Greenham Common | 4 Mar-28 Apr 54 |
| | RAF Fairford, England | 28 Apr-5 June 54 |
| 306th BMW | Ben Guerir AB, French Morocco | Jan-Feb 55 |
| 310th BMW | RAF Upper Heyford, England | 10 Mar-8 June 55 |
| 320th BMW | RAF Brize Norton, England | 5 June-4 Sept 54 |
| 321st BMW | RAF Lakenheath, England | 9 Dec 54-5 Mar 55 |

In support of America's policy of containment, these 10 B-47 wings were deployed to the noted forward operating locations during the civil unrest in French Morocco.

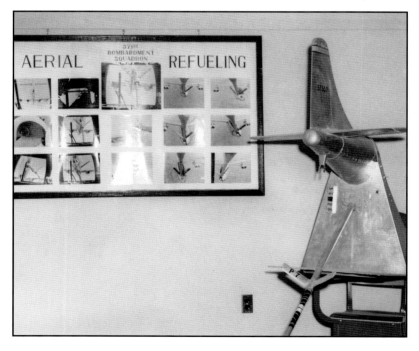

*Local training was a continual process. The 371st BS, 307th BMW, Lincoln AFB, Nebraska, employed is shown here. Note the UP, AFT, FWD, and DN light indicators that replicated the pilot directional panel on the belly of a KC-97. (SAC Combat Crew Magazine)*

lost an engine. One of the receivers was unable to take on fuel in its center tank but proceeded on to the Moroccan refueling area. Three other aircraft aborted for maintenance issues. Forty-two KC-97 tankers from the 2nd and 308th AREFSs performed the refuelings over Lajes.

The refueled bomber force of 63 B-47s continued on to their assigned targets in France and Italy. One of the bombers was unable to take on fuel in the bomb bay tank, but continued on the bombing mission and altered its withdrawal route to conform to its reduced fuel load. The post-strike recovery base was Sidi Slimane. In the Moroccan area, tankers from the 308th and 305th AREFSs provided the refueling services, with the latter based at Ben Guerir.

For the redeployment to Hunter, the bombers were launched in three main elements. Air refueling was again accomplished over Lajes. One B-47, in the first wave, was directed to deliver a duplicate package of strike photographs and logs to Headquarters Second Air Force at Barksdale AFB, but weather caused the crew to divert to MacDill AFB.

Lessons learned from this exercise included the possibility of fog developing in the Mascot, French Morocco, refueling area caused concern because the tankers would not have sufficient fuel to divert to an alternate base and off-load sufficient fuel to the bombers for a long-range mission. Consideration was given to a fog dispersal system at the bases in Morocco. The FIDO fog dispersal system was subsequently installed at the three SAC bases at Sidi Slimane, Ben Guerir, and Nouasseur. Another concern was the designation of alternate refueling areas that were within range of the tankers.

## Exercise FREE THROW

Some SAC exercises were orchestrated as a show-of-force in response to on-going events around the world. One of these would occur in French Morocco.

When the French government exiled Sultan Ben Youssef in August 1953, there was considerable unrest in French Morocco. Supporters of the Sultan conducted a campaign of terror primarily against the pro-French elements of the native population. The situation became extremely volatile in August 1954, and several French officials were assassinated. Martial law was declared and the French sent in 60,000 troops to quell the riots. The political situation was considered to be critical and was expected to become particularly tense on 28 July 1955, the second anniversary of the Sultan's exile.

As a show of force, SAC conducted Exercise FREE THROW. All personnel deploying overseas were warned of the potential dangers in cities, such as Casablanca, and aircrews were briefed on survival and what identification to carry with them. The intelligence documents normally given to the 2nd AREFS at Hunter AFB were held at the base while the unit was deployed. The 5th Air Division provided all intelligence briefs in-country.

The 2nd AREFS was deployed to Sidi Slimane with 22 KC-97s on 16 July 1955 for a 90-day deployment. Additional support personnel were provided from the 2nd Field Maintenance Squadron, 2nd Periodic Maintenance Squadron, and the 2nd Armament & Electronic Squadron. Headquarters SAC directed the 1st Strategic Support Squadron from March AFB to provide a pair of C-124 Globemaster IIs to support this deployment, although they remained at Lajes to provide spare engines as required. During this period, SAC had a number of B-47 wings deployed to forward operating locations in the event the Soviets attempted to use the civil unrest to their advantage.

When the 509th BMW, Roswell AFB, New Mexico, began transitioning from the B-50s to the B-47s, it dispatched its first crew to Wichita to accept the wing's initial aircraft on 10 June 1955. In the photo are (left to right): R. S. Sasnett, Assistant Manager of Boeing Military Sales; Colonel James P. Ferrey, AF Plant Representative; Clifford E. Roberts, Engineering & Sales Representative for Boeing in Washington, D.C.; Colonel Clifford F. Macomber, 509th BMW Commander; Captain W. M. Remmington, Bombardier-Navigator; and Lieutenant Colonel R. C. Householder, Instructor Pilot. The aircraft was named City of ROSWELL at the factory. (Boeing BW93104)

It wasn't all flying. SAC flight crews were required to attend classes and pass examinations on a myriad of subjects. Here these pilots and navigators, in their summer silver tans, were taking a test on survival. (SAC Combat Crew Magazine)

This B-47 crew from 97th BMW, Biggs AFB, Texas, were checking their parachutes prior to a TDY as denoted by their B-4 bags. This final check ensured that all of the pins for the ripcord were properly secured. (SAC Combat Crew Magazine)

It was time for a time hack prior to takeoff for this 97th BMW crew stationed at Biggs AFB, Texas. Note the photo ID badges on each person, years before terrorism was a worry. The B-4 bags were indicative of a deployment. (SAC Combat Crew Magazine)

*Taxiing B-47s generated vast quantities of black smoke that made it more difficult for following aircraft to remain on the taxiways. Note the list to the left on the aircraft to the left that had just made a right turn onto the runway. (SAC Combat Crew Magazine)*

## SAC Alert Operations

For almost 10 years SAC enjoyed the luxury of performing most of its operations from within the continental United States, albeit with temporary deployments to England, North Africa, and the Far East. However, during this period, the Soviets had gained a thermonuclear offensive capability, vastly increased the size of their bomber force, and began developing intercontinental ballistic missiles (ICBM). SAC planners took notice and determined that the Soviets might resort to one of the basic principles of war – the element of surprise. Under General LeMay's guidance, a plan was developed which would pro-

*This 68th BMW B-47E-60-LM, s/n 53-1869, was taxiing out for a REFLEX deployment while another wing aircraft was billowing smoke from its RATO during takeoff. (Via SAC Combat Crew Magazine)*

vide a quick retaliatory response to any Soviet aggression, protect SAC's strategic forces, and maintain the philosophy of deterrence as a viable strategy. If a portion of the SAC force was on alert, it could launch in a very short period and thereby reduce the possibility that it would be destroyed on the ground.

All SAC alert schedules were governed by SAC Regulation 51-9. A wing's readiness status was predicated on strict adherence to these times. A great expenditure of maintenance man-hours was required to prepare an aircraft for alert status. Field maintenance squadron personnel checked out the various aircraft systems. When satisfied that the aircraft was ready, personnel from the Armament & Electronics Maintenance Squadron performed sequential checkouts of the bomb/nav system, loaded and checked the RATO system, loaded the 20-mm ammunition for the tail guns, then loaded and checked out the special weapon. Each step had to be performed in a precise order to ensure completeness and safety. For security reasons, the special weapon had to be held in a secure location until the aircraft was ready for loading. Should a wing have sufficient deviations from the 51-9 procedures, it would be removed from the Emergency War Order (EWO) and be declared non-combat ready. Such a condition could be career limiting for those involved. If a wing was dropped from the EWO, other wings were tasked with taking up the slack.

Members of the Armament & Electronics Maintenance Squadron had to be certified in the loading procedures for the special weapon. These weapons were stored in highly secure areas across the field from the alert flight line. Squadron personnel would obtain a C-21 ground power unit and trundle it to the storage area. There they would pass through two security checkpoints, sign for the keys, unlock the double-locked igloo, and enter the storage unit. The weapon would be loaded onto a transport vehicle and attached to a 2-1/2-ton BC-164 truck. The entry process was then reversed. Under escort from a security police detail, the ground power cart and transport vehicle would be trundled to the alert line. Towing was restricted to five mph.

While the Armament & Electronics Maintenance Squadron personnel were allocated one hour to load the special weapon, 45 minutes to install the RATO rack, and 15 minutes to load the tail guns, in reality it required 12 hours to place one B-47 on alert and remove another aircraft from alert status. Generally the same personnel performed an entire aircraft change-out.

If there was an Air Defense Command (ADC) fighter-interceptor squadron co-located at the SAC base, personnel from the Armament & Electronics Maintenance Squadron would also be tasked with certifying, loading, unloading, and maintaining the nuclear-tipped GAR-2 Genie rockets for the fighters.

**Operation OPEN MIND** – Six B-47 and six KC-97 crews from the 2nd Bombardment Wing validated the alert concept during the first week of February 1955. During this continual 24-hour alert, the bomber crews were permitted to go home, but were required to remain by a telephone. This was because the bombers were not to launch for 4 hours and 50 minutes after receiving the alert. The tanker crews, however, had to remain in the alert barracks and were authorized absences only for pre-flighting the aircraft, briefing, and dining. The tankers would launch earlier to place them ahead of the bombers for making the refueling rendezvous. One aircraft of each type was cycled through the alert status on a 24-hour basis to ensure their mission capability.

Base munitions personnel, under the direction of the 2nd Armament & Electronics Maintenance Squadron's loading supervisors, loaded three of the B-47s with Mk. VI training weapons and the other three bombers with T-59 training bombs. These crews made daily checks of the training weapons. Unloading and reloading the bombers took approximately an hour and a half.

The wing received an execution message for this exercise at 19:07 hours on 7 February. The tankers taxied out within 30 minutes of the wing receiving the message and were lined-up on the runway ready for takeoff when they were notified that the exercise was terminated. The bomber crews assembled for their briefing within 30 minutes of the alert. The briefing was completed in one hour and eight minutes, and then the crews were notified that the exercise had been terminated. However, the B-47s still had to start engines, taxi out, do a 100-percent power run-up, and check out the K-system at the end of the

*These Eighth Air Force B-47Bs were taxiing out the runway for a pre-dawn takeoff at Thule AB, Greenland, during a SAC wing deployment. The censor had scrambled the tail number on the lead aircraft. (USAF 148957AC)*

*A 379th BMW crew from Homestead AFB aborted a takeoff on 1 October 1957, resulting in the distruction of this B-47B-50-BW (51-2317). Fortunately the base fire department was able to quench the flames, allowing the crew to egress. The crew blew the canopy when the aircraft came to a rest, allowing the pilots to climb out of the cockpit. The navigator popped his escape hatch and was able to egress the aircraft. (USAF)*

*The first* City of Savannah *was a B-47E-75-LM (53-1944) from the 2nd BMW at Hunter AFB. Note the skids filled with RATO bottles.* (2nd Bomb Wing History Office)

*Another* City of Savannah *was a B-47E-125-BW (53-2381) assigned to the 308th BMW at Hunter AFB. Note the Rebel battle flag flying from the navigator's window.* (Eighth Air Force History Office)

runway. Combat crews, on aircraft loaded with Mk. VI training bombs, performed IFI/IFE cycles during the taxi out and return to the flight line. (IFI is an in-flight insertion of the bomb's arming device. An in-flight extraction is the reverse of an IFI, and means disarming the bomb.) All of the bombers taxied on schedule and completed this phase of the exercise satisfactorily.

*This technical sergeant was checking out a hydraulic jack, equipped with an electric motor-driven pump, used to raise the main gear. The device was centered on a jack pad located on the bottom of a gear axle. The hydraulic pressure caused the jackscrew to rotate, thereby raising the wheels off the ramp.* (SAC Combat Crew Magazine)

The final mission report for Operation OPEN MIND concluded that the basic operational concept was feasible and that the alert periods for any single crew should not exceed seven days. Next came a series of three tests to determine the feasibility of the alert concept.

**Operation TRY OUT** – The 38th Air Division at Hunter AFB supervised the 2nd and 308th Bombardment Wings as they kept one-third of their B-47 and KC-97 force on 24-hour ground alert between November 1956 and March 1957. These tests proved that ground alert operations were feasible. The wing's efforts during this operation contributed to them being awarded the Air Force Outstanding Unit Award for the period of 1 November 1956 to 1 April 1957.

**Operation WATCH TOWER** – The 825th Air Division at Little Rock AFB oversaw the 70th Strategic Reconnaissance Wing, 384th Strategic Bombardment Wing, 70th Air Refueling Squadron, and 825th Combat Support Group between April and November 1957. This test validated the organizational structure that would be required to accommodate alert operations without jeopardizing SAC training programs. Their efforts in these tests contributed to the 384th Bombardment Wing receiving the Air Force Outstanding Unit Award for the period of 15 February to 30 December 1957.

**Operation FRESH APPROACH** – Between July and December 1957 the 9th Bombardment Wing at Mountain Home AFB refined the organization that had been evaluated during Operation WATCH TOWER. The wing was the only SAC unit to evaluate the deputy commander concept under alert conditions. Between October 1957 and January 1958, portions of the 9th BW and the 9th AREFS operated from Elmendorf AFB and Andersen AFB to work out the details of the deputy commander concept. The 9th Strategic Bombardment Wing was recognized with the Air Force Outstanding Unit Award for the period of 1 January 1957 to 31 January 1958. After these tests, the wing continued to operate under the deputy commander concept.

## On Alert

SAC-wide alert operations commenced on 1 October 1957 under the leadership of General Thomas S. Power, SAC's third commander. In order to maintain the requisite aircrew and aircraft rotations for the alert operations, SAC increased the size of the B-47 wings from three tactical squadrons to four. The fourth squadron began appearing on 1 December 1958 or 1 January 1959. As the B-47s were being phased out, many of these fourth squadrons only had aircrews to support the monthly alert schedules. The fourth squadrons were eliminated by 1 January 1962 with the demise of the alert program.

During the alert tests individual aircrews, for both the bombers and tankers, stuck together for an entire week. Each aircrew lived in the alert facilities and traveled as a unit for medical check-ups, barbershop visits, etc. Sometime during the week the crew was scrambled and had to get their aircraft powered-up and taxi out to the runway. Only then they would learn if they would take off or return to the ramp. The aircraft were rotated through the alert ramp on a regular basis to ensure that the aircraft were always ready.

## Yo-Yo Missions

During combat operations it might have been necessary to refuel and rearm returning aircraft for a second strike. These types of operations were designated Yo-Yo missions. To practice these missions, the Deputy Commander for Maintenance would select certain aircraft that would be scheduled to fly before 17:00 hours, and earlier if possible. This time was set to permit the required maintenance to be performed during a normal duty day.

The flight crew was responsible for alerting the wing command post of the maintenance status of their aircraft. Any maintenance write-ups that might affect the second sortie were reported by the command post to maintenance job control at least 45 minutes prior to the aircraft landing. As required, maintenance would have the command post query the flight crew for additional information.

### NUCLEAR WEAPONS STORAGE FACILITIES

| AFLC Storage Facility | SAC Base |
| --- | --- |
| Deep Creek AFS | Fairchild AFB, Wash. |
| Mt. Rushmore AFS | Ellsworth AFB, S. Dak. |
| Caribou AFS | Loring AFB, Maine. |
| Stony Brook AFS | Westover AFB, Mass. |

Until the mid-1950s, AFLC retained special weapons at these four facilities adjacent to these SAC bases. It should be noted that all of these SAC bases had B-36 wings assigned.

A B-47E-66-BW (51-7045) was the charge of this SAC security policeman armed with his 9.5-pound M-1 Garrand rifle. The 66 block number meant that this B-47E-65 had undergone modification during an IRAN visit. On 20 February 1955, the aircraft was assigned to the 68th BMW, Lake Charles AFB, when it attempted a landing and crashed into a trailer park, killing all three crewmen aboard. (USAF)

The bombers would fly a prescribed mission and return to base within 10 minutes of the planned schedule and taxi into a refueling pit. There a debriefing team would meet the flight crew and a maintenance debriefing would be conducted on the spot. The bomber would be given required maintenance, serviced, preflighted, and launched on a second sortie.

## SAC REFLEX Operations

As each new SAC B-47 wing received its Stratojets, they entered a period of intensive training. At the end of the program the wing would be certified as combat-ready by a team of SAC inspectors. In a graduation-like ceremony, the entire wing would mobilize for a 90-day deployment to a base in England or North Africa.

SAC wing 90-day rotations to Morocco ceased in July 1957 and were replaced by REFLEX actions where wings sent bombers and tankers on shorter TDY rotations. On 1 October 1957 REFLEX bombers at Sidi Slimane were placed on ground alert along with the aircraft within the continental United States. Similar deployments to the Pacific began when Major General Sweeney, Fifteenth Air Force Commander, led a formation of B-47s from the 22nd Bombardment Wing at March AFB to Yokota AB, Japan. This non-stop 6,700-mile flight occurred on 21 June 1954. Subsequent B-47 wing deployments to the Pacific went to Andersen AFB, Guam. There were four REFLEX action routes: REFLEX – England and French Morocco, ALARM BELL – Spain, GLASS BRICK – Far East, and AIR MAIL – Alaska.

A typical SAC wing was equipped with 45 B-47s. While the REFLEX program was in effect, 18 aircraft would be on alert at the home station, while another 12 aircraft stood on alert at a forward operating location for a period of three weeks. This meant that every week six B-47s would deploy or redeploy between their home base and a forward operating location. The remaining aircraft were in some phase of maintenance or allocated for local training. With such a schedule, a great amount of work was placed upon the organizational maintenance squadron to ensure the aircraft could be operationally ready per schedule. In addition, the field maintenance squadrons were tasked with maintaining the operationally-ready aircraft on a daily basis.

By 31 December 1965 REFLEX operations in England, Guam, and North Africa had been replaced by B-52s. In 1966, the B-47 REFLEX operations in Spain were terminated.

## Low-Level Training Routes

The Strategic Air Command had gotten spoiled. Since the introduction of the high-altitude B-36 immediately after World War II, all high-altitude airspace was assigned to the military primarily for SAC training. This changed when the jet-powered Boeing Model 707 Stratoliner went into revenue service on 26 October 1958.

Coincidentally, by 1958 the Soviet air defenses had improved considerably, making high-altitude penetrations more risky. As a result, SAC developed plans for low-altitude penetrations in an effort to fly beneath the Soviet air defense radar network. In November 1959 SAC and the Federal Aviation Agency (a predecessor of today's Federal Aviation Administration) announced the establishment of seven low-level training routes that were dedicated to the SAC bomber training. These Oil Burner routes were located in unpopulated areas and were generally 20 miles wide, up to 500 miles in length, and were restricted to less than 1,000 feet altitude.

Earlier, General LeMay had established a series of 13 fixed radar bomb scoring (RBS) sites across the United States that were used for training and scoring the capabilities of the bomber crews. Over time, flying against these well-known sites became less challenging for the radar navigators and a new program had to be developed. SAC instituted mobile RBS sites that traveled across the country in trains known as the RBS Express.

In 1961, SAC contracted with the U.S. Army Ogden General Depot in Utah to build three RBS trains for use by the 1st Combat Evaluation Group (1CEVG). The RBS trains had a radar car and another car that housed plotting equipment. These trains were designed to move to existing military bases where they were parked on a siding and operated. The RBS Express crews were locally billeted and messed at the base.

Between 16 and 18 August 1961, Captain Bill D. Little, from the RBS Operations Section, and Major R. F. Luttman, Chief of the

On 6 May 1959, the crew of a B-47E-75-BW (51-7041) from the 306th BMW at MacDill AFB aborted a takeoff, resulting in this conflagration. Miraculously three of the crew managed to escape, but the copilot was not so lucky. (USAF)

Cheri-Lynn, a B-47B-45-BW (51-2295) from the 367th BS, 306th BMW, had a red tail band. Note that the Square P tail marking had been removed and its scars remain etched into the aluminum. (Boeing HS-920)

Plans Division, visited the FAA regional offices at Fort Worth, Texas, and Kansas City, Missouri, to coordinate future RBS Express locations. As a result of these meetings, radio frequencies, routes, altitudes, and separations with civilian air traffic were established. This allowed the FAA to issue Notices to Airmen (NOTAM) advising of the airspace restrictions.

SAC personnel maintained and operated the trains, while motive power was contracted from commercial railroads. The train would pull onto a siding and the crews would begin setting up the equipment. A B-25 accompanied the train and provided a radar calibration target until the RBS equipment was up and running. Then the B-25 crew took a break until the next site relocation. These mobile RBS sites provided SAC bomber crews with much needed experience in finding and bombing unfamiliar targets, thereby enhancing their mission capabilities. The radar-navigator had to account for wind drift, ground speed, true air speed, altitude, and absolute altitude using radar, visual, optical, computer, celestial, and dead reckoning techniques. One of the toughest jobs for the radar-navigator was to check his wind drift before commencing the bomb run, thereby reducing the circular error probability (CEP) to an acceptable score. He had to learn to make the drift correction prior to the final portion of the bomb run to ensure that the bombs would hit the target and not be adversely affected by the wind. In radar bombing, the bombardier would allow for two sweeps of the radar to ensure his drift correction angle prior to locking on to the target.

The first two RBS Express trains to be deployed were No. 3 on 21 August 1961, and No. 2 the following day. The Union Pacific Railroad provided the motive power and the tracks. The next several weeks were used for familiarization, and the No. 2 train was operational at Ives

*These crewmembers from the 340th BMW, Sedalia AFB, Missouri, were being debriefed by wing intelligence specialists. (SAC Combat Crew Magazine)*

Crossing near Rhame, North Dakota, on 16 September 1961 to support the SAC Annual Bombing & Navigation Competition.

Initially, the No. 1 train was assigned to the Second Air Force, 10th RBS Squadron. It supported the Second Down Oil Burner route

*A pair of B-47B-75-BWs (51-7062 and 51-7071) from the 22nd BMW had completed their flight from March AFB to Yokota. Aircraft 51-062 was carrying an earlier tail band from the arrow. This No. 4 engine belonged to a C-124 Globemaster II from one of SAC's strategic support squadrons that supported the mission. (USAF 152037AC)*

*This B-47E-75-BW (51-7071) from the 33rd BS, 22nd BMW, at March AFB taxied into Yokota AB, Japan after completing a 6,700-mile flight. GLASS BRICK missions that mirrored the REFLEX operations to England and French Morocco would replace such wing deployments to the Pacific. (USAF 152036AC)*

## 1CEVG OPERATING LOCATIONS DURING APRIL-JUNE 1962

| Unit | Oil Burner Route | Location |
|------|-----------------|----------|
| **1CEVG** | | *Barksdale AFB, Louisiana* |
| 10th RBS Squadron | | Carswell AFB, Texas |
| Det. 2 | Rough Road | Joplin, Missouri |
| Det. 7 | Sea Horse | Matagorda Island, Texas |
| Det. 10 | Clear View | U.S. Naval Ammo Depot – Hastings, Nebraska |
| Det. 12 | | Bayshore, Michigan |
| RBS Express No. 1 | | Emhouse, Texas & Newport, Arkansas |
| | | |
| 11th RBS Squadron | | March AFB, California |
| Det. 1 | Clay Bank/Tar Pail | La Junta, California |
| Det. 2 | | Scenic Badlands, South Dakota |
| Det. 9 | Clay Bank | St. George, Utah |
| Det. 10 | | Bismarck, North Dakota |
| Det. 12 | | U.S. Naval Ammo Depot – Hawthorne, Nevada |
| Det. 13 | | Wilder, Idaho |
| RBS Express No. 2 | | Gallop, New Mexico & Creston, Wyoming |
| | | |
| 12th RBS Squadron | | Turner AFB, Georgia |
| Det. 3 | Gun Load | Statesboro, Georgia |
| Det. 8 | Green Valley | Richmond, Kentucky |
| Det. 11 | Hangover | Camp Drum – Watertown, New York |
| RBS Express No. 3 | | Lake City, South Carolina & Broma, Illinois |

*A B-47B-5-BW (50-004) employs the ribbon chute for approach. Just before touchdown the crew deployed the braking chute. Note the fully open drogue chute and the deploying braking chute. (Via SAC Combat Crew Magazine)*

### Wing Dispersal

SAC had as many as 70 B-47s and 40 KC-97s or 45 B-52s and 20 KC-135s at a single base. Such overcrowding made a tempting target for the Soviets and resulted in extremely long launch times. In an effort to further complicate Soviet planning, SAC began dispersing aircraft to other bases beginning in 1958 and continuing into the early 1960s. The cumbersome two-wing B-47 bases were downsized and one wing was relocated to another base. The seed wing remained at a SAC base, whereas the spin-off wings were usually co-located at bases operated by other Air Force commands. By scattering the

located near the Naval Ammunition Depot in McAlester, Oklahoma. The No. 2 train was assigned to the Eighth Air Force, 11th RBS Squadron, and supported the Bitter Battle Oil Burner route near Bowman, North Dakota. The No. 3 train was also assigned to the Eighth Air Force, but this time to the 12th RBS Squadron. It supported the Tree Trimmer Oil Burner route near the Alabama Ordnance Works in Childersburg, Alabama.

By January 1967 the assignments had changed considerably. The No. 1 train was still assigned to the Second Air Force, 10th RBS Squadron, but now supported the Go Buy Oil Burner route near Corsicana, Texas. The No. 2 train and 11th RBS Squadron had been transferred to the Fifteenth Air Force and supported the Dusty Desert Oil Burner route near Thoreau, New Mexico. The No. 3 train was assigned to the Eighth Air Force and 12th RBS Squadron, supporting the Here's How Oil Burner route near the Blue Grass Ordnance Depot in Richmond, Kentucky.

*This B-47E-85-BW (52-462) from the 98th BMW was parked in the snow at Lincoln AFB. Note the protective shield over the navigator's compartment and the canvas engine plugs. (SAC Combat Crew Magazine)*

bomber force, Soviet targeting plans were complicated and the launch time for the alert force was markedly reduced.

Several KC-97 squadrons were separated from their parent B-47 wings and assigned to northern tier bases. For example, the 305th Bombardment Wing (Medium) at Bunker Hill AFB remained there with its B-47s; however, the 305th AREFS with its KC-97s went to McGuire AFB on 15 January 1960.

### Emergency Dispersal Plan

As the Soviet Union's long-range nuclear capability grew, SAC bases became more vulnerable. At the direction of the Joint Chiefs of Staff, SAC developed a two-pronged program to protect its bomber force from a second strike. First, the B-52s were placed on 24-hour airborne alert under Project CHROME DOME. The second part of the plan involved B-47s dispersing to remote sites during periods of crisis. By way of example, when notified of a crisis, the 2nd Bombardment Wing at Hunter AFB would launch all available bombers to orbit in specified areas until directed by the command post to either return to base or fly to the dispersal base. The off-base dispersal area for mobility personnel (those personnel required for unit operations) and equipment was in the vicinity of Pooler, Georgia. Local civil defense authorities would be alerted and provide clear passage for the convoy. Robins AFB, Georgia, would take up to 20 KC-97s and have fuel and lubricant capability to service these aircraft with 7,500 gallons of 115/145-octane aviation gasoline and 4,000 gallons of JP-4 jet fuel. Shaw AFB, South Carolina, would receive up to 45 B-47s and have the fuel and lubricant capability to service each aircraft with up to 11,000 gallons of JP-4. The Base Public Affairs Officer would have a canned statement that "this was a routine mobility training exercise" if asked by the press, as would undoubtedly happen. This plan was established on 1 October 1954 and first tested on 17 December.

*Early ground refueling operations were conducted manually at each tank – a tedious and time-consuming process. Note the grounding wires attached to the outrigger gear. (SAC Combat Crew Magazine)*

## B-47 DISPERSAL BASES

| Wing | Base | Dispersal Base | Host |
|------|------|----------------|------|
| **Second Air Force** | | | |
| 40th BMW | Forbes AFB, Kans. | Atlantic City, N.J. | Civilian |
| | | Andrews AFB, Md. | HQ, USAF |
| 68th BMW | Chennault AFB, La. | England AFB, La. | TAC |
| | | Birmingham, Ala. | Civilian |
| | | Dobbins AFB, Ga. | CONAC |
| 98th BMW | Lincoln AFB, Neb. | Phelps Collins, Mich. | Civilian |
| | | Niagara Falls, N.Y. | Civilian |
| | | Bradley Field, Conn. | Civilian |
| 307th BMW | Lincoln AFB, Neb. | Chicago O'Hare, Ill. | Civilian |
| | | Mitchell Field, Wisc. | Civilian |
| 340th BMW | Whiteman AFB, Mo. | Lambert Field, Mo. | Civilian |
| | | Langley AFB, Va. | TAC |
| | | Minneapolis, Minn. | Civilian |
| 384th BMW | Little Rock AFB, Ark. | Memphis, Tenn. | Civilian |
| | | Hulman, Ind. | Civilian |
| **Eighth Air Force** | | | |
| 2nd BMW | Hunter AFB, Ga. | Charleston AFB, S.C. | MATS |
| | | Philadelphia, Pa. | Civilian |
| | | Suffolk Co. AFB, N.Y. | ADC |
| 19th BMW | Homestead AFB, Fla. | Patrick AFB, Fla. | ARDC |
| 306th BMW | MacDill AFB, Fla. | Hurlburt Field, Fla. | ARDC |
| | | Brookley AFB, Ala. | AMC |
| | | Dannelly, Ala. | Civilian |
| | | New Hanover, N.C. | Civilian |
| | | Palm Beach, Fla. | Civilian |
| 321st BMW | McCoy AFB, Fla. | Olmstead AFB, Pa. | AMC |
| 509th BMW | Pease AFB, N.H. | Logan, Mass. | Civilian |
| **Fifteenth Air Force** | | | |
| 9th BMW | Mountain Home AFB | Portland, Oreg. | Civilian |
| | | Spokane, Wash. | Civilian |
| 22nd BMW | March AFB, Calif. | McClellan AFB, Calif. | AMC |
| | | Oxnard AFB, Calif. | ADC |
| 96th BMW | Dyess AFB, Tex. | Tinker AFB, Okla. | AMC |
| | | Tulsa, Okla. | Civilian |
| | | Truax AFB, Wisc. | ADC |
| 303rd BMW | Davis-Monthan AFB | Hill AFB, Utah | AMC |
| | | Luke AFB, Ariz. | TAC |
| 310th BMW | Schilling AFB, Kans. | Detroit-Wayne, Mich. | Civilian |

## Operation CLUTCH PEDAL

B-47s achieved their dispersal capability by being assigned to select commercial and military airfields within the continental United States, and through deployments to overseas bases. In what was known as Operation CLUTCH PEDAL, a pair of B-47s from each wing flew without weapons to a dispersal base every quarter. They remained there 12 to 72 hours to familiarize crews and maintenance personnel with the base before returning to their home station. By July 1961 these operations were part of the normal routine. The Operation CLUTCH PEDAL dispersal bases for July through December 1961 are shown in the accompanying tables.

*These three crewmembers and their crew chief proudly stood at parade rest in front of a B-47B-30-BW (51-2122). The crewmembers were (left to right): Captain Swenson, Captain Kring, Captain Koski, and Staff Seargent Lynch. The aircraft had been through an IRAN where it was upgraded to eliminate the windows in the navigator's compartment. For a period during the late 1950s and early 1960, Day-Glo Orange conspicuity paint was the order of the day. The conspicuity paint was applied to the nose, wingtips, and waist. The aircraft had a partial white anti-radiation finish. (SAC Combat Crew Magazine)*

*This A1/C from the 301st BMW Armament & Electronics Squadron at Barksdale AFB was working on equipment in one of the electronics bays. Extreme care had to be taken when positioning the workstand next to the aircraft to prevent ramp rash. (SAC Combat Crew Magazine)*

The Air Force Reserve Recovery Squadrons were tasked with receiving aircraft at civilian dispersal fields. In addition to parking and servicing the aircraft, the reservists were trained in chemical, biological, and radiological warfare and could provide aircraft recovery services under all conditions. Such training became routine summer camp exercises for these units. For two weeks the reservists established a base of operations, activated the requisite communications systems, and performed routine base operations such as administration, security, and medical. At the end of the exercise, a B-47 would land at the airport where the reservists would perform recovery operations. During the summers of 1962 and 1963, one such squadron operated at Fort Mifflin, adjacent to the Philadelphia International Airport, and this author was able to participate in the exercises. Cadet and senior members of 908 Squadron, Pennsylvania Wing, Civil Air Patrol, providing additional administrative, communications, medical, and transportation support augmented this undermanned Reserve squadron.

## Operation TEXAS STAR

SAC designated its bomber stream missions as Operation TEXAS STAR. Records indicate that units frequently used these to satisfy many of the SAC Regulation 50-8 training requirements during a single mission. Ultimately, these operations were far more successful with B-52 units than with B-47 wings.

*On 15 May 1962, a B-47E-135-BW (53-6230) assigned to the 340th BMW, at Whiteman AFB, Missouri, was completely engulfed in black smoke and flames. The fireball engulfed all of the firemen within 100 feet of the aircraft. The aircraft was being fueled with 10,000 gallons of JP-4 fuel when it exploded, killing 4 firemen and injuring 18 others. Here a fire truck was almost in the flames as the firemen attempted to get the blaze under control. (USAF)*

From Air Force records it appears that SAC conducted Operation TEXAS STAR with its bomber forces between January 1957 and March 1964. The 341st Bombardment Wing from Dyess AFB was the first B-47 unit to fly in Operation TEXAS STAR.

During January 1957 the wing scheduled five missions, but only four were executed. Each of these missions required extensive coordination within the wing and with outside organizations for such things as tanker support, RBS scheduling, and air traffic control. When dates

*While on a flight line outing on a delightful day at Lake Charles AFB these 68th BMW technicians were maneuvering one of the Marathon Electric MD-3 ground power carts into position under a B-47E-65-BW (51-5252). To the rear were B-47Es, 51-2439 and 51-5248. This picture dates from 20 October 1953. Aircraft 51-5252 was deployed to Sidi Slimane, French Morocco, and was on a routine training flight on 10 June 1954. During refueling, the B-47 went into a spin and crashed near Oujda, killing one of the crewmembers. Aircraft 51-5248 was subsequently reassigned to the 307th BMW at Lincoln AFB; on 8 October 1959 the aircraft crashed on takeoff, killing all four aboard. (SAC Combat Crew Magazine)*

and times were selected, they had to be meshed with other wing requirements such as REFLEX deployments, training, scheduled maintenance, crew leave, and higher headquarters tasking.

Crews for an Operation TEXAS STAR mission assembled three-and-a-half hours prior to takeoff for a weather briefing. After a thorough crew briefing, aircraft preflight inspection, and aircraft loading, engines were started 2 hours and 35 minutes after arriving at the aircraft. Taxi commenced 10 minutes later, followed by takeoff in another 15 minutes. Aircraft took off at 90-second intervals.

After conducting the four Operation TEXAS STAR missions in January 1957, the 341st Bombardment Wing rated, at best, a fair grade. The night mass refuelings results were not satisfactory. However, the bombing and navigation results were graded as adequate. It was believed that greater wing readiness could be accomplished through better diversification of flying time that was dedicated to specific mission requirements rather than bomber stream missions.

*This Master Sergeant assigned to the 341st A&E Squadron was using an AN/UPM-11A range calibrator set. A test cable was connected to the aircraft. Signals generated by the calibrator set were directed at the aircraft through a rectangular-section used to change the polarity of the antenna horn from horizontal to vertical as required. The rectangular-section antenna horn was attached to the wave-guide output. With this test set, the technician could provide simulated radar signals to any radar transmitter operating within a given frequency range. Its use permitted the calibration and adjustment of radar range-tracking circuits, and when used with necessary associated equipment, accurately boresighted the radar's antenna. In the background was a B-47E-35-BW (51-2169) and a pair of C-124 Globemaster IIs from SAC's 4th Strategic Support Squadron also based at Dyess AFB. (SAC Combat Crew Magazine)*

*While attempting a MITO takeoff from Pease AFB, New Hampshire, on 4 February 1961, a 100th BMW crew lost control of the aircraft shortly after takeoff. They were No. 2 in a 3-ship cell. The aircraft, the last B-47E-130-BW (53-4244), was captured in this aerial photo. It appears the aircraft came down flat, and the right wing ripped off without slicing the trees. The aircraft nose is visible just forward of what appears to be the No. 5 engine. Lost in the crash were Captain Thomas C. Weller, aircraft commander; 1st Lieutenant Ronald Chapo, copilot; 1st Lieutenant J. A. Wether; and Staff Sergeant Stephen J. Mikva, crew chief. (USAF)*

### PACE SETTER Exercises

While SAC conducted command-wide exercises, the numbered air forces had their own training and evaluation programs. By way of example, the Eighth Air Force conducted a number of PACE SETTER exercises during the mid-1950s to hone the various skills within their organization. The program was continually developed and refined in order to measure the performance of Eighth Air Force units under carefully controlled conditions. Lieutenant General Walter C. Sweeney, Jr.,commanded the Eighth Air Force between 6 August 1955 and 30 September 1961. Sweeney stated that the competitive bomber stream missions were designed to: evaluate the ability of the individual wings to plan all phases of the mission; prepare crews and aircraft for their wartime mission; evaluate the performance of the combat crews; determine the reliability of the aircraft and allied equipment; check the performance of the crews in securing radar scope bomb run and bomb burst photography; and assess the ability of intelligence personnel to complete timely and accurate indirect bomb damage assessments.

The requirements for the first five PACE SETTER exercises included three record radar RBS runs, one photo-scored grid celestial navigation leg, and bomb scoring of one of the runs by photo-interpreters. PACE SETTER I was flown in December 1955.

All Eighth Air Force combat wings, except the 55th Strategic Reconnaissance Wing, participated in the PACE SETTER exercises. The 55th was exempted because of its specialized role in electronic and weather reconnaissance missions.

Soon, the overall proficiency of Eighth Air Force personnel had improved to the point were more difficult tactical requirements were warranted. Hence, starting with PACE SETTER VI various more difficult tasks were added, including bravo type targets, ground controlled intercept (GCI)-scored grid navigation legs, Mach 0.81 bomb runs, and hi-jinx breakaway maneuvers.

PACE SETTER VI was flown between 21 January and 4 February 1957. To further hone their skills, the participation of integral non-ready crews was encouraged. The RBS targets for this exercise were located at Omaha, Nebraska, St. Louis, Missouri, and Binghamton, New York. Participants included the 40th, 98th, 307th, 310th, 340th, and 380th Bombardment Wings and the 26th, 90th, and 91st Strategic Reconnaissance Wings.

For the third consecutive year, the 340th Bombardment Wing won the Brigadier General Jack Roberts Memorial Trophy for best wing performance, thereby giving them permanent possession of the trophy. A new trophy established for PACE SETTER VI was the Major Lacie C. Neighbors Memorial Trophy for the best reconnaissance wing, won by the 26th Strategic Reconnaissance Wing. It was even more significant because Major Neighbors had been the aircraft commander of a 26th Wing RB-47 lost over the Bering Sea in April 1955.

PACE SETTER VII was conducted between 9 April and 17 May 1957. The RBS targets were located at Atlanta, Little Rock, and Seymour, Indiana. Eighth Air Force participants included the 40th, 42nd, 98th, 100th, 307th, 310th, and 340th Bombardment Wings and the 26th, 90th, 91st, and 100th Strategic Reconnaissance Wings. The 380th Bombardment Wing was deployed to RAF Brize Norton and was, therefore, exempted from the exercise. The 100th Strategic Bombardment Wing was added because they became combat-ready on 1 March 1957. This marked the first participation of a B-52 wing in the exercise with the addition of the 42nd Strategic Bombardment Wing.

### Cuban Missile Crisis

During early 1962, a B-47E from the 96th Bomb Squadron, 2nd Bombardment Wing, was on a routine training mission over Florida when its copilot noted that a Soviet-built Fan Song radar was painting them. When the aircraft landed, the copilot reported his findings to the debriefing intelligence officer who assumed that the signal had come from a test at Eglin AFB. When it was learned that there were no such tests being conducted at Eglin, the copilot was subjected to a series of evaluations to determine if he could really identify the Fan Song radar signals on his APS-54 equipment. Each test was positive. Now that the intelligence community was convinced of the copilot's story, they began earnestly checking the source of the transmission.

The Joint Chiefs of Staff ordered a reconnaissance overflight of Cuba on 14 October 1962 using a Lockheed U-2 from the 4080th Strategic Wing. On the morning of 15 October 1962 quick readout teams from the National Photographic Interpretation Center (NPIC) in Washington analyzed the photographs and identified major components of Soviet medium range ballistic missiles (MRBM) in a field at San Cristobal. Further analysis by NPIC resulted in identification of all but one of the 24 SAM sites on the island. In addition, the analysts observed the uncrating of Il-28 Beagle bombers at San Julian. Continued analysis on the following day revealed that the missiles found were not SS-3s, but longer range SS-4s. At that time no nuclear warheads were seen in the photographs. An evaluation conducted by the Guided Missile and Astronautics Intelligence Committee (GMAIC) resulted in conclusions that the missiles were clearly under Soviet control and confirmed that no nuclear warheads were present.

At the request of President John F. Kennedy the 4080th Strategic Reconnaissance Wing flew high altitude reconnaissance missions over Cuba for the next several days gathering more intelligence data. The Wing deployed its U-2 from Laughlin AFB to McCoy AFB for this operation. Subsequently, an RB-47E from the 55th Strategic Reconnaissance Wing photographed a Soviet freighter loaded with missiles bound for Cuba.

On 22 October President Kennedy ordered an arms embargo against Cuba and demanded the removal of the missiles. The U.S. Navy and Coast Guard set up a naval blockade and SAC responded

*Major General Walter C. Sweeney, Jr., Eighth Air Force Commander, and Colonel Harold E. "Bus" Humfeld, Eighth Air Force Director of Operations, inspected the Brigadier General Jack Roberts Memorial Trophy. (Eighth Air Force Historian)*

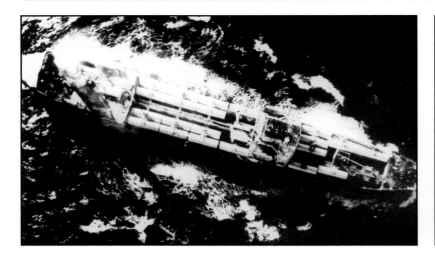

The Soviet freighter PV Grozny was photographed while returning missiles from Cuba. The photo was taken at 23 degrees 50 minutes North and 61 degrees 10 minutes West at 12:07 hours Zulu on 27 October 1962. (SAC Historian)

This B-47B-20-BW (50-076) from the 320th BMW was returning to March AFB after being dispersed for the Cuban Missile Crisis. Note the pilot chute resting against the billowing drag chute. (SAC Combat Crew Magazine)

Honorable Susie was an RB-47H-BW (53-4300) assigned to the 55th SRW. Shown here with her lead crew L-48 consisting of: Captain J. T. Bennington, aircraft commander; 1st Lieutenant N. L. Riggin, copilot; Major R. D. King, navigator; Captain G. W. Johnson III, EWO; Captain E. E. Posa, EWO; 1st Lieutenant G. A. Head, EWO; Staff Sergeant Joe Perrault, crew chief; and Airman 2/C Joe Kroboth, assistant crew chief. Captain Eugene E. Posa would be lost during the 1 July 1960 shoot down with Major Willard Palm's crew. (Bruce M. Bailey)

to the threat by ordering its bomber fleet to dispersal areas around the United States and overseas. Commercial airports had airline ramp space lined with B-47s and KC-97s, replete with air police security supported by dogs. Florida became a virtual arsenal.

The standoff continued until 28 October, when the Soviet Union agreed to remove its offensive missiles from Cuba. SAC reconnaissance aircraft monitored the dismantling of the missiles, their crating, and shipboard loading. On 20 November, the Russians also agreed to remove their medium-range Tu-16 Badger bombers from Cuban air bases. (The Tu-16 was roughly equivalent to the B-47.)

During the crisis, the B-47s from the 2nd Bombardment Wing at Hunter AFB were dispersed to Charleston AFB, South Carolina, while the KC-97s from the 2nd AREFS were deployed to Lajes AB, Azores. The major problem confronting the units that were deployed to non-SAC bases was communications. SAC's command structure required secure communications between various headquarters levels, wing command posts, and operational crews. Only part of the requirement could be met by commercial landline telephone. The most effective means of communications was found in the AN/ARC-21 single-side-band (SSB) radio, developed by Collins Radio as part of Project BIRDCALL.

When the crisis was over, the bombers were ordered home. As with all redeploying nuclear-armed bombers, strict requirements were imposed for the operations. The weapons were to be disarmed and carried in the ferry configuration. No en-route training was to be exercised on the return flight and populated areas were to be avoided. Preparations for the return to Hunter were completed on 7 November 1962, and preflights were initiated on 24 November. Returning crews were placed on telephone alert at their quarters. SAC was back to its usual activities, but was still at heightened alert.

## Lieutenant Obenauf's Flight

On 28 April 1958 a B-47 from the 341st Bombardment Wing at Dyess AFB took off on a flight that became famous in the annals of SAC. The B-47E-35-LM (52-278) carried its normal three-man crew; Major James M. Graves, aircraft commander; First Lieutenant James E. Obenauf, copilot; Lieutenant John P. Cobb, navigator; plus an instructor navigator, Major Joseph Maxwell. The aircraft took off at 19:55 hours on a routine training mission that included celestial navigation and bombing technique as part of an evaluation of Lieutenant Cobb. Major Maxwell had completed grading the navigator and the lieutenant gave Maxwell a heading for the next leg to Denver. The aircraft was flying at 34,000 feet where the outside air temperature was -32 degrees Fahrenheit.

Three hours into the flight one of the engines exploded. The aircraft shuddered and Graves saw flames flickering under the left wing. In such a condition, the engine could begin shedding hot turbine blades into the fuselage containing the fuel tanks. Per SAC's standard operating procedures, the aircraft commander gave the bailout order. Under these conditions, the crews were trained to react and immediately egress the aircraft. The navigator went out the downward hatch while the aircraft commander blew the canopy and, assuming the rest of the crew had departed the aircraft, initiated an ejection. His seat failed to fire. Graves disconnected his oxygen and headed for the open navigator's hatch. En route he spotted Lieutenant Obenauf and believed he too was on his way out. Graves dove for the open hatch and departed the aircraft. Obenauf attempted to eject but his seat failed also, so he then proceeded down the catwalk to bail out of the navigator's hatch. On the way he found the unconscious body of Major Maxwell who had been knocked out by the air blast when the

canopy was jettisoned. Attempts to revive him were unsuccessful, as was a search for a spare parachute.

Lieutenant Obenauf climbed back into his seat where he faced gale-force winds, hoping the seat would not fire. He plugged in his oxygen and surveyed the situation. The No. 6 engine had blown. It would now become a desperate effort to get the aircraft to a safe altitude and to get the aircraft back on the ground. Obenauf placed the crippled jet into a dive, approaching its structural limits, and he recovered at 5,500 feet.

Initiating a shutdown of the ailing engine, Obenauf called a Mayday over the guard channel. Altus AFB, in the Oklahoma panhandle, picked up the distress call and gave him vectors. The controllers pleaded with Obenauf to land at Altus, but he opted for familiar territory and requested vectors to Dyess, which were provided. Obenauf desperately needed his landing lights. He felt a tug on his leg and looked down to see Maxwell. Obenauf instructed Maxwell to get into the forward seat and find the landing light switch. Unfortunately, Maxwell's unfamiliarity with the pilot's station forced him to give up after several futile attempts in the darkened cockpit. Maxwell finally found a flashlight and was able to locate the landing light switch.

Major Doyle Reynolds, 341st Bombardment Wing Chief of Flying, was in the tower at Dyess. Reynolds had been one of Obenauf's instructors. By this time Obenauf was out of position with the runway that was paralleled by a row of 30 parked B-47s, but he was too close to make major directional changes. The GCA controller called for a go-around but Obenauf was too exhausted and continued the approach. Major Reynolds calmly called over the radio: "It would be better if you could move a little to the left." Obenauf struggled with the sluggish controls. He spotted the rows of landing lights and planted the aircraft between them. It was the best landing of his career.

*This B-47E-125-BW (53-2398) from the 380th BMW at Plattsburgh AFB, New York, suffered a failure of the forward main landing gear on 2 Dececember 1964 and skidded off the right side of the runway. The crew exited via the main entry hatch and the navigator's emergency hatch. The aircraft was reclaimed on 13 January 1965. (USAF)*

Immediately he chopped the power, deployed the landing chute, and applied the brakes, successfully stopping the aircraft.

Both men were taken to the hospital for observation. They were then driven to the base theater where 800 base personnel and their families gathered for a special presentation. CINCSAC General Thomas S. Power, who had been listening to their ordeal over the radio, had flown to Dyess. For his actions, Lieutenant Obenauf was presented the Cheney Award for heroism. General Power also presented him with the Distinguished Flying Cross. After recovering from injuries sustained during the flight, Lieutenant Obenauf was upgraded to aircraft commander – then the youngest SAC bomber aircraft commander.

## SAC Bombing Competition

When LeMay became SAC Commander, he inherited a poorly trained and motivated organization. LeMay employed his wartime experience leading B-17 and B-29 units to develop a realistic training program. From the time LeMay took command of SAC, it trained the way it would fight. There is an old Army adage – *Train hard, fight easy; train easy, fight hard.* As a consequence, SAC's training missions were long and arduous to simulate the long distances that would have to be covered to reach a target, and bombing would be scored to meet the requirements for getting the most bombs on target the first time. The SAC Bombing Competition became an annual event to improve overall bombardment performance and to develop a competitive spirit among the crews.

The first competition where B-47s participated was held at Davis-Monthan AFB for the Stratojets, while the B-29s, B-36s, and B-50s operated out of Walker AFB. This competition was held between 25 and 31 October 1953. Events were prepared so that not only would there be an overall winner, but also categories dedicated to specific aircraft types, bombing, navigation, bomber/tanker team, etc. During the 1953 competition the 303rd Bombardment Wing from Davis-Monthan took the Best B-47 Crew Trophy, while the 44th Bombardment Wing from Lake Charles AFB garnered the Best B-47 Wing Trophy.

Colonel Michael N. M. McCoy had led the 306th Bombardment Wing at MacDill AFB through their transition and service evaluation of the Stratojet. He then went on to command the 321st Bombardment Wing at Pinecastle AFB near Orlando. On 9 October 1957 McCoy was demonstrating the speed characteristics of the B-47 to RAF Group Captain John Woodroffe, commander of the RAF contingent at the 1957 SAC Bombing Competition, and literally pulled the wings off the aircraft, killing the entire crew. Colonel McCoy was replaced by Colonel William L. Gray and Pinecastle AFB was renamed McCoy AFB the following year. Its ICAO designator is MCO, and today, as Orlando International Airport, it retains this code.

The 1957 SAC Bombing Competition was held at Pinecastle AFB between 30 October and 5 November. There were twenty-eight B-47, five RB-47, five B-36, and five B-52 wings in the competition. In addi-

*Early B-47 flight crews wore the dark blue flight suits of the day. They were not liked and more than one crewmember opined that he never saw a blue tree behind which to hide if he ever went down in enemy territory! Note the three hats – a wheel hat with a 50-mission crush, a flight cap, and a baseball cap. (SAC Combat Crew Magazine)*

*This flight crew wore the blue flight suits and the short blue winter flight parkas with wolverine hood trim. (SAC Combat Crew Magazine)*

*This 6th BMW flight crew was performing a final briefing before going aviating. They were wearing the sage green nylon summer flying suits that replaced the blue suits. Note how the SAC Milky Way band came through the crew entry hatch on this aircraft, denoting this was an early application of the marking. (SAC Combat Crew Magazine)*

*The City of MERCED was a B-47E-85-BW (52-436) from the 93rd BMW. This aircraft represented the wing at the 1954 SAC Bomb Comp held at Barksdale AFB. This crew scored a total of 853 points out of a possible 1,000. The crew consisted of (left to right): Lieutenant Colonel J. L. Holquin, navigator; Lieutenant Colonel H. C. Traylor, Jr., aircraft commander; and Lieutenant Colonel M. A. Speiser, copilot. Ground support was provided by Staff Sergeant Joseph D. Armstrong, crew chief; and Airman 1/C William E. Scott, radar maintenance specialist. This photograph was taken during the wing-level competitions leading up to the SAC Bomb Comp. It was here the crew garnered the Top Jet Crew in Fifteenth Air Force award. Note the early UNITED STATES AIR FORCE marking on the forward fuselage. This was replaced by U.S. AIR FORCE and the SAC Milky Way band and SAC insignia for the SAC-level Bomb Comp. (Lieutenant Colonel Jose Holquin via Rick Rodriguez)*

tion, the RAF had four crews flying Valiant and Vulcan bombers. In honor of Colonel McCoy, SAC instituted the McCoy Trophy, which was only awarded in 1957 and was won by the 321st Bombardment Wing. Out of a possible 2,000 points, this Pinecastle AFB-based unit scored 1,744 points (87.2 percent) beating out the 100th and 384th Bombardment Wings, which scored 1,691 and 1,680 points, respectively. The 321st also garnered the Fairchild and Best B-47 Trophies.

During the 12 years that the B-47 flew in the SAC Bombing Competition, it earned trophies in the 10 years in which the event was held. The competition was suspended during 1962, 1963, and 1965 due to other commitments. The most coveted award was the Fairchild Trophy, and B-47 wings took this trophy during four competitions.

CITY of ORLANDO II *was a B-47E that represented the 321st BMW at the 1957 SAC Bomb Comp that was held at Pinecastle AFB shortly after the death of its commander Colonel Michael N. M. McCoy. The aircraft was marked to recognize the wing's outstanding accomplishments at the competition. (SAC Combat Crew Magazine)*

Pride of the Adirondacks *was a B-47E-125-BW (53-2385) from the 380th BMW at Plattsburgh AFB. This aircraft represented the wing in the 1965 Bomb Comp, taking three of the top four B-47 awards. The aircraft is on display at the former air base. (SAC Combat Crew Magazine)*

The last SAC Bombing Competition in which the B-47s participated was held at Fairchild AFB in September 1965. That year a B-47E crew from the 509th Bombardment Wing at Pease AFB earned the Best B-47 Wing – Navigation Trophy. Most spectacular was the 380th Bombardment Wing, winning three of the awards – Best B-47 Crew, Best B-47 Wing, and Best B-47 – Bombing. A B-47E-125-BW (53-2385), named *Pride of the Adirondacks*, was flown by Major Charles W. Patrick, aircraft commander, Captain John V. Wilcox, copilot, and Major Robert A. Wickland, navigator. Within three weeks of this win, the 380th's B-47s became swept up in Project FAST FLY. On 14 December 1965 the last three operational B-47s departed Plattsburgh AFB for the boneyard at Davis-Monthan. *Pride of the Adirondacks* was spared, and placed on display at the entrance to the base on 8 February 1966.

## Project FLY FAST

Secretary of Defense Robert McNamara was determined to replace the strategic bomber with intercontinental ballistic missiles (ICBM) and ordered Project FLY FAST to retire the B-47. The once prolific B-47 medium bomber force continued to shrink under this

### PROJECT FLY FAST DRAWDOWN

| Date | Wing | Base | Note |
|---|---|---|---|
| 1 Apr 63 | 2nd BW | Hunter AFB, Ga. | 1 |
| 1 Apr 63 | 305th BW | Bunker Hill AFB, Ind. | 2 |
| 1 Apr 63 | 306th BW | MacDill AFB, Fla. | 1 |
| 15 Mar 63 | 22nd BW | March AFB, Calif. | 3 |
| 15 Mar 63 | 96th BW | Dyess AFB, Tex. | 1 |
| 15 Apr 63 | 4347th CCTW | McConnell AFB, Kans. | 4 |
| 1 Sept 63 | 340th BW | Whiteman AFB, Mo. | 1 |
| 15 June 64 | 301st BW | Lockbourne AFB, Okla. | 5 |
| 15 June 64 | 303rd BW | Davis-Monthan AFB, Ariz. | 1 |
| 1 Sept 64 | 40th SAW | Forbes AFB, Kans. | 4 |
| 1 Sept 64 | 384th BW | Little Rock AFB, Ark. | 4 |

This is a summary of the B-47 drawdown during Project FLY FAST between 1 April 1963 and 1 September 1964, by date of inactivation or mission change.

NOTES:
1. Transitioned into B-52s at another base.
2. Transitioned into B-58s.
3. Transitioned into B-52s at same base.
4. Deactivated.
5. Transitioned into KC-135s.

*General Curtis E. LeMay, CINCSAC, presented actor Jimmy Stewart a chrome B-47 desk model for his efforts in promoting strategic airpower. The award was presented at the 1956 Air Force Association Convention in New Orleans. This was the first year the AFA presented their annual Outstanding Airmen award to the top enlisted personnel in SAC. At the time Stewart was a colonel in the Air Force Reserve. Stewart was rated in the B-36 and the B-47 when he made the movie Strategic Air Command; however, he did not actually fly these aircraft during the filming. At right, Jimmy Stewart flew into Barksdale AFB in a VB-25 Mitchell bomber when he attended B-47 transition training with the 376th BMW. Note that Stewart had scrambled eggs on the bill of his service cap, whereas the rather old looking public information captain had none. (left: Via Air Force Association; right: Eighth Air Force Museum)*

program. At its peak in 1958, SAC had 1,367 B-47s in its inventory; through 1963, a total of 267 B-47s were retired, and those remaining were concentrated in 22 medium bombardment wings. Eleven B-47 wings were either inactivated or converted to B-52s, B-58s, or KC-135s during 1963 and 1964. Two of the remaining wings were equipped with EB-47s. Another 222 B-47 bombers were dropped from the inventory the following year, along with reductions in the EB/RB-47 fleets. The ultimate goal of Project FLY FAST was to eliminate all B-47s by 1966.

## Strategic Air Command – The Movie

While the movie *Strategic Air Command* dealt primarily with the Convair B-36, it concluded with the lead character, played by Jimmy Stewart, beginning the introduction of the B-47 into SAC's arsenal. A wartime leader flying B-24s, Stewart continued in the Reserve where he was rated in the B-36, B-47, and B-52. He retired from the Air Force as a brigadier general, the highest rank attained by an actor. The film depicts the rigors of Cold War flying by members of SAC and its effects on family life. In addition, the flying scenes are superb. The B-47 cockpit procedures trainer that was used in the movie is currently on display at the March AFB Museum in Riverside, California.

## A Tale of Two Aircraft

A B-47E-135-BW (53-6244) was the last Stratojet off the Boeing-Wichita assembly line on 18 February 1957. The aircraft was first assigned to the 40th Bombardment Wing at Smoky Hill AFB. It had competed a scheduled Inspect and Repair As Necessary (IRAN) visit at Lockheed-Georgia before its last assignment in SAC with the 307th Bombardment Wing at Lincoln AFB. The aircraft arrived at Lincoln on 31 October 1959.

During 1965, the 307th Bombardment Wing was in the midst of Project FLY FAST, the phase-out of B-47s from the inventory. Aircraft 53-6244 was pulled from the alert ramp and its weapons downloaded. Maintenance personnel from the 307th Organizational Maintenance Squadron and 307th Aircraft Generation Squadron ensured that the aircraft was in pristine condition and readied for its last flight – not to the boneyard, but to be enshrined at the U.S. Air Force Museum at Wright-Patterson AFB.

On 22 January 1965 the aircraft (53-6244) was preflighted by her crew chief, A1C James R. Sine, and turned over to the flight crew – Captain Eugene T. Hackman, aircraft commander; Captain Harold W. "Pete" Todd, copilot; and Captain Alfred F. Ottaviano, navigator. The flight crew was selected for this mission because they were winners of the Emergency War Order (EWO) knowledge competition. Also aboard was A1C Sine. With the polish and elbow grease applied by the maintenance personnel from the 307th, the aircraft flew 15 knots faster than normal.

Over time, Wright-Patterson had a fleet of as many as 15 B-47s for their rigorous test programs. When it became time for Aeronautical Systems Division to rid themselves of their Stratojets in 1969, they opted to have an NB-47E-120-BW (53-2280) placed on display at the Air Force Museum.

Now there was a dilemma. To solve the problem, the Air Force Museum relegated 53-6244 to the base fire department. This ignominious assignment resulted in the aircraft being used for fire training, where it was eventually destroyed. Needless to say, the members of the 307th Bombardment Wing Association were not very pleased with this action.

## B-47 Spirit – Last Flight

Douglas delivered a B-47E-25-DT (52-0166) to the Air Force on 25 October 1954, with its initial assignment to the 9th Bombardment Wing at Mountain Home AFB. Subsequently it served with the 509th Bombardment Wing at Walker AFB and the 509th Bombardment Wing at Pease AFB. Its last assignment was with the 40th Bombardment Wing at Forbes AFB. The aircraft was dropped from the Air Force inventory in August 1964 and transferred to the Naval Weapons Center China Lake to serve as an electronic bomb target.

Retired Air Force Chief Master Sergeant Russell G. Morrison had formerly served as the director of the Castle AFB Museum. While looking for another aircraft for the museum, he found the generally

This B-47E-135-BW (3-6244) was the last B-47 produced and last served with the 307th BMW, Lincoln AFB, Nebraska. This aircraft was flown to Wright-Patterson AFB, Ohio, to join the collection at the Air Force Museum; however, it was upstaged by a test Stratojet from the base. The aircraft was transferred to the base fire department and met its demise as a fire-training device. (Robert Joe Loffredo)

intact B-47. The aircraft was transferred to the Air Force Museum Programs and work began on its restoration. A team of 160 civilian and military personnel (including 75 volunteers) expended some 36,000-man-hours to get the aircraft back into flying condition.

Using old technical orders provided by The Boeing Company and retirees, the team went to work restoring the aircraft. They used parts cannibalized from other non-flyable B-47s at China Lake, and museum aircraft, to complete the project. Though the dated manuals were used for the restoration, all work was performed in accordance with the current Air Force standards.

Seasoned B-47 pilots were selected for the ferry crew. Major General J. D. Moore, an airline captain and Air Force Reservist had logged 3,200 hours in the aircraft. Lieutenant Colonel Dale Wolfe, an FB-111 instructor pilot from the 380th Bombardment Wing at Plattsburgh AFB, was the copilot. He had flown 2,000 hours in the Stratojet. Their most recent B-47 flights had taken place in January 1962 and December 1965, respectively.

When the team approached General Earl T. O'Laughlin, commander of the Air Force Logistics Command, for permission to make the flight, they were denied for safety reasons. Then General Larry D. Welch, CINCSAC, in coordination with the Fifteenth Air Force Commander, Lieutenant General James E. Light, Jr., granted approval; after all this was the 40th anniversary of SAC.

It was far cheaper to fly the aircraft than to truck it. A 1984 estimate determined that to disassemble the aircraft, truck it, and reassemble it at Castle would have cost $183,000. On 17 June 1986 the B-47 made its last flight from China Lake to Castle AFB.

Per Federal Aviation Administration directives, the aircraft was flown gear down at 280 knots, with a maximum altitude of 18,000 feet.

Engine specialists from the 320th BMW, March AFB used this ingenious device to haul a serviceable J47 engine across the ramp to an aircraft in need. The engine and dolly would be properly positioned and the tow bar would be disconnected from the vehicle. Next the men would use the crane end to lift the engine into place. This picture dates from 8 February 1958. (SAC Combat Crew Magazine)

These 321st BMW engine technicians from Pinecastle AFB were performing coordinated maintenance on the No. 1 and 2 engines during the 23-29 August 1954 SAC Bomb Comp. For this event, the B-47s staged out of Barksdale AFB. (SAC Combat Crew Magazine)

After takeoff, the aircraft made a final pass over China Lake and headed towards Bakersfield. Using tried and true IFR (I Follow Roads) procedures, the crew followed Highway 99 to Castle. Shortly after takeoff they lost airspeed indications, and down elevator control was lost. A pair of T-33s joined with the bomber to provide airspeed data.

A series of 45-degree S-turns were made to allow the aircraft to descend to approach altitude. After the 1.5-hour flight, an arrival pass was made at Castle. Without elevator control, pitch could only be maintained by airspeed control. Using prudent airmanship, the crew flew a rectangular approach pattern to better gauge the field. A long final approach to Runway 35 was used to ensure a stabilized flight. The approach was normal until the flaps were extended. Sequentially, the crew lost the left aileron, then both flaperons. At 500 feet, the T-33s broke off leaving the B-47 crew to fend for themselves. A 15- to 20-knot crosswind at 45 degrees came up when the aircraft was only 200 feet above the ground. Rudder inputs induced a Dutch roll and the aircraft set down on the rear main gear first. Immediately Moore deployed the drag chute. This was not the standard B-47 drag chute, but a combination of three F-105 Thunderchief ribbon chutes. Using superior airmanship the crew was able to land the aircraft without further incident. A post-flight inspection revealed that the No. 6 nacelle had scraped the runway. The system failures were in no way attributable to the preflight crew, but were the result of the aircraft languishing in the desert for 20 years.

A 93rd Bombardment Wing insignia was applied to the right side of the nose, denoting its last official assignment, and a tribute to those who made this restoration possible.

Certain field-level jet engine maintenance could be performed at the bomb wing base. These technicians were performing inspections and local repairs before sending the engine back out to the flight line. (USAF 152936AC)

Members of the 22nd BMW, March AFB were installing the nose cone on the No. 6 engine of one of their entrants in the 1955 Bomb Comp that was held on their home turf. It is interesting to note that the sister wing at the base, the 320th BMW, won the Fairchild Trophy that year with their YRB-47B. (SAC Combat Crew Magazine)

At Smoky Hill AFB, these jet engine mechanics were making adjustments on the No. 1 engine of this aircraft in one of the base maintenance docks. Note the engine burner cans located at convenient places around the workstands. (SAC Combat Crew Magazine)

On-wing jet engine maintenance was performed from any position that permitted access. At the forward-most end of the engine was the starter-generator. (SAC Combat Crew Magazine)

Dedicated SAC maintainers worked on the B-47s under all weather conditions. Here the mechanic on the left was wearing a standard issue field parka, while the mechanic to the right was wearing a cold-weather nylon flight parka with its wolverine hood trim. The latter parka was extremely warm and the wolverine fur did not freeze. These parkas were later replaced with lighter weight flight parkas with rabbit fur hood trim because too many enlisted men were being eaten by snow blowers that they could not hear. (SAC Combat Crew Magazine)

Extreme care had to be exercised when aligning and latching the engine cowl panels in place. Note the inlet cowl with its landing light lens resting away from the work area. The Master Sergeant to the extreme right was wearing his low quarter shoes, while the mechanic on top of the engine was wearing brogans. Demarcation of the partial white anti-radiation paint on the belly, outrigger doors, aft engine strut, wing trailing edge, and horizontal tail are clearly shown. (SAC Combat Crew Magazine)

*This B-47E-30-BW (51-5233) assigned to the 341st BMW at Dyess AFB, Texas, careened off the runway during a landing on 24 November 1956. The 341st had begun transitioning into the B-47 on 1 September 1955. The rear view reveals the flaps in a takeoff position, probably configured for a go-around. Neither the approach nor the brake chute compartments were open. Note that the entire left inboard nacelle was ripped from the wing and was facing aft. Note the rudder was deflected to the right, indicating that the crew was attempting to turn the aircraft back onto the runway. The crew appears to have exited through the crew entryway hatch. (USAF)*

*This B-47B-35-BW (51-2151) had touched down to the left of the runway. The crew attempted to correct their alignment and the aircraft careened completely across the runway. They continued along a divergent path from the runway centerline before coming to rest here. Engines No. 2, 3, and 6 had departed the aircraft. Training in the hot bomber resulted in numerous accidents. (USAF)*

*On 8 October 1959 this B-47E-65-BW (51-5248) assigned to the 307th BMW at Lincoln AFB, Nebraska, crashed during a RATO take-off, killing Major Paul R. Ecelbarger, instructor pilot; 1st Lieutenant Joseph R. Morrisey, aircraft commander; Captain Lucian W. Nowlin, navigator; and Captain Theodore Tallmadge, navigator. (USAF)*

## RECONNAISSANCE OPERATIONS

Five SAC strategic reconnaissance wings were equipped with a variety of RB-47s between 1950 and 1966 and flew innumerable peripheral reconnaissance missions of the Soviet Bloc nations. For security reasons, all RB-47 operations were conducted in radio silence although crews monitored certain frequencies for code words that would give them en-route instructions. The tower gave the crew a single green light flash for clearance to start engines. Ten minutes prior to takeoff, the tower gave the crew two green flashes for taxi clearance. Then the tower gave landing clearance to a fictitious aircraft that contained all of the relevant weather data for the crew to calculate their takeoff performance. The RB-47 was taxied to the end of the runway and awaited a steady green light from the tower one minute prior to takeoff. Presidential approval was required for these missions that should have been received one hour prior to launch. If the order did not arrive, the mission proceeded as planned until takeoff time. If the order still did not arrive, the tower gave the crew a steady red light and the mission was cancelled.

All refuelings were also conducted in radio silence. The tanker orbited in a predetermined refueling track, and the RB-47 used its navigational aids and homed in on the tanker's rendezvous beacon. Typically the RB-47 took on fuel early in the run with the aircraft commander flying. Then the copilot would be given a chance to make some practice hook-ups. Near the end of the refueling track, the RB-47 took on its full fuel load. On occasion, the copilot would get the RB-47 into an unusual attitude, scaring the boom operator who would call for an immediate breakaway. Then the tanker scampered away leaving the Stratojet short on fuel. Being radio silent, there was no way for the RB-47 to tell the tanker to come back.

The jet stream has compromised the fuel state of many a flight. One day a KC-135 encountered the jet stream and did not have enough fuel to get into Eielson AFB, Alaska. The RB-47s were always refueled after a mission and sat in an alert configuration. The solution was to launch the RB-47 and reverse refuel the tanker. The pumps on the RB-47 were not designed for high-flow-rate operation; hence the offload was just a bit better than the tankers fuel burn. The two aircraft remained hooked up for over an hour-and-a-half during this mission. Both aircraft landed safely.

On 29 December 1967 SAC retired its last RB-47H (53-4296) from the 55th SRW at Offutt AFB, Nebraska.

### First Soviet Jet Overflight

During the fall of 1952, Major General Frank Armstrong, Commander of the 6th Air Division at MacDill AFB, directed Colonel Donald E. Hillman, Deputy Commander of the 306th BMW, to attend a briefing with him at SAC Headquarters at Offutt AFB. General LeMay personally briefed them. Because of the level of secrecy, the only other key staff personnel involved were Major General John B. Montgomery, Director of Operations, and Brigadier General

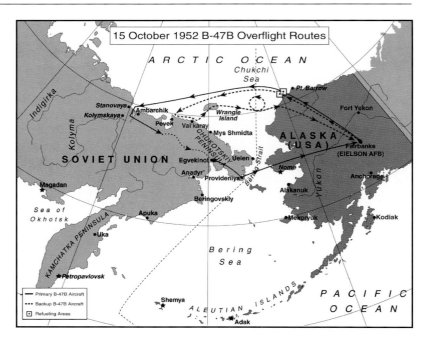

*A map of the route used by Project 52 AFR-18, flown by Colonel Donald E. Hillman.*

James Walsh, Director of Intelligence. Armstrong and Hillman were directed to discuss the matter with no one but themselves. The mission was identified only as Project 52 AFR-18. Because this was the

*Plans for the first Soviet overflight by a B-47 were made in the utmost secrecy. Three of those privy to the information stationed at MacDill AFB were (left to right): Major General Frank Armstrong, 6th AD Commander; Lieutenant Colonel Donald E. Hillman, 306th BMW Deputy Commander; and Lieutenant Colonel Charles Wolfendale. Hillman flew the mission. (Via Colonel Donald E. Hillman)*

first SAC overflight mission of the Soviet Union, a special briefing was held for President Harry S. Truman.

Intelligence reports from several sources indicated that the Soviets were building a number of air bases along the Kamchatka Peninsula that were suitable for bomber operations. At the time the Soviets had the Tu-4 Bull (copy of the B-29). The United States had no suitable reconnaissance aircraft to perform a mission in this area, so a pair of 306th BW B-47Bs was specially modified by the personnel at Wright-Patterson AFB with the installation of a new camera system and radar in the bomb bay.

The plan called for the two B-47s to stage out of Eielson AFB, Alaska. One aircraft was the penetrator; while the other orbited to the north of Siberia outside of Soviet territory to act as a relay. In the event the first aircraft aborted, the second aircraft would conduct the overflight. Intelligence had reported that a MiG 15 regiment was based in the target area and that anti-aircraft artillery could be expected. The B-47 would rely on tactics, aircraft performance, tail guns, ECM, and, most of all, the element of surprise. Two KC-97s were also deployed to Eielson to transport the requisite support personnel and equipment, and to provide refueling for the mission.

Armstrong and Hillman selected all mission and support personnel, which totaled approximately 15 officers and 55 airmen, including the B-47 and KC-97 crews. While the seasoned pilots were selected from the 306th BMW, the navigators were loaned from the 91st SRW at Lockbourne AFB. Camera repair technicians from the 91st were also assigned to the mission. Members of the 544th Recon Tech Squadron based at Offutt AFB provided reece tech support. The flight crews were not briefed on the mission until approval was granted from the Joint Chiefs of Staff (JCS).

Two aircraft participated in Project 52 AFR-18. The first was a B-47B-20-BW (50-073) piloted by Colonel Hillman, with Major Lester E. "Ed" Gunter as copilot and Major Edward A. "Shakey" Timons as navigator. The other was a B-47B-15-BW (50-028) piloted by Colonel Patrick D. Fleming, with Major Lloyd S. "Shorty" Field as copilot, and Major William J. "Red" Reilly as navigator.

On 15 October 1952 both B-47Bs took off and refueled from the waiting tankers. Hillman headed for Wrangel Island, several hundred miles off the north coast of Siberia. He then flew on a southwesterly heading to the penetration point about 500 miles into the Soviet Union. After making landfall, the aircraft headed southeast to appear as if it were a friendly aircraft coming from the western Soviet Union.

With fuel burned off Hillman's B-47 was able to cruise at a respectable airspeed above 40,000 feet. They proceeded over the various targets and took their pictures. During this mission it was learned that the Russians were operating Tu-4 Bulls from airfields at Mys Shmidta and Providenceiya. From these bases, they could make one-way flights from Arctic staging bases on the Chutkosky Peninsula to targets on the North American continent, using a direct route across Alaska. After passing the second target complex, the B-47 crew determined that they were being tracked on Soviet radar. Gunter soon called out that he had visual contact with a MiG 15

*Lieutenant Colonel R. D. Fleming was part of Project WIBAC. When the first jet overflight of the Soviet Union was directed, he flew the backup aircraft. (Boeing P11299)*

climbing towards them. Because their cover had been broken, they called the second B-47 to inform them of the situation. The MiGs never reached the B-47 because of their airspeed and altitude. After completing their eight-hour, 3,500-mile flight, 800 of which were over Soviet territory, the two B-47s returned to Eielson. There, the photo lab immediately began processing the film and making a duplicate set of photographs prior to shipping them to Washington.

On the following day the B-47s crews learned that the Soviets had added another MiG regiment to the area and that the Soviet regional commander had been replaced, presumably for his failure to shoot down the intruder. Six months later Colonel Hillman was reassigned to SAC Headquarters. One day Hillman was called to the boss's office where General LeMay pinned a Distinguished Flying Cross on him. When he saw the puzzled look on Hillman's face, LeMay said with a rare smile: "It's secret."

### Mission to Murmansk

During 1954, American and British leaders became concerned that the Soviets might begin basing their new jet bombers on the Kola Peninsula. Another Soviet overflight was conceived to confirm or deny their suspicions.

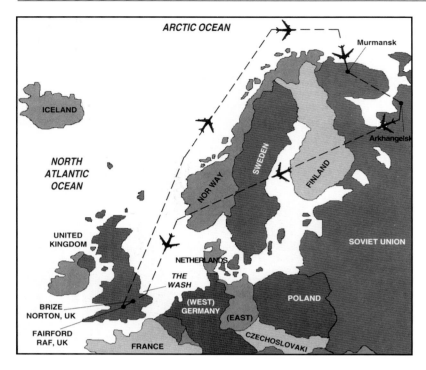

*Flight path used by the 91st SRW mission to Murmansk.*

On 6 May 1954 a feint of seven RB-47Es from the 91st Strategic Reconnaissance Wing at RAF Fairford began taking photographs of the Spitsbergen Islands in northwest Norway, well above 75 degrees north latitude. This feint, unbeknown to the crews, was to set up a mission that was flown on 8 May. Three crews received independent briefings by a pair of SAC colonels from Intelligence. The mission for a crew consisting of Captain Harold "Hal" Austin, Captain Carl Holt, and Major Vance Heavlin was to penetrate Soviet airspace and photograph nine Soviet airfields.

Three RB-47Es took off at 07:00 hours, refueled from KC-97s, and headed toward Norway in a loose cell. When the formation was about 100 miles from Murmansk, two of the aircraft headed back to base. By noon the single RB-47E headed in at an altitude of 40,000 feet and Heavlin turned on his O-15 radar camera and three K-17 large area visual photo cameras. Over each specified airfield target he activated two K-36 cameras with 36-inch focal length lenses for detailed photographs. Their first target consisted of two large airfields near Murmansk. As they were finishing the photo run on the second airfield, the RB-47E was joined by a flight of three MiGs that flew off their wing. About 25 minutes later a flight of six MiGs showed up and were soon joined by two more flights of three MiGs; making a hornets' nest with which the RB-47 had to contend. By then the RB-47E had photographed two more airfields near Arkhangelsk and started heading south towards the last two targets.

The RB-47E had been at 40,000 feet over Soviet territory for about an hour and was indicating a true airspeed of 440 knots. The fighters were not MiG 15s as described by Intelligence – they were MiG 17s. Soon the lead fighter began a firing run on the RB-47E with tracers flashing above and below the reconnaissance aircraft. Austin nosed the RB-47E down and gained about 20 knots of airspeed when the second MiG began its firing run. Holt turned around to activate his guns and began firing on the third MiG. At General LeMay's order, SAC aircraft did not carry tracers. The MiG pilot must have seen the guns tracking as the 20-mm cannon began firing. A fourth MiG made his firing run on the RB-47 and a lucky shot went through the top of the left wing flap, about eight feet from the fuselage. The exploding 23-mm cannon shell knocked out the RB-47's intercom. Suddenly the fighters broke off, presumably due to a lack of fuel. The RB-47 continued toward the coast.

A KC-97 was waiting for the RB-47E near Stavanger, Norway, but when it did not receive a radio transmission, the tanker departed. The fuel state became critical and the RB-47E crew began calling on the command post frequency – the only one that worked. One of their strip alert tanker pilots recognized their broken transmission and tried to get permission from the RAF to launch. Permission was denied because the Brits were engaged in some sort of exercise; the tanker launched anyway and refueled the fuel-starved RB-47E. The RAF station commander threatened the KC-97 pilot with a court-martial and the British air traffic control people filed a violation against him. General LeMay cleared both issues. The general would not let the crew see the photographs, but informed them that they were excellent. During the running gun battle, one of the MiG 17s had tried to ram the bomber and stalled. As it fell away, the cameras got some excellent close-up shots for Intelligence to ponder in their quest for differences between the MiG 15 and MiG 17. General LeMay awarded the entire crew Distinguished Flying Crosses for this mission. LeMay wished he could have given them the Silver Star, but that would have to be approved by Headquarters USAF and they'd screw it up: "I'd have to explain this mission to too damn many people who don't have a need to know. Try explaining two of the same decoration being awarded on the same day for the same event! You better keep a set of orders in your own 201 file."

## Project HOME RUN

Between 21 March and 10 May 1956, SAC RB-47Es flew almost daily reconnaissance sorties over the entire northern slope and interior of the Soviet Union, from the Kola Peninsula to the Bering Strait. Each Project HOME RUN sortie was approximately 3,400 miles long. Brigadier General Hewitt T. Wheless, 801st Air Division Commander, ran the operation. His deputy was Colonel William J. Meng, 26th SRW Commander. Major George A. Brown was HOME RUN's project officer and mission planner. For security reasons, the missions were listed as SAC cold weather tests.

SAC established a special detachment at Thule AB, Greenland, for Project HOME RUN. Two wings provided the requisite RB-47s and two full squadrons of tankers. Support personnel and cargo

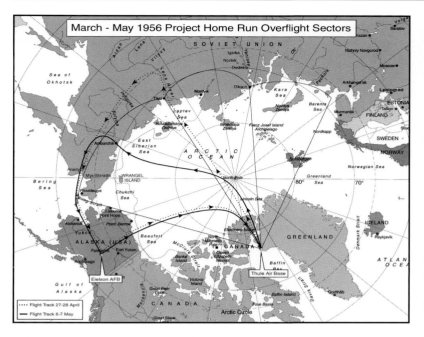

March - May 1956 Project Home Run Overflight Sectors

Flight Track 27-28 April
Flight Track 6-7 May

*This map shows the route used by Captain Harold Austin during his overflight of Project HOME RUN.*

zero temperatures at Thule made it weigh around seven pounds per gallon. Hence the normal fuel load of 98,000 pounds became 107,000 pounds. However, the engines performed far better in the cold, thereby reducing the takeoff distance. Operating an aircraft on a snow-covered airfield is no picnic. The first aircraft creates water out of the snow that immediately turns into ice. Then the following aircraft must negotiate this slippery surface.

For Project HOME RUN, a 3,500-mile area of the Soviet Arctic was divided into three sectors: Kola Peninsula to Dikson, on the Kara Sea; Dikson to Tiski, on the Laptev Sea; and Tiski to the Bering Strait.

The aircraft were usually paired as an RB-47E and an RB-47H for photographic and electronic reconnaissance, respectively. Each formation had one KC-97 to support each reconnaissance aircraft, however, two tankers were sometimes required. Four or five missions were flown daily with rotating aircraft and crews. All missions were flown in daylight, and secrecy required that each RB-47 crew be briefed separately. When flying together, the RB-47Hs trailed the RB-47Es and recorded the radar transmissions. The RB-47Hs also flew solo missions outside of Soviet airspace lighting up their defenses and recording their radar transmissions.

from the two wings were sent via Douglas C-124 Globemaster IIs provided by SAC strategic support squadrons from the Fifteenth Air Force. Including aircrews, the 55th Strategic Reconnaissance Wing deployed 115 personnel.

In preparation for deploying to Thule, in March 1956 the 55th SRW sent its flight crews, crew chiefs, and a senior maintenance supervisor to Lockbourne AFB for a week of arctic indoctrination. A bit later, their arrival at Thule was a real eye opener. With the -35 to -40 degree Fahrenheit temperatures and the potential for 60- to 70-knot winds, survival training became essential. Upon arriving at Thule, they were given further training that included two nights of sleeping outdoors. Survival instructors preached that meat was the best way to stay alive in the frozen north; hence steak three times a day became the norm. Small survival shacks with food and medical supplies were located all over Thule in case one was caught outside during a sudden white out.

Forty-eight aircraft were assigned to HOME RUN. Sixteen RB-47Es came from the 10th SRS, 26th SRW, at Lockbourne AFB. Four RB-47Hs came from the 343rd SRS, 55th SRW, at Forbes AFB. The 26th ARS from the 26th SRW at Lockbourne and the 55th ARS from the 55th SRW at Forbes contributed 28 KC-97 tankers.

The arriving aircrews spent their first week undergoing arctic survival training and practiced flight operations on the ice-covered runways and taxiways, polar navigation, air refueling, and radio-silence operations. While the North Pole was only one flying-hour away, the nearest alternate base was Goose Bay, Labrador, some 1,200 miles away.

Jet fuel weighs about six pounds per gallon; however, the sub-

*This 301st BMW fuel specialist was using the single-point hydrant system for refueling a B-47E-50-LM (53-3357). Note the ground wire plugged into the jack above and aft of the refueling nozzle. The airman on the headset was in contact with someone in the cockpit who was monitoring the fuel gauges. (USAF 158885AC)*

During a REFLEX deployment to RAF Chelveston in early 1959, the 301st BMW, 32nd BS was short a copilot, so 1st Lieutenant Augustine "Gus" Letto from the 353rd BS was sent to fill the slot. Here "Gus," in a blue hat, was flanked by the 32nd BS crew he supported who wore their red hats. The pilot wore a leather flying jacket, Letto had a nylon jacket with a fur collar, while the navigator's jacket had a knit collar. The crew wore leather gloves with wool inserts. Behind them was one of the British Bedford trucks that served as an alert vehicle. The truck had a right-hand drive that was awkward for American personnel. They brought their own support vehicles for subsequent wing deployments. For the REFLEX missions, all ground support equipment was assigned to the resident combat support group. (Augustine "Gus" Letto)

These shiny new International double-cab trucks served as alert crew vehicles at RAF Brize Norton during 1962. The lettering on the right side of the bumper read SAC BNAFB – the Brits either didn't notice the AFB or chose to ignore it. (Augustine "Gus" Letto)

The first mission on 5 April 1956 was inauspicious. While four RB-47Es and two RB-47Hs took off on schedule and arrived at the air refueling rendezvous point on time, only two of the KC-97s were there. Five or six other tankers were either late or had aborted. General Wheless cancelled the mission. It was learned that two complete tanker crews and several individuals from other tanker crews missed the pre-flight briefing. After a serious reprimand by Colonel Meng, the mission was rescheduled and the tanker squadron commander was instructed to order all of his crews to attend the briefings.

The second mission was scheduled, however, once again several tanker crews had something more important to do and missed the briefing. Colonel Meng arrived and was advised of the absentees. He concurred with the briefers' delay and departed, but the tanker squadron commander was again on the receiving end of Meng's anger. The derelict tanker crews finally appeared and the briefing commenced. All aircraft got off on schedule and the requisite refuelings were completed on time.

All of the Project HOME RUN missions were flown under radio-silent conditions. The tankers departed about two hours ahead of the RB-47s and headed towards the refueling rendezvous points. Then the RB-47s took off and the RB-47 navigator would acquire the tanker's rendezvous beacon and direct his aircraft to the tanker. The RB-47, which would descend to about 15,000 feet to meet the tanker, flew at Mach 0.74. At approximately four minutes out, the RB-47 was flying 100 knots faster than the tanker. Each minute the RB-47 would bleed off 25 knots to arrive at the pre-contact position at the same speed as the tanker. As much as 20,000 pounds of fuel would be transferred during the refueling. For the longer missions, two tankers would off load fuel to the RB-47s.

Captain John Lappo caused a stir during one of the missions when he was 45 minutes late returning to base. At the command post, Major Lloyd Field, 10th SRS Commander, Colonel Meng, and General Wheless were getting nervous. Wheless finally said: "Lloyd, let's break radio silence. I want you to call John and see how and where he is." Major Field got on the radio and asked: "John, how much fuel do you have?" Captain Lappo replied: "I have enough." After a repeat of these transmissions, Field asked: "John, how many pounds of fuel do you have?" The reply was: "I have 8,000 pounds." SAC regulations stipulated that a B-47 on the ramp could have no less than 8,000 pounds of fuel. In flight, the B-47 burned about 6,600 pounds of fuel per hour. Now came the crucial question: "John, how far are you from the base?" The response was "Forty-five minutes." When asked if he wanted a tanker, the answer was no, and Lappo advised that if he missed the tanker he would really be in trouble. Lappo landed on fumes. At the debriefing he was asked what had happened and Lappo said that the weather obscured the target and he missed it on the first pass. He circled back for a second try and got the photos. He commented that in his opinion there was no need to send another aircraft to the target another day. General Wheless commented: "Captain Lappo, I wish I had an air division of pilots like you." Lappo received the Distinguished Flying Cross for his actions that day. Regardless of the fact that the mission was successful, General LeMay received a letter of reprimand from Air Force Vice Chief of Staff, General Thomas D. White, for not following instructions and the risk it entailed. Only one secretary in the office had a clearance to type the letter. General White signed the letter and told Colonel Roger Rhodarmer, from the Office of the Deputy Chief of Staff, Operations, to fly out to Omaha and hand-deliver the eyes-only letter. White also quipped: "You'd better wear your iron suit."

A long mission was flown on 27 and 28 April 1956 when a flight of RB-47s took off from Thule and flew straight towards Tiski near the mouth of the Lena River, which they followed until heading east to fly over Indigirka and Koiyma. They exited near Anadyr and recovered at Eielson AFB, Alaska. On the following day they returned to Thule.

The final HOME RUN mission was flown on 6 and 7 May 1956. The RB-47Hs were redeployed to Forbes AFB while a formation of six RB-47Es took off from Thule, crossed the North Pole, and entered Soviet airspace near Ambarchik. The aircraft flew in a line-abreast formation and headed south at 40,000 feet. They turned towards the east and exited Soviet airspace at Anadyr near the Bering Strait. The aircraft recovered at Eielson AFB where they remained overnight before returning to Thule the next day.

The detachment flew a total of 156 missions from Thule. Excepting the first, not one mission was missed. This was a testament to the aircrews that operated from a 10,000-foot ice and fog covered runway and the maintenance personnel who worked in subzero temperatures on the open ramp. No aircraft were lost during Project HOME RUN.

### Operation TEXAS STAR

Like its bomber brethren, the 55th Strategic Reconnaissance Wing flew a number of TEXAS STAR missions between 1959 and 1963. During January 1959 the 3920th Combat Support Group at RAF Brize Norton began to provide logistical support for RB-47H operations of the 55th SRW under Operation TEXAS STAR. The first two RB-47Hs arrived on 5 January to provide overseas ELINT support for SAC operations in the theater. KC-97s deployed from the 55th Air Refueling Squadron provided the air refueling support for these missions. Aircraft and crews were on a 90-day rotational schedule. Operation TEXAS STAR missions were flown from operating locations at RAF Brize Norton, England, Yokota AB, Japan, Eielson AFB, Alaska, and Incirlik AB, Turkey.

For security reasons, all unclassified correspondence during the operations identified the aircraft as B-47s, not RB-47s. Operation TEXAS STAR was an unclassified codename.

### Operation COMMON CAUSE – The Cuban Missile Crisis

Some SAC reconnaissance units were heavily involved in the Cuban Missile Crisis, which was known as Operation COMMON CAUSE. Of importance were the U-2s flown by the 4080th SRW, and RB-47s from the 55th SRW. While the 4080th had been deployed to

B-47E-135-BW, s/n 53-6244, was the last B-47E produced. It was assigned to the 307th BMW as identified by its wing insignia displayed on the right side of the nose. (Robert Joe Loffredo)

MacDill AFB from Davis-Monthan AFB, the 55th SRW operated from its home base at Forbes AFB or from Kindley AFB, Puerto Rico, where a number of aircraft had been forward deployed. To place the RB-47s closer to the action, some 55th SRW aircraft were redeployed to MacDill AFB. RF-101A Voodoos from the Tactical Air Command and Navy F-8 Crusaders also flew reconnaissance missions over Cuba.

The RB-47Hs flew ferret missions to obtain SIGnals INTelligence (SIGINT) data on the Soviet radar and communications systems located on Cuba. RB-47Ks, while configured for weather reconnaissance, retained all of the photographic capabilities of the RB-47Es that had long-since been retired. These aircraft carried a fourth crewmember that used a hand-held camera to shoot through the canopy. The additional crewmember may have been a photographic specialist, a crew chief, or a skilled amateur photographer. It was one of these aircraft that detected a Soviet ship carrying missiles on its deck.

Flying during the Cuban Missile Crisis was an agonizing ordeal for the RB-47H and RB-47K crews that flew several missions per day. Informally, they renamed the mission Operation LOST CAUSE. On a typical day, the crews attended a briefing at 08:00 hours, followed by mission planning. After the crew briefed the staff around 14:00, they were freed for crew rest around 15:00. The crew returned to preflight their aircraft around 21:00 hours. The primary crew took off at 01:40 for a boring 12-hour mission. If the primary crew aborted within the first four hours of the mission, a secondary crew was launched. If the secondary crew were fortunate, they would be relieved at 07:00 – making for a 24-hour duty day. It became extremely grueling if the secondary crew was launched because they had already been up for 18 hours and then faced a 12-hour mission.

After takeoff, the RB-47 would head towards New Orleans where they met a tanker to top-off for their long mission. The Stratojet would set up an orbit over the island of Cuba. The first circuit was usually uneventful. During subsequent orbits, they were subject to anti-aircraft fire, like that that brought down Major Rudolph Anderson flying a U-2 on 27 October 1962. After the shoot down, the Cubans were sure another incident would provoke an invasion; hence the reconnaissance birds were never fired upon again. In addition, they never made any transmissions that the SIGINT aircraft could gather.

The 55th SRW lost three aircraft during this period.

On 27 September 1962 an RB-47K (553-4327) lost power on the No. 6 engine during takeoff from Forbes AFB and crashed. The cause was contaminated water-alcohol in the assisted-takeoff system. All four crewmembers: Lieutenant Colonel James Woolbright, aircraft commander; First Lieutenant Paul Greenwalt, copilot; Captain Bruce Kowol, navigator; and S/Sgt. Myron Curtis, crew chief, were killed. This is the aircraft that spotted the Soviet freighter with missiles on its deck earlier in the day.

On 27 October 1962 an RB-47H (53-6248) experienced continual loss of thrust and crashed at Kindley AFB, also because of contaminated water-alcohol, killing all four crewmembers: Major William A. Britton, aircraft commander; First Lieutenant Holt J. Rasmussen, copilot; Captain Robert A. Constable, navigator; and Captain Robert C. Dennis, observer.

On 11 November 1962 an RB-47H (53-4297) crashed at MacDill AFB killing all three crewmembers: Captain William E. Wyatt, aircraft commander; Captain William C. Maxwell, copilot; and First Lieutenant Rawl, navigator. The aircraft lost power on an outboard engine, rolled, and crashed within the confines of the base.

RB-47H crews from the 55th SRW continued to fly surveillance missions over Cuba for several months after the Soviets had agreed to

*Mobile air police patrolled the flight line and were in constant contact with the command post with their 2-way radio. They not only ensured flight line safety and security, but also were an integral part of the overall SAC EWO. (SAC Combat Crew Magazine)*

remove the weapons from the island nation. With only a cockpit crew, and maybe a fourth man observer/photographer, they monitored the withdrawal of the missiles carried on the decks of the ships until the United States was sure all had been accounted for.

## Operation GYPSY FIDDLE

The 55th SRW was routinely tasked by the Second Air Force as part of Operation GYPSY FIDDLE to provide photography of the continental United States as directed by the Department of the Interior.

On the evening of 27 March 1964 a large earthquake occurred in Alaska, and the following day Headquarters USAF directed SAC to conduct aerial reconnaissance of the damage. A pair of B-58s from the 43rd BMW at Carswell AFB was tasked with this low-level mission. Within two hours of notification, the aircraft departed with their special reconnaissance pods attached on the centerline pylon. Their round-trip flight covered 5,751 miles, and overflew Gulkana, Valdez, Seward, Whittier, Kodiak, and Anchorage.

On the same day SAC also dispatched two RB-47Ks from the 55th SRW stationed at Forbes AFB and three U-2s from the 4080th SRW from Davis-Monthan AFB to perform high-level photography of the quake area. Within 14.5 hours SAC had processed the film from the RB-47s, B-58s, and U-2s, and had photographs of the quake area available in Washington, D.C. The last GYPSY FIDDLE mission was flown on 5 May 1964. Less than 10 of these missions were flown in any given month.

## Operation IRON WORK

During Operation IRON WORK, EB-47E(TT)s would gather information on Soviet missile launches from the Tyuratam space center and the missile test center at Kapustin Yar. The aircraft were deployed to Turkey in pairs so that one could fly as the primary aircraft while the other stood by as a backup. The second crew sat in their aircraft for the first hour with the engines running in case they had to make an immediate launch. Then they would shut down and remain near the aircraft for another three hours, serving as a backup for the flying aircraft. If the first aircraft aborted on the ground or in the air, the second aircraft was launched.

Between 15 and 23 December 1965 the 55th SRW deployed a pair of EB-47E(TT)s and an RB-47H to Incirlik with a cover mission of air-sea rescue for a missing RB-57. During this period, the three aircraft logged 274.6 hours of flying time during clandestine missions to gather data on the Soviet launches.

On 3 April 1955 an EB-47E(TT) (53-2320) from the 55th SRW was on an electronic surveillance mission along the Soviet border, and fought a running gun battle with MiG fighters. Upon returning to Turkey, the aircraft was attempting to land at Incirlik, while a second EB-47E(TT) was held from taking off because of high crosswinds. The airborne aircraft orbited until the winds abated and the aircraft was cleared to land. During the approach the winds changed again, but the crew was not notified. Immediately after touch down the aircraft was blown off the side of the runway. The pilot attempted a go-around, but an outboard engine contacted the ground, ingested dirt, and flamed-out. The aircraft bounced into the air, lost control, and it was blown 90-degrees to the runway. The ensuing fire consumed the aircraft. Captain Gary L. Jacobs, the navigator, died in the crash. Major Walter E. Savage, the aircraft commander, suffered a ruptured diaphragm. Raven Two, Captain Albert T. Parsons, was critically burned and later died of his injuries. The copilot, Captain John W. Dubyak, and Raven One, Captain Barry L. Hammond, escaped without injury.

The Soviets became enraged upon learning that Turkey provided a forward operating location for Tell Twos and threatened retaliatory action against the Turks. The flight and maintenance crews of the 55th had departed before they were asked to leave on 24 December 1965. By then it was a moot point, because the crews of the 55th SRW had gained the sought-after data.

The 6th SRW at Eielson AFB flew RC-135s for the LISA ANN mission from their forward operating location at Shemya AFB on the far end of the Aleutian chain. The LISA ANN mission involved both electronic and optical tracking of Soviet missile tests. To meet regularly scheduled maintenance programs, these aircraft were taken out of service and returned to Tinker AFB. To bridge the gap in 1966, the 55th SRW dispatched an EB-47E(TT) to fly the missions. Whereas the RC-135 was equipped for both photographic and electronic surveillance, the mission was degraded because the Tell Twos only had an electronics capability.

Tell Twos also were deployed to Wheelus AB, Libya, to perform surveillance work during the Arab-Israeli Six-Day War in June 1967. The EB-47E(TT)s were retired from service late in 1967 and the 338th SRS was stood down on 25 December 1957.

### RB-47E Shoot down

In 1955, the 26th SRW deployed RB-47Es to Eielson AFB for cold weather training and peripheral reconnaissance of the Soviet Union. One YRB-47B-25-BW (51-2054) from the 4th SRS flew a peripheral reconnaissance mission along the Kamchatka Peninsula on 18 April 1955. Soviet radars began tracking the aircraft around 09:40 local time, with the aircraft located in the vicinity of Cape Lopatka at the southern end of the peninsula. The aircraft was reported to be 43 miles southeast of Cape Vasliev at 10:57 hours. Soviet records indicate that the aircraft had not violated their borders.

Two MiG 15s from the Soviet Istrebitel'naya Aviasta Protivovozdushnoi Oborony (IA-PVO) [fighter aviation/anti-air defense] intercepted the aircraft at 11:25 hours and shot it down about 32 miles east of Cape Kronotski. The crewmembers were Major Lacie C. Neighbors, Captain Robert N. Brooks, and Captain Richard E. Watkins, Jr. A search for the aircraft and crew by the 3rd and 10th Air Rescue Groups was not successful. While the Air Force contended that it was a routine weather reconnaissance flight at the time, in 1992

Here 13 B-47s from the 320th BMW flew over Dayton, Ohio, en route on a non-stop redeployment from RAF Brize Norton to March AFB, California. This flight was accomplished in under 15 hours. The wing's deployment was between 5 June and 4 September 1954. (Boeing P14681)

it was acknowledged that the aircraft was on an intelligence-gathering mission. At the time of the incident, the Soviets knew that the Americans were searching in the wrong sector. Members of the Soviet Border Guard had recovered aircraft parts, a life vest, topographical maps of Chikhota and Alaska, and portions of the aircraft manuals. These items were turned over to the Soviet military intelligence organization (GRU). There was no mention of survivors.

### RB-47H Shoot down

On 1 July 1960 the 55th SRW dispatched an RB-47H (53-4281) from RAF Brize Norton on a surveillance mission from which it never returned; it was shot down while flying over the Barents Sea.

*Unwanted company was always a possibility for crews of the 55th SRW. This a belly shot of a MiG-17 Fresco C that was pulling away from a 55th SRW. RB-47 reveals its long nose cannon. (Via Bruce M. Bailey)*

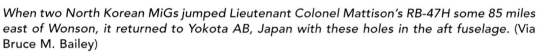

*When two North Korean MiGs jumped Lieutenant Colonel Mattison's RB-47H some 85 miles east of Wonson, it returned to Yokota AB, Japan with these holes in the aft fuselage. (Via Bruce M. Bailey)*

The aircraft was crewed by Major Willard G. Palm, Captain Eugene E. Posa, Lieutenant John R. McKone, Lieutenant Dean B. Phillips, Freeman B. Olmstead, and Lieutenant Oscar L. Goforth.

This mission was flown just two months after CIA pilot Francis Gary Powers was shot down in his U-2 while overflying Russia. Meetings were held at the UN Security Council where U.S. Ambassador Henry Cabot Lodge argued in defense of the aircrew and accused the Soviet Union of air piracy. Finally, on 28 January 1961, McKone and Olmstead were released from the infamous Lubyanka Prison. Major Palm's body was also released and he was buried at Arlington National Cemetery with full military honors. The bodies of Goforth, Phillips, and Posa were not recovered.

### More Hostile Action

Another 55th SRW RB-47 was flying a mission off the coast of Korea on 28 April 1965 when it was attacked by a pair of North Korean MiG 17s. At the time of the incident, the RB-47H Silver King (with the AN/ALD-4 pod installed) (53-4290) was flying 50 miles over the Sea of Japan, paralleling the coastline near Wonsan, North Korea. The two MiGs jumped the Stratojet without warning. The copilot returned fire but saw no hits. During his last visual contact he reported seeing one of the fighters coming through a cloud layer in a high-speed dive.

The RB-47H sustained damage from the cannon rounds. Two engines were lost and a third was only delivering partial power. Hydraulics and other systems were also damaged. Fuel tanks in the waist were holed, as was the aft fuselage. Fuel drained from the damaged tanks causing a severe nose-heavy condition. Lowering the flaps for landing would have only exacerbated the condition, so the crew elected to make a high-speed, no-flap landing at Yokota AB,

Japan. No crewmembers were injured during the attack and they landed without incident. The aircraft was subsequently scrapped. The crew consisted of Lieutenant Colonel Hobert D. Mattison, aircraft commander; First Lieutenant Henry E. Dubuy, Jr., copilot; Captain Robert A. Rogers, navigator; Captain Robert C. Winters, electronic warfare supervisor (R1); First Lieutenant George V. Beck, electronics warfare officer (R2); and First Lieutenant Joel J. Lutkenhouse, electronics warfare officer (R3).

### B-47 ECM UNITS

| Capsule | Wing/Squadron | Years |
|---|---|---|
| Phase IV ECM | 376th BMW | 1954-1966 |
| | 512th BS | 1954-1964 |
| | 513th BS | 1954-1965 |
| | 514th BS | 1954-1961 |
| | 515th BS | 1954-1966 |
| Phase V ECM (Blue Cradle) | 301st BMW | 1957-1964 |
| | 32nd BS | 1958-1964 |
| | 321st BS | 1957-1964 |
| | 352nd BS | 1958-1964 |
| | 419th BS | 1957-1964 |

These two wings were equipped with EB-47Es. While the 376th was at Barksdale AFB, Louisiana, until 1957, both wings were assigned to Lockbourne AFB, Ohio, between 1957 and 1966.

## KNOWN RB-47 LOSSES TO HOSTILE ACTION

| Date | Type | Serial No. | Unit | Location | Crew | KIA | MIA | Note |
|------|------|-----------|------|----------|------|-----|-----|------|
| 18 Apr 55 | YRB-47B | 51-2054 | 26th SRW | Off Kamchatka Peninsula | 3 | | 3 | 1 |
| 1 July 60 | RB-47H | 53-4281 | 55th SRW | Barents Sea | 6 | 4 | 2 | 2 |
| 27 Sept 62 | RB-47K | 53-4279 | 55th SRW | Kindley AFB, Puerto Rico | 4 | 4 | - | 3 |
| 27 Sept 62 | RB-47H | 53-6248 | 55th SRW | Kindley AFB, Puerto Rico | 4 | 4 | - | 3 |
| 11 Nov 62 | RB-47H | 53-4297 | 55th SRW | MacDill AFB, Fla. | 3 | 3 | - | 3 |
| 3 Apr 65 | EB-47E (TT) | 53-2320 | 55th SRW | Incirlik, Turkey | 6 | 4 | - | 4 |
| 27 Apr 65 | RB-47H | 53-4290 | 55th SRW | Near Korea | 6 | - | - | 5 |

Known RB-47 losses due to hostile action during the Cold War are shown in this table. Notes: 1. Shot down while on a PARPRO mission off Kamchatka Peninsula. 2. Aircraft shot down and crew interned in USSR. 3. Operational losses associated with the Cuban Missile Crisis. 4. Fought a running gun battle with MiGs and crashed on landing. 5. Fought a running gun battle with MiGs and managed a safe landing at Yokota AB.

## WEATHER OPERATIONS

The Air Weather Service (AWS) was part of the Military Air Transport Service (MATS). However, the initial cadre of WB-47 aircrews came from SAC and began their WB-47 training at McClellan AFB, California, in July 1963. Instruction was provided by both the WB-47 Maintenance Training Detachment (MTD) and 55th WRS. Classes for the pilots included courses in hydraulics, heating and pressurization, special equipment, weather observing, and the new AMQ-19 MET system. Navigators received instruction in the APN-102 Doppler navigation system, PN-70 LORAN system, mission requirements, special equipment, performance charts, grid navigation, weather observing, AMQ-19 MET system, and log and chart procedures.

An S-6A flight simulator was shipped from SAC's 4347th CCTW at McConnell AFB to McClellan for use as a proficiency and emergency procedures trainer by the 55th WRS. Upon completion of MTD training at McClellan AFB, the 777A MTD departed for Japan to conduct WB-47 training for the 54th and 56th WRSs at Johnson AB. The 53rd WRS received its training at Hunter AFB.

Unclassified nicknames were applied to the various types of Air Weather Service missions to provide easy recognition of the mission while retaining their security.

**ARC LIGHT** – Weather reconnaissance missions flown in support of B-52 bombing missions in Southeast Asia.

**CREW CUT** – Low to maximum altitude atmospheric sampling at various latitudes between 45 degrees south and 75 degrees north. On 20 December 1967 this mission was renamed COLD CUT.

**DD** – Weather reconnaissance missions flown in support of Department of Defense commitments to various treaty organizations such as NATO.

**DELTA LARK** – This was a daily weather track flown between McClellan AFB and Eielson AFB, Alaska.

**GEMINI** – Weather reconnaissance missions flown in support of the Project Gemini manned space program.

**HURRICANE & TYPHOON** – Weather reconnaissance and tracking of tropical storms.

**LOON ALPHA** – These weather reconnaissance missions were flown from Clark AB, Philippines, in support of B-52 refueling during ARC LIGHT operations. The WB-47s flew two tracks – one approximately 200 miles north of Luzon and the other 200 miles south of the island. These missions were limited to seven hours because the in-flight refueling system on the WB-47s had been inactivated.

**MILROW** – During the third quarter of 1968, the 9th WRW provided support for an underground nuclear detonation on Amchitka Island in the Aleutian Islands. The entire operation was classified.

**PTARMIGAN** – A ptarmigan is an arctic bird for which the mission was named. This was one of the oldest flying missions for the Air Weather Service, starting with WB-29s on 7 March 1947. The mission was modified to better fit the WB-47's capabilities and, under no-wind conditions, could be flown in 5 hours and 20 minutes. On 20 December 1967 this mission was renamed STORK ROUTE to meet the new computer spacing requirements of the National Weather Service.

**CLAY FEET** – In early 1966 the 55th WRS initiated weather reconnaissance of the Western Pacific areas using two WC-130s from the 54th WRS deployed to Ubon AB, Thailand, WB-47s operating from Clark AB, Philippines, and WC-135s from the 56th WRS based at Yokota AB, Japan.

### WB-47 Accidents

Considering the missions, the WB-47s had a remarkable safety record during their 13 years of Air Weather Service operations, with only five major accidents.

The first Air Weather Service Stratojet accident occurred in 1963 when a WB-47E-60-BW (51-2420) assigned to the 55th WRS crashed

*Ye Ole Turkey was a B-47B-40-BW (51-1225) from the 306th BMW. The aircraft was taxiing out for the return flight during Operation SKY TRY. (USAF)*

at Lajes AB, Azores. The aircraft was en route to Tripoli, Libya, and ran low on fuel. Four engines were shut down and a two-engine landing was attempted through an overcast at night. While considered crew error, there were extenuating circumstances. The N-1 compass malfunctioned, allowing the crew to become lost. This extended the flight time and placed them in a serious fuel state. To make matters worse, only the No. 1 and No. 4 engines were operating, causing an asymmetrical condition from which the pilot could not recover. The right wing struck the ground during landing. The copilot ejected during touchdown and was the only crewmember to sustain injuries.

The second occurred in April 1964 when a WB-47E-65-BW (51-7049) assigned to the Det. 1 of the 55th WRS crashed at Eielson AFB. The aircraft was attempting a takeoff on a PTARMIGAN mission when it crashed and was destroyed by fire. Both pilots managed to egress the aircraft and suffered burns on their hands and faces; the two navigators and a special equipment operator were killed.

A WB-47E-55-BW (51-2397) assigned to Det. 2 of the 53rd WRS, crashed at Ramey AFB, Puerto Rico, on 5 December 1966.

Another WB-47E-55-BW (51-2366) was assigned to the 55th WRS when the forward main landing gear collapsed on landing at Clark AB in the Philippines. Inspection revealed that the damage was beyond local repair capabilities and the aircraft was scrapped on-site. This accident occurred on 20 June 1967.

On 26 February 1968 a WB-47E-55-BW (51-2373) assigned to the 57th WRS at Hickam AFB, Hawaii, was involved in an accident with a Cessna 140. The Stratojet was practicing tough-and-go landings when the tower cleared a Cessna (registry N2929N) to hold on the active runway. With its engine idling, the light plane was struck by the WB-47, with the former sustaining substantial damage. Minor damage was inflicted on the Stratojet. The accident report concluded that there was insufficient visual opportunity for the WB-47 to see and avoid the Cessna, and tower personnel failed to advise either aircraft of the traffic. The WB-47 was subsequently retired to Davis-Monthan AFB in October 1969.

## WB-47 Disposal

The Air Force was directed to reduce its FY70 budget by $1 billion as part of the DoD's $3 billion total. A decision to eliminate 209 aircraft included retiring the 24 remaining WB-47s from the Air Weather Service. The announcement came as a complete shock at the 25 August 1969 Air Weather Service morning reconnaissance briefing. Major General Russell K. Pierce, Air Weather Service Commander, stated that he believed that this order stemmed from General John D. Ryan, then USAF Vice Chief of Staff, who had questioned the extent of weather reconnaissance support needed for the ARC LIGHT missions. (General Ryan had been CINCSAC between 1 December 1964 and 31 January 1967. Earlier he had commanded SAC wings equipped with B-36s and B-50s.)

The accelerated departure of these aircraft from the Air Weather Service inventory occurred between 7 September and 30 October 1969. One WB-47E (51-7066) departed Hickam AFB, Hawaii, for McClellan AFB on 29 October, and on the following day was flown to Boeing Field in Seattle where it was released to the Pacific Northwest Aviation Historical Foundation (since renamed the Museum of Flight) for permanent display.

## FLIGHT CHECKING

The Airways & Air Communications Service (AACS) resulted from the 11 September 1946 redesignation of the Air Communications Service and was responsible for all Air Force communications and navigation facilities. On 1 June 1948 the AACS was reassigned from the former Air Transport Command to the newly formed Military Air Transport Service (MATS). AACS was further redesignated Air Force Communications Service (AFCS) on 1 July 1961, and was relieved of subordination to MATS and elevated to major command status.

With the large influx of jet aircraft into the Air Force inventory during the 1950s a perplexing problem regarding safe navigation and flow control within the airways arose. During 1955 SAC alone had 205 piston-powered B-36s and 1,104 jet-powered aircraft – 1,086 B-47s and 18 B-52s in its inventory. Operating large numbers of dissimilarly performing aircraft in the same airspace presented monumental challenges. In the January through June 1955 history of AFCS, historian Louis B. Jones, stated:

"AACS was at a loss in its development of navigational aids and control procedures for high-flying conventional and jet aircraft without knowledge of exactly how the navigational aids would perform at high altitudes. Falling behind in the development of navigational aids and control procedures for these fast, high-flying modern aircraft would be much like the development of adequate highway systems lagging far behind the development of the automobile."

The Civil Aeronautics Agency (CAA) – predecessor of the Federal Aviation Administration (FAA) – had no jet aircraft capable of performing facility flight checking; hence the task fell to the Air Force.

Under guidance provided by Air Force Regulation 80.14, the AACS and the Air Proving Ground Command began evaluating the multitude of ground-based navigational facilities operated both by AACS and the CAA. The Air Proving Ground Command published the initial test directive. This directive was entitled *High-Speed, High-Altitude Evaluation of Ground Navigational Aids*, but was generally called the *B-47 Flight Check Project* or *High Altitude Project*. The objectives were to evaluate air traffic control procedures and recommend new procedures as required, determine the capabilities of ground navigational aids at altitudes between 20,000 and 40,000 feet, and develop high-altitude flight checking procedures to supplement the low-level procedures already in existence. The existing low-altitude flight checks were conducted by C-47s and C-54s operated by the CAA.

Project planners originally estimated that 12 months would be required to complete the project, but a combination of inclement weather and aircraft availability severely hampered the program. The sole high-performance aircraft assigned to the project was constantly down for modification and maintenance. In June 1955 mission responsibility was transferred to the AACS, and the Air Proving Ground Command withdrew from the project.

Two sets of navigation materials for pilots came out of the project. A set of full color, low-altitude charts was already in existence and used for flights below 18,000 feet. A new set of jet navigation charts was developed for altitudes between 18,000 and 40,000 feet. In addition, a set of airfield approach plates was developed and tailored for the higher speeds used by jet aircraft.

To provide continual checks of the navigation aids, the AACS operated two different B-47s, one at a time, between 1955 and 1962. The aircraft were assigned to the 1800th Airways and Air Communications Wing at Tinker AFB. The first aircraft was a B-47B-10-BW (50-017) that arrived at Tinker on 5 June 1955 after having been fitted with a suite of navigation flight check equipment.

During November 1955 the AACS celebrated its 17th anniversary and sponsored an aircraft-naming contest. Staff Sergeant Dale E. Icke from the 3rd AACS Squadron (Mobile) submitted the winning entry – *The Navaider*. The name was applied to the B-47B and Icke's wife had the honor of breaking a bottle of seawater on the aircraft's nose during the celebration. A $25 U.S. Savings Bond was awarded to Sergeant Icke and he subsequently went on an orientation flight. The aircraft was subsequently modified into a TB-47B as part of Project EBB TIDE.

The second aircraft was a B-47B-30-BW (52-2120) that had been delivered to the 3520th Flying Training Wing at McConnell AFB in May 1953. It served as a transition trainer until June 1956 when it was transferred to the 1800th AACW at Tinker. Shortly after its arrival, the aircraft was named *Sweet Marie*. During the late 1950s she was renamed *The Sooner*, in deference to Oklahoma that is known as the Sooner State. On 9 October 1962 Captain John C. Kwortnik flew the B-47 from Tinker to Whiteman AFB where it was reassigned to the 340th BMW. This aircraft was stricken from the active inventory on 20 March 1963, and was placed on permanent display at the base museum. Five Lockheed C-140 Jetstars replaced the B-47 in the flight check role.

*This B-47B-30-BW (52-2120), later named* Sweet Marie, *was assigned to the 1800th AACW at Tinker AFB, Oklahoma, where it served as a flight check aircraft. Painted overall Gloss White, the aircraft had a Day-Glo Red lightning bolt, edged in black, running the length of the fuselage. A MATS insignia was applied to the waist. (OCAMA Historian)*

The GAM-63 missile was suspended at a slight angle on the YDB-47E's pylon. Note that the tip of the folded ventral fin was below the main gear axle. (Boeing P14229)

# Chapter 9

# *EXPERIMENTAL STRATOJETS*

The 1950s were filled with experimentation. Fears generated by the Cold War drove Congress to authorize funds for a wide variety of defense-related aerospace projects. While at times these expenditures appeared to be being spent on dead-end projects, the information gleaned from each program permitted a leapfrogging of technology to ever-higher levels. Spin-offs from these projects not only enhanced military programs, but also opened up a profusion of concepts that had civilian and humanitarian benefits.

## YB/RB-47C

Initial work for the B-47C (Boeing Model 450-24-26) began in Seattle under contract AF33(038)-12883, Work Order 9329, dated 17 May 1950. This contract covered preliminary design, mock-up construction, and detailed development work.

The early versions of the Stratojet were all severely underpowered, and in pursuit of a more powerful Stratojet, Boeing proposed the Model 450-19-10 powered by four 9,700-lbf Allison J35-A-23 engines mounted in single nacelles. The design was subsequently redesignated YB-56 because of its different engine configuration. A reconnaissance version, known as the RB-56A, was also planned. For a time, the YB-56 was intended to be the definitive Stratojet. According to the original planning, the 88th B-47B (50-092) was scheduled for conversion to the YB-56 configuration.

Supplemental Agreement #9 to contract AF33(038)-12883 ordered 266 B-47Bs, 175 B-47Cs, and 35 RB-47Cs on 14 August 1950. The RB-47C Project was established under Edward Duff to oversee the production engineering of the photoreconnaissance components of the new aircraft. Concurrently, components related to the RB-47C propulsion and fuel systems were assigned to the YB-47C Project headed by Roy Ostling. Boeing had already expended some 12,000 engineering man-hours on the B-47C.

On 15 August 1950 Boeing received Amendment #1 to Supplemental Agreement #9 that revised the order, which now called for the production of 294 B-47Bs, 21 B-47Cs, and 86 RB-47Cs. Then, on 27 December 1950, Amendment #4 further altered the order to 445 B-47Bs, no B-47Cs, and 19 RB-47Cs.

All of this was superseded by contract AF33(038)-21407 dated 12 April 1951 when the Air Force revised the order to include 471 B-47Bs, 48 RB-47Bs, and 19 RB-47Cs. On 3 July 1953 contract Amendment #1 changed production to 510 B-47Bs, 52 RB-47Bs, and no RB-47Cs, effectively ending this iteration of the B-47C project.

## YB-47C/B-47Z

A further extrapolation of the basic B-47 design was the Boeing Model 450-155-33 that was commonly known as either the YB-47C or B-47Z. Work on the new design, which was a substantial modifi-

ETB-47B-1-BW, s/n 49-2643, was taking off on a test flight with J57 engines in the No. 1 and 6 positions, as part of the tests for both the YB-47C/B-47Z program and the B-52. (Boeing BW91702)

cation of the original B-47C project, began on 12 March 1952. The aircraft was generally the same size as the B-47E and had a maximum gross weight of 125,000 pounds. As with the B-52, this design featured spoilers for control, with five spoiler panels located on top of each wing.

Initially, propulsion for the Model 450-155-33 was to have been four 10,090-lbf Allison J71-A-5 turbojets, essentially an evolved version of the J35-A-23s featured on the earlier Model 450-24-26. The J71 engine was later found to be unsuitable for the Stratojet, and a switch was made to the new 11,100-lbf Pratt & Whitney J57-P-1W. However, these engines were not yet available, and, in any case, they were already earmarked for the B-52, severely slowing work on the B-47C program. The outboard nacelles were to be mounted essentially like those on production Stratojets, but the inboard strut/nacelle configuration was considerably different. Longer struts

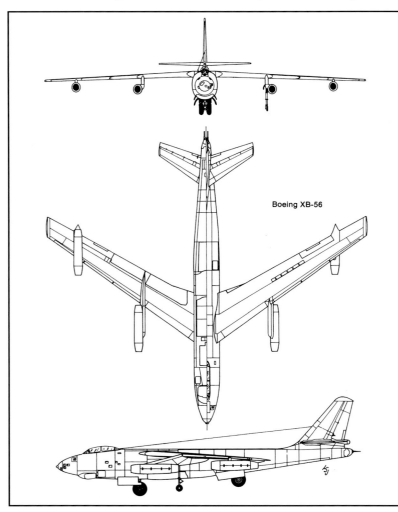

Boeing XB-56

Three-view drawing of the XB-56/B-47Z that was to have been powered by four J57 turbojets. (L. S. Jones)

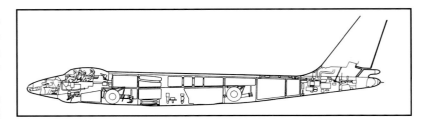

RB-47C inboard profile.

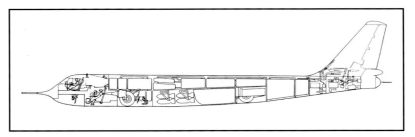

B-47C inboard profile. This design was closer to the B-52 with side-by-side pilot seating on the upper deck and side-by-side seating for the navigators on the lower deck.

cantilevered the engines much farther forward and the nacelles were mounted to the outboard side of the struts.

A crew of four consisted of a pilot, copilot, navigator-gunner, and bombardier-assistant navigator. The cockpit was rearranged to have side-by-side seating as in the B-52. The two pilots were in the upper deck, while the navigators were seated in a similar fashion on the lower deck. All four crewmembers had ejection seats.

## XB-47D

Boeing and other aircraft manufacturers were driven into producing a series of turboprop aircraft because of the opinion of Gene Root from the RAND Corporation. His theory was that only a small cross-sectioned aircraft powered by turboprops could penetrate Soviet airspace and he envisioned large fleets of turboprop bombers. A large part of the desire for turboprops was that RAND saw the engines as a good compromise between speed and fuel economy – the early turbojets guzzled jet fuel at tremendous rates.

| CURTISS-WRIGHT YT49-W-1 POWER OUTPUT | | | | | |
|---|---|---|---|---|---|
| Setting | ESHP | SHP | Thrust | RPM | Min. of Operation |
| Takeoff | 9,710 | 8,500 | 3,025 | 8,000 | 5 |
| Military | 9,710 | 8,500 | 3,025 | 8,000 | 30 |
| Normal | 8,770 | 7,700 | 2,600 | 7,700 | Continuous |

The Air Force was interested in determining the feasibility of producing a high-speed, long-range turboprop-powered bomber like that envisioned at RAND. In support of this goal, the Air Force ordered Boeing to convert two B-47Bs into high-speed, long-range composite turbojet/turboprop test beds to provide data on the installation of turboprops in swept-wing aircraft. Design efforts began in February 1951, and the contract was signed two months later. A mock-up was completed in January 1952 and two B-47Bs (51-2046 and 51-2103) were diverted from the production line and converted into XB-47Ds (Boeing Model 450-162-28).

New pylons and nacelles that housed a turboprop version of the J65 axial-flow turbojet replaced the normal inboard engines. The Curtiss-Wright engines, derived from the Rolls-Royce Sapphire turbojet, were designated YT49-W-1 and drove 15-foot-diameter Curtiss C-846SA propellers. Each blade featured a four-foot chord, and the units were reversible only on the ground. The automatic feathering propellers precluded a rapid yaw that could snap off the vertical stabilizer if they were suddenly stopped. At military power, the engines produced 8,500 shaft horsepower and 3,025-lbf of residual thrust for up to 30 minutes. At normal continuous power, the engines produced 8,770-shp and 2,600-lbf. The two outboard J47-GE-23 engines were retained.

*For the flight test program, a B-47B-30-BW (51-2103) had a camera installed at the top of the vertical fin and tufts attached to the right wing for airflow evaluations. In the background was a pair of the bombers General LeMay was really looking for – the B-52. (Boeing P14970)*

*The modified B-47B-30-BW (51-2103) in a SEBAC hangar. Note the prop index markers on the No. 2 nacelle. The markers on the nose represented the eight engine and two propeller changes done on the aircraft. The engine/propeller combination made an unusual noise leading to the crews saying that is sounded like a goat eating cans, hence the insignia on the nose depicts a winged goat biting an XB-47D. (Boeing FA16269)*

*Raymond McPhearson and Lew Wallick were the Boeing project pilots for the XB-47D program. Here the aircraft was taking off to the south on Runway 13 at Boeing Field, Seattle. In the background was a B-52 with its flaps extended and vertical fin folded down on its right horizontal stabilizer. (Boeing)*

In many respects the aircraft were brought up to a standard similar to the later B-47Es. Provisions were included for installation of external fuel tanks, and other improvements consisted of an automatic heating, cooling, and pressurization system, boosted hydraulic flight controls, and single-point ground refueling.

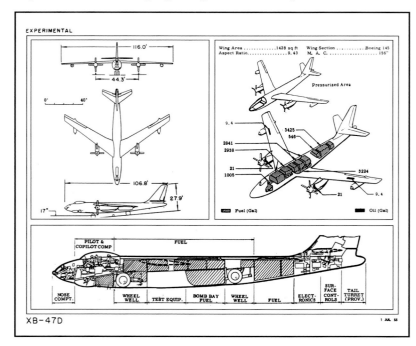

*XB-47D inboard profile.*

The first flight of the XB-47D was scheduled for early 1953, but recurring engine difficulties kept the schedule sliding to the right. When the engine failed its 50-hour qualification run, the Wright Air Development Center (WADC) estimated that the first flight would not occur until January 1954. Shortages in government-furnished aircraft equipment also slowed the program. On 16 May 1955 the engine finally successfully completed its integration tests at WADC. The maiden flight was made at Boeing Field on 26 August 1955, with Boeing engineering test pilots Raymond L. McPhearson and Lew Wallick at the controls. The second aircraft did not fly until 15 February 1956. While the XB-47Ds handled reasonably well in the air, vibration induced by the huge propellers was quite noticeable.

The XB-47Ds were plagued by engine/propeller problems and after 18 months of testing had only accrued a total of 50 flight hours. Nevertheless, the maximum speed achieved by the XB-47D during these tests was 597 mph at 13,500 feet, the fastest yet achieved in level flight by a propeller-driven aircraft. When the Air Force asked Boeing to ferry the aircraft to Tinker AFB where they would be reconverted to bombers, Boeing stated that they would have to make one, if not two, en route stops to replace one or both engines and/or propellers. The subject was dropped by the Air Force and the aircraft were scrapped in Seattle.

*Captured during a 1955 test flight, this XB-47D (51-2103) was flying with its gear extended. Below the airplane taxis to the north at Boeing Field. (Gordon S. Williams)*

*Opposite Page Top and Above: This massive 15-foot-diameter, 4-foot-chord propeller replaced the two inboard J47s on each side of the XB-47Ds. The engine was direct-geared to the propeller, hence the DO NOT ROTATE PROPS placard on the blade. (Above: Gordon S. Williams; other: Boeing A71130)*

*This 1955-vintage profile view of the XB-47D reveals the propeller index marks and a turbine warning stripe on the nacelle. (Gordon S. Williams)*

The relative size of the broad-chord propellers shows up well here compared to the ground crew. (Tony Landis Collection)

This front view of the composite-powered XB-47D shows the general engine arrangement. (Boeing FA24417)

## DRONE DIRECTOR PROJECT

In an effort to enhance the striking capabilities of the B-47, the Air Force ordered Boeing to modify the B-47 to carry and launch the Bell GAM-63 RASCAL missile. This missile was also tested on the Convair B-36.

### Bell GAM-63 RASCAL

Bell Aircraft in Buffalo, New York, developed the GAM-63 guided missile. The name RASCAL was derived from its **R**adar **SCA**ning **L**ink navigation technique. The GAM-63 was a "supersonic pilotless parasite bomber" capable of carrying a 3,000- or 5,000-pound nuclear warhead at speeds between Mach 1.5 and 2.5. This all-weather device was designed to strike any tactical or strategic radar target within 100 nautical miles of its launch point. In essence, it was a precursor to the Boeing AGM-69 Short Range Attack Missile and Boeing AGM-89 Air Launched Cruise Missile (ALCM).

The RASCAL was developed under the 1940s-vintage MX-776 designator. On 26 April 1946 the system was approved under Project No. R-448-48 and the missile then carried the B-63 bomber designation. The Air Force eventually decided that the B-designation would only apply to manned aircraft, and the RASCAL and several other missiles were redesignated as Guided Air Missiles.

The RASCAL was 4 feet in diameter, 32 feet long, and spanned 16.7 feet. At launch, the missile weighed 18,500 pounds. A set of three 4,000-lbf Bell XLR67-BA-1 liquid-propellant rocket engines used 293 gallons of JP-4 fuel and 600 gallons of white fuming nitric acid oxidizer. The total fuel and oxidizer weight was 9,600 pounds. All three chambers of the XLR67 operated during the one-to-two-minute boost phase immediately after launch, then the upper and lower chambers shut down and the missile continued its flight on the center chamber alone.

When carried by the B-47, the launch altitude for the missile was between 25,000 and 35,000 feet after which the missile climbed to between 50,000 and 60,000 feet. Approximately 20 miles from its target, the missile would dive at an angle of 30 degrees.

Guidance for the RASCAL was divided into three phases. The B-47 would use standard K-system navigation procedures up to the launch point. For mid-course guidance after it was launched, a single-axis inertial guidance system aboard the missile was used. During the final phase, a radar image of the target was relayed from the missile to the director aircraft where course corrections were determined by the missile operator and relayed back to the RASCAL. The closer the missile got to the target the better the radar resolution was. The circular error probable (CEP) was anticipated to be within 500 feet. A large dome antenna in a retractable bay on the bottom of the B-47 fuselage, and the missile relay antenna in the trailing edge of the lower aft stabilizer, provided the data link. Optionally, the bombardier could allow the onboard inertial guidance to fly the missile throughout the mission, but accuracy was compromised by the crude state of the art at the time.

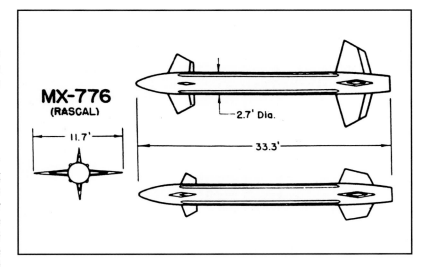

*Three-view drawing of the MX-776 supersonic RASCAL development prototype.*

The first RASCAL air launch took place on 30 September 1952 from a modified Boeing DB-50D. The Strategic Air Command was never very enthusiastic about the RASCAL program, believing that the missile was far too complex, with a guidance system that was likely to be prone to frequent failures and which would be relatively easy for an enemy to jam. However, the Air Staff pushed hard for the RASCAL concept, and SAC was forced to go along.

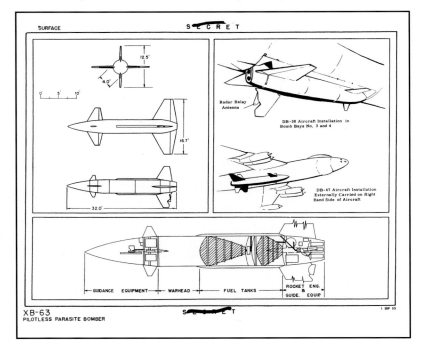

*Final GAM-63 RASCAL (still called the XB-63) inboard profile.*

*This mock-up was employed for developing the external strut for carrying the GAM-63 RASCAL. (Boeing A52535)*

*This bottom view of the strut for the GAM-63 RASCAL reveals the forward restraining lock and the aft lateral supports. An air inlet in the leading edge of the strut was for equipment cooling. (Boeing A53421)*

*Munitions specialists from the 321st BMW were hanging this 1,700-pound GAM-63 RASCAL on the waist pylon installed on this DB-47B-35-BW, (51-2179). (SAC Combat Crew Magazine)*

## YDB-47B

As originally conceived the RASCAL missile was earmarked for the B-36, B-47, and B-52. In March 1952 the list of candidate aircraft for the RASCAL was reduced to just the B-36 and B-47, with the B-47 being assigned the first priority. Despite official resistance from SAC, in 1953 a B-47B (51-2186) was modified as a RASCAL carrier under the designation YDB-47B. The missile was suspended from the starboard side of the fuselage. At launch, the missile would be released from its supports; with the rocket motor firing once the RASCAL had dropped a safe distance away from the YDB-47B.

As the RASCAL program proceeded, SAC's sense of unease increased still further. SAC felt that equipping the B-47 fleet with the large and bulky externally mounted RASCAL would degrade performance to such extent as to make the whole concept of dubious value. SAC also feared that the guidance system would never work very well, and they were reluctant to add even more complex electronic equipment to an already overloaded B-47. The million-dollar per aircraft modification costs were high, and personnel training demands were considerable. Nevertheless, in June 1955 the Air Force decided that 30 B-47B-BWs (51-2160, 51-2162/2174, and 51-2176/2191) originally earmarked for the EBB TIDE trainer program would instead be converted to the DB-47B configuration.

## YDB-47E

As progress was made on developing the B-47E, it became obvious that it would make a much better RASCAL carrier than the B-47B did. It was decided to pull two B-47E-60-BWs (51-5219 and 51-5220) off the production line and convert them into YDB-47Es

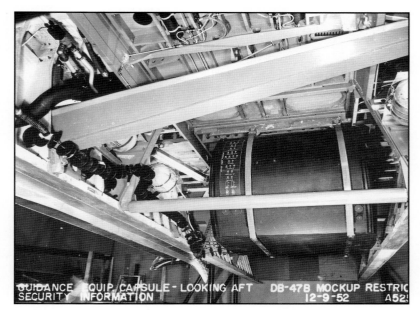

A guidance equipment capsule was installed in the aft portion of the bomb bay. (Boeing A52524)

This grid-antenna mounted in the nose permitted the crew to control the missile being launched from the aircraft. (Boeing FA11468)

A new retractable relay antenna had to be installed in the fuselage. It is shown here in the extended position. When the relay antenna was retracted, sliding panels closed off the opening. Rollers on the doors moved along the tracks seen on the aft frame. (Boeing A52528 and A52519)

3/4 FRONT VIEW EXTERNAL STORES YDB-47E MOCKUP
RESTRICTED SECURITY INFORMATION   1-21-53   A53416

*Bell Aircraft designed this piece of ground support equipment that allowed the GAM-63 missile to be hoisted into position for mounting on the B-47's pylon. (Boeing A53416)*

*This GAM-63 was nestled against the fuselage of the YDB-47E. Details of the staggered RATO exhaust nozzles are evident in this view. (Boeing P14227)*

*The massive 17,000-pound GAM-63 is shown in its true proportion to a YDB-47E-BW (51-5219) as it sat at the north end of Boeing Field during the test program. (Gordon S. Williams)*

*The 445th BS, 321st BMW was the only unit to operate the B-47 with the GAM-63 RASCAL. Here an operational missile was attached to one of the unit's B-47s from Pinecastle AFB, Florida. With the Marine helicopters in the background and the Fairchild R4Q Flying Boxcar in the background, this photo was most likely taken at MCAS Cherry Point, N.C., home of VMF-122. (Peter M. Bowers/Victor D. Seeley Collection)*

*The YDB-47E mock-up was also used to properly locate the additional equipment for the navigator. The panel with the actual instrument faces was from the existing aircraft. To the right was a new guidance control panel. A new guidance sight was placed on the extreme left, while a control stick was added to the inboard forward corner of the navigator's table. (Boeing A53414)*

(Boeing Model 450-167-50). The modifications were performed under contract AF33(600)-22108, dated 23 July 1952. The design for the YDB-47E had actually begun in April 1952, and the mock-up was ready for inspection in December 1952.

The modifications to carry the RASCAL were designed to be as minimal as possible so that the aircraft could be their normal bombing configurations without too much effort. The most obvious change was a removable missile support strut installed on the right side of the aircraft. Internal structural supports had to be installed to accommodate the loads imposed by the strut and missile, and new supporting structure had to be added to the bomb bay for the guidance equipment capsule. Structural provisions were also added between Body Stations 1024 and 1090 for mounting the relay antenna unit. Lastly, doors were added to fair over the opening when the relay antenna was retracted.

Wiring was installed to interface between the various guidance system components, and an umbilical plug was added in the missile pylon to mate with the connector on the missile. A relay antenna, transmitter, and receiver were installed in the fuselage between Body Stations 1024 and 1090. A ram air duct was installed to afford cooling of the missile and revise the pneumatic duct system as required by relocation of the U-2 bomb rack. Guidance equipment was installed in a capsule mounted in the bomb bay and at the navigator's station. Portions of the K-4 bombing system were replaced with modified units furnished by the government.

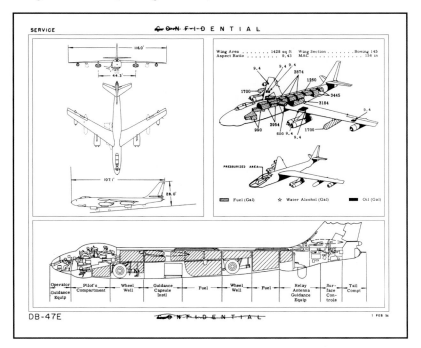

*This DB-47E inboard profile reveals the locations for the various components of the missile guidance system.*

YDB-47E-BW, s/n 51-5219, had a large white rectangle painted on the side of the fuselage to give greater contrast to the GAM-63 during launch tests in 1954. (Vern Manion via Gordon S. Williams)

This GAM-63 was captured shortly after launching from the YDB-47E mothership. Note that the U.S. national insignia was hand-applied to the photograph. (Via L. S. Jones)

An auxiliary hydraulic system was installed to provide operation of the missile hydraulic system while in captive flight. An extension and retraction mechanism and a door actuator for the relay antenna were installed. Hooks and associated linkages were installed to secure and release the missile. Both a manual control and emergency release systems for the missile were added. Changes were also required for the bomb bay fuel tank to permit clearance of the missile support beam.

The first YDB-47E made its maiden flight in January 1954, and both YDB-47Es were dispatched to Holloman AFB, New Mexico, for testing. One aircraft was briefly used in radio noise tests conducted at Roswell AFB, New Mexico. Major Guy Townsend was once asked how the aircraft flew with the RASCAL missile. His response was: "Like any other B-47 with 1,700 pounds of horse manure strapped to the side." Nevertheless, the testing was successful and plans continued for production DB-47Es.

It was expected that the 445th Bombing Squadron from the 321st Bomb Wing would operate with the RASCAL from Pinecastle AFB. Formal acceptance of the first production GAM-63 took place at Pinecastle on 30 October 1957. However, the program soon encountered snags and delays, and even by early 1958, RASCAL facilities were still not yet in place at Pinecastle.

Disenchanted with the program, the Air Staff terminated the entire RASCAL program on 29 September 1958. AMC was tasked with the disposal of 78 experimental and 58 production missiles that had been accepted by the Air Force.

The YDB-47E-BW (51-5219) underwent refueling tests with this SAC KC-97G replete with its SAC Milky Way band and Insignia Red Arctic trim. Note the partially extended flaps on the drone director. This aircraft was bailed to Martin Aircraft in Baltimore, Maryland, for other tests. On 25 September 1958, the aircraft departed Patrick AFB, Florida, for Baltimore. On landing, the aircraft porpoised and the pilot opted to perform a ground loop. All three aboard survived the accident; however, the aircraft was reclaimed on 20 October 1958. (Boeing BW117212)

## DB-47E

The DB-47E (Boeing Model 450-172-52) differed from the YDB-47E in that a capability to carry an ECM capsule was added. In addition, the K-4 bombing and navigation system was replaced by an MA-8 system that necessitated replacing the 5-inch radarscope with a 10-inch scope. The DB-47Es were also equipped with IFF and ECM equipment, which had been lacking on the prototypes.

Despite the first successful RASCAL launch from a DB-47E in July 1955, it was decided during early 1956 that initial production of the DB-47E would be limited to only two aircraft (53-2345 and 53-2346). Looming plans to produce a large number of DB-47Es were abandoned when the GAM-63 program was cancelled in 1958.

## GAM-67 CROSSBOW

The Radioplane Company of Van Nuys, California, designed and built the RP-54D Crossbow to serve as a remotely controlled target drone. Its size and versatility allowed it to be converted into an ECM vehicle with the designation GAM-67. Its empty weight was 1,650 pounds and it grossed 2,800 to 2,900 pounds when loaded. The GAM-67 had a 12.5-foot wingspan, was 19.1 feet long, and 4.6 feet high. Powered by a single 1,000-lbf Continental J69-T-17 turbojet engine, the missile could attain a speed of Mach 0.99 (676 mph at sea level), and cruise at an altitude of 40,000 feet for approximately 300 miles. Guidance was provided by a modified ARW-59 command-control receiver system. Two DB-47Es (51-2328 and 51-2350) could each carry four Crossbows suspended from large pylons

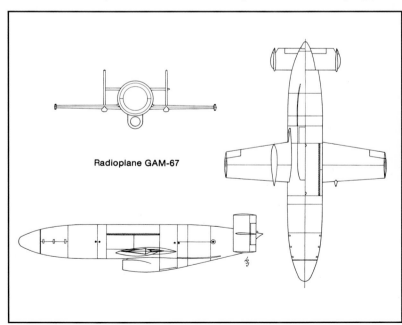

*Three-view drawing of the GAM-67 Crossbow. (L. S. Jones)*

*The YDB-47B carried four GAM-67 Crossbow missiles on large underwing pylons. The bottom shows the GAM-67 on its ground transportation dolly. (Top: Boeing BW94088; others: Via L. S. Jones)*

YDB-47B carried four Radioplane GAM-67 Crossbow missiles on large underwing pylons. (Boeing BW94089)

*This GAM-72 Quail missile was undergoing systems checkout by a member of the aircraft munitions maintenance squadron. While the Quail was only tested on the B-47, it became a staple in the B-52's ECM arsenal. (Via SAC Historian)*

located between each of the engine nacelles. Confusingly, these DB-47Es had nothing in common with the similarly designated aircraft used on the RASCAL program.

## ADM-20/GAM-72 QUAIL

The McDonnell ADM-20 Quail decoy missile was in service between 1960 and 1978. (ADM is the USAF designation given to an Aerial Decoy Missile.) When launched, the Quail could confuse, dilute, saturate, or reduce the effectiveness of enemy radar-controlled air defense and infrared detection systems. The missile, with its fiberglass fuselage, was 13 feet long and had a wingspan of 5 feet 5 inches when extended and 2 feet 5 inches when stowed. The single 2,450-lbf General Electric J85 turbojet engine produced a small infrared target for heat-seeking missiles. The decoy had a gross weight of 1,198 pounds. The Quail had a range of approximately 250 miles that could be covered in a period of 30 minutes. Two ADM-20 Quails could be carried in the bomb bay of a B-52. At its peak, there were 492 ADM-20 missiles in SAC's arsenal.

While the ADM-20s were carried operationally on the B-52s, they were initially tested on a pair of DB-47Es (52-538 and 53-2104) over Holloman AFB, New Mexico. Again, these DB-47Es had little in common with the RASCAL or Crossbow carriers.

Members of the 3205th Drone Group at Eglin AFB, Florida, used this MRW-5A gear to control the QB-47s. A ground power cart provided electric power. Note the telemetry pod on the wing between the outboard and inboard nacelles. (Boeing BW119415)

This QB-47E-45-BW (53-4250) was photographed while taking off for a mission from Tyndall AFB, Florida. Portions of the vertical tail, waist, wing, engine struts, and nacelles were painted Day-Glo Red for added visibility during flight tests. (Boeing 1194181)

## QB-47E

Developed in cooperation between Lockheed-Marietta and Sperry Gyroscope, the QB-47E was a drone intended to improve the targeting ability of the Boeing IM-99 BOMARC interceptor missile.

Initially considered to be a relatively simple retrofit, considerable equipment engineering was required. The contract was let to Lockheed-Marietta in December 1958 and flight-testing began in May 1959. The 3205th Drone Director Group at Eglin AFB became operational with the QB-47E in July 1960.

A QB-47E-45-BW (53-4254) being escorted to the runway at Eglin AFB, Florida, while control was about to be transferred to the ground controllers on the truck. The aircraft was equipped with a Pitot boom installed in the nose, and telemetry pods attached to stubby pylons where the external fuel tanks would have been installed. The QB-47 was being controlled by the DT-33 that was flying in an offset trail. (Boeing P26178)

This QB-47E-45-BW (53-4253) was rolling out on landing at Eglin at the 1,000-foot marker. The arresting gear hook had just snagged the arresting cable. The snubber in the foreground decelerated the aircraft. Note that the canopy was cracked for cooling of the crew. These aircraft could be flown by a crew or operated in a No Onboard Live Operator (NOLO) mode. Note the bright Day-Glo Red paint that was applied to the empennage. (USAF)

*This QB-47E (53-4256) has three "kill" marking on the nose in the shape of a YF-12A. In this case the "kills" indicated the drone had been shot at three times by the Lockheed interceptor – at least one AIM-47 missile scored a direct hit on the leading edge of the horizontal stabilizer. (AFFTC History Office via Tony Landis)*

The QB-47E offered the BOMARC a target that accurately represented offensive bomber systems without the necessity for electronic augmentation. With flight duration of around 5.5 hours, the drone bomber also afforded greater test mission flexibility. Because of its size, the QB-47 could carry a large array of intricate scoring and ECM equipment. The program called for a pair of prototypes and 12 production QB-47Es.

These aircraft retained their manned crew positions for missions requiring human operation of the scoring and telemetry equipment, and ferry operations. Just in case control of the drone was ever lost, explosives were carried so that the aircraft could be intentionally destroyed before it could wander into a populated area.

Command guidance was provided by an AN/ARW-65 UHF radio that could initiate 46 major commands through 16 direct and 28 multiplexed channels. By stepping some of the functions, a total of 66 command functions could be achieved. The AN/UKR-2 telemetry receiving equipment displayed the flight parameters for the ground controllers. While this system was capable of receiving 12 channels of data, signal stepping afforded an additional 27 data channels. Ground controllers had a total of 18 proportional functions and 45 on-off functions available to them.

In addition to receiving external commands from either a ground or airborne director, the aircraft was equipped with a basic stabilization system that provided complete normal maneuvering control, and control of basic aircraft subsystems such as flaps, landing gear, and brakes. The UHF command link also actuated the ECM and scoring equipment. To slow the aircraft on landing, a cable engagement hook was installed to the aft landing gear outer cylinder.

Because the runway at Eglin Auxiliary Field #3 was only 8,000 feet long, the 18-bottle RATO system had to be employed to get the aircraft airborne. Two director pilots stood on the top deck of an MRW-5A, one controlling the elevator and the other the rudder, and controlled ground operations and takeoff. (The MRW-5A was a modified pick-up truck with an electronics box mounted in the bed and an exposed upper deck with antennas and controller stations.) Exhaust from the RATOs obscured the aircraft from the two director pilots, hence a second remote station located in the Duke Field (Eglin Auxiliary Field #3) tower maintained visual contact with the QB-47E and made the requisite azimuth corrections.

After takeoff, control of the QB-47E was transferred to a DT-33A flying overhead. This director aircraft guided the drone to its operating area where control was transferred to another ground station. The DT-33 then broke off and orbited the coastline while the ground controllers vectored the drone to the desired intercept area with precise airspeed, altitude, and heading.

Just before the intercept, the ECM and scoring equipment was started. Optical scoring equipment consisted of 12 Bell & Howell 16-mm cameras operating at 200 frames per second with effective ranges of 1,200 to 1,500 feet. Mounting the cameras in under-wing pods provided spherical coverage. Electronic scoring equipment consisted of an Aerojet AN/USQ-7 system that picked up a signal from the BOMARC via wing-mounted antennas with an effective range of 4,000 feet. This signal was in turn relayed to a ground station. A highly accurate scoring system provided space/time data on the BOMARC trajectory to within 10 feet.

For return to base, control was transferred to the DT-33A that guided the QB-47 to within four miles of the runway. Control was then transferred to the ground station. The effectiveness of the ground controllers was demonstrated during the first QB-47 targeting mission. Wind gusts interfered with the landing and the controllers executed a go-around and made a successful landing.

Because of their $1.9 million unit cost, these aircraft were not considered expendable. The plan was for the BOMARC missiles to make near misses, thereby saving the drone bomber. In spite of such precautions, a QB-47E was inadvertently destroyed when members of the Royal Canadian Air Force No. 447 Squadron, under the command of Wing Commander Art Laflamme, learned their trade too well. During a practice session at Hurlburt Field (Eglin Auxiliary Field #9), the RCAF personnel assembled their missile, set the tracking, and fired the BOMARC across the Eglin Missile Range. Loitering in the area was a QB-47E; the missile exploded within lethal range, sending the QB-47 into a fireball that plunged into the ocean. Eventually, most of the drones were destroyed during later missile tests.

However, two survived to become JQB-47Es for use as targets for the Hughes AIM-47 long-range air-to-air missile fired from the Lockheed YF-12A Blackbird interceptor. On 25 April 1966 the first and third YF-12As were flown to Eglin for firing trials. Later the same day, Lockheed test pilot Jim Eastham, in the first YF-12A, fired an unarmed AIM-47 against a JQB-47E (53-4256) flying 60,000 feet below the Blackbird (which was flying at 75,000 feet and Mach 3.2). The missile passed through the JQB-47's horizontal stabilizer –

*An NB-47E-80-BW (52-0412) arrived at Douglas-Tulsa for retrofit for its new Navy mission. The photograph dates from 29 April 1966. A large pylon was mounted at the former external fuel tank locations and smaller pylons were mounted between the fuselage and inboard nacelles. (Douglas-Tulsa T34268)*

Eastham believes the missile impacted there because the intersection of the horizontal and vertical stabilizers produced the greatest radar reflection. If the missile had been armed, the bomber would have been destroyed. As it was, the ground crew managed to land the bomber, which, ironically, would be hit by another AIM-47 over the White Sands Missile Range on 21 September 1966.

## NAVY B-47S

The U.S. Navy operated a pair of NB-47E-80s (52-0410 and 52-0412) as electronic surrogates for the Navy's surface warfare fleet. These aircraft were modified to carry a variety of electronic sensors and telemetry equipment, often carried on the former drop tank pylons. Among the most notable tests conducted by these aircraft was during the development of the Aegis missile systems. When the aircraft

*This NB-47E-80-BW (52-0410) became part of the Navy's missile tracking fleet. The Navy merely added a 0 to the tail number that then became 24100. This picture dates from 20 December 1977. Later a McDonnell Douglas insignia replaced the Douglas markings on the nose. (Douglas-Tulsa T62130)*

### U.S. NAVY FLIGHT TEST PROGRAMS

| Model/Series | Serial No. | Remarks |
|---|---|---|
| NB-47E-80-BW | 52-0410 | Served with the Navy until its retirement in 1977 when it was ferried to Pease AFB, N.H. |
| NB-47E-80-BW | 52-0412 | Served with the Navy until its retirement in 1977 when it was ferried to Dyess AFB, Tex. |

*NB-47E-45-DT, s/n 53-2104, was airborne with a TF34 turbofan installed at the external fuel tank hard point. The remains of the partial white anti-radiation finish may be seen on the bottom of the horizontal tail. NAVY replaced the U.S. AIR FORCE on the forward fuselage, while the USAF tail number was retained. (General Electric Flight Test)*

*General Electric engineers prepared to start NB-47E-45-DT, s/n 53-2104, for a test flight with the TF34 turbofan engine. (General Electric Flight Test)*

were retired during 1977, 52-0410 was ferried to Pease AFB. When Pease closed, the aircraft was disassembled and trucked to Ellsworth AFB. Unfortunately, funds did not exist to reassemble it and it has since been parted-out to restore other B-47s. Also during 1977, 52-0412 was ferried to Dyess AFB where it is currently on display.

During early 1971, the Navy also operated an NB-47E-45-DT (53-2104) as a test bed for the General Electric TF34 turbofan engine. Suspended from the left drop tank pylon, the 9,065-lbf TF34 was 49 inches in diameter, 100 inches long, and weighed 1,440 pounds. While it was being developed, the TF34 was expected to be

used extensively on a wide variety of aircraft types, but ultimately, only the Lockheed S-3 Viking and Republic A-10 Thunderbolt II (aka, Warthog) used the engine.

The aircraft was retired from service and in 1979 was donated by the Naval Air Systems Command to the Pueblo Historical Aircraft Society museum in Colorado. The aircraft was returned to flying condition with civil registry N1045T and flown to Pueblo where it is currently on display.

## YB-47F/KB-47G

From the inception of the B-47 program, it had been recognized that the development of efficient in-flight refueling techniques would be absolutely essential for the full success of the relatively short-ranged Stratojet. The first Air Force in-flight refueling tankers were converted B-29 and B-50 bombers, but by the mid-1950s the standard tanker was the piston-engined Boeing KC-97. However, the use of the propeller-driven KC-97 as the tanker for the jet-powered B-47 had its drawbacks, since it could not climb to the B-47's best altitude, forcing the Stratojet to descend down to the tanker's level, wasting time and fuel. In addition, the KC-97 tanker was so slow that the B-47 tended to stall during the refueling operation. In order to keep the B-47 from stalling, the slower KC-97 would often enter a shallow dive to pick up speed – a hair-raising operation for all concerned while the two aircraft were linked.

Clearly, aerial tankers with greater speeds would be required. In early 1953, two B-47Bs were allocated for tests with the British-developed probe-and-drogue aerial refueling system. The YB-47F (50-069) was fitted with a probe in the nose for in-flight refueling via the probe-and-drogue system. During the refueling operation, a hose and drogue system was unreeled from the bomb bay of the KB-47G (50-040), and the YB-47F would fly below and behind and use a nose probe to engage a basket trailed from the end of the hose. On 1 September 1953 these two aircraft performed the first all-jet aerial refueling.

Unfortunately, the probe-and-drogue refueling method did not prove to be effective for the B-47, and subsequent models were refueled by the established flying-boom system. Adding auxiliary jet engines to the piston-engined KB-50 and KC-97 tankers, which were used to provide additional bursts of speed during the refueling operations, eventually solved the speed problem.

The Stratojet tanker concept was briefly revisited in mid-1956, when it was found that the KB-50s of the Tactical Air Command lacked the speed and altitude performance to refuel the new Century Series fighters. On 23 July 1956 the Air Force authorized the development of a KB-47 tanker with a drogue system installed under each wing where the B-47E carried its drop tanks; this was conceptually similar to the system used on the KB-50s. However, the $2.7 million cost of the KB-47 conversion was too high, and it was found that the addition of two auxiliary jet engines to the KB-50 provided a satisfactory albeit temporary solution to the speed problem. The Air Force cancelled the KB-47 program on 11 July 1957.

*A single B-47B-5-BW (50-069) was converted into a probe and drogue refueling receiver test bed and redesignated the sole YB-47F. An instrumented refueling probe was installed in the nose. These photos date from 5 May 1953. (Boeing)*

*The hose reel and drogue basket are shown in this picture of the KB-47G. (Boeing FA12281)*

*The hose-refueling drum was mounted in the bomb bay of the KB-47G. (Boeing A56394)*

Hook-up was complete for this air refueling test. (Boeing)

The KB-47G employed this flight refueling control panel. (Boeing A56389)

A camera mounted in the tanker shows the drogue attached to the receiver's probe. (Boeing P12407)

*The YB-47F (50-009) flew with all gear, except the forward main, extended to slow-fly the aircraft in this refueling test with the KB-47G. (Boeing P23420)*

*Using the Flight Refueling, Ltd., probe and drogue system, the sole KB-29G (50-040) was refueling the only YB-47F (50-069). (Boeing P13353)*

### YB-47J

The single YB-47J was a B-47E modified to evaluate the MA-2 radar bombing-navigation system that had been designed for the B-52.

## PROJECT **BOLD ORION**

In 1958 the Air Force awarded a contract to Martin Aircraft in Baltimore, Maryland, to determine if an air-launched ballistic missile (ALBM) was feasible. Cruise missiles then under development flew much like a conventional aircraft, while the ALBM was to be dropped from an aircraft and fly a ballistic trajectory through space to its target. The $5 million Project BOLD ORION was designated WS-199. George Smith headed the small Martin laboratory running the project and Joe Verlander was in charge of flight-testing.

The BOLD ORION 1, designated WS-199A, was a single-stage missile powered by a Sergeant TX-20 rocket motor. The larger BOLD ORION 2, designated WS-199B, was a two-stage missile approximately 37 feet long. A Sergeant TX-20 was its first stage and a Vanguard rocket motor made up its second stage.

*Hose and probe refueling tests were also tried with a Republic F-84 Thunderjet. The fighter had a probe mounted in the nose of each tip tank. The receiver pilot would fill half of the tip tank then slip the aircraft using crossed-controls to fill the opposite tip tank, then slip back to the other side to top off the first tank. A camera was mounted in the No. 4 nacelle of a KC-97 to record the operation. (Boeing P12422)*

The Air Force bailed the YDB-47B-60-BW (51-5220) to Martin as a carrier aircraft for BOLD ORION. Martin test pilot Bill Johnson was assigned to fly the aircraft with an all-Martin crew, and Martin personnel also performed all loading and system checkouts. A dozen BOLD ORION flights took off from Baltimore and were launched over the Air Force Missile Test Center at Cape Canaveral, Florida. The results from the BOLD ORION program were subsequently incorporated into the requirements for the WS-138A operational ALBM program (leading to the GAM-87/AGM-48 Skybolt).

The final WS-199B launch tested the BOLD ORION ALBM as an anti-satellite missile. On 13 October 1959 the YDB-47B flew north along the Florida coast towards Wallops Island, Virginia. The BOLD ORION was launched from an altitude of 35,000 feet and achieved an apogee of 160 miles. To record its flight path, the BOLD ORION transmitted telemetry to the ground, ejected flares to aid visual tracking, and was continuously tracked by radar. The missile came to within four miles of the *Explorer VI* satellite that was at an altitude of 156 miles.

## PROJECT BRASS RING

Early testing of the thermonuclear weapons known as hydrogen bombs began in 1949. Knowledge of the capabilities of the delivery systems extant during that period indicated that it would be extremely difficult for a manned bomber to deliver such a weapon and make a successful exit from the target area. It would be a number of years before a missile capable of delivering such weapons would be developed. Under Project BRASS RING, thoughts turned to an unmanned bomber, with the logical choice being the B-47.

Two terminal flight scenarios were conceived. The first envisioned the aircraft being flown by a crew who would perform several in-flight refuelings en route, then bail out over friendly territory and allow the B-47 to continue on to the target. This thinking obviously came from the World War II experience with Project APHRODITE in which B-17s and B-24s loaded with Torpex were launched at German submarine pens and V-weapons sites in France. The wartime project was only marginally successful. The second idea was to control the B-47 "bomb" with a second, manned B-47.

A decision in early 1950 called for one B-47A to be converted into a director aircraft with the designation DB-47A. In addition, two B-47Bs would be converted into MB-47 delivery systems. This was called Project BRASS RING.

The MB-47 was to have a highly sophisticated navigation and flight control system. While Boeing developed the requirements, North American Aviation was awarded a contract to develop the equipment. Design requirements were for the navigation system to be fully automatic, non-jammable, and have precise accuracy. Unfortunately, the North American project had continual developmental problems, and after the expenditure of $850,000, it was cancelled in mid-1952. The Air Force turned next to Sperry Gyroscope, and this system was ultimately worked after an expenditure of some $2.3 million.

With the remote flight control and stabilization equipment installed, the MB-47 made its first flight on 7 May 1952. By 30 June 1952 both the MB-47 and its DB-47A director had conducted several test flights with rewarding results. However, forecasted costs for the program rose from $4.9 million to $10.3 million in 1952.

Fortunately, while the MB-47 development program struggled, it was learned that the B-36 would be perfectly capable of dropping a thermonuclear weapon with an appropriate parachute retarding system. The advantages of BRASS RING were further eroded by the

The mount used for the GAM-63 RASCAL was adapted to carry the Martin Aircraft WS-199B Project BOLD ORION missile. Note the last four digits of the tail number on the forward gear door, identifying the aircraft as a YDB-47B-60-BW (51-5220). (USAF)

### BOLD ORION TEST LAUNCHES

| Date | Vehicle | Remarks |
|---|---|---|
| 26 May 58 | BOLD ORION 1 | Phase I test. Successful. |
| 27 June 58 | BOLD ORION 1 | Phase II test. Failed due to high pitch attitude resulting in erratic flight. |
| 18 July 58 | BOLD ORION 1 | Phase II test. Failed due to 90-degree roll tumbling gyro resulting in erratic flight. |
| 25 Sept 58 | BOLD ORION 1 | Phase II test. Failed due to rocket shut-off motor failing at T+19 seconds. |
| 10 Oct 58 | BOLD ORION 1 | Phase II test. Failed due to rocket shut-off motor failing at T+126 seconds. |
| 17 Nov 58 | BOLD ORION 1 | Phase II test. Successful. |
| 8 Dec 58 | BOLD ORION 2 | Phase III test. Failed because the rocket motor was a dud. |
| 16 Dec 58 | BOLD ORION 2 | Phase III test. Successful. Flew 1,100 miles down range. |
| 2 Apr 59 | BOLD ORION 2 | Phase III test. Failed due to second stage ignition failure. |
| 8 June 59 | BOLD ORION 2 | Phase II test. Successful. |
| 19 June 59 | BOLD ORION 2 | Phase III test. Successful. |
| 13 Oct 59 | BOLD ORION 2 | Phase III test. Successful. Achieved an apogee of 160 miles, and came to within 4 miles of Explorer VI satellite. |

acquisition of forward operating locations in England, Spain, and French Morocco. Despite efforts by WADC to continue the program, the Air Staff terminated Project BRASS RING on 1 April 1953.

## PROJECT WEARY WILLIE II

The idea would not go away, however. In August 1966 the Air Force investigated Project WEARY WILLIE II (the name derived from the WEARY WILLIE missions during World War II as part of Project APHRODITE). This project involved using an unmanned QB-47 drone to attack hard targets. In preliminary trials under Project SOD BUSTER, an off-the-shelf television camera and zoom lens were installed in the nose of a QB-47 and used to transmit video to a DF-100F drone director whose back-seater was flying the Stratojet. The project evaluated the distances achievable between the drone and director aircraft, and also the accuracies that could be expected during an attack. The perceived uses of this combination were against well-defended targets in North Vietnam, such as the Thanh Hoa Bridge.

It was found that the QB-47 could acquire a target with the television camera at distances of approximately 10 miles, and that the director aircraft could follow about 15 miles in trail, although distances as great as 50 miles were demonstrated.

The Air Force anticipated filling some of the B-47 fuel cells with the same slurry-type explosive used in mining operations. Approximately 35,000 pounds of the slurry could be carried without severely compromising the range of the B-47. Sandia National Laboratory would provide a fusing system derived from the nuclear program. The estimated cost of the television and telemetry systems was $150,000, and QB-47s could be modified from retired aircraft for $514,000 each. Assuming a single QB-47 could destroy a target such as the Thanh Hoa Bridge, it would be much more cost effective than attacking the bridge with F-105s. The Air Force estimated that to ensure a 0.85-probability of killing the bridge, a total of 140 2,000-pound bombs would need to be dropped. This would require 73 F-105 sorties, resulting in the loss of three Thunderchiefs and their pilots. The total cost for the mission (excluding the human cost) would be $9,610,280, versus $664,000 for a single QB-47.

Despite the seemingly good economics, the program was not pursued further and no QB-47s were used against North Vietnam.

## OTHER B-47 TEST USES

The adaptable B-47 permitted it to be used in a number of interesting test programs for Boeing, the Air Force, the Navy, and other aircraft and engine manufacturers.

### Boeing Tests

In addition to routine production flight testing, Boeing operated extensive experimental flight test facilities both at WIBAC and SEBAC

The B-52 Dog Ship was retrofitted with spoilers attached to the rear spar of the wings between engine struts. Three fingered panels were installed per side. When used symmetrically, they acted as speed brakes. Differential deflection caused them to perform like ailerons. Note the camera pod that was mounted on top of the fuselage aft of the wing trailing edge. (Gordon S. Williams)

for the development of design improvements for the B-47 program and for other follow-on programs. At least 20 B-47s are known to have participated in various tests at Boeing. For instance, a B-47A-BW (49-1901) was used to test the crosswind landing gear destined for the B-52, and a B-47-25-BW (51-2052) was used as a *Dog Ship* to evaluate a variety of engineering innovations destined for the Stratofortress.

During the summer of 1953 Boeing modified a B-47B-1-BW (49-2643) to test the Pratt & Whitney J57 for both the YB-47C/B-47Z and B-52 programs. These tests were conducted under contract

This B-47B-25-BW (51-2052) was known as the B-52 Dog Ship. It was used to test a variety of engineering innovations for the future B-52. Photo markings were applied to the sides of the fuselage. (Gordon S. Williams)

*A B-47B-20-BW (50-054) was used as a test bed for the Pratt & Whitney J57 engines that would be used on the KC-135. The No. 1 nacelle is almost identical to that installed on the KC-135A Stratotanker. The aircraft was assigned to ARDC and was operated by the Wright Air Development Center. The brake chute was billowing behind the aircraft. (Boeing P14761)*

*The KC-135 test bed B-47B-20-BW (50-054) was assigned to ARDC and was photographed on Boeing Field in Seattle in 1954. Operated by the Wright Air Development Center, the aircraft carried the unit insignia on the nose. Within the insignia was a red and blue triangle that was repeated on the vertical tail. (Vern Manion via Gordon S. Williams)*

AF33(038)-21407. The modifications included removing the two outboard J47 engines and replacing them with J57s in nacelles reworked from an XB-52 cowling. This installation required the modification of the existing fire seals, the installation of new engine mounts, and the deletion of or blocking off of existing water injection, pneumatic bleed ducts, single-point starting, nose inlet deicing, and J47 oil system. In addition, the ailerons were reinforced for approximately 60 inches each side of the engine centerline, and two additional rows of vortex generators were added to the wing's upper surface.

A second B-47-20-BW (50-054) was also modified to test the J57 destined for the KC-135 program. These tests provided valuable data for the forthcoming KC-135 Stratotanker and Model 707 Jetliner. While the J47s were plagued with low service life, the J57 proved to be a most reliable engine and permitted development of large transport aircraft, both military and commercial.

During 1958, a joint Air Materiel Command, Bell Aircraft Avionics Division, and Lockheed-Marietta project pursued the development of an automatic landing system to assist in getting aircraft

*At left, this B-47B-25-BW (51-2061) passed an antenna associated with the Bell Aircraft automatic landing system. At right, USAF and RCAF officers, Lockheed engineers, and AMC civilian personnel observed a touchdown during an automatic landing of this Stratojet. The autoland transmitting equipment was located in the Bell Aircraft van to the left. (Lockheed-Marietta)*

*This side view of the B-47B-20-BW (50-054) reveals a profile of the No. 1 nacelle that is almost identical to that later installed on the KC-135A. Note the significant difference in size between the J57 nacelle and the inboard nacelle that housed a pair of much less powerful J47s. (Vern Manion via Gordon S. Williams)*

*This B-47A-BW (49-1901) was fitted with a crosswind landing gear system being evaluated for the B-52. Both main landing gear could be swiveled such that the aircraft touched down with the fuselage pointing into any crosswind. The painted tires were for braking tests. A camera pod was mounted on top of the vertical fin. (Boeing BW65386)*

down during adverse weather conditions. A single B-47B-25-BW (51-2061) was used for the tests. A van contained most of the equipment and a portable dish antenna was placed next to the runway. Receiving equipment was installed in the Stratojet to drive the flight controls during landing. A normal flight crew was employed for take-off and routine flight, and to monitor the automatic landing. By all accounts the tests were relatively successful and contributed to the body of knowledge on the subject.

*Air Force Tests*

Between 1950 and 1969, the various organizations at Wright-Patterson AFB operated as many as 15 B-47s at any one time.

A B-47B-20-BW (50-053) performed numerous tests at Wright-Patterson over the years, and was subsequently tasked to participate in Project SWORD FISH – an Air Defense Command penetration test. The bomber departed the Air Defense Identification Zone

*These B-47s at Wright-Patterson were used in an unusual ASD test involving satellites and aircraft during 1965. The aircraft to the rear is NB-47E, s/n 53-4257. The aircraft carried a standard Day-Glo Orange tail band, AFSC insignia on the nose, and the unusual black and white stripes on top of the aircraft. (USAF)*

*This former 55th SRW RB-47H, s/n 53-4296, became the test bed for the General Dynamics F-111 radar system. The Air Force Avionics Laboratory insignia was applied to the right side of the fuselage and the last four digits of the tail number were applied to the forward main landing gear door. (Boeing HS6062)*

*ARDC employed this B-47 for use in development tests for the North American XB-70 Valkyrie escape capsule drop tests over Edwards AFB. A pair of stabilizer booms was extended from the capsule. Note that the bomb bay doors had been removed from the Stratojet. (left: Boeing HS6060; right: Boeing via Tony Landis)*

(ADIZ), dropped below the radar, and then attempted to penetrate the ADIZ undetected. During one of these tests, the aircraft experienced an engine failure and diverted to Westover AFB, Massachusetts. The following morning, 8 February 1958, the crew attempted a five-engine takeoff for the return flight to Wright-Patterson. With a 120,000-pound gross weight the takeoff should have been uneventful, but somehow the crew lost control of the aircraft and it crashed, killing all three aboard. Instead of retaining the accident investigation within the command, it was turned over to SAC who determined the cause was crew error. However, many in the flight test community believe that the crew experienced a failure in the elevator-rudder hydromechanical servo that they could not overcome.

*These individuals were responsible for the fly-by-wire tests at Wright-Patterson AFB, Ohio. The full white anti-radiation belly finish is indicative of other tests performed by this aircraft. Note that it had the early UNITED STATES AIR FORCE markings on the forward fuselage and the later Air Force System Command emblem. (AFMC Historian)*

The Air Force Flight Test Center (AFFTC) at Edwards AFB, California, also used B-47s for many tests over the years. One of the more interesting of these was following the jet stream. Equipment onboard a B-47E-100-BW (52-0514) followed the jet stream and kept the aircraft in the area of maximum speed. One flight from Edwards to Wright-Patterson was made in only 2.5 hours. On another occasion, the aircraft was flown to England using the jet stream. This same B-47E accompanied U-2s on overseas deployments to provide radio relay, and also provided Discovery satellite recovery guidance.

Between March and December 1958, an AFFTC B-47 was involved in Project HOT HAND to develop an improved aerial recovery system for re-entry vehicles. The B-47 flew at high altitude and dropped missile nose cones that deployed parachutes to arrest their descent. Using a trapeze snare, a Fairchild C-119 Flying Boxcar equipped with flight-operable Beavertail doors, would intercept the falling nose cone and capture the parachute with the snare. Then the nose cone would be reeled into the C-119, completing the recovery cycle. These tests were conducted over the Edwards AFB test range.

A B-47B-20-BW (50-0064) from the AFFTC was used for various bomb drop tests, but also conducted a couple of more unusual tests. During 1959 it was used eight times to drop a B-58 escape capsule to test the parachute recovery systems. Similar tests were conducted using the same aircraft to verify that the more-sophisticated XB-70A escape capsule would function as expected.

During the middle of 1956, a pair of B-47s was modified to test the Emerson Electric MD-7 fire control system and General Electric T-171 (later redesignated M61) 20-mm rotary cannon destined for the Convair B-58 Hustler. The tests conducted at Eglin AFB determined gunfire effects, ballistics dispersion, and tracking and aiming accuracy.

In 1959, a mothballed RB-47H-1-BW (53-4296) was modified to test equipment for the F-111 program. The ALD-4 pod and its supporting strut were removed from the right waist, and the strut mounting holes were faired over. The tail guns were removed and the nose modified to house the Mk. I AN/AJQ-20A bomb/nav system. The characteristic F-111 nose radome was installed, and avionics pods that would be installed on the F-111s replaced the external fuel tanks. After the test program was completed, the unique nose was replaced by a standard B-47E nose, making this Stratojet something of a bastard configuration. The aircraft is currently on display at the Air Force Armament Museum at Eglin AFB, Florida.

Also in 1959, the Air Force Aerospace Medical Research Laboratory at Wright-Patterson conducted a series of extended flight experiments on aircrew habitability and crew fatigue. The copilot's station of a B-47 was modified with the first tiltable ejection seat equipped with a pulsating seat cushion, an inflatable lumbar cushion, and a massaging G-suit. The pilot remained in the seat for the entire flight. His physiological condition was read and electronically transmitted to a recording device that was continuously transmitted to a ground receiving station for analysis. A world record for nonstop jet flight was established during an 80-hour, 36-minute flight covering a distance of 39,200 miles.

When a Russian MiG 15 was turned over to the United States by a Polish defector, it presented an opportunity to evaluate the fighter against a host of American aircraft. The MiG went to Eglin AFB and was flown by various American pilots. While they were not particularly happy with the comfort or control system of the aircraft, they were pleased with its maneuverability. One of the evaluations pitted the MiG against a B-47. Both Air Proving Ground and SAC pilots flew the B-47, with SAC Operations Analyst (Ops Annie) Richard J. Camp, crammed behind the copilot. No matter how hard the B-47 tried, it could not shake the MiG. Camp, with his stopwatch in-hand,

timed each attack and took notes on the events. Camp could not get behind the copilot without first removing his parachute. He had instructions that if they had to bail out he was to retrieve his parachute, don it, and exit after the pilots – talk about expendability! During one flight at 42,000 feet, in a last ditch effort to shake the MiG, the pilot threw the B-47 into a series of sharp banks to the left and right. The B-47 went uncontrollable for about two minutes. Camp fought the g-forces in a failed attempt to don his parachute. Later on the ground, the fighter pilot wondered what was going on inside of the B-47. Needless to say, these tests showed that the B-47 was defenseless against the MiG and something else had to be done to improve survivability.

The Flight Dynamics Laboratory at Wright-Patterson AFB modified an NB-47E-110-BW (53-2280) to serve as a fly-by-wire test bed. It was the first aircraft to incorporate a primary fly-by-wire analog flight control system, albeit only for the pitch axis. Between 14 December 1967 and November 1969 the aircraft accrued 100 flight hours with the system. Colonel Wilbur Giesler headed the program. For Phase I of the B-47 fly-by-wire program a transducer on the control column was used. This device controlled an electro-hydraulic actuator in parallel with the normal hydromechanical elevator actuator. Phase II of the program incorporated a sidestick controller for both fly-by-wire pitch and roll control. Tests had previously been conducted on other aircraft with a sidestick controller. The B-47 sidestick controller was adapted from an inexpensive radar controller that had been reclaimed from salvage. For Phase III, a dual-fail-operative

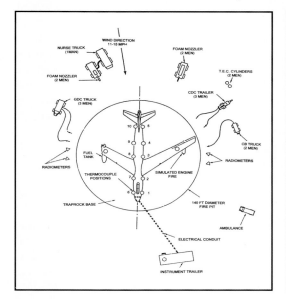

For the first FAA experiment, NAFEC personnel removed the right wing outboard of the external fuel tank and placed a variety of equipment around the aircraft. Only the No. 1 engine remained on the aircraft. (FAA-NAFEC)

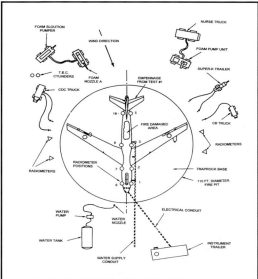

For Experiment No. 4, a whole B-47 with only the No. 1 engine remaining on the aircraft, NAFEC personnel used this equipment configuration. The removed engines were used for separate tests. (FAA-NAFEC)

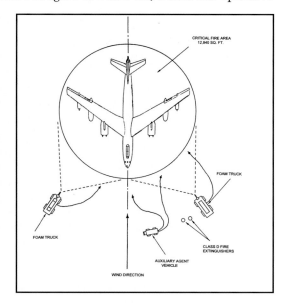

NAFEC personnel employed his equipment configuration when attempting to protect the aircraft when the wind was parallel to the fuselage. (FAA-NAFEC)

*The sole CL-52, carrying minimal RCAF markings, was employed in tests for the Orenda Iroquois engine that was planned for the Avro of Canada CF-105 Arrow. The mammoth size of the engine is readily apparent in this view. (Left: SAC Combat Crew Magazine; Right: Boeing)*

redundant elevator actuator was installed in the aircraft. In a report, Giesler stated that the fly-by-wire B-47 was "superior in every respect concerning ease of control" and that "best of all the fell is good." One of the program objectives was to increase the acceptance of the fly-by-wire concept within the community of military aviators.

### Federal Aviation Agency Tests

The FAA National Aviation Facilities Experimental Center (NAFEC) in Atlantic City employed a pair of B-47E-95-BWs (52-542 and 52-554) for experiments with JP-4 fuel. The Air Force and FAA jointly funded the program to evaluate new firefighting extinguishants and equipment between August 1967 and July 1971. These tests employed known and newly developed firefighting agents, both blanketing and auxiliary, and dispensing equipment. Only agents meeting Federal or Military Specifications or those approved by recognized laboratories were used in the testing. The objective of the full-scale fire tests on the B-47s was to determine the minimum application rate and quantity of each class of fire-extinguishing agent necessary to prevent the aluminum skin on a medium-sized aircraft from melting under severe fire conditions. Test findings were then extrapolated up or down to determine the requirements for smaller and larger aircraft. Subsequently these airframes were used in fire and crash rescue tests.

### Orenda Iroquois Engine Tests

In spite of the large numbers of B-47s built, none of them ever ended up in the service of foreign air forces. There is, however, one significant exception – a TB-47B-25-BW (51-2051) loaned to the

Royal Canadian Air Force (RCAF) as a flying test bed for the 20,000-lbf Orenda Iroquois turbojet. A pair of Iroquois engines was to power the projected Avro CF-105 Arrow long-range interceptor, which was then under development in Canada.

Prior to modification of the aircraft, tests were conducted in Boeing's transonic wind tunnel at speeds up to Mach 0.85. Low speed tests of the nacelle were done at the Convair plant in San Diego. Final low speed tests were performed at the University of Wichita facility.

After delivery, the RCAF turned the TB-47B over to Canadair on 16 February 1956 to complete the required modifications. A separate nacelle – 29 feet 5 inches long, 5 feet 4 inches in diameter, and weighing 1,380 pounds – for the test engine was installed on a stub pylon on the starboard side of the rear fuselage underneath the horizontal tail. To reduce the effects of asymmetrical thrust at low power settings, the nacelle was toed out 5 degrees. A pair of steel supports was installed at Body Stations 1068 and 1166. In addition, a drag strut was installed at Station 1118. Hydraulically operated close-off doors were installed in the nacelle nose to prevent FOD during takeoff and landing, and windmilling in flight.

An external 3-inch-diameter fuel line for the Iroquois engine was installed along the aft fuselage and was covered by a fairing. External stiffeners were added to the fuselage from the forward wheel well to the aft fuselage. Skin doublers were installed over the aft fuselage. Existing bulkheads were stiffened and new bulkheads were added. A 4,680-lb lead ballast was installed in the nose to counter the weight of the aft-mounted Iroquois engine and nacelle. Test instrumentation was installed in the bomb bay. The copilot's station was converted into a flight test engineer's station.

Canadair assigned model number CL-52 to the project. While on loan, the aircraft carried the RCAF roundels on the waist and four wing positions. A red/white/blue fin flash was applied, but the aircraft retained the last three digits of its USAF serial number, which followed a proceeding "X" to become the RCAF serial number.

The Iroquois engine was operated at altitude for the first time on 13 November 1958. At higher thrust settings the asymmetrical thrust was most noticeable. The thrust of the Iroquois engine was sufficient to maintain flight with the J47s shut down. The CL-52 spent a total of 31 hours in the air with the Iroquois engine. Most flights were routine, but on its only full-power flight the Iroquois engine suffered a fan blade failure that damaged the elevator and rudder of the CL-52. The aircraft, however, landed safely.

The first five Arrows (RCAF serials 25201 through 25205) were powered by Pratt & Whitney J75 turbojets for the initial flight tests. The first Iroquois-powered Arrow was to be number 25206, which was being readied for its first flight when the entire Arrow/Iroquois project was cancelled by the Canadian government on 20 February 1959.

Following cancellation of the program, all Arrow airframes were scrapped, including those in partially completed states on the production line. All that survives today is the front end of Arrow 25206 plus a couple of outer wing panels on display at the National Aviation Museum of Ottawa. A pair of Iroquois engines still survives, one in the National Aviation Museum and the other at the Canadian Warplane Heritage Museum in Hamilton, Ontario.

After the termination of the Arrow program, the Iroquois engine was removed from the CL-52 and the aircraft was returned to the United States in August 1959. The aircraft was subsequently scrapped at Davis-Monthan AFB.

## STILLBORN B-47 CONCEPTS

Naturally, there were many variations of the basic B-47 design explored during the gestation and service career of the Stratojet. A few of the more interesting designs are detailed here.

### Project MX-948

Boeing was already looking to the future by January 1948 with four alternate aircraft concepts that were derived from the B-47 under Project MX-948. These design concepts capitalized on current aerodynamic and structural experience. By using the basic B-47 wing, strategic engine locations and bicycle landing gear could be adapted to a variety of new configurations. Both turbojet and turboprop versions were proposed.

**Model 474 Basic Proposal Aircraft A** – Powered by four Allison T40-A-2 turboprops, this would be the smallest practicable aircraft that would meet all of the design requirements and have excellent takeoff characteristics. This design was assigned the designation of XB-55 and was the only fully turboprop bomber to receive a government MDS designation. A crew of 10 would have manned the aircraft. Defensive armament was to have a dozen 20-mm cannons mounted in three turrets.

**Model 464-33-1 Alternate Aircraft B** – Powered by four Wright XT35-W-3 turboprops, its high speed would exceed the design requirements. The basic design could have been used for normal long-range missions or for an extended range mission through use of refueling and/or forward operating bases. The aircraft would have been highly effective for shorter-range missions of the type anticipated by Project MX-948 requirements. The aircraft would have possessed outstanding takeoff performance and had space provisions for heavier loads.

**Model 450-5-5 Alternate Aircraft C** – Basically a modified XB-47, six Westinghouse X40E2 turbojet engines would have provided power. Its high speed offered inherent defense, greater flexibility, and less crew fatigue. The forward fuselage length was increased by 36 inches for added fuel capacity. The internal RATO system was deleted and additional fuel tanks installed. All defensive armament was eliminated, thereby reducing weight and offering a 95-mph increase in cruise speed.

**Model 479 Alternate Aircraft D** – Essentially, this aircraft was like the Model 450-5-5 except that two inhabited tail gunner positions were added and the bomb bay capacity was increased. In addition the wing area was increased, but the heavier aircraft resulted in performance penalties with respect to high speed and rate of climb.

### Boeing Model 450-150-30

On 27 December 1951 Boeing began designing the Model 450-150-30 long-range patrol bomber for the U.S. Navy. While retaining the same general size and shape of the B-47, the aircraft had significant changes to meet the Navy's requirements. The crew consisted of a pilot, copilot, navigator-minelayer, radio-radar ECM operator, and gunner. Most unusual was the high cockpit blister that housed the two pilots. While constructed mostly of sheet metal, three panels made up the forward windscreen, and there were two windows on each side of the cockpit. One eyebrow window was located aft each of the forward windscreen panels.

Structural reinforcing would permit the aircraft to have a maximum gross weight of 166,600 pounds and an alternate gross weight of 168,200 pounds. Six spoilers were located on top of each wing in line with the outboard flap. The tail turret was revised to accommodate the Navy's usual pair of 20-mm cannon with 500 rounds of ammunition.

Four 15,000-lbf Pratt & Whitney J57-P-1 turbojets provided power. The outboard nacelles were to be mounted essentially like those on production Stratojets; however, the inboard pylons were shorter and the engines were not cantilevered as far as those on the YB-47C/B-47Z. The inboard nacelles were positioned on the outer edge of the pylons.

### Boeing Model 450-166-38

Still another version of the Stratojet was the Boeing Model 450-166-38. Based on the B-47E, this version would have been powered

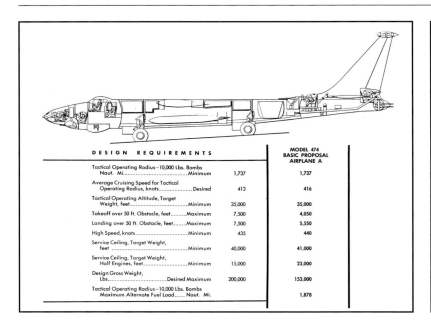

| DESIGN REQUIREMENTS | | MODEL 474 BASIC PROPOSAL AIRPLANE A |
|---|---|---|
| Tactical Operating Radius–10,000 Lbs. Bombs Naut. Mi. .................... Minimum | 1,737 | 1,737 |
| Average Cruising Speed for Tactical Operating Radius, knots .............. Desired | 413 | 416 |
| Tactical Operating Altitude, Target Weight, feet ...................... Minimum | 35,000 | 35,000 |
| Takeoff over 50 ft. Obstacle, feet ...... Maximum | 7,500 | 4,050 |
| Landing over 50 ft. Obstacle, feet ...... Maximum | 7,500 | 5,550 |
| High Speed, knots ..................... Minimum | 435 | 440 |
| Service Ceiling, Target Weight, feet ...................... Minimum | 40,000 | 41,000 |
| Service Ceiling, Target Weight, Half Engines, feet ................ Minimum | 15,000 | 23,000 |
| Design Gross Weight, Lbs. ................... Desired Maximum | 200,000 | 153,000 |
| Tactical Operating Radius–10,000 Lbs. Bombs Maximum Alternate Fuel Load .... Naut. Mi. | | 1,878 |

*Model 474 Basic Proposal Airplane A inboard profile.*

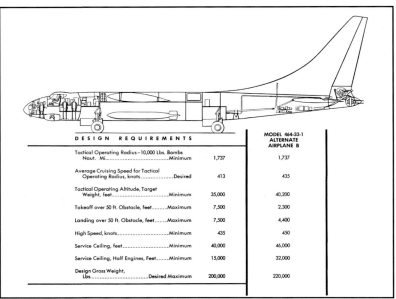

| DESIGN REQUIREMENTS | | MODEL 464-33-1 ALTERNATE AIRPLANE B |
|---|---|---|
| Tactical Operating Radius–10,000 Lbs. Bombs Naut. Mi. .................... Minimum | 1,737 | 1,737 |
| Average Cruising Speed for Tactical Operating Radius, knots .............. Desired | 413 | 435 |
| Tactical Operating Altitude, Target Weight, feet ...................... Minimum | 35,000 | 40,200 |
| Takeoff over 50 ft. Obstacle, feet ...... Maximum | 7,500 | 2,300 |
| Landing over 50 ft. Obstacle, feet ...... Maximum | 7,500 | 4,400 |
| High Speed, knots ..................... Minimum | 435 | 450 |
| Service Ceiling, feet ................. Minimum | 40,000 | 46,000 |
| Service Ceiling, Half Engines, Feet ..... Minimum | 15,000 | 32,000 |
| Design Gross Weight, Lbs. ................... Desired Maximum | 200,000 | 220,000 |

*Model 464-33-1 Alternate Airplane B inboard profile.*

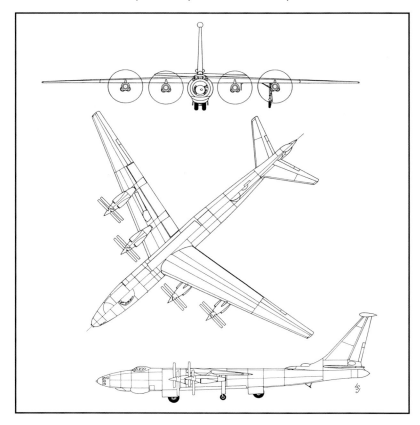

*Three-view drawing of the XB-55. This was the only fully turboprop bomber design to receive a government MDS designation. (L. S. Jones)*

by four 15,000-lbf Pratt & Whitney J57-P-1 turbojets, incorporate strengthened landing gear, have a 33.5 percent increase in wing area, and a 45 percent increase in horizontal stabilizer area. The maximum takeoff weight would have been 221,090 pounds and the combat weight would have been 133,400 pounds.

The engine/nacelle arrangement would have been similar to the Model 450-150-30. Thirty-three externally mounted RATO bottles would have augmented takeoff thrust. A pair of 20-mm M24A1 cannon served by 700 rounds of ammunition was in a tail turret.

### Almost Aussie

Since the formation of the Malaysian Federation in 1963, Australia has been the recipient of open hostility from the new nation. Australia was in the awkward position of having the English Electric Canberra as its main bomber. This aircraft did not have the range to provide a viable deterrent to Malaysia. On 24 October 1963 the Australian Government placed an order for 24 General Dynamics F-111s; however, the aircraft was in the midst of a political battle in the United States. The other alternative at the time was the British Aircraft Corporation's TSR-2, but its operational readiness was too far out in the future. As a palliative, the United States offered a no-charge lease of two squadrons of B-47E and RB-47Es. Between 15 November and 4 December 1963, three B-47Es (52-0348, 53-1822, and 53-1845) gave 10 familiarization flights to 26 Royal Australian Air Force pilots and navigators. The Australian Government, probably due to the complexity of the aircraft, declined the offer for the B-47s and leased two-dozen McDonnell F-4E Phantom IIs while awaiting their F-111Cs.

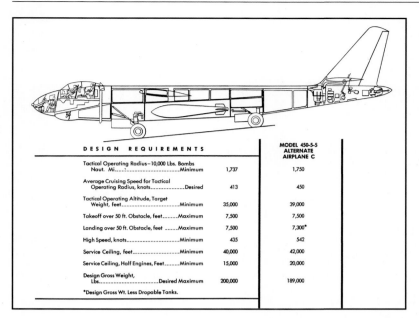

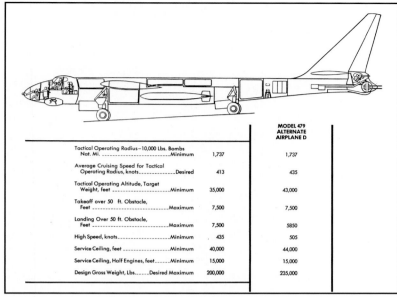

Model 450-5-5 Alternate Airplane C inboard profile.

Model 479 Alternate Airplane D inboard profile.

## PROJECT MX-948 AIRCRAFT PROPOSALS

| Parameter | Model 474 Basic Aircraft A | Model 464-33-1 Alternate Aircraft B | Model 450-5-5 Alternate Aircraft C | Model 479 Alternate Aircraft D |
|---|---|---|---|---|
| Length | 119 ft. 10.8 in. | 132 ft. 9 in. | 110 ft. 5.8 in. | 131 ft. 5 in. |
| Wing Span | 135 ft. | 185 ft. | 116 ft. | 150 ft. |
| Height | 33 ft. 8 in. | 45 ft. 11 in. | 27 ft.10 in. | 35 ft. 3 in. |
| Wing Area | 1,500 sq. ft. | 2,600 sq. ft. | 1,428 sq. ft. | 2,500 sq. ft. |
| Horizontal Tail Area | | 615 sq. ft. | 268 sq. ft. | 470 sq. ft. |
| Vertical Tail Area | | 430 sq. ft. | 230 sq. ft | 370 sq. ft. |
| Empty Weight | 78,020 lbs. | 122,500 lbs. | 77,370 lbs. | 96,760 lbs. |
| Design Useful Load | | 97,500 lbs. | 111,630 lbs. | 138,240 lbs. |
| Design Gross Weight | 153,000 lbs. | 220,000 lbs. | 189,000 lbs. | 235,000 lbs. |
| Engines | 4 x Allison T40-A-2 turboprops | 4 x Wright XT35-W-3 turboprops | 6 x Westinghouse X40E2 turbojets | 6 x Westinghouse X40E2 turbojets |
| Operating Radius with 10,000 lb. Bombs (Minimum 1,737 NM) | 1,737 nm | 1,737 nm | 1,750 nm | 1,737 nm |
| Average Cruising Speed for Operating Radius (Desired 413 Kts.) | 416 Kts. | 435 Kts. | 450 Kts. | 435 Kts. |
| Tactical Operating Altitude, Target Weight (Minimum 35,000 ft.) | 35,000 ft. | 40,200 ft. | 39,000 ft. | 43,000 ft. |
| Landing Over 50' Obstacle (Maximum 7,500 ft.) | 5,550 ft. | 4,400 ft. | 7,300 ft. | 5,850 ft. |
| High Speed (Minimum 435 Kts.) | 440 Kts. | 450 Kts. | 542 Kts. | 505 Kts. |
| Service Ceiling (Minimum 40,000 ft.) | 41,000 ft. | 46,000 ft. | 42,000 ft. | 44,000 ft. |
| Service Ceiling (1/2 Engines) (Minimum 15,000 ft.) | 23,000 ft. | 32,000 ft. | 20,000 ft. | 15,000 ft. |
| Design Gross Weight – (Maximum 200,000 lbs.) | 153,000 lbs. | 220,000 lbs. | 189,000 lbs. | 235,000 lbs. |

Factory technicians were checking out the flight controls in this B-47. Without the canopy, many of the interior components are visible. A separate windscreen was installed for the copilot. (Boeing BW93258 via SAC Combat Crew Magazine)

# Chapter 10

# *DEFINING THE AIRPLANE*

The Air Force employed the Mission-Design-Series (MDS) designation system to identify an aircraft. In defining the B-47E: **B** = bomber mission, **47** = the 47th bomber type, and **E** = the fifth model in the series.

Further definition comes from the block number that defines running production line changes. Normally, these numbers are not sequential – usually five or ten numbers are skipped to allow further definition if required at a later date. Boeing normally used every fifth block number (i.e., they would have blocks 90, 95, 100, but skip 91, 92, 93, etc.). Lastly is the suffix identifying the manufacturer; i.e., **BW** = Boeing-Wichita, **DT** = Douglas-Tulsa, and **LM** = Lockheed-Marietta.

The physical layout of an aircraft follows traditional shipbuilding terminology with increments being in one-inch intervals. The fuselage is laid out with its fore and aft dimensions being stations; station zero is usually well ahead of the nose of the aircraft to allow future modifications or the use of flight-test booms or other protuberances. With the B-47, the standard bomber nose began at Station 42.50; whereas the RB-47E/K nose began at Station 10.00. Buttock lines define its inboard and outboard location, while its vertical measurements are defined in waterlines. The wings and empennage locations are defined with their own station numbers increasing in the outboard direction from the centerline.

Yet another definition is applied to the aircraft. These are section numbers that were developed during World War II by Boeing for cost accounting. The accompanying illustration identifies the various sections of the B-47.

## B-47 DESIGN

The design of the B-47 required a great number of technological innovations in order to meet its design objectives and be mission-capable. Capitalizing on the lessons learned from the B-29, Boeing expended great effort in developing structural materials and systems capable of operating at high speeds and altitudes over long ranges, while carrying the required bomb load.

More than just structural materials provided challenges. Something as simple as a rubber seal around the canopy or hatches required special lubricants to be applied to prevent damage occurring when opening the components after the aircraft had been cold-soaked at altitude.

While the early B-47s were limited to a maximum gross taxi weight of 185,000 pounds, a number of structural improvements resulted in later aircraft being capable of a 230,000-pound gross weight. These changes began as a result of the range extension program where additional fuel tanks were added to the aircraft. Just

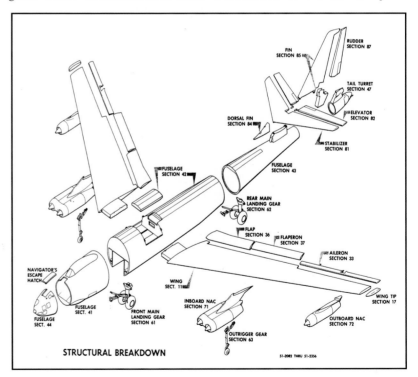

*The major structural breakdown of the B-47 is depicted in this exploded view drawing. Note that each major section has its nomenclature followed by a number. This number is the section number used for production identification and cost accounting breakdown. This system was developed by Boeing with the B-17 during World War II.*

## B-47 TRIVIA

The cooling capacity of the B-47's air conditioning system would service five five-room houses. Its heating system for both the cabin and anti-icing would heat 22 five-room houses. The fuel requirement for engine start, warm-up, and taxi (a distance of approximately 1.5 miles) was 300 gallons.

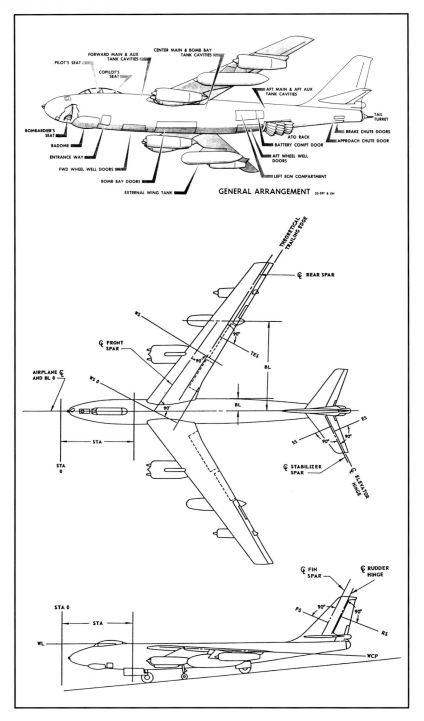

*This plan view drawing shows the locating plane designations for the B-47. STA = Station. BL = Buttock Line. WS = Wing Station. CL = Centerline. TES = Trailing Edge Station. ES = Elevator Station. WL= Waterline. FS = Fin Station. RS = Rudder Station. WCP = Wing Chord Plane.*

strengthening the aft main gear vertical beam and installing 32-ply tires could increase the gross weight to 200,000 pounds. To gain the full 230,000-pound gross-weight capability, the Station 861 bulkhead was reinforced and both the water-alcohol injection system and external RATO racks were installed. Still, if the aft center of gravity exceeded 34-percent of the mean aerodynamic chord, the aircraft was prohibited from taking off.

### Structures

Designing the B-47 afforded ample opportunities for the use of dissimilar materials. Strength, durability, thermal environments, and weight limitations dictated the use of specific materials, many of which were relatively new in the post-World War II era. While wartime aircraft were built using 24 and 24ST aluminum alloys, the B-47 required stronger materials such as 2014, 2024, 2024ST, and 7075 aluminum, magnesium, and titanium. Forged steel and corrosion resistant steel (CRES) were employed in high strength areas such as landing gear and engine mounts. Each of the metals has unique characteristics in their basic form; with heat-treating the range of these properties increases considerably.

A variety of finishes were applied in production to inhibit corrosion of the aluminum alloy structural components. Accumulated debris such as exhaust gas residue and environmental pollutants formed hygroscopic particles that retained moisture that collected in crevices where it induced corrosion. Operating in areas of industrial pollutants and saltwater environments exacerbated the effects of such debris. To ensure structural integrity, the airframe was washed at regular intervals to remove mud, water, gravel, and other debris accumulated from the operating environment.

### Wings

The fully cantilevered B-47 wing consisted of the center and two outboard sections. No production breaks were incorporated into the outboard wing sections, thereby increasing strength and reducing weight because there is no need for complicated structural joints. The center section spars were perpendicular to the fuselage, whereas the outboard wing spars were swept back in conformance with the wing planform. The control surfaces (ailerons, and inboard and outboard flaps) were attached to the wing trailing edge.

The wing was designed with two spars joined by a stressed skin that was constructed in one piece to form a box beam. The 35-degree swept wing had a thin airfoil section with a heavy inboard skin tapering along the span from a maximum of 0.563-inch at the root to 0.188-inch at Buttock Line 683, near the tip. Inspar ribs were nominally installed at 35-inch intervals. The stressed skin was stiffened by I- and Z-section extrusions running span wise along the internal surfaces of the skins. This wing box was attached to the fuselage with four large taper pins, known as bottle pins, located at Buttock Line 45 (the wing/fuselage joint). All wing shear loads were transferred into the fuselage through these pins. Additional shear fasteners were incorporated along the upper and lower wing inspar areas where the wing attaches to the fuselage. The double-skin aluminum alloy construction leading edge formed a duct for thermal anti-icing.

Fowler-type flaps were installed along the wing inboard trailing edge and modified Fowler-type flaperons were located outboard on the wing. While the outboard flap had several intercostals near the inboard nacelle fairing, the inboard flap had none and the spar carried all of the bending loads. Each flap had conventional ribs spaced approximately at nine-inch intervals. While three carriages and tracks supported the inboard flaps, the outboard flaps had four carriages and tracks. The tracks were attached to the wing trailing edge structure.

The ailerons were aluminum alloy structures supported by six hinge ribs. Each aileron was divided into an inboard and outboard segment connected by a common torque box in the wing's outboard nacelle region. An aluminum and magnesium alloy tab was hinged to each aileron. To ensure increased balance action

and control, the ailerons incorporated a balance seal along the leading edge. The wingtips, access doors, and leading edges were all removable for maintenance.

B-47s were equipped with one of two different wingtip configurations. Initially there was an aluminum sheet metal tip that served no function other than to provide aerodynamic smoothness and a place to install the navigation light. Later came a laminated fiberglass skin with internal rib chords and stiffeners serving as an antenna for multi-purpose electronic countermeasures (ECM) equipment. The fiberglass tip increased the wingspan by four inches and slightly increased performance.

The swept wings tended to experience a loss of lift at high speeds due to airflow separation along the outboard wing section, causing the aircraft to pitch upwards. Two rows of vortex generators were

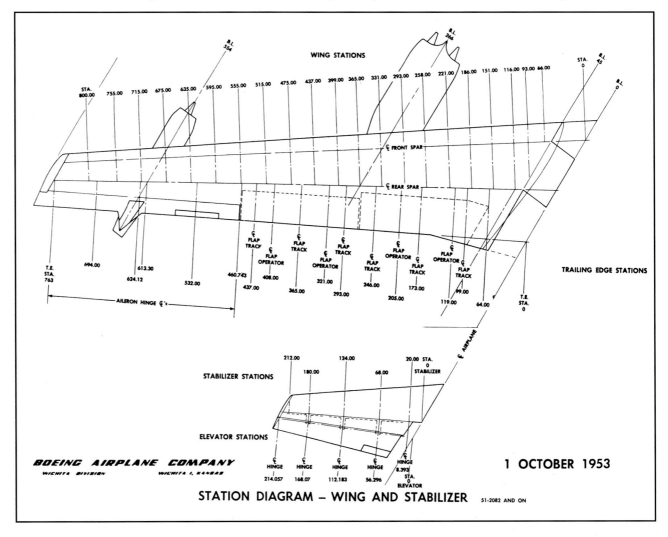

*This plan view reveals the wing station and wing buttock line numbers. Note that the station numbers are perpendicular to the swept wing; whereas the buttock lines are parallel to the aircraft centerline.*

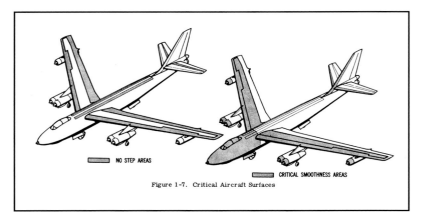

Figure 1-7. Critical Aircraft Surfaces

NO STEP AREAS

CRITICAL SMOOTHNESS AREAS

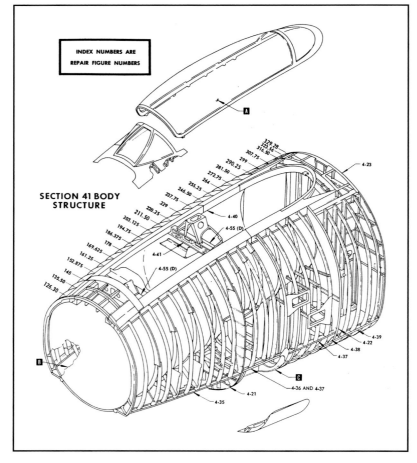

INDEX NUMBERS ARE
REPAIR FIGURE NUMBERS

SECTION 41 BODY
STRUCTURE

*Typical fuselage construction is shown in this isometric drawing. The Station Numbers are in one-inch increments. This view shows the frame layout for Section 41. The pressure vessel for the crew compartment is basically cylindrical. The space to the left of the crew compartment housed the entryway and hatch, and the crawlway back to the hellhole in the bomb bay. The canopy depicted is the early sliding version.*

installed along the upper surface of each wing, just aft of the front spar, to keep the boundary layer close to the wing. These small pieces of bent metal were nominally spaced at three-inch intervals and screwed into threaded inserts in the wing skin. So critical were these devices, they had to be inspected prior to each flight and only two per wing could be missing in order to dispatch the aircraft. Because these small devices cure major headaches for designers, they have been called aspirin for aerodynamicists.

Aerodynamic smoothness of the wings was extremely critical. For the B-47, scuffed wing skin surfaces could result in a 20-knot reduction in speed.

## Empennage

The horizontal stabilizer consisted of a single spar with a stressed skin without span-wise stiffeners. Ribs, installed perpendicular to the spar, were nominally spaced at eight-inch intervals. The horizontal was of single-piece construction that penetrated the vertical stabilizer without a break. The horizontal was attached to the fuselage at Station 1090.6 by a single bolt, and to the stabilizer attachment terminal fitting at Station 1169.83 by a pair of bolts. The stabilizer had the same sweepback as the wing and a slightly smaller thickness ratio. As with the wing, a double-skin construction afforded a leading edge anti-icing duct.

The elevators were of monospar stressed-skin construction and were installed without span-wise stiffeners. An auxiliary spar afforded support for the elevator tabs. Four hinge support ribs, cantilevered from the auxiliary spar, supported the elevator.

The vertical stabilizer was essentially of the same monospar construction as the horizontal stabilizer; however, a short auxiliary spar was installed below the horizontal stabilizer cutout. Ribs were nominally installed at nine-inch intervals. The leading edge was swept back at 40 degrees. Once more, a double-skin leading edge formed the anti-ice duct. The fin was attached to the fuselage at three points. The forward attach point was common to the horizontal stabilizer connection, and a pair of aft terminal fittings was located at Station 1172.45. The vertical fin was topped with a laminated fiberglass tip that contained the VOR antenna.

The rudder and elevators also consisted of monospar stressed-skin construction without span-wise stiffeners. The ribs were nominally spaced at seven-inch intervals and were perpendicular to the spars. Five hinge ribs were cantilevered from the fin spar and a hinge was attached directly to the rudder stub structure. Both the elevators and rudder incorporated balance seals.

## Fuselage

The fuselage was divided into five major sections for production reasons. The nose and lower fuselage sections determined the aircraft's mission configuration. Although the fuselage configuration varied for each B-47 series, the primary structure was identical for all

*This B-47B was under construction at WIBAC. While the fuselage was stabilized on jacks, the built-up wing assembly was being lowered into place. The aft right wing attach point is visible in the Station 5110.50 bulkhead. Four milk bottle pins held the wing to the fuselage. These pins would later become the subject of a major modification program after the aircraft was flown at higher gross weights than originally planned, and used for toss bombing. The waist cutout would accommodate nine RATO bottles. The forward jack was placed against the longeron for the radar compartment. (Boeing BW60223)*

aircraft. A semi-monocoque design was constructed around bulkheads and four longerons that provided bending strength. A pair of short longerons located under each wing cutout afforded additional bending strength. The fuselage skin served as a web between the longerons that acted as chord beams providing tension and compression strength. The skin panels were joined with lap joints. The walkway members located above the upper deck provided additional fuselage bending strength. Each circumferential frame and bulkhead was nominally spaced at nine-inch intervals.

The Station 425 and 515.50 bulkheads incorporated 2014 aluminum alloy forgings with additional 7075 aluminum sheet and other structural members to form the wing attachment fittings. A similar design was employed for attachment of both the forward and aft main

landing gears. The outer gear struts contained a trunnion that rotated within support fittings attached to the wheel well sidewalls. The trunnion acted as a horizontal beam between the bulkheads. A vertical beam located on the forward bulkhead of each wheel well carried the loads from the drag strut and retraction mechanism into the bulkhead.

The main fuel tank decks were located above the forward wheel well and the bomb bay. These decks consisted of longitudinal and transverse beams with skin attached to bulkheads. Because these decks formed an integral part of the fuselage torsion box, the access doors also acted as structural members. In addition, the tank access doors below the lower longerons between Stations 861 and 1024 (aft of the aft main wheel well to the fin leading edge fillet) were also structural members.

The pressurized crew compartment was located within the two forward-most fuselage sections. The tapered forward fuselage was basically cylindrical in cross-section and tapered like a cone. The front and rear of the cone were truncated to form the crew compartment. The pressure area for this compartment was designed in the form of a frustum enclosed within the outer shell and was attached adjacent to the beams along the canopy cutout. The frustum was closed at the front by the nose section and at the rear by the bulkhead at Station 329.26. Clad aluminum 2024 alloy was used for the interior skin and stiffener channels. A hatch, located beneath the navigator's seat, permitted downward ejection in the event of an emergency. In addition, a hatch above the navigator allowed emergency egress on the ground. This hatch also incorporated a sextant port on early B-47s. The crew areas were designed for a pressure differential up to 6.55 psi.

The canopy was formed from laminated plastic sheets composed of 0.20-inch face plies and a 0.20-inch butyral inner layer. The XB-47s, B-47As, and early B-47Bs were equipped with a sliding canopy that could be operated either hydraulically or pneumatically and could be ejected in an emergency. When open, the canopy was secured to the fuselage by rollers at the forward end and by hooks at the operating arms. When closed, the canopy rested on a pressure seal and was secured by 14 latch hooks. The sliding canopy was installed on aircraft 51-2092 through 52-611, and 51-2092 through 52-825.

Later B-47Bs and all later models used a clamshell canopy. For normal operation, the clamshell canopy was operated with an electrically actuated hydraulic system. In an emergency, pneumatic pressure and ballistics operated the canopy. If the canopy were opened in flight, the force of the slipstream would lift the canopy and break a 5,000-pound tension shear pin, resulting in loss of the canopy. Alternately, the canopy could be jettisoned in an emergency. A periscopic sextant mount was incorporated into the clamshell canopy above the copilot's seat; the copilot would trade places with the navigator while the latter performed his sextant shots or performed the shot for the navigator. Aircraft 52-612 and subsequent had the clamshell canopy installed as did 52-3374 and on.

### Landing Gear

Because the high-speed airfoil of the wing was so thin, there was no room to stow the landing gear as had traditionally been done on large aircraft. Instead, Boeing opted for a bicycle landing gear arrangement. Each main gear consisted of an inner and outer cylinder, the former containing the axles and the latter the trunnion. The air-oil (or oleo) shock struts were designed to provide a 12-inch stroke. The main gear was cantilevered in the lateral direction by the trunnion, and supported in the fore and aft direction by a drag strut and link. The gear rotated about the trunnion for retraction and extension. The drag strut and link were pinned to form a knee joint at which one end of the retraction actuator was attached. Bendix built the forward gear strut and Cleveland Pneumatic manufactured the aft strut. Beginning with the B-47B, a taxi light was mounted on the forward gear strut.

*Early B-47s were equipped with a fixed windscreen and sliding canopy that rolled forward and down to latch. Note the radio antennas in the top of the canopy above the copilot. This crew from the 303rd BMW was going through their preflight checklist. (USAF 12-54-35)*

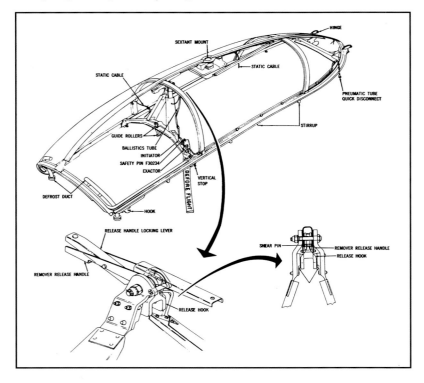

*Later B-47s were equipped with a clamshell canopy that greatly increased safety for the pilots.*

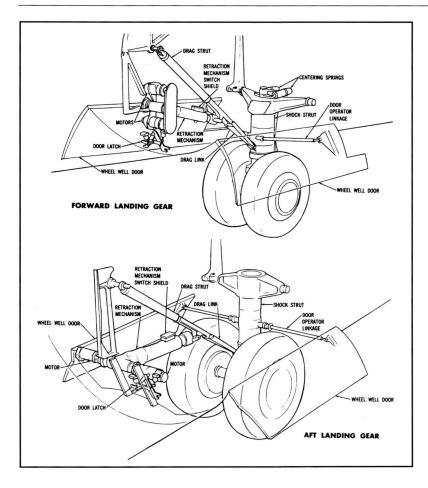

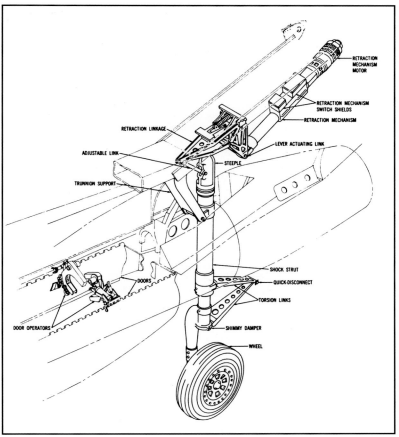

*Major components of forward and aft main landing gears are shown in these illustrations.*

*Major components of outrigger landing gear are shown in this illustration. Note how the anti-skid electrical conduit and hydraulic lines are installed to articulate with the gear torque links.*

An electric motor drove a Thompson Saginaw ballscrew actuator that operated the gear during retraction and extension. Locks at either end of the ballscrew held the gear in either the extended or retracted position. To preclude damaging the gear, the flight crew observed the airspeed limits on a placard in the cockpit; 305 knots (350 mph) for extension and 215 knots (250 mph) for retraction.

Goodrich designed and manufactured the wheels, tires, and brakes. Each main gear had two wheels with 56-inch tires. When operating below 185,000 pounds, the B-47 was equipped with 24-ply tires. At higher gross weights, 32-ply tires that carried a 200-pound weight penalty were used. The main gear wheel base was 36 feet, 4 inches.

Hydraulically powered steering cylinders on the forward strut permitted turning of the aircraft during ground operations. This steering system also served as a shimmy damper for the forward gear. Steering control inputs were made through the rudder pedals. Hydraulic pressure drove the steering cylinders at a rate defined by the ratio selector. Upon retraction, the hydraulic system depressurized and rendered the steering system inoperative. For takeoff and

landing, steering was limited to 12 degrees (6 degrees either side of center). When the TAXI position was selected, the forward gear could traverse a 60-degree arc to either side of the centerline. With the TOW mode selected, the forward gear could travel through 120 degrees. A red stripe on each of the forward gear doors indicated the limit for gear travel. Placing the gear in the TOW position was a two-handed operation reserved for maintenance personnel, and precluded the flight crew from inadvertently selecting the TOW configuration.

Installation of the forward gear doors was critical to preclude in-flight opening. While the forward edge of the door contacted the fuselage, the inboard portion of the aft edge required a 0.50-inch gap to preclude unlatching in flight.

The landing gear brake system employed six duplex expander tube-type brakes. Two brakes were installed on each of the forward wheels and one on the inboard side of each of the aft wheels. No brakes were installed on the outrigger gears. Toe pressure on the tops of any one of the four rudder pedals would actuate all of the brakes. In the event of a condition involving the loss of hydraulics, sufficient pressure on either

Maj. William J. Schneider, from HQ 43rd BW at Davis-Monthan AFB, Arizona, was inspecting the aft main landing gear of this B-47. The torque links that keep the inner and outer cylinders of the strut together moved as compression loads on the strut changed, thereby offering a shock absorber. The black flexible hoses were for the brake pressure and return lines. Note the two different tire treads. Maj. Schneider was wearing a pair of capeskin gloves. The canteen was a must to keep the crew hydrated on long high altitude flights. The photograph dates from 7 May 1958. (USAF)

This photograph of a B-47B clearly shows the forward gear turning capability for taxiing. The outrigger gears were free to caster. Note the absence of the NLG towing stripe on the gear door. (USAF)

of the pilot's brake pedals would activate the emergency braking system. Upon gear retraction an automatic braking valve and automatic brake actuator stop wheel rotation at the start of retraction relieved the pilots of this action and eliminated possible damage to the retraction mechanism caused by sudden braking during retraction. The B-47 was equipped with a Hydro-Aire Mark I antiskid system that prevented tire skidding thereby reducing the chances for blown tires.

To stabilize the aircraft during ground operations, a pair of outrigger gear was employed. A long strut, with a single 26 x 6.66-inch tire, was mounted within each inboard nacelle. The outrigger gear track was 44 feet, 4 inches. The gear retracted forward, and a pair of long doors in the bottom of the nacelle faired the gear in when retracted. Each outrigger strut had a 24-inch stroke, accommodating up to seven degrees of wing droop. A shimmy damper was incorporated into each outrigger strut. A pair of torsion links joining the inner and outer cylinders restricted castering to 28 degrees inboard and 93 degrees outboard for normal operations. To ease ground handling, the torsion links could be disconnected permitting the outrigger gear to caster through 360 degrees. On occasion, B-47s developed shimmy in the outrigger landing gear that could result in severe structural damage to not only the gear, but also the inboard engine mounts. If shimmy was reported, maintenance had to immediately inspect the outrigger gear. However, regular inspections would preclude the condition before it became noticeable.

With aircraft gross weights ranging between 80,000 and 185,000 pounds, the main gear tires would be inflated to between 7 psi and 179 psi, accordingly. Should the aircraft gross weight be less than 150,000 pounds, the outrigger gear tires would be inflated to 150 psi. Tire pressure would be increased to 180 psi for higher gross weights.

### Nacelles and Pylons

The four nacelles of the Stratojet housed six General Electric J47 turbojet engines; two engines, separated by a titanium firewall, were located in the inboard nacelles. Each engine was supported at two points. A semicircular saddle of rectangular cross-section formed the forward support. The aft support consisted of a pin connected to a pad on the turbine case. The outboard nacelle saddle was supported by a brace assembly that attached to the saddle on either side of the engine centerline and to fittings on the wing front spar. A steel beam supported the inboard nacelle saddle, located between the two saddles in a plane perpendicular to the engine centerline, by steel drag struts that ran diagonally and connected the nacelle strut through the rear engine fitting.

The two inboard nacelles were cantilevered below and forward of the wing by a pylon. This configuration allowed rapid engine changes and greatly eased engine maintenance tasks. The pylon was basically a single cell semi-monocoque unit of two-spar construction with a structural leading edge. The lower end of the strut was made from sheet steel to withstand the high engine operating temperatures. The front spar was made from 7075 aluminum extruded chords with a clad 7075 web over two-thirds of the length. For thermal fatigue reasons, the front spar was made from sheet steel within the wing contour where the thermal anti-icing duct passed through the spar. The rear spar was fabricated from 7075 extruded chords and clad 7075 webs. Loads from the strut were transmitted through single pin terminals at the upper end of each spar chord. The loads were transmitted to 2014 aluminum fittings located on the wing front spar and wing lower surface between the spars.

Both inboard and outboard nacelles were of similar construction with a cantilevered nose cowl, side panels, and tail cone shroud. Only the geometry of the inboard and outboard nacelles differed. The nose cowl was of double wall construction to form an anti-icing duct. The nose cowls were attached by cowl rings to the engine case and were readily removable for maintenance. The tail cone shrouds were fabricated from either corrosion resistant steel (CRES) or titanium. The tail cone was attached to the engine by four quick-disconnect pins and steel fittings that were bolted to the engine turbine flange. The inboard nose cowls were highly polished and served as mirrors for the pilots to observe the position of the landing gear and bomb bay doors.

It is interesting to note that when later models of the Convair B-36 required additional thrust, the B-47 inboard nacelles and struts were employed. Bell Aircraft manufactured the entire installation. The only difference was that the outrigger gears were omitted and the gear doors were secured closed. When a Boeing inspector assigned to Bell Aircraft was confronted with these nacelles and struts he refused to buy them off with his inspector's stamp. It was only after he was shown the drawing that tabulated specific serial number units for the B-36 that he applied his stamp of approval.

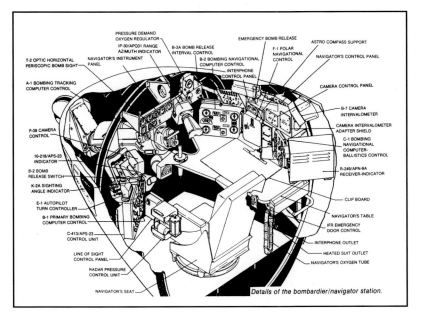

*Details of the bombardier/navigator station.*

*The nose section of the B-47 was formed as a frustum of a right circular cone.*

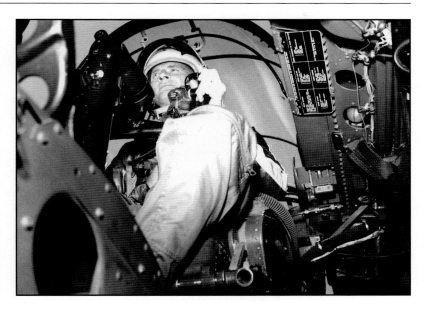

*Pilots' stations were located above the catwalk, with some controls located along the left sidewall across the catwalk. (Via SAC Combat Crew Magazine)*

### Crew Accommodations

The radar-bombardier-navigator-radio operator's position occupied the forward-most portion of the crew compartment. To the left were the bombing system controls. Directly forward was the T-2 optic horizontal periscopic sight for the Y-4 bombsight. The primary navigation instruments were located on the forward instrument panel. To the right was the IP-30/AN/APQ-31 range azimuth indicator, followed by the bomb intervalometer control. Farther to the right were the controls for the bomb/nav computer, polar navigation system, astrocompass, camera intervalometer, and ECM receiver. The navigation table located on the right side of the crew compartment had a joystick for the bomb computer and a large surface for performing navigational duties. The seat rotated to permit access to the various controls. While the B-47As were delivered with Republic upward ejection seats for the radar bombardier-navigator-radio operator they proved to be ineffective. Hence B-47Bs were initially delivered without ejection seats for this position. Beginning at Line Number 731 (52-508), new Stanley downward ejection seats were incorporated in production. These seats were retrofitted during Project TURNAROUND.

A downward ejection hatch was located beneath the navigator's ejection seat to provide an opening during the egress operation. The hatch was a structural element formed to match the external fuselage contour, a pressure seal, with latching and release jettison mechanisms incorporated. A 2,000-psi air cylinder was employed when jettisoning the hatch.

The pilots were located high in the cockpit beneath the canopy in tandem seats. The main instrument panels were located in front of

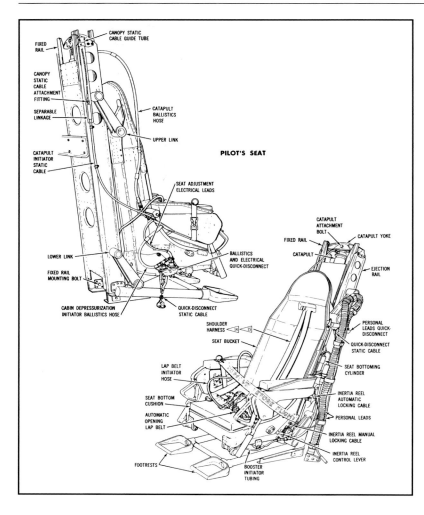

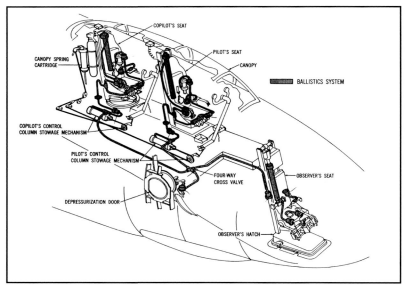

*The highly complicated flight crew ejection system was designed to permit egress in the most expeditious manner. It was a two-step system. First to function was the cabin depressurization door, and the pilots' control columns were stowed to afford maximum clearance. In the second sequence, the canopy was jettisoned and the pilots could be ejected upwards. For the navigator, the observer's hatch would be jettisoned; the seat had to be centered forward, followed by the downward ejection of the seat and navigator.*

*The ejectable components of the pilots' seats are depicted in these illustrations.*

each pilot. A throttle console, one for each pilot, was located beneath the right canopy rail. Rudder pedals were located in the conventional position as was the control wheel. Each pilot's seat had a vertical adjustment feature. The copilot's seat could be rotated 180 degrees to permit operation of the defensive tail armament. While both XB-47s and the B-47As were equipped with Republic ejection seats, they were inactivated on the all B-47Bs until Line Number 731 (52-508) when improved Weber seats were introduced. These were also retrofitted under Project TURNAROUND.

The ejection seats had two components: a fixed structure and an ejectable structure. The fixed rail structure supported the seat, remained in the aircraft, and provided a trajectory line for an ejection. Each seat was equipped with adjustment controls for crew comfort, and ejection controls, located in the right armrest, for initiating the ejection sequence. The seat control handles were painted red. Each seat also had a shoulder harness and an automatically opening lap belt.

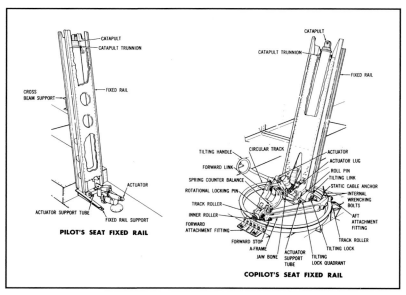

*The fixed rail components of the pilots' seats remained in the aircraft during an ejection. Note that the aircraft commander's seat was fixed, while the copilot's seat could rotate 180 degrees to permit access to the gunnery station.*

Quick-disconnect fittings were installed for the ballistics, electrical, and oxygen systems. Footrests installed on the seats helped ensure proper posture for the ejection. During ejection, the copilot's seat had to be in the forward-facing position.

To ensure adequate clearance for the pilots' legs during maintenance, normal seat ingress/egress, or the ejection sequence, a control column emergency stowage mechanism was incorporated into the system. This system automatically centered the control wheel and stowed the column in the forward-most position. A T-handle at either pilot's station operated the system under normal conditions. During an emergency egress, the columns automatically stowed as part of the ejection sequence. An alarm bell sounded when the emergency operation was initiated.

During the pre-ejection sequence, the seat was prepared for ejection. In the second sequence, the seat and occupant were ejected from the aircraft. Independent ballistics were incorporated into each seat. Raising the right seat handle initiated the first sequence, while squeezing the catapult firing trigger located within the right handgrip initiated the second sequence. Safety pins precluded firing of the ballistics system during aircraft ground maintenance.

The B-47 was equipped with a life raft located opposite the aft portion of the wing in the right cable well. The normal procedure was to ditch the aircraft and jettison the canopy. A door located just aft of the canopy was opened to access the external release T-handle. Pulling the T-handle unlatched the life raft compartment door, and then discharged a $CO_2$ bottle that inflated the raft. Inflation of the

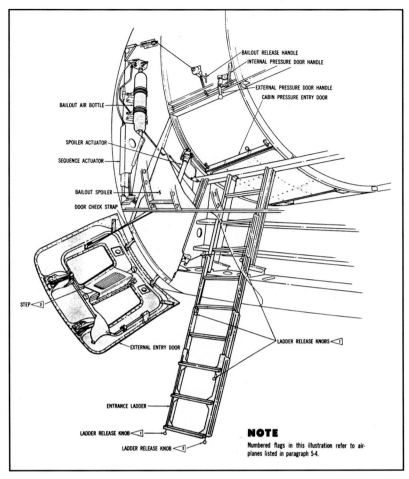

NOTE

Numbered flags in this illustration refer to airplanes listed in paragraph 5-4.

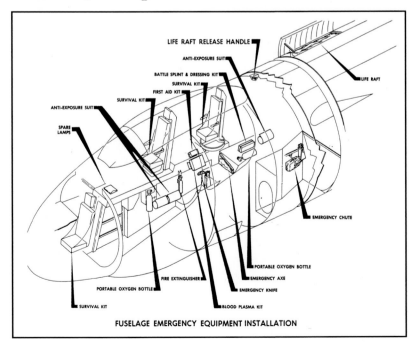

FUSELAGE EMERGENCY EQUIPMENT INSTALLATION

*This illustration reveals the locations for the various pieces of emergency equipment that were carried in the cockpit of the B-47.*

*This illustration depicts the salient features of the cabin entrance and bailout system. The exterior door was contoured to conform to the fuselage and was hinged along the forward edge. A collapsible crew ladder could be extended from the entryway. In the event of an emergency, a pneumatically actuated spoiler deployed behind the door to provide a modicum of safety as the individual entered the slipstream.*

raft pushed the door open and launched the life raft. A secondary release system was incorporated into the door and compartment, where a handle was rotated to open the compartment and a $CO_2$ release cable was pulled to activate the raft.

The external entry door, located aft of the radome on the left side of the fuselage, housed the cabin entrance and bailout system. The door hinged forward and when closed formed an aerodynamic seal for the entryway. The extension ladder was located on the inboard wall of the entranceway. A cabin pressure entry door was located at the top of the entranceway; it moved on rollers and was secured at the forward end by a pair of latches. In the event of an emergency bailout, the entry door was forced open against the slipstream by the bailout spoiler that was operated by a pneumatic actuation system.

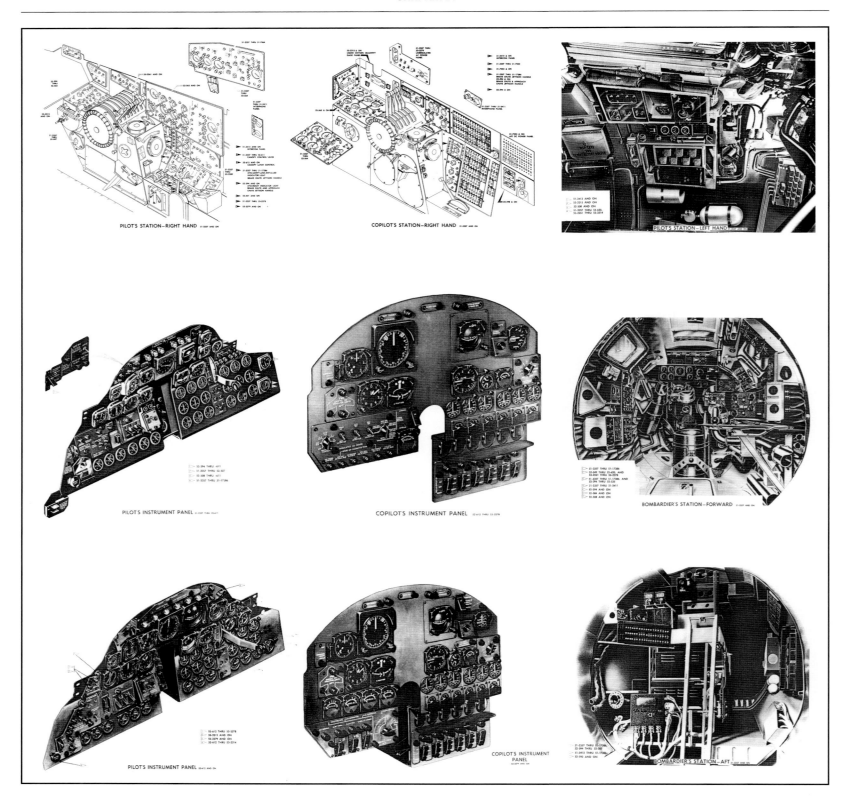

The B-47 instrument panels.

A catwalk along the left side of the crew compartment interconnected the radar bombardier-navigator-radio operator compartment and pilots' compartment. A door in the aft wall of the entranceway permitted access to the left crawlway known as the hellhole. On early B-47s, the bombardier-navigator had to gain access through this panel to arm and disarm the nuclear weapon while in flight in what was known as in-flight insertion and in-flight extraction (IFI/IFE).

Both pilots' main instrument panels contained flight instruments, engine instruments, and rudimentary navigation instruments. The copilot had hydraulic and electrical system indicators and controls. The new jet aircraft were virtually vibration free thereby greatly enhancing crew comfort. The main drawback of this environment was that instrument needles tended to stick. To counter this condition, motor-driven vibrators were installed on each crewmember's instrument panels. These vibrators were located on the backside of each of the instrument panels.

An A-12D automatic pilot, manufactured by Sperry Gyroscope, was installed in the B-47. This system reduced pilot workload during cruise and assisted in making an instrument landing system (ILS) approach. In addition, the autopilot was coupled to the bombing/navigation computer to provide a stable bombing platform. The pilot would stabilize and trim out the aircraft prior to engaging the autopilot.

### Flight Controls

As with any aircraft, the flight control systems were divided into primary and secondary systems. While primary controls were required for directionally controllable flight, the secondary controls provided assistance to the pilot in the form of reduced control surface loads and lower airspeed requirements.

The primary flight control system included the ailerons, flaperons (when the flaps were extended), elevator, and rudder. With flaps extended, the outboard flaps operated in conjunction with the ailerons moving differentially for roll control while providing increased lift. These controls were cable actuated and hydraulically boosted. When operated in the boosted mode, all air loads were transmitted into the aircraft structure and an artificial feel system provided control force feedback to the pilots.

In the event of hydraulic system power loss, the hydraulic system was locked out and the pilots flew the aircraft in manual reversion – relying completely on the unboosted cable system. An aerodynamic balance feature was incorporated into the primary flight controls to aid in overcoming high force loads on the control surfaces under all flight conditions. To further assist the pilots, trim tabs were installed on each primary flight control surface.

A torsional spring in the left aileron control linkage provided artificial feel for the ailerons. The elevator and rudder utilized a Q-spring artificial feel mechanism. Separate systems served each control surface. A bellows assembly – the Q-spring – was expanded by ram air introduced through an inlet located at the base of the vertical stabilizer leading edge. The ram air force acted through a cable system and

Q-tab linkage to oppose the movement of the control system torque tube induced by the pilot. The resultant pilot-perceived control force was proportional to the control system deflection and indicated airspeed (ram air pressure, or Q). Mathematically, with boosted power control, the Q-spring provided artificial control feel proportional to the square of the indicated airspeed.

Additional lateral control was provided by the flaperon at low airspeeds when the flaps were fully extended to 35 degrees, when the aileron movement exceeded 5 degrees, plus or minus 1 degree. The total flaperon deflection range was 25 degrees, plus or minus 3 degrees, in conjunction with aileron movement.

The secondary controls consisted of the flaps and trim tabs. The inboard flaps were located along the wing's trailing edge between the fuselage and the inboard engine strut. Trim tabs were installed on each aileron, each elevator, and the rudder.

### Hydraulic Systems

Main and emergency hydraulic systems provided hydraulic power for the B-47. Several utility systems, powered by either the main or emergency systems, were employed for some subsystems. Each hydraulic system provided primary power to specific systems, and backup power for others.

A pair of engine-driven hydraulic pumps was mounted to the accessory cases of the No. 3 and No. 4 engines. These pumps pressurized the main system that powered the ailerons, brakes, canopy, steering, air refueling slipway door, and bomb bay door systems.

An electric-driven pump, located in the forward wheel well, powered the emergency hydraulic system. This back-up system provided power to all systems, except the ailerons, that would be used in manual reversion. In addition, emergency hydraulic power packages in the wings afforded back-up pressure for the ailerons.

While powered by the engine-driven pumps, the flight control systems provided power to position the primary flight controls and the flaperons when used in conjunction with the ailerons. Two critical functions of these systems was to prevent the transmission of forces on the flight control surfaces to their control cable systems and to prevent control surface flutter at high speeds.

The rudder/elevator hydraulic system was a component of the flight control hydraulic system. To ensure critical pitch and yaw control, a separate rudder/elevator hydraulic system was installed in the aft fuselage. In addition, a separate emergency system was dedicated to the elevators only.

Swept-wing jet aircraft have a tendency to oscillate along the vertical (yaw) and longitudinal (pitch) axes. As the aircraft yaws, the span of the two swept wings effectively changes. The longer wing generates more lift than the shorter wing causing the aircraft to yaw towards the shorter wing. Concurrently the vertical fin gains a lift component that causes the aircraft to roll into the shorter wing. The natural dampening effect of the fixed flying surfaces causes the aircraft to reverse direction. If these oscillations go unchecked, the aircraft gets into a

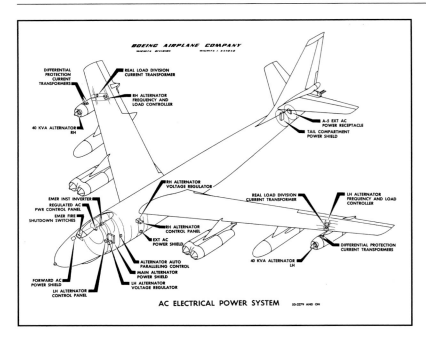

*The main components of the alternating current (AC) electrical system are shown in this isometric view.*

Dutch roll condition, particularly at low airspeeds and high altitudes, which can go divergent. The yaw damper system was an electro-mechanical mechanism that transmitted control forces to the rudder through the rudder control rod.

The system consisted of a control switch on the pilot's main instrument panel, a lock switch, rate gyro, amplifier, calibration unit, and servomotor. As the aircraft heading began to deviate, the rate gyro sensed the rate of deviation and sent a proportionate signal to the amplifier. The amplifier interpreted the signal, amplified it, and transmitted it to the servomotor. The servomotor acted upon the rudder control rod to move the rudder surface (through the rudder power control unit) to the opposite deviation.

### Electrical Systems

Many of the B-47 systems were powered by either a direct current (DC) or alternating current (AC) electrical system, depending upon their specific requirements.

The DC system was generally a single-wire ground return bus system that received power from six engine-driven 400-ampere starter-generators. Also connected in series to this bus was a pair of 12-volt, 34-ampere-hour, high-rate discharge batteries. The batteries provided emergency starting power in the case of generator failure and, when the aircraft engines were running, provided continuous partial voltage stabilization. Carbon-pile voltage regulators and generator control relays served to automatically maintain 28 (+/- 0.25)-volt output from the generators and place the generators in or out of

the system in the event of an undervoltage or overvoltage or ground fault condition. The copilot's instrument panel had a voltmeter and voltmeter selector switch to permit his checking the status of the forward bus, left bus, right bus, and each generator. Engines Nos. 1 and 2 supplied the left main bus, Nos. 3 and 4 supplied the forward main bus, and Nos. 5 and 6 the right main bus. DC power distribution was accomplished by a triangular arrangement of feeder lines, buses, and power shields.

In the AC system each alternator was driven by an engine through a constant speed hydraulic transmission that regulated the output frequency to 400 cycles per second. [During the early 1960s scientific convention to describe frequency changed from cycles per second (cps) to Hertz (Hz) in honor of German physicist Heinrich Rudolph Hertz who worked in electricity and electromagnetic research.] In the event both alternators failed, an emergency instrument inverter provided power to the AC instruments necessary to maintain limited flight.

The exterior lighting system consisted of landing and taxi lights, air refueling and wing illumination lights, and navigation and fuselage lights. Landing lights were mounted in the leading edge of the inboard nacelles between the engines. A taxi light was installed on the forward main gear strut. The maximum intensity range of the landing lights was 400 feet, whereas the taxi light range was 230 feet. For night refueling, one light was located on the air-refueling door and three were in the refueling receptacle and slipway. During the early 1960s, two rotating anti-collision beacons were installed on the vertical fin tip and on the lower fuselage forward of the forward landing gear. These rotating lights could interfere with the pilots' vision at night or while flying in clouds, and would normally be turned off.

Interior lighting consisted of edge-lighted control panel lights for the crew – instrument panel lights, spot lights, flood lights, camera compartment lights, entrance and walkway lights, and bomb bay and tunnel dome lights. Red lights were used to protect the crews' night vision; and white lights were employed during daylight, low light level conditions, and during thunderstorms to reduce the effect of lightning flashes. Rheostats at each crew position controlled the light intensity.

### Oxygen Systems

Two different crew oxygen systems were employed on the B-47. Early B-47s were equipped with a low-pressure gaseous oxygen system that provided oxygen to the crewmembers through diluter demand regulators located at each crew position. When serviced with an initial charge of 425 psi, the total capacity of the system was capable of sustaining a crew of three for about 6.5 hours when flying at an altitude of 25,000 feet. Six bottles, weighing 459 pounds apiece, each contained 29 cubic feet of oxygen at sea level.

Beginning with Line Number 898 (B-47E-115-BW, 53-2315), a 305-psi high-pressure-type liquid oxygen (LOX) system provided oxygen to the crewmembers through diluter demand regulators located at each crew position. Two or three A-2, 8-liter converters stored the LOX and converted the liquid into a gas as required to meet the crew requirements. In addition, portable A-1 or MA-1 oxygen bottles were available to meet the crews' needs as required; i.e., seat changes or working emergencies. The portable bottles were refillable at recharging stations located throughout the crew compartment. The LOX system occupied only one fifth of the space of the gaseous system and its two 8-liter converters provided 739.6 cubic feet of oxygen – equivalent to 25 gaseous cylinders; thereby almost doubling the crews' oxygen supply.

## Air Conditioning and Pressurization

An air conditioning and pressurization system was installed on the B-47. Crew comfort and the electronic system-operating environment were automatically controlled by the air conditioning and pressurization system. Input for these systems came via the 12th stage compressor bleed from the Nos. 1, 2, and 3 engines. The maximum bleed pressure was 100 psi.

A refrigeration unit operated by energy exchanged during the heat transfer cycle cooled a portion of the bleed air supplied to the air conditioning and pressurization system. The remaining hot bleed air was routed through a valve bypassing the refrigeration unit into a mixing chamber where it was blended with the cold air to the desired temperature. This conditioned air was discharged into the cabin through an upper and lower outlet located at each crew position. Airflow rate could be controlled at each crewmember's station. To provide ventilation, the air was automatically exhausted from the cabin by the cabin pressure regulators during pressurized flight. A cabin pressure safety dump valve was employed for exhausting cabin air during unpressurized flight.

## Propulsion Systems

The B-47 propulsion systems consisted of six turbojet engines, supported by a pair of thrust augmentation systems that were employed for takeoff.

The engines on the B-47s were General Electric J47 axial-flow turbojets. The engines were podded (two in each inboard nacelle and a single in each outboard nacelle) and slung beneath the wings. In the event of a catastrophic failure, the engines could explode, burn, and fall off the aircraft without causing fatal damage to the primary structure. Fuses in the fuel lines would prevent a loss of fuel if an engine departed the aircraft.

To eliminate induced drag caused by a windmilling engine, nacelle close-off doors were installed in the engine nose cowls on the first 86 aircraft that were powered by J47-GE-11 engines. When closed, the doors formed the frustum of a right circular cone. Due to incomplete sealing, the airflow through the engine was reduced to about four percent when closed off. This feature reduced bearing wear on a shutdown engine, reduced drag, and prevented possible severe vibration caused by damaged engine parts. Because the J47-23 and J47-25

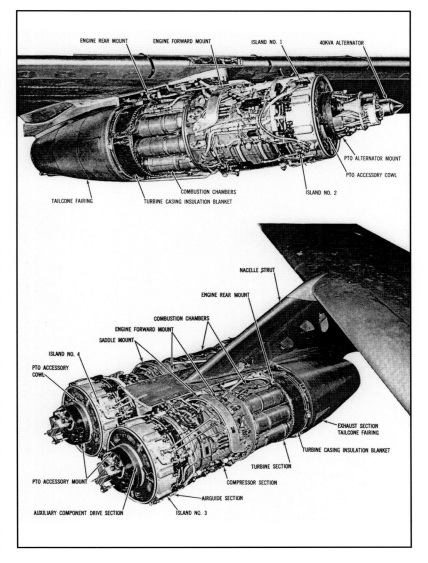

*The right outboard No. 6 engine (top), with its cowling removed, reveals the mounts and major components. The right inboard No. 4 and 5 engines (bottom), with the cowlings removed, reveal the strut that cantilevered the engines away from the wing and the major components.*

engines had hydraulically actuated friction brakes to prevent windmilling of a stopped engine, the nose cowl doors were deleted beginning with aircraft 51-2045.

The engine build-up and transportation dolly served to support an engine during build-up and ground handling, and could be used to air transport an engine aboard a transport or within the B-47's bomb bay. For carriage in a B-47, the dolly would be rolled under the bomb bay and a bomb hoist mechanism would be used to lift the engine into the bomb bay. There, it would be secured with sway braces and cables.

## *B-47 ENGINE USEAGE BY MODEL*

| Aircraft Series | Engine Series | No. of Aircraft | Thrust Rating | Thrust (lbf) | RPM | Minutes of Operation |
|---|---|---|---|---|---|---|
| XB-47 No. 1 | J35-GE 7 (TG-180 B1 Series) | 1 | Maximum | 3,750 | | Continuous |
| XB-47 No. 2 | J47-GE-9 (TG-180 C1 Series) | 1 | Maximum | 3,750 | | Continuous |
| B-47A B-47B | J47-GE-11 | 1-86 | Maximum | 5,200 | 7,950 | 5 |
| | | | Military | 5,200 | 7,950 | 30 |
| | | | Normal | 4,730 | 7,630 | Continuous |
| B-47B | J47-GE-23 | 87-233 | Maximum | 5,910 | 7,950 | 5 |
| | | | Military | 5,620 | 7,800 | 30 |
| | | | Normal | 5,270 | 7,630 | Continuous |
| B-47B B-47E | J47-GE-25 | 289-Subs | Maximum | 7,000 (wet) | 7,950 | 5 |
| | | | | 6,000 (dry) | 7,950 | 5 |
| | | | Military | 5,700 | 7,800 | 30 |
| | | | Normal | 5,350 | 7,630 | Continuous |
| B-47E-II B-47E-IV | J47-GE-25A | | Maximum | 7,200 (wet) | 7,950 | 5 |
| | | | | 5,970 (dry) | 7,950 | 5 |
| | | | Military | 5,570 | 7,800 | 30 |
| | | | Normal | 5,320 | 7,630 | Continuous |
| RB-47B | XJ47-GE-25 | 24 | Maximum | 7,200 (wet) | 7,950 | 5 |
| | | | | 5,970 (dry) | 7,950 | 5 |
| | | | Military | 5,570 | 7,800 | 30 |
| | | | Normal | 5,320 | 7,630 | Continuous |
| RB-47E RB-47H RB-47K | J47-GE-25 | 240 32 15 | Maximum | 7,000 (wet) | 7,950 | 5 |
| | | | | 6,000 (dry) | 7,950 | 5 |
| | | | Military | 5,700 | 7,800 | 30 |
| | | | Normal | 5,350 | 7,630 | Continuous |
| YDB-47E DB-47E | J47-GE-25 | 2 2 | Maximum | 7,000 (wet) | 7,950 | 5 |
| | | | | 6,000 (dry) | 7,950 | 5 |
| | | | Military | 5,700 | 7,800 | 30 |
| | | | Normal | 5,350 | 7,630 | Continuous |
| RB-47C | J33-A-23 | 0 | Maximum | 9,700 | 6,100 | 5 |
| | | | Military | 9,700 | 6,100 | 30 |
| | | | Normal | 8,200 | 6,100 | Continuous |

Note: Wet = 650 lb. water/minute.

*Members of the 320th BMW were working on the No. 2 and 3 engines of this B-47. This view reveals the struts supporting the engine inlet within the surrounding ducts. The sparse interior of the outrigger landing gear wheel well is also visible. (Fifteenth Air Force History Office)*

### Assisted Takeoff System (ATO)

The Assisted Takeoff System (ATO) consisted of two components: the Water-Alcohol Injection (WAI) System and the Rocket Assisted Takeoff (RATO) System. Each system had to be initiated at precisely the right time and distance during the takeoff roll. Too soon, and the systems dropped out before achieving the proper speed and would result in an aborted takeoff. Too late, and the systems would not allow the aircraft to achieve the requisite speed until it passed the end of the runway. In either case, it was a dangerous situation.

For added thrust to ensure takeoff at nominal gross weights, the XB-47s, B-47As, and B-47Bs were equipped to carry 18 internally mounted rocket assisted takeoff (RATO) bottles located aft of the aft wheel well. Later B-47s had either a droppable horsecollar, or split-mounted RATO racks with 33 or 30 bottles, respectively. When spent, these racks were dropped along corridors off the ends of the runways.

The external RATO system almost doubled the takeoff power of the B-47 by adding some 32,500 pounds of thrust. The 33-bottle ATO system was introduced in production at Line Number 664 (B-47E-85-BW, 52-441) and Line Number 47 (RB-47E-15-BW, 51-15848). Many earlier aircraft were retrofitted through modification programs. The original 18-bottle system reduced the ground take-off roll to 5,400 feet, and a 50-foot obstacle could be cleared in 6,750 feet. The later 33-bottle system reduced the ground take-off roll to 4,250 feet, and a 50-foot obstacle could be cleared in 5,500 feet.

Being droppable, the racks offloaded several thousand pounds of weight after use, but aircraft began experiencing skin damage when the racks were dropped. To correct this situation, Boeing designed a set of four displacement arms that were mounted at the four upper corners of the rack. As the rack was jettisoned, the rack rollers moved down inclined planes formed by the body rollers. When the rack

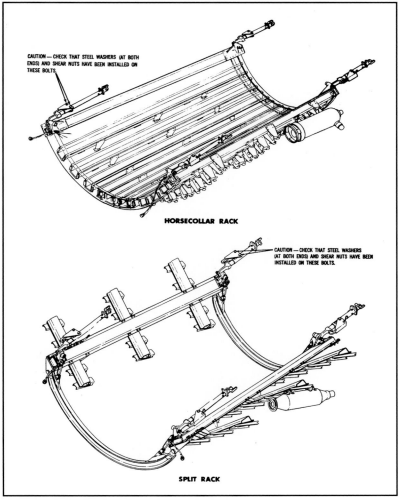

*These two illustrations reveal the differences between the horsecollar and split RATO racks.*

The 33-rocket horsecollar rack was affixed directly to the waist of the aircraft. Subsequently it was learned that the dark Insignia Blue in the national insignia absorbed the heat of the rockets, causing structural damage. (Boeing BW58429)

The scars from the national insignia are barely visible in this view of the 30-rocket split RATO rack. Note the rails and articulating arms that allowed the rack to ease away from the aircraft, reducing heat damage. This aircraft commander, Capt. Glen E. Stribling, from the 446th BS, 321st BMW, McCoy AFB, Florida, was inspecting the Aerojet General 15KS1000 RATO bottles on this rack. Note that only two-thirds of the rockets had been installed. This is not an unusual configuration, depending upon the gross takeoff weight of the aircraft. (USAF)

moved to the point that it was no longer supported by the aft cams, the rack fell away from the aircraft without contacting the fuselage. The rack displacement system was incorporated in production with Line Number 761 (B-47E-95-BW, 52-538) and Line Number 117 (RB-47E-25-BW, 52-749). The system was retrofitted to aircraft 51-2192 through 52-537 and RB-47E 51-5258 through 52-748. The speed restrictions for jettisoning the rack were a maximum of 305 knots for aircraft with or without the displacement system. However, it was further recommended that the racks not be jettisoned above 260 knots with the displacement gear installed, or above 200 knots on aircraft without the displacement gear.

On early jet engines, takeoff power could be increased through the injection of a water-alcohol mixture into the burner section (this is often called "wet" thrust). The water-alcohol increased the mass flow of gases through the engine by vaporizing the water. The alcohol provided the additional heat needed to vaporize the water. This mixture for jet engine applications was typically between 22.5 percent to 25 percent alcohol. Three tanks, located in the inboard wing root area, contained 300 gallons of a water-alcohol mixture. Because of the limited fluid quantity, its use was limited to 120 seconds of operation.

All B-47s carried 56.4 gallons of Grade 1005 MIL-L-6-81A engine oil. One tank was installed in each inboard pylon and in the wing's leading edge just inboard of the outboard engines. The remaining tanks were located in the inboard pylons. While the aircraft could be refueled in flight, engine oil became a limiting factor on mission endurance.

## Fuel System

The fuel carried by the B-47 contributed almost 50 percent of the maximum gross weight of the aircraft. With the wings being too thin to accommodate fuel tanks, all main fuel tanks were located within the fuselage. Ten main fuel cells were located: aft of the pilot's seats, above the bomb bay, and aft of the aft main wheel well. In addition, another pair of auxiliary tanks was located beneath the pilots and below the forward cell of the forward main tank. Each of the main and auxiliary fuel cells was constructed as bladders that were suspended within the various areas of the fuselage. The material used in these bladders was dual plies of pliocel, nylon impregnated with nylon resin. These 0.015-inch-thick cells were extremely vulnerable to damage resulting from mishandling, which in turn resulted in serious fuel leakage.

The almost 40 tons of fuel was distributed across a distance of 68 feet, but the aircraft's center of gravity had to remain within three feet. During takeoff the fuel pumps forced more than 10 pounds per second to each engine. The original fuel transfer system left something to be desired and an improved system was incorporated in production starting with Line Number 335 (B-47B-50-BW, 51-2312). The improved system was retrofitted on all previous aircraft.

A 1,700-gallon droppable external fuel tank was installed on each wing of the B-47Es at Buttock Line 419.7. Each tank was 24 feet 11 inches long and 50 inches in diameter. The fuel in these tanks offered a range increase of about 10 percent. These tanks were non-self-seal-

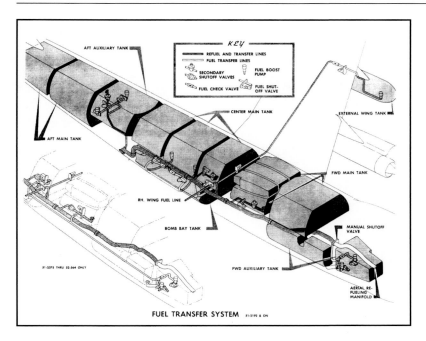

*To afford the requisite range of the B-47, the fuselage was crammed with fuel tanks that were interconnected by an elaborate plumbing system. The single-point ground refueling receptacle, plumbed into the air refueling system, was located in the aft wheel well.*

ing and incorporated a stabilizing ribbon chute in the tail cone. When jettisoned, the tank tail cone separated and the chute billowed to its eight-foot diameter; its drag separated the tank and its strut from the wing. Both flutter tests and flight testing revealed that wing flutter could be induced at higher speeds when the external tanks were not full. Four companies manufactured these tanks. Goodyear and Ryan produced what were commonly called Boeing tanks, and Beech and Fletcher rounded out the manufacturers. Pioneer produced the parachutes for all but the Fletcher tanks that used Steinthal chutes.

A single-point refueling system was installed on the B-47s to reduce aircraft refueling time and minimize the filling equipment requirements. Tapping into the air refueling system plumbing was a filler neck located just forward of the right aft landing gear hinge. One of four different modular refueling panels was connected electrically to receptacles within the wheel well. This was a semi-automatic system capable of replenishment rates of 600 gallons per minute at 40 psi. This system also permitted ground fuel transfer between two aircraft.

An in-flight refueling receptacle was added to the B-47s. Because of the critical nature of the weight and takeoff performance of the aircraft, it was not unusual to take off with a light fuel load and required bomb load, and then take on the required fuel load once in the air. The receptacle for the in-flight refueling system was located in the nose to the right of the navigator. A manifold from the receptacle carried fuel to the B-47's fuel tanks. The receptacle/manifold joint was located above the navigator's electronic equipment. On occasion a major fuel leak

occurred at this joint (much like what one sees when water is spewing in a submarine movie); at which point the navigator attempted to torque down the bolts securing the joint with a box/open-end wrench. If his efforts failed, he called for a breakaway from the tanker. The receptacle was lighted and had an anti-icing system.

### Anti-Icing System

Hot engine bleed air was employed for anti-icing the wings, empennage, nacelle struts, and the air refueling door. Twelfth stage bleed air as high as 100 psi and in excess of 500 degrees Fahrenheit was employed. Pressure regulators reduced the air pressure to 12.5 psi to preclude damage to the ducts. Ducts ran up the nacelle struts and into the D-duct forming the leading edge of the wing. Other ducts ran aft along the length of the fuselage to the D-ducts forming the leading edges of the vertical fin and horizontal stabilizers. Another duct ran forward to the air-refueling door.

Early in 1962, a series of B-47 losses led to an investigation that concluded that the anti-icing ducts had deteriorated due to corrosion, fatigue, chaffing, and mechanical defects in the ducts. The system had deteriorated below a reasonable confidence level and a two-phase improvement program was implemented. In Phase I, the ducts in the body fuel tank area were blocked due to the explosive environment caused by proximity of the hot air and fuel vapors. For Phase II, all high-pressure anti-icing ducts in the wing leading edge were replaced. Subsequently it was learned that anti-icing was not required for either the wings or the empennage, and all ducts in these areas were blocked.

### Approach and Brake Chute Systems

The B-47 liked to fly. It was an aerodynamically clean aircraft and slowing it for approach and landing was difficult at best. Whereas propeller-driven aircraft have an almost instantaneous response to thrust changes, jet engines tend to lag. Spool-up in an emergency can be extremely critical for making a successful go-around. To solve this conundrum, a dual parachute system was developed for the B-47.

The pilot could maintain the requisite power to provide the margins required for a go-around, yet slow the aircraft for approach and landing using the approach chute. This 16-foot-diameter ring-slot-type parachute was stowed in a compartment in the aft fuselage and was pulled out by a 30- or 36-inch-diameter pilot chute. The approach chute, with its 68-square-foot area, could withstand an opening shock associated with a 200-knot approach speed. The main chute risers were attached to a release latch and link assembly. The pilots could jettison the approach chute during the landing rollout, or in flight if a missed approach had to be executed. During the later situation, the crew had to cope with the next landing without the aid of the approach chute. The approach chute was incorporated in production beginning with Line Number 755 (B-47E-95-BW, 52-532) and Line Number 44 (RB-47E-15-BW, 51-15845). Retrofit was accomplished on B-47Bs 51-292 through 51-2356 and B-47Es 51-2357 through 52-431.

The landing roll of a B-47 decelerating with brakes alone was about twice that of a propeller-driven bomber of equivalent weight. A 32-foot-diameter ribbon-type braking parachute was located in a separate compartment in the aft fuselage. Either pilot could activate the cable-operated chute deployment system. While designed for operation at 156 knots landing speed, risers were known to have failed as low as 120 knots. Hence crews were advised to not deploy the brake chute above 115 knots. When the aircraft speed had dissipated sufficiently during the rollout, either pilot could jettison the brake chute.

## Pitot Static System

The pitot static system provided ambient pressure data for the various instruments on the B-47. One pitot probe was installed on either side of the forward fuselage below the pilots' stations. Ram air through the pitot tube provided air speed information for the airspeed indicators and the bombing/navigation computer. A series of eight static ports mounted singly and in pairs was located in a circular area between the wing leading edge and the rear limit of the canopy. A red border stripe surrounded these static ports. Inputs from these ports

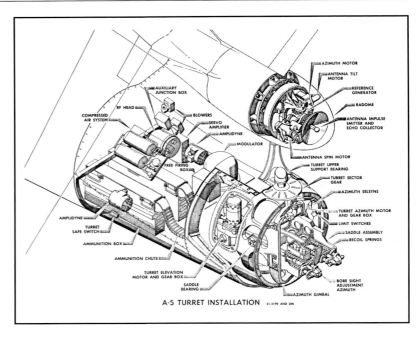

*Details of the A-5 tail turret are shown in this illustration.*

were used for the airspeed indicators, altimeters, cabin pressurization system, autopilot, radar fire control, and the bombing/navigation computer. To ensure delivery of true air pressure by the pitot tubes under all operating conditions, heating coils were installed in the pitot tube head to prevent icing.

## Defensive Armament

The development of the defensive tail gun system was fraught with difficulties. The initial Emerson A-2 was cancelled in 1951 in favor of the General Electric A-5 fire control system. It would not be before 1953 that the A-5 system would be available; therefore, SAC opted for an interim installation of the B-4 system with a pair of 0.50-caliber machine guns and tail warning radar that offered a modicum of harassing fire for defense. The definitive A-5 system incorporated a pair of 20-mm M24A-1 cannon coupled to a gun-laying radar. This system was adapted from the Convair B-36 and was incorporated on the B-47Bs under Project HIGH NOON. In August 1953 Line Number 938 (B-47E-120-BW, 53-2355) was delivered with an improved A-5 system known as the MD-4. The MD-4 system was retrofitted into the last 14 B-47s going through Project HIGH NOON, and was installed on all subsequent production B-47s.

While many of the fire control system functions were performed automatically, the copilot had many duties to defend the aircraft. For instance, he had to activate the system, set altitude, airspeed, and air temperature data into the computer; manually select a specific target for tracking; monitor the tracking operation; and fire the guns when the radar scope indicated that the target was within 1,500 yards range.

*These armorers were checking the 20-mm tail turret on this B-47. (SAC Combat Crew Magazine)*

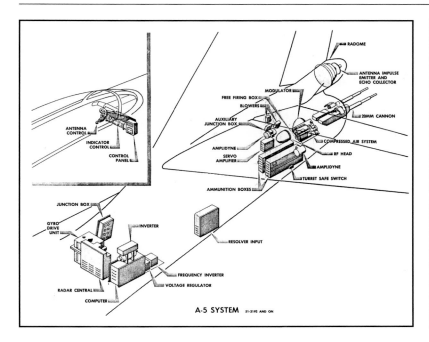

The major components of the A-5 are shown in this illustration.

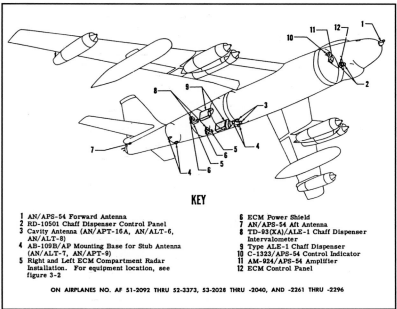

**KEY**

| | | | |
|---|---|---|---|
| 1 | AN/APS-54 Forward Antenna | 6 | ECM Power Shield |
| 2 | RD-10501 Chaff Dispenser Control Panel | 7 | AN/APS-54 Aft Antenna |
| 3 | Cavity Antenna (AN/APT-16A, AN/ALT-6, AN/ALT-8) | 8 | TD-93(XA)/ALE-1 Chaff Dispenser Intervalometer |
| 4 | AB-109B/AP Mounting Base for Stub Antenna (AN/ALT-7, AN/APT-9) | 9 | Type ALE-1 Chaff Dispenser |
| 5 | Right and Left ECM Compartment Radar Installation. For equipment location, see figure 3-2 | 10 | C-1323/APS-54 Control Indicator |
| | | 11 | AM-924/APS-54 Amplifier |
| | | 12 | ECM Control Panel |

ON AIRPLANES NO. AF 51-2092 THRU 52-3373, 53-2028 THRU -2040, AND -2261 THRU -2296

Typical ECM equipment installations for the B-47.

The normal rate of fire for the 20-mm cannon was 750 to 900 rounds per minute. While the maximum range of the projectiles was 5,750 yards, the maximum effective range with the fire control system was 1,500 yards. The ammunition load for the A-5 system was 350 rounds per gun, while the MD-4 system had a capacity of 450 rounds per gun.

### Electronic Countermeasures

The art of radio countermeasures was developed during World War II. Using both passive and active measures, aircrews were able to detect, analyze, and defeat enemy radars and radio communication systems. In 1949, the term was officially changed to electronic countermeasures, when a Joint Electronic Countermeasures Policy defined electronic countermeasures (ECM) as: "That major subdivision of the military use of electronics involving actions taken to reduce the military effectiveness of enemy equipment and/or tactics employing or affected by electromagnetic radiations."

Electronic warfare is a cat and mouse game. One nation builds sophisticated communications and navigation radios, and radars. Then the opposing nation develops the requisite electronics to defeat these systems. The first stage in defeating the systems is to understand them. Hence, sensitive receiving equipment is developed to detect the new signals. Once analyzed as to frequency ranges and mission, a suitable countermeasure can be developed. With this new defensive equipment installed, the aircraft can more safely perform its mission – whether it is bombardment or reconnaissance. These back and forth cycles of electronic measures and countermeasures result in phased systems

development. The B-47 had five iterations of countermeasures identified as Phase I through Phase V. The mission equipment was divided into three categories: warning receivers, chaff, and jammers.

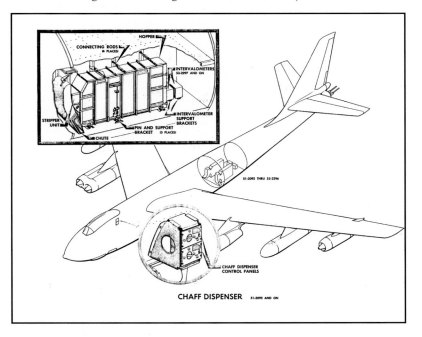

Controls for the chaff dispenser were located below the right canopy rail next to the copilot, while the chaff dispensers were installed in the waist aft of the aft main landing gear.

## B-47 ELECTRONIC COUNTERMEASURES EQUIPMENT USEAGE BY MODEL

| Series | ECM Phase | Equipment | Function |
|---|---|---|---|
| B-47B | I | 2 x AN/APT-5A | B-D band jammers |
| | | 2 x AN/ALE-1 | Chaff dispensers |
| | | 1 x AN/APS-54 | Warning receiver |
| B-47E-I | II | 2 x AN/ALT-6 | E-F band jammers |
| | | 2 x AN/ALE-1 | Chaff dispensers |
| | | 1 x AN/APS-54 | Warning receiver |
| B-47E-II | III | 2 x AN/ALT-6B | E-F band jammers (slow sweep) |
| | | 2 x AN/ALT-7 | A band jammer (slow sweep) [in extended wingtip] |
| | | 2 x AN/ALE-1 | Chaff dispensers |
| | | 1 x AN/APS-54 | Warning receiver |
| EB-47E | IV | 2 x AN/ALT-6 | E-F band jammers |
| | | 2 x AN/ALT-6B | E-F band jammers (slow sweep) |
| | | 2 x AN/ALE-1 | Chaff dispensers |
| | | 1 x AN/APS-54 | Warning receiver |
| | | 16 x AN/ALT-6B | E-F band jammers (slow sweep) [in the Blue Cradle pod] |
| EB-47E | V | 9 x AN/ALT-6B | E-F band jammers (slow sweep) [in the Blue Cradle pod] |
| | | 1 x AN/ALT-6B | G-H-I band jammer |
| | | 1 x AN/ALT-6B | D band jammer |
| | | 1 x AN/ALT-7 | A band jammer (slow sweep) [in extended wingtip] |
| | | 1 x AN/ALT-8B | E-F band jammer |
| | | SUBSEQUENTLY INSTALLED IN LIEU OF SOME OF THE ABOVE | |
| | | AN/QRC-49 | E-F band carcinotron jammer |
| | | AN/QRC-65 | VHF communications jammer |
| | | QRC-96 | D band carcinotron barrage jammer |
| | | QRC-139 | AN/ALT-22 modulator to make it more effective against Fan Song radar |
| | | AN/ALT-13 | F-I band jammer |
| | | AN/ALT-15 | A-B band jammer |
| | | AN/ALT-16 | D band jammer |
| | | 2 x AN/APR-9 | Set-on receiver |
| | | 1 x AN/APR-14 | Set-on receiver |
| | | 2 x AN/ALA-7 | Set-on receiver |
| | | 2 x AN/ALE-1 | Chaff dispensers |
| | | 1 x AN/APS-54 | Warning receiver |

Much like a radar detector in one's car, warning receivers are passive devices that detect certain frequencies of electromagnetic waves. An electronic tone is generated in the crews' headsets advising of the threat. Generally the copilot was assigned to monitor the AN/APS-54 radar receiver system that consisted of an amplifier, a control indicator located aft of the copilot, a forward antenna on the fuselage nose above the periscopic bombsight cover, and an aft antenna located above the A-5 or MD-4 gun turret.

Developed during World War II, chaff consists of packages of various sizes of aluminum foil strips that are housed in the aircraft. Under the control of the flight crew, mechanical strippers peel off the packages and dump them into the slipstream. There the packages open

| Series | ECM Phase | Equipment | Function |
|---|---|---|---|
| **B-47E-I Tee Town** | I + | Phase I ECM + | (As above) + |
| | | 4 x AN/ALT-6B | E-F band jammers (slow sweep) [carried in each Tee Town pod] |
| **EB-47E Tell Two** | | 16 x AN/ALT-6B | G-H-I band jammers [in the Blue Cradle pod] |
| | | AN/ALT-8 | E-F band jammer |
| **RB-47H** | | AN/APD-4 | 3-man capsule in bomb bay [ECM pod] |
| | | AN/APR-17 | ELINT receiver |
| | | SUBSEQUENTLY INSTALLED IN LIEU OF SOME OF THE ABOVE | |
| | | 2 X AN/ALT-6B | E-F band jammers |
| | | 2 x AN/ALE-1 | Chaff dispensers |
| | | 1 AN/APS-54 or | Warning receiver |
| | | 1 x AN/ARC-91 | Warning receiver |
| | | 1 x AN/ALD-4 | Automatic ELINT package in an externally mounted Silver King pod |
| **ERB-47H** | | | [2 men in the ECM pod |

**B-47 ELECTRONIC COUNTERMEASURES EQUIPMENT USEAGE BY MODEL (CONTINUED)**

and the foil strips are dissipated behind the aircraft. When radar detects the billowing strips of aluminum, it detects a massive reflective cloud that essentially masks the incoming aircraft. Two chaff dispenser systems were installed on the B-47. Each system had an RD-10501 control panel, a TD-93 (XA)/ALE-1 intervalometer, and an ALE-1 chaff dispenser consisting of a hopper, stripper unit, and chute. The chaff dispensers were located in the forward section of the left and right ECM compartments in the waist of the aircraft.

Jammers actively emit signals at a given frequency that defeat enemy radar or communications radios. Designed during World War II, these systems required skilled personnel to manually operate them. Subsequently, systems were developed that automatically engaged the threat, thereby permitting the crew to continue with more pressing events related to the success of their mission. The AN/APT-9, AN/APT-16A, AN/APT-6, AN/ALT-7, and AN/ALT-8 jamming sets could be used interchangeably depending upon the tactical situation. Two or four external stub antennas and one or two cavity antennas could be mounted to the underside of the aircraft for this equipment. On Phase III and later aircraft, ECM antennas were installed in the blister fairing on the belly just forward of the empennage.

B-47As were not equipped with ECM equipment. However, beginning with the B-47Bs, ECM gear was standard equipment. A major campaign was initiated to install ECM equipment into the B-47 fleet. In the end, 978 aircraft were equipped with Phase I ECM equipment, 197 with Phase II, 328 with Phase III, 181 with Phase IV, 205 with Phase IVA, 25 with Phase V, and another 12 with the Phase V capsule. A summary of the ECM equipment installed on the various B-47 series is shown in the accompanying table.

Some B-47s were equipped with a two-man capsule in the bomb bay to provide defensive electronic countermeasures. Communication between the electronic warfare (EW) crew and the other members of the crew was provided by an interphone system. In case of an emergency, the pilots, by means of an emergency communications light and an alarm system, could alert the EW crew. Downward ejection seats were provided for the EW operators (called ravens). The ECM capsule had an independent oxygen system and pressurization and air conditioning system. DC and AC electrical power for the capsule was provided by the aircraft electrical system. The following basic instruments were provided to the EW crew: remote compass repeater indicator, altimeter, airspeed indicator, clock, and cabin pressure altitude gauge.

**NUMBER OF B-47s EQUIPPED WITH ECM**

| ECM Phase | Number of Aircraft |
|---|---|
| I | 978 |
| II | 197 |
| III | 328 |
| IVA | 205 |
| IV | 181 |
| V Capsule | 12 |
| V | 25 |

## B-47 COMMUNICATION AND NAVIGATION EQUIPMENT USEAGE BY MODEL

| Equipment | B-47A | B-47B | B-47B-II | B-47E | B-47E (Heavyweight) | B-47E-II | B-47E-IV |
|---|---|---|---|---|---|---|---|
| AN/ARC-3 VHF Command | X | X | | | | | |
| AN/ARC-27 VHF Command | | | X | X | X | X | X |
| AN/ARN-6 Radio Compass | X | X | | | | | |
| AN/ARN-6A Radio Compass | | | X | X | X | X | X |
| AAF Combat Interphone | X | X | | X | | | |
| AN/AIC-1 Interphone | | | | X | | | |
| AN/AIC-10 Interphone | | | | | X | X | X |
| RC-193A Marker Beacon | X | | | | | | |
| AN/ARN-12 Marker Beacon | | X | X | X | X | X | X |
| AN/ARN 6 Glide Path Receiver | | X | | | | | |
| AN/ARN-5A Glide Path Receiver (Provisions only) | | | | | | | |
| AN/ARN-5B Glide Path Receiver | | X | | | | | |
| AN/ARN-18 Glide Path Receiver | | | X | X | X | X | X |
| SCR-695B IFF (Provisions only) | X | | | | | | |
| AN/APX-6 IFF | | X | X | X | X | X | |
| AN/APX-6A IFF | | | | | | | X |
| AN/ARN-14 VHF Omni-Directional Receiver | | X | X | X | X | X | X |
| AN/APN-9A LORAN | | X | | | | | |
| AN/APN-68 or AN/APN-76 Radar Beacon | | X | | | | | |
| AN/APN-76 Radar Beacon | | | | X | X | X | X |
| Type K-2A Bomb/Nav Radar or Type K-4 Bomb/Nav Radar | | X | | | | | |
| Type K-4A Bomb/Nav Radar | | | X | X | | X | |
| Type K-4A or Type MA-7A Bomb/Nav Radar | | | | | X | | X |
| AN/APG-27 Gunlaying Radar | | X | | | | | |
| B-4-400 Fire Control System | | X | | X | | | |
| A-5 Fire Control System | | | | X | X | | |
| A-5 or MD-4 Fire Control System | | | | | | X | X |
| AN/ARA-26 Emergency Keyer | | | X | X | X | X | X |
| AN/ARC-21 HF Liaison Radio | | | | X | X | | |
| AN/ARC-21X HF Liaison Radio | | | | | | X | X |

A variety of communications and navigation systems were carried onboard the B-47s. This matrix shows the standard configuration for B-47As, B-47Bs, and B-47Es. A similar table will be found in other chapters describing the TB-47s and RB-47s.

The AN designation stood for an Army/Navy design; whereas SCR was for Signal Corps Radio. The second part of the AN designation indicated the use, with: ARN = Aircraft Radio Navigation; AIC = Aircraft Interphone Communications; and ARC = Aircraft Radio Communications.

ECM operators' capsules presented an extreme challenge for the egress system engineers. Of concern were the cutters employed with the ejection seats for the ravens. The initial systems could not guarantee a successful bailout from the capsule, thereby forcing the ravens to crawl forward and bail out via the entry hatch. By November 1955 a new system of knife cutters beneath the seats and incorporation of two M-4 thrusters permitted cutting through the fiberglass skin panel to permit a clean departure of the ejection seat. The cutter created a hole of sufficient size to permit a clean egress of the seat and occupant. Testing was accomplished on a B-47E-65-BW (51-7043) and an RB-47H-BW (53-4280).

### Offensive Systems

At the heart of the offensive system of the B-47s were the K-2 or MA-7 bombing systems and the large-capacity bomb bay. Of major importance was the offensive armament system that was based around the K-2 bombing and navigation system and a bomb bay that was capable of carrying a variety of either conventional or nuclear stores.

### Bomb Bay

While designed as a nuclear weapons carrier, a few B-47s were equipped to carry conventional stores. The B-47 was designed with a long bomb bay that was capable of accepting the out-sized nuclear weapons of the day or a single 25,000-pound general-purpose bomb. With the reduction in size of the nuclear weapons, a 3,230-gallon fuel tank could be installed in the aft portion of the bomb bay. Only three SAC B-47 wings had a conventional bombing capability. When the B-47 was employed for low-altitude toss bombing, a major structural problem developed. Several B-47s were lost before cracks were found in the bottle pins that attached the wings to the fuselage. A major modification program known as Project MILK BOTTLE was developed to resolve the problem.

The bomb bay doors were equipped with wide-open supports to facilitate ground activities within the bomb bay. In addition, lessons learned from the B-29 fast-acting doors resulted in bomb bay door safety locks that were installed to prevent inadvertent closure of the doors while the aircraft was on the ground. The locks were installed on the door actuators.

The B-47 could be equipped with two different-sized bomb bays, and ground crews could – in theory, at least – switch between them relatively quickly depending on tactical needs. All B-47Bs from Line Number 88 (B-47B-25-BW, 51-2045) were delivered with the normal bomb bay configuration. In the field, SAC personnel could modify the aircraft to the special configuration in 60 man-hours, or from the normal to alternate configuration in 15 man-hours. Kits for the alternate configuration were furnished by Boeing; whereas the special configuration kits were provided by the Air Force.

Most of the time, the B-47s flew with the short bomb bay that included a 3,230-gallon fuel tank in the aft part for increased range.

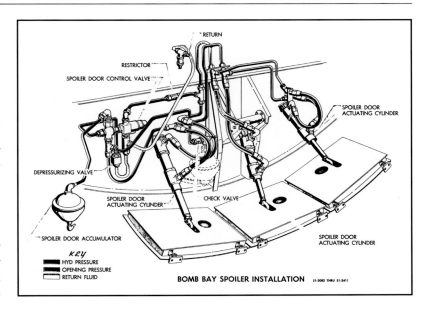

*The major components of the bomb bay spoiler system are depicted in this drawing. This view is looking forward.*

With the long bomb bay, the fuel tank and its supporting structure were removed and longer doors replaced the short bomb bay doors. An additional set of door actuators was also installed at the aft end of the doors. In this configuration, an additional 300 inches in room was gained permitting the carriage of outsized weapons. When this configuration was employed, a buffeting fairing, fuel drains, electrical wiring, and additional hydraulic components had to be installed.

Within each size of bomb bay, several different bomb-carrying configurations could be selected. The primary bomb bay configuration was designed for a single special weapon and included sway braces and fin rails, platform, equipment support and stowage straps, and bomb hoist beams. The Special Purpose Bomb System was capable of supporting a 10,000-pound bomb load when using the primary bomb bay configuration. The system consisted of a pneumatic bomb release system, emergency bomb release system, U-2 bomb rack release system, bomb arming control unit, and a bomb arming safe control. The pneumatically operated U-2 special purpose bomb rack incorporated a safety lock and electric gun-type heaters to ensure positive operation at low temperatures. A manual release cable system could be employed to drop the weapon in an emergency.

Various special weapons could be carried by the B-47B, based largely on when they were built and what phases of ON TOP they had been through. Initially, Line Numbers 1 through 30 could carry the Mk. IV, Line Numbers 31 through 87 could carry the Mk. IV and Mk. VI, and Line numbers 88 and subsequent could carry the Mk. IV, Mk. V, Mk. VI, and Mk. VIII. The B-47E could carry a great number of types, including the Mk. 15, Mk. 18, Mk. 21, Mk. 28, Mk. 36, Mk. 39, Mk. 41, Mk. 43, and Mk. 53. (Note that Arabic numerals were used for the Mk. 9 and later; Roman numerals for earlier weapons.)

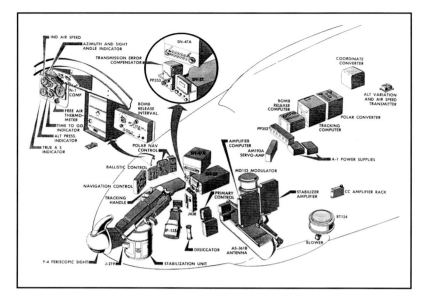

*The major components of the K-4 bombing and navigation system are depicted in this illustration. While most of the components were installed in and around the navigator's compartment, a number of other pieces of related equipment were scattered throughout the forward portion of the aircraft. This dispersal of components resulted in system checkout times of as much as eight hours.*

The Alternate Bomb Bay Configuration was used for the loading of general-purpose bombs. The same release controls used for the primary bomb bay configuration were employed in the alternate system. Installation of the alternate bomb bay configuration required removal of the bomb bay platform, special purpose bomb rack, bomb hoist beams, special purpose bomb sway braces, arming control unit, and emergency bomb-arming safe bracket. Some aircraft also required removal of the H-1 equipment support and stowage straps. The bomb rack indicator switch was also removed and stowed on the beam deck. This configuration could support eight 1,000-pound bombs, three 2,000-pound bombs, or a single 4,000-pound bomb.

The High-Density Alternate Bomb Bay Configuration permitted a variety of bomb load configurations to be carried. It was used to carry a larger number of conventional bombs in the short bomb bay or outsized weapons in the long bomb bay configuration. This configuration employed two bomb racks in the short bomb bay and four racks in the long bomb bay.

During early testing it was found that the special weapons tended to bounce in and out of the bomb bay due to the turbulence generated by the open bomb bay. To rectify this condition, a three-segment spoiler system was installed just forward of the bomb bay opening that directed the slipstream below the aircraft thereby permitting the bomb to separate from the aircraft. Hinged at the forward edge, these spoilers were operated by three actuating cylinders utilizing pressure from the main hydraulic system. The spoilers were automatically locked out

on the ground and were only operable for maintenance with the aircraft on jacks or with the system electrically disabled.

### Bombing System

The K-2 or K-4 bombing system (usually called the K-system since it was constantly being modified and changing precise designations) consisted of the H-21D automatic pilot, a large computer, interconnecting equipment, an AN/APS-23 radar, and the Y-4 or Y-4A bombsight. Initially developed in 1944, the K-2 system underwent a series of modifications that resulted in the K-4 system. The K-4 system was extensively tested under Project SKY TRY, the results of which became Project RELIABLE, an intensive modification program to incorporate improvements into the system beginning in 1953.

The K-system consisted of 41 major components with some 370 vacuum tubes and approximately 20,000 separate parts that were scattered throughout the aircraft. Some components, by necessity, had to be located outside of the pressurized cabin thereby precluding any in-flight maintenance. On the ground, system checkout took up to eight hours versus one hour on the B-36 (which was a much larger aircraft with many of the components located near each other).

The MA-7A bombing navigational system (BNS) provided radar or optical sighting of targets, dual off-set, AN/APS-64 radar with tunable magnetron and 10-inch PPI indicator, AN/AWA-2 position mark generator of IBDA purposes, switch and dial illumination, and automatic computation of bombing and navigational problems enabling the navigator to fulfill his multiple function job.

### Cameras

The bomber versions of the B-47 had provisions for vertically mounting a variety of aerial cameras in the aft lower fuselage directly below the fin leading edge, mainly for use in bomb-damage assess-

### ALTERNATE (HIGH DENSITY) BOMB CONFIGURATIONS

| Bomb Weight (Pounds) | Short Bomb Bay Capacity | Long Bomb Bay Capacity |
|---|---|---|
| 500 | 13 | 28 |
| 750 | 7 | 21 |
| 750 (Chemical Cluster) | 6 | 18 |
| 1,000 | 6 | 18 |
| 2,000 | 3 | 6 |
| 3,000 | 2 | 4 |
| 5,000 | 2 | 4 |
| 10,000 | 1 | 1 |
| 12,000 Tall Boy | 1 | 1 |
| 22,000 Grand Slam | 1 | 1 |

ment. The B-47As could carry a K-17, K-19B, K-22, or K-24 camera. The B-47B could carry a K-17C, K-22A, K-37, or K-38 camera. The TB-47B and B-47E could carry a K-17C, K-22A, or K-38 camera.

The K-17 could be equipped with 6-, 12-, or 24-inch lenses. The K-19B was an automatic night camera. The K-22 could be equipped with 6-, 24-, 36-, or 48-inch lenses. The K-24 was an orientation camera, and the K-37 was an updated night camera. The K-38 had a 36-inch lens. The aerial camera could be used automatically in conjunction with the bombing system to record and determine the accuracy of the bomb drop, or used independently for photoreconnaissance. Controls for the camera system were located at the navigator's station.

Electric heater blankets with automatic temperature control prevented moisture condensation and ice formation within the cameras. Defrosting of the camera window was accomplished either by ducted ram air from the fin leading edge or by a defroster blower.

A pair of camera doors was located in the belly of the aircraft to protect the camera window from debris damage. These doors were slaved to the bomb bay doors and opened when the bomb bays were opened. However, the doors could be opened by the navigator should the system be needed for reconnaissance.

### Aircraft Color Schemes and Markings

Like most Air Force aircraft during the 1950s, B-47s were delivered in Natural Metal Finish. Basic B-47 markings included the radio call number on each side of the vertical stabilizer and walkway markings along the upper surface of the wings and upper fuselage. Red turbine warning stripes were applied around each engine nacelle. A dark anti-glare green or flat black anti-glare panel was painted around the cockpit canopy. A red warning stripe was applied around the RATO panels on aircraft equipped with internally mounted bottles.

B-47As, TB-47Bs, and early B-47Bs carried the four national insignia (stars and bars) located on the top left and lower right wings, and on both sides of the waist. USAF was applied to upper right and lower left wings. Early aircraft carried UNITED STATES AIR FORCE in black on the forward fuselage. Later this was changed to U.S. AIR FORCE in black. The USAF and U.S. AIR FORCE began in black then became Insignia Blue.

For security reasons, SAC aircraft markings were rather limited. Only the 305th and 306th Bombardment Wings carried large geometric tail markings consisting of an open black square with the letter "P" or "G" within the square, respectively. Some of these aircraft carried the squadron insignia on the left side of the nose and wing insignia on the right side of the nose.

Later, SAC B-47s had Gloss White anti-radiation applied to the lower surfaces to protect crews from the effects of nuclear blasts. First came the partial white scheme that began aft of the radome, covered the lower portion of the fuselage, the entire wing lower surfaces, and the outboard portions of the horizontal tail planes. The USAF and national insignia were only carried on the upper surfaces of the wings. The national insignia was only applied on the waist on B-47s with the

partial white anti-radiation finish that extended up to the gear and bomb bay hinge lines. On B-47s with the full white anti-radiation paint, the national insignia was deleted from the waist. Anti-radiation paint was never carried on RB-47s or WB-47s.

B-47s assigned to Air Training Command (ATC) carried the ATC insignia on both sides of the nose and a large colored band on the tail to identify the squadron.

Air Weather Service WB-47s had the Military Air Transport Service insignia on the waist and had an Insignia Yellow-edged Insignia Blue band with WEATHER in white on the vertical tail.

During the early 1960s, the last three digits of the tail number were carried in large numerals below the tail number. A SAC Milky Way band was applied to the forward fuselage, and the left side almost always carried a SAC insignia. Occasionally, the wing insignia was applied on the right side of the nose centered on the SAC band. Some aircraft had names painted on the nose.

With the deletion of the geometric tail markings came a variety of colored stripes on the vertical tails that identified both the wing and the squadrons within the wing. In addition, the stripe orientation offered some semblance of wing identification.

*Mechanics were making some last minute inspections in the raceway. Control cables for the empennage and wings ran through the raceway. (Boeing BW55026)*

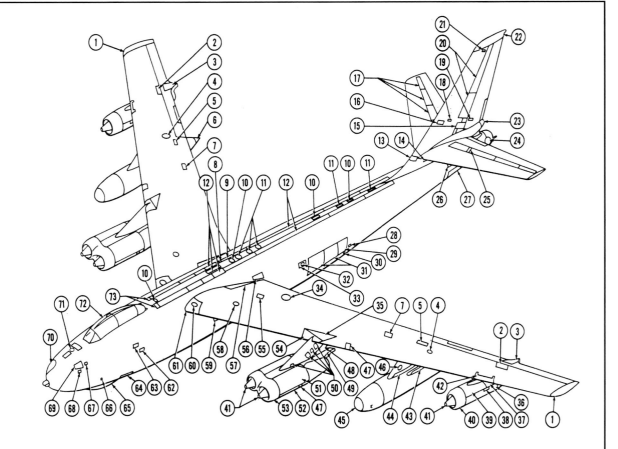

# KEY

1 WING TIP
2 AILERON POWER CONTROL UNIT & QUADRANT ACCESS
3 TAIL CONE FAIRING
4 EXT FUEL TANK REAR FITTING ACCESS
5 FLAPERON DISCONNECT ACCESS
6 EXT FUEL TANK TAIL CONE
7 FLAPERON POWER CONTROL ACCESS
8 LIFERAFT RELEASE DOOR
9 LIFERAFT DOOR
10 DUAL HIGH LEVEL CONTROL VALVE ACCESS
11 FUEL PROBE ACCESS
12 CONTROL CABLE ACCESS
13 FITTING VERTICAL STABILIZER
14 STABILIZER ANTI-ICING DUCT ACCESS
15 RUDDER SURFACE POWER CONTROL ACCESS
16 N-1 COMPASS TRANSMITTER ACCESS
17 ELEVATOR BALANCE ACCESS
18 RUDDER CONTROL TORQUE TUBE ACCESS
19 RUDDER TRIM TAB ACTUATOR ACCESS
20 RUDDER BALANCE ACCESS
21 ANTENNA COUPLING ACCESS
22 FIN TIP
23 A-5 RADOME
24 TAIL TURRET ACCESS
25 ELEVATOR TAB ACCESS
26 APPROACH CHUTE DOOR
27 BRAKE CHUTE DOOR
28 ATO RACK ADJUSTMENT
29 BATTERY COMPARTMENT
30 EXT ATO PULLOUT PLUG
31 LEFT ECM COMPARTMENTS
32 BOOST PUMP & FUEL TANK SUMP DRAIN
33 BOMB BAY TANK NAME PLATE ACCESS
34 FLAP SCREW DISCONNECT ACCESS
35 INBOARD STRUT GAP COVER
36 SIDE PANEL ACCESS
37 OUTBOARD STRUT SIDE ACCESS
38 FIRE EXTINGUISHER DOOR
39 FORWARD CENTER SECTION
40 NACELLE NOSE COWL
41 ACCESSORY DOME

42 OUTBOARD STRUT GAP COVER
43 SWAY BRACE ACCESS
44 STUB STRUT ACCESS
45 EXT FUEL TANK NOSE ACCESS
46 MAIN STRUT FUEL HOSE ACCESS
47 THERMAL ANTI-ICING VALVE ACCESS
48 FUEL VALVE ACCESS
49 INBOARD STRUT REAR ACCESS
50 INBOARD STRUT ACCESS
51 INBOARD NACELLE UPPER ACCESS
52 INBOARD NACELLE LOWER ACCESS
53 INBOARD NACELLE NOSE COWL
54 INBOARD STRUT SUPPORT ACCESS
55 FUEL FLOW RATE TRANSMITTER ACCESS
56 CENTER MAIN TANK FORWARD CELL
57 WING TRAILING EDGE GAP COVER

58 WATER INJECTION TANK FILLER CAP
59 CENTER MAIN TANK FWD SUMP DRAIN
60 WING BREAK INSPECTION PLATE
61 WING LEADING EDGE GAP COVER
62 CABIN AIR CONDITIONING INTAKE
63 CABIN AIR CONDITIONING EXHAUST
64 ENTRANCE DOOR
65 FORWARD RADOME
66 BOMB SIGHT ACCESS
67 CANOPY EXT RELEASE PULL
68 HATCH EXT RELEASE HANDLE
69 NAVIGATOR'S ESCAPE HATCH
70 AIR REFUELING DOOR
71 PERISCOPE SEXTANT MOUNT
72 CANOPY
73 ELECTRICAL ACCESS DOORS

# ACCESS DOORS AND OPENINGS SLIDE 1 OF 2  52-597

Upper isometric view of the external access doors and openings on the B-47E as of 1 October 1955.

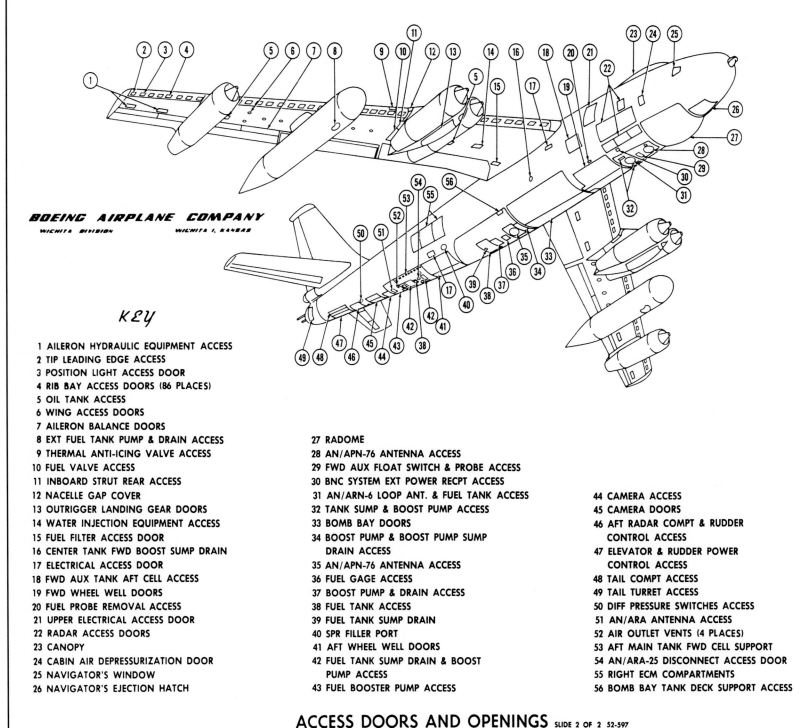

**BOEING AIRPLANE COMPANY**
WICHITA DIVISION          WICHITA I, KANSAS

## KEY

1 AILERON HYDRAULIC EQUIPMENT ACCESS
2 TIP LEADING EDGE ACCESS
3 POSITION LIGHT ACCESS DOOR
4 RIB BAY ACCESS DOORS (86 PLACES)
5 OIL TANK ACCESS
6 WING ACCESS DOORS
7 AILERON BALANCE DOORS
8 EXT FUEL TANK PUMP & DRAIN ACCESS
9 THERMAL ANTI-ICING VALVE ACCESS
10 FUEL VALVE ACCESS
11 INBOARD STRUT REAR ACCESS
12 NACELLE GAP COVER
13 OUTRIGGER LANDING GEAR DOORS
14 WATER INJECTION EQUIPMENT ACCESS
15 FUEL FILTER ACCESS DOOR
16 CENTER TANK FWD BOOST SUMP DRAIN
17 ELECTRICAL ACCESS DOOR
18 FWD AUX TANK AFT CELL ACCESS
19 FWD WHEEL WELL DOORS
20 FUEL PROBE REMOVAL ACCESS
21 UPPER ELECTRICAL ACCESS DOOR
22 RADAR ACCESS DOORS
23 CANOPY
24 CABIN AIR DEPRESSURIZATION DOOR
25 NAVIGATOR'S WINDOW
26 NAVIGATOR'S EJECTION HATCH

27 RADOME
28 AN/APN-76 ANTENNA ACCESS
29 FWD AUX FLOAT SWITCH & PROBE ACCESS
30 BNC SYSTEM EXT POWER RECPT ACCESS
31 AN/ARN-6 LOOP ANT. & FUEL TANK ACCESS
32 TANK SUMP & BOOST PUMP ACCESS
33 BOMB BAY DOORS
34 BOOST PUMP & BOOST PUMP SUMP
   DRAIN ACCESS
35 AN/APN-76 ANTENNA ACCESS
36 FUEL GAGE ACCESS
37 BOOST PUMP & DRAIN ACCESS
38 FUEL TANK ACCESS
39 FUEL TANK SUMP DRAIN
40 SPR FILLER PORT
41 AFT WHEEL WELL DOORS
42 FUEL TANK SUMP DRAIN & BOOST
   PUMP ACCESS
43 FUEL BOOSTER PUMP ACCESS

44 CAMERA ACCESS
45 CAMERA DOORS
46 AFT RADAR COMPT & RUDDER
   CONTROL ACCESS
47 ELEVATOR & RUDDER POWER
   CONTROL ACCESS
48 TAIL COMPT ACCESS
49 TAIL TURRET ACCESS
50 DIFF PRESSURE SWITCHES ACCESS
51 AN/ARA ANTENNA ACCESS
52 AIR OUTLET VENTS (4 PLACES)
53 AFT MAIN TANK FWD CELL SUPPORT
54 AN/ARA-25 DISCONNECT ACCESS DOOR
55 RIGHT ECM COMPARTMENTS
56 BOMB BAY TANK DECK SUPPORT ACCESS

## ACCESS DOORS AND OPENINGS SLIDE 2 OF 2 52-597

*Lower isometric view of the external access doors and openings on the B-47E as of 1 October 1955.*

## B-47 DIMENSIONS

| Parameter | Dimension | Parameter | Dimension | Parameter | Dimension |
|---|---|---|---|---|---|
| | | Flaperon Span | 15' 8.4 " | Horizontal Stabilizer Root Chord | 11' 5" |
| | | Flap Span | 16' 7.5" | Horizontal Tail Area | 199.5 sq. ft. |
| Wing Span | 116' | Flap Area | 249.6 sq. ft. | MLG Tire Diameter | 56" |
| Wing Span (with ECM tips) | 116' 4" | Length | 107' 1.5" | MLG Wheel Base | 36' 4" |
| Wing Root Chord | 17' 4" | Height | 28' | Outrigger Tire Diameter | 26" |
| Wingtip Chord | 7' 3.6" | Rudder Height | 14' 9.8" | Outrigger Tire Track | 44' 4" |
| Wing Area | 1,428 sq. ft. | Vertical Stabilizer Height | 18' 10" | | |
| Aileron Span | 27' 9.2" | Vertical Tail Area | 230 sq. ft. | | |
| Aileron Area | 53' 9" | Horizontal Stabilizer Span | 33' | | |

## B-47 WEIGHTS

| Series | Empty | Basic | Design | Combat | Max. T.O. (1) | Max. In Flight | Max. Ldg. (2) |
|---|---|---|---|---|---|---|---|
| XB-47-BO | 75,186 | | 125,000 | 109,000 | 162,500 | | |
| B-47A-BW | 73,240 | 74,524 | 125,000 | 106,060 | 157,000 | | 157,000 |
| B-47B-BW | 78,102 | 80,512 | 125,000 | 122,650 (3) | 185,000 | 198,000 (3) 221,000 (4) | 180,000 |
| B-47B-II-BW | 78,102 | 80,512 | 125,000 | 122,650 (3) | 184.908 | | |
| B-47E-BW | 78,620 | 80,590 | 125,000 | 123,080 | 200,000 | 202,000 | 180,000 |
| B-47E-BW (heavyweight) | 79,074 | 81,044 | 125,000 | 133,030 | 230,000 | 221,000 | 180,000 |
| B-47E-II-BW | 80,756 | 82,726 | 125,000 | 124,875 | 200,000 | 221,000 | 180,000 |
| B-47E-IV-BW | 79,074 | 81,044 | 125,000 | 133,030 | 230,000 | 221,000 | 180,000 |
| B-47E-DT | 80,756 | 82,726 | 125,000 | 124,875 | 200,000 | 221,000 | 180,000 |
| B-47E-LM | 80,756 | 82,726 | 125,000 | 124,875 | 200,000 | 221,000 | 180,000 |
| RB-47E-BW | 81,100 | 83,190 | 125,000 | 130,800 | 200,000 | 221,000 | 180,000 |
| RB-47H-BW | 83,642 89,230 (5) | 84,661 | 125,000 | 136,995 | 220,600 | 221,000 | 125,000 198,000 (3) |
| RB-47K-BW | 81,100 | 83,190 | 125,000 | 130,800 | 200,000 | 202,000 | 180,000 |
| RB-47B-BW | 81,992 | 86,768 | 125,000 | 130,100 | 180,000 | 202,000 | 180,000 |
| TB-47B-BW | 76,617 | 79,407 | 125,000 | 120,000 | 179,292 | | 179,292 |
| YB-47C-BW | 80,811 | 83,953 | 125,000 | 128,400 | 180,000 | 202,000 | 180,000 |
| RB-47C | 74,540 | | 125,000 | | | 202,000 | |
| XB-47D-BW | 79,800 | 82,409 | 125,000 | 121,850 | 184,428 | | 180,000 |
| YDB-47E | 81,020 | 85,255 | 125,000 | 119,300 | 185,300 | 212,000 | 125,000 |
| DB-47E-BW | 82,424 | 85,527 | 125,000 | 130,955 | 230,000 | 221,000 | 125,000 |
| QB-47E | 81,100 | 83,190 | 125,000 | 130,800 | 200,000 | 221,000 | 180,000 |
| ETB-47E | 78,620 | 80,590 | 125,000 | 123,080 | 200,000 | 202,000 | 180,000 |
| WB-47E | 78,620 | 80,590 | 125,000 | 123,080 | 200,000 | 202,000 | 180,000 |
| YB-47F-BW | 78,620 | 80,590 | 125,000 | 123,080 | 200,000 | 202,000 | 180,000 |
| KB-47G-BW | 78,620 | 80,590 | 125,000 | 123,080 | 200,000 | 202,000 | 180,000 |
| ERB-47H-BW | 83,642 89,230 (5) | 84,661 | 125,000 | 136,995 | 220,600 | 221,000 | 125,000 198,000 (3) |

NOTES: (1) Limited by strength of landing gear; (2) For Basic Mission; (3) w/o External Tanks; (4) w/ External Tanks; (5) Including Silver King Pod.

## B-47 PROPULSION

| Series | Engines (6 each) | Thrust (Lbf) each | RATO | Number | Thrust (Lbf) each | Duration (Seconds) |
|---|---|---|---|---|---|---|
| XB-47-BO | J35-GE-7 or J35-GE-9, then J47-GE-11 | 3,750 5,200 | Aerojet No. 12 | 18 | 1,000 | 12-14 |
| B-47A-BW | J47-GE-11 | 5,200 | Aerojet 15KS-1000 | 18 | 1,000 | 15 |
| B-47B-BW | J47-GE-23 | 5,910 | Aerojet 15KS-1000 | 18 | 1,000 | 15 |
| B-47B-II-BW | J47-GE-25 | 5,970 | Aerojet 15KS-1000 | 18 | 1,000 | 15 |
|  |  |  | Aerojet 15KS-1000 | 33 | 1,000 | 14 |
| RB-47B | J47-GE-25 | 7,200 | Aerojet 15KS-1000 | 18 | 1,000 | 15 |
| B-47E-BW | J47-GE-25 | 7,200 | Aerojet 15KS-1000 | 33 | 1,000 | 15 |
| B-47E-BW (Heavyweight) | J47-GE-25 | 7,200 | Aerojet 15KS-1000 | 33 | 1,000 | 15 |
| B-47E-II-BW | J47-GE-25 or J47-GE-25A | 7,200 | Aerojet 15KS-1000 | 33 | 1,000 | 15 |
| B-47E-IV-BW | J47-GE-25 or J47-GE-25A | 7,200 | Aerojet 15KS-1000 | 33 | 1,000 | 15 |
| B-47E-DT | J47-GE-25 | 7,200 | Aerojet 15KS-1000 | 33 | 1,000 | 15 |
| B-47E-LM | J47-GE-25 | 7,200 | Aerojet 15KS-1000 | 33 | 1,000 | 15 |
| RB-47E-BW | J47-GE-25 | 7,200 | Aerojet 15KS-1000 | 33 | 1,000 | 15 |
| RB-47H-BW | J47-GE-25 | 7,200 | Aerojet 15KS-1000 | 33 | 1,000 | 15 |
| RB-47K-BW | J47-GE-25 | 7,200 | Aerojet 15KS-1000 | 33 | 1,000 | 15 |
| DB-47B-BW | J47-GE-23 | 5,910 | – | – | – | – |
| TB-47B-BW | J47-GE-23 | 5,910 | Aerojet 15KS-1000 | 18 | 1,000 | 15 |
|  |  |  | Aerojet 15KS-1000 | 33 | 1,000 | 14 |
| WB-47B-BW | J47-GE-25 | 7,200 | – | 0 | – | – |
| XB-47D-BW | YT49-W-1 (2) J47-GE-23 (2) | 9,710 (ESHP) 5,910 | – | – | – | – |
| YDB-47E | J47-GE-25 | 7,200 | Aerojet 15KS-1000 | 33 | 1,000 | 15 |
| DB-47E-BW | J47-GE-25 | 7,200 | Aerojet 15KS-1000 | 33 | 1,000 | 15 |
| QB-47E | J47-GE-25 | 7,200 | – | – | – | – |
| RB-47E-BW | J47-GE-25 | 7,200 | – | – | – | – |
| ETB-47E | J47-GE-25 | 7,200 | – | – | – | – |
| WB-47E | J47-GE-25 | 7,200 | – | – | – | – |
| ERB-47H-BW | J47-GE-25 | 7,200 | Aerojet 15KS-1000 | 33 | 1,000 | 15 |
| EB-47L | J47-GE-23 | 5,910 | – | – | – | – |
| CL-52 | J47-GE-23 and Orenda Iroquois (1) | 5,910 26,000 | – | – | – | – |

The Boeing Model 367 Stratofreighter (and KC-97) went through a number of design iterations in a search for a more efficient transport aircraft. The result of these engineering efforts was the Model 367-80 – turning a straight-winged, four-engined propeller-driven aircraft into a sweptwing, four-engined jet. Seen here over Lake Washington, the airplane was in its original brown and yellow company colors and was powered by four Pratt & Whitney JT3D engines. The inboard wing trailing edge chord had been increased, hence its double sweep. The aircraft was the progenitor of both the commercial Model 707 and the military Model 717 (KC-135). (Boeing K21051)

# Chapter 11

# *EFFECT ON THE FUTURE*

The B-47 was truly an innovative aircraft incorporating a plethora of new designs that had a direct and lasting impact on future jet aircraft, both military and commercial. Unlike fighters and smaller research aircraft, the B-47s roamed the upper edges of the stratosphere for long hours thereby providing ample time to gather reliability data on the various components.

A Boeing report, dated 9 March 1954, summarized a study of B-47 accidents relative to the Model 707, showing that such an aircraft would have good safety characteristics. The extensive data available on B-47 accidents through 1 January 1954 was analyzed and presented by phase of flight hazards, and the principal contributing causes. These data also applied to the Boeing Model 367-80 – forerunner of the Model 717 (USAF KC-135) and the Model 707 Jetliner.

Design changes implemented in the B-47 program led engineers to believe that it was reasonable to assume that the Model 707 would avoid all of the operational accidents that led to damage or destruction of the B-47s during the study period.

While asymmetrical gear-up landings with the B-47 had not been serious, they could be a factor with the low wing pod engine design of the Model 707. (Subsequent commercial history has shown this not to be the case.)

Fire hazards remained a concern, therefore Boeing engineers believed that the fire detection should be retained, and a suppression system added. Ground refueling with such large quantities of fuel resulted in an ever-present fire hazard.

## COMMON MILITARY AND COMMERCIAL INNOVATIONS

The B-47 provided Boeing, and the aircraft industry, with the requisite background for future systems and structures designs, and manufacturing tooling and techniques.

**Producibility –** A major challenge in designing the B-47 was to achieve not only superior performance, but also rapid producibility. Through the combined efforts of aircraft engineers, tool designers, and production planners new manufacturing techniques compatible with aircraft performance were developed. The result was a minimum compromise between performance and producibility.

**Antiskid System –** Braking a speeding heavy jet aircraft is no easy chore for any pilot. Add some crosswind and water and the problem rapidly grows in magnitude. Improper braking can result in blown tires that make the landing even more difficult. To solve this problem Boeing engineers worked with Hydro-Aire to develop the first antiskid system that was installed on the B-47. This system prevents the wheels from locking and the tires from skidding thereby markedly reducing the possibility of a blown tire. An unplanned benefit was increased braking efficiency. A skidding tire is far less efficient than a rolling tire with metered braking. The Hydro-Aire Mark I system was a mechanical inertial rate on-off system. Braking efficiency is a measure of how much of the available runway friction is used to stop the aircraft. The Mark I system had a braking efficiency somewhere around 60 percent. The Mark II system, introduced in 1960, was a modulating rate design that produced a 70 to 85 percent braking efficiency. To have an antiskid system be effective, the weight of the aircraft had to be on the wheels. With the B-47 this required the pilot to firmly plant the aircraft on the runway.

**Electrical Generators –** The early alternating current generators were fraught with problems associated with high altitude flight. Westinghouse spent some 10 years developing an 18-kVA generator system. This, too, had initial problems with its brushes and bearings. Once rectified, these generators paved the way for newer and more powerful alternating current generators. By the 1960s, aircraft were flying with 120-kVA generators.

**Turbine Engines –** While early turbine engines were not so powerful and had long spool-up times, they pointed the way to the future. Engine manufacturers have been able to continuously improve turbine engine performance. An offshoot was the highly efficient turboprop that is employed on a large number of aircraft, both military and commercial. The J35-GE-7 engines that powered the XB-47 developed a mere 3,750-lbf of static thrust, whereas the J47-GE-25 turbojets on the later B-47s mustered 7,000-lbf. These engines were straight turbojets – a single shaft with a compressor section at one end and a turbine section at the other.

Over time engine technology advanced and the low bypass turbofan engine evolved. This design incorporates a sleeved shaft with two compressor and two turbine sections. The longer inner shaft has a low-stage compressor and a low-stage compressor at either end; whereas the inner shaft comprises the high-stage section. Examples of these engines are the 14,000-lbf static thrust P&W JT8D that powered the Boeing 727 and early 737 family of jetliners. Later JT8Ds developed 18,000-lbf. A still larger low-bypass engine was the 43,000-lbf static thrust P&W JT9D that powered the original Boeing 747-100s.

During the late 1970s, 1980s, and 1990s, jet engine performance was substantially increased along with their reliability with the introduction of large high-bypass engines. Some of these engines develop in excess of 100,000-lbf.

**Swept Wing** – The swept wing design was key to high subsonic speeds. The 35-degree sweep introduced with the B-47 has essentially been carried forth to all future jet-powered aircraft. This design reduces drag by reducing the frontal area, but more importantly, delays compressibility and increases the achievable Mach number. A swept wing in effect increases its chord and aerodynamically acts like a thinner wing.

Experience showed that the extremely thin wing was not a requirement for efficient flight. With a thicker wing root tapering to a thinner tip, aerodynamic efficiencies could be retained. Such a design allowed the wings to also serve as fuel tanks. In addition, in a low wing design, landing gear could be mounted in a more efficient manner.

A swept wing made up of heavy tapered stressed skins with flush high-strength fasteners not only provided a clean wing, but permitted a simpler wing interior. A pair of heavy spars with a minimum of ribs coupled with the heavy skins formed the wing torque box and eliminated the requirement for complicated rib designs. All requisite aerodynamic leading edges, engine mounts, and flight controls could be attached to this wing box.

**Yaw Damper** – This simple device, known as Little Herbert, reduced pilot workload, maintained stable flight along the vertical axis, reduced Dutch roll, and assured safe flight by preventing the aircraft from getting into divergent flight. This was the first active flight control system and was essential for the B-47.

**Flight Controls** – The B-47 had an irreversible hydraulic boost system. Lessons learned with the B-47 showed that the elevators and rudder required tabs to ease manual flying of the aircraft, spoilers were far more effective than ailerons, and a moveable horizontal stabilizer was essential for longitudinal trim.

**Podded Engines** – Not only did podded engines significantly reduce drag and airflow distortion; they were a major aid to aircraft maintenance. Podded engines could be mounted either directly under the wing or suspended from pylons without detrimental aerodynamic effects on the wing. More so, podded engines provided additional safety in the event of an engine fire or explosion. Flames were kept away from critical aircraft components, and fuse-pin mounts would allow the engine to break away during high load conditions. In the event of a catastrophic engine failure its seizure would fail the cone bolts attaching the engine to the strut and permit it to safely separate from the aircraft. This design permitted retrofit of higher performance engines without affecting the basic wing structure.

**Spoilers** – While not standard on the Stratojet, a B-47B-25-BW (51-2052) was retrofitted with spoilers at a time when it was too far into the B-47 program for them to be incorporated in production and retrofit in an economical fashion. However, spoilers became the primary speed brakes and roll axis controls for the B-52 and subsequent jet transports. In fact, the B-52 could not have been flown without a spoiler system. Spoilers improve approach performance and rapidly get the weight on the wheels for the antiskid system to be effective.

**Vortex Generators** – The bane of aerodynamicists is airflow separation that may result from attempting to achieve optimum drag loss. The solution is the vortex generator, also known as aspirin for aerodynamicists. These miniature airfoil-shaped devices are mounted to critical areas to help smooth airflow in specific areas. On the B-47, a double row of vortex generators was installed aft of the front spar of the wing upper surface, in line with the ailerons. With these devices, the boundary layer was kept intact thereby permitting effective aileron operation. Vortex generators may be found on a number of later aircraft. Unusual locations were along the aft fuselage of the Boeing 737 to control vertical bounce, and the large engine ears on the outboard side of the engine cowls on 737s powered by high-bypass engines.

**Thermal Anti-Icing** – Thermal anti-icing systems were designed for wing and empennage leading edges, canopy, and engine inlets. Anti-icing of the engine inlet is critical – when static air conditions may not produce icing conditions, the increased airflow into the engine may easily result in a local icing condition. This is particularly true when a cold-soaked engine inlet enters a cloud with a great amount of moisture. Over time it was proven that this feature was not required for the empennage and was deleted from future designs. However, it was retained for the other areas.

**Fly-by-Wire** – The first successful fly-by-wire flight testing was accomplished on a B-47. Albeit only a single, then two, axis system, it proved that such systems were feasible. Fly-by-wire became essential on modern jet fighters and Boeing introduced fly-by-wire into production aircraft with the Model 757 engine control system. The Model 777 incorporates fly-by-wire in the engine control system and flight controls, albeit the elevator still has a manual reversion capability. Boeing's commercial fly-by-wire design concepts retain pilot override capability, unlike the Airbus products where the computer rules.

**Moisture Separator** – In 1951 WIBAC had developed the first water separator for high-altitude jet aircraft. As the aircraft climbs from a relatively warm and humid airfield to the cold of high altitude, moisture separates out of the air and can form as snow, rain, or fog within the pressurized cabin. While the jet's air conditioning system could account for temperature, it had no effect on humidity. In flight this moisture could be expelled on critical electrical connectors. On landing, the entrained moisture could form a dense fog that impaired or completely obscured the crew's vision. Boeing engineers developed a centrifugal-type water separator with a cyclonic rotor attachment. This system had an 80 percent efficiency that more than adequately controlled the moisture. If 100 percent efficiency were achieved, there would be a detrimental effect of drying the lungs of the aircrew. One problem with the system is that it could freeze if the temperatures got below 33 degrees Fahrenheit. Subsequently a 35-degree switch was developed to keep the system above freezing.

**Maintenance Access –** While earlier aircraft had access panels attached with a plethora of screws, the B-47 featured hinged access panels incorporating push-button Hartwell latches. Not only were aerodynamic requirements retained, but also maintenance access was greatly enhanced. Engine cowls could be removed in a matter of seconds. Tubing or mounting hardware did not block components.

**Structural Integrity –** Lessons learned from the B-47 led to new branches of metallurgy including a better understanding of fatigue life, crack length and progression, and stress corrosion.

**Damage-Tolerance Inspections –** Experience with the B-47 paved the way for developing damage tolerance inspection programs to ensure the safe operational life of the aircraft.

**Lead-the-Fleet Programs –** By looking at high-time airframes, both Boeing and the Air Force learned how to predict potential failures in the rest of the fleet and take preemptive corrective action. This action could take several forms: redesign, increased inspection intervals, or more detailed maintenance programs.

## IMPACT ON FUTURE BOMBER DEVELOPMENT

The B-47 also provided guidance for design of future bombers.

**Tapered Wing –** Through the B-47 program it was learned that an extremely thin wing was not required to achieve the desired aeroelastic qualities; hence the B-52 was designed with a thick wing root that tapered towards the tip. This design permitted incorporation of integral wing fuel tanks that further helped to distribute the operational loads on the airframe.

**Bicycle Landing Gear –** The efficient bicycle landing gear with a bomb bay between allowed use of a high wing design to ensure critical center of gravity requirements. In addition, it made the bomb bay design less complicated by having the wing carry-through structure located above the bomb bay. The bicycle gear design was chosen because of the requirement for maximum speed. This design precluded the need for long, heavy landing gear that had to be accommodated in fairings that would have resulted in increased drag.

**Bomb Bay Clip-in System –** The B-47 employed a number of clip-in bomb rack systems that came in kit form and could be easily changed to suit mission requirements. A direct result of these designs was the highly efficient Big Belly system installed on the B-52Ds for the war in Southeast Asia.

**Electronic Countermeasures (ECM) –** Design changes in electronic countermeasures evolve in three- to five-year increments to meet the ever-changing threat. The B-47 went through five phases of upgrades. Data gathered by the RB-47s helped make these changes possible and paved the way for future ECM development.

**Ejection Seats –** From an arduous beginning, safe and efficient ejection seats were developed for the B-47 and have been installed on every future bomber.

**Deceleration Parachute –** The deceleration or drag chute was incorporated early in the B-47 program and became standard equipment. This system was subsequently incorporated in the B-52 Stratofortresses, other bombers, most high-performance fighters, and even the Space Shuttle.

## IMPACT ON FUTURE COMMERCIAL JETLINERS

Essentially all future commercial jet transports were based on the design philosophy of the B-47. This philosophy optimized the high subsonic flight characteristics while permitting an economical payload. Albeit for the BAC Concorde supersonic transport, all commercial jet transports fly at speeds between Mach 0.8 and 0.9.

The general planform of Boeing commercial jetliners and those of Boeing's competitors retain the basic shape of the B-47 with its swept wing and empennage.

Podded engines are the norm for multi-engined jet aircraft.

RATO was used on some Boeing 727s that operated out of high altitude airports.

## PROVEN CONCEPTS

By employing the proven concepts developed for the B-47 program, numerous long lines of bombardment, reconnaissance, refueling military aircraft, and successful jet-powered commercial transports have evolved. These were all the result of daring and innovative engineering concepts being driven to fruition in a relatively short time frame. Boeing engineers working in concert with Air Force personnel at various research and development units and with reliable suppliers designed and built a truly innovative and revolutionary aircraft.

*The Boeing 747-400F shows its obvious heritage to the B-47.* (Boeing)

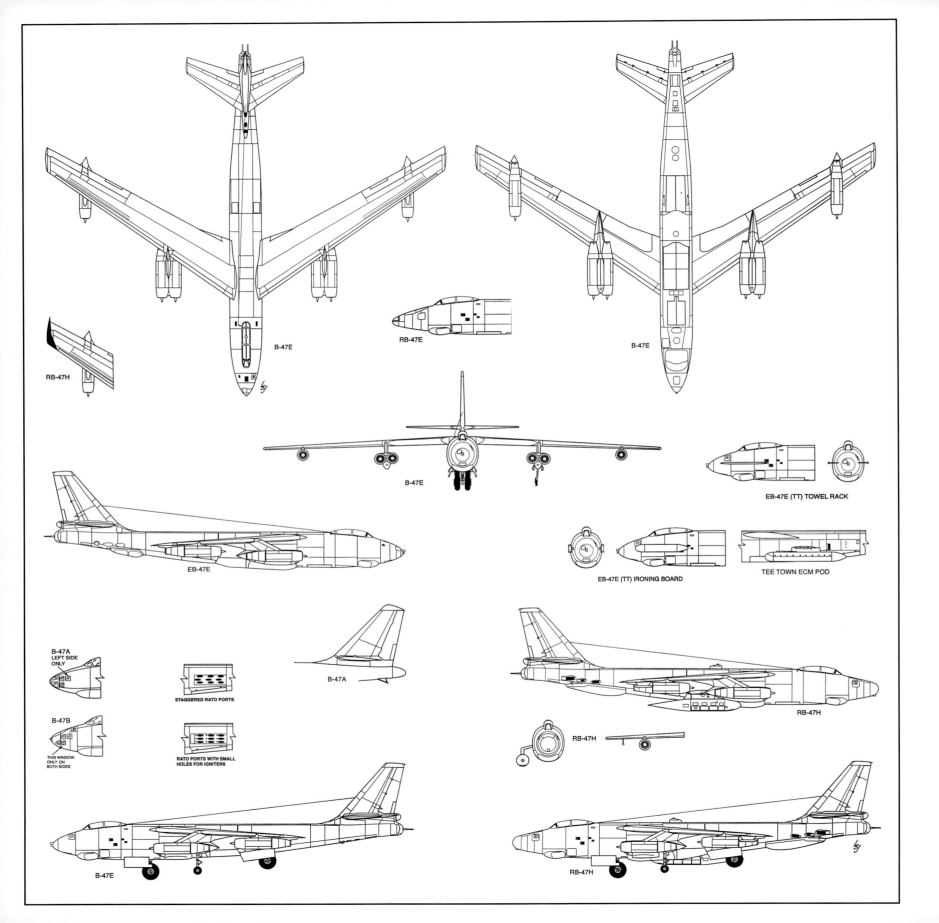

B-47E

RB-47E

B-47E

RB-47H

B-47E

EB-47E (TT) TOWEL RACK

EB-47E

EB-47E (TT) IRONING BOARD

TEE TOWN ECM POD

B-47A
LEFT SIDE
ONLY

STAGGERED RATO PORTS

B-47A

RB-47H

B-47B

THIS WINDOW
ONLY ON
BOTH SIDES

RATO PORTS WITH SMALL
HOLES FOR IGNITERS

RB-47H

B-47E

RB-47H

# Appendix A

# *STRATOJETS IN COLOR*

These shock waves were generated on the top of a B-47 wing during a high altitude, high speed test conducted in April 1955. (Edward King)

Aerojet performed a static test of their liquid-fueled RATO system on this B-47B-1-BW (49-2644). (Aerojet General via Charles Ehresman)

Here the Aerojet liquid-fueled RATO system was fired during a takeoff test at Edwards AFB. (Aerojet General via Charles Ehresman)

The final RATO system installed on the B-47s was the 32-rocket split rack or 33-bottle horsecollar rack. This B-47E-90-BW (52-509) was equipped with the 33-bottle horsecollar rack. Note that the national insignia was still applied to this test aircraft. Camera blisters were located aft of the bottles and heat sensor tape was applied to the fuselage aft of the bottles. Tests showed that the heat from the rockets was absorbed by the national insignia, which caused skin buckling. (SAC Combat Crew Magazine)

This TB-47B-30-BW (51-2098) was assigned to the 3520th FTW (M) at McConnell AFB, Kansas. The aircraft sported an ATC insignia on the nose. The last three digits of the tail number appeared on the fin to assist personnel in locating the correct aircraft amongst a sea of birds on the ramp. (USAF K9326)

A copilot from the 306th BMW photographed this refueling operation with a KC-97E that was devoid of any unit markings. (George A. Johnson)

These Stratojets were assigned to the 367th BS, 306th BMW, MacDill AFB, Florida, as denoted by the blue tail band. Barely visible are the scars etched in the tail sheet metal from the former Square P wing tail marking. In the lead was a B-47B-45-BW (51-2287) followed by a B-47B-20-BW (51-081). Note the early 0.50-caliber tail guns. (George A. Johnson)

This flight of B-47Bs was from the 442nd BS, 320th BMW at March AFB, California. The aircraft in the background had the full white anti-radiation finish. The blue tail stripes identified the 442nd BS, while the red was for the 441st BS. Note the vortex generators on the outboard portion of the wing. These devices controlled airflow over the wing and helped prevent blanking of the aileron. (Edwin Bailey)

Early SAC B-47s carried the wing insignia on the left side of the nose and oftentimes a squadron insignia on the right side. This B-47E-65-BW (51-2539) had the last four digits of the tail number applied to the forward gear doors. The red gear doors indicate that the aircraft was assigned to the 44th BS, 40th BMW, Smoky Hill AFB, Kansas. The brake rider was standing up in the cockpit. (USAF K9421)

Classy local cars were the mode of transportation for SAC personnel when they deployed to England. When the 306th BMW deployed to RAF Fairford between June and September 1953, this B-47B-30-BW (51-2094) was assigned to the 369th BS. It carried the squadron's Fightin' 'n' Bitin' insignia on the left side of the nose. (George A. Johnson)

Here is an example of the Day-Glo Orange conspicuity paint applied to this B-47E-110-BW (53-2275). The orange paint was applied to the nose, waist, and wingtips. The aircraft had a full white anti-radiation finish and was devoid of any unit insignias, although it was likely assigned to the AFFTC. (Via MSgt. D. W. Menard)

This B-47E-10-BW (53-2271) from the 310th BMW at Schilling AFB took on fuel from a KC-135A (52-3567). Note the colored bands on the refueling boom that helped the receiver pilot judge his distance from the tanker. Refueling with the KC-135 was a vast improvement over the slower piston-powered KC-97. (SAC Combat Crew Magazine)

This view of a B-47-45-BW (51-2288) reveals the SAC Milky Way band and insignia, crew names, and air conditioning system inlets and exhaust outlets. The aircraft commander was P. S. Friedrich, pilot; 1st Lieutenant J. I. Granger, AOB; Captain I. Terry, crew chief; L. S. Morris; and assistant crew chief, R. L. Keebaugh. Listing both flight and ground crews on the aircraft greatly enhanced morale, and individual and personal pride. (Paul S. Friedrich)

This B-47E-30-LM (52-274) sported the original SAC Milky Way band that was narrower and more swept back than the later ones. The aircraft had red squadron trim on the fin and forward gear doors, and the last four digits of its serial number on the forward gear doors. Taken at an airshow in the 1950s, a Chance Vought F7U-3M Cutlass (a.k.a. ensign killer) was in the foreground and a Blue Angels TV-1 (T-33A) was in the background. (Gordon S. Williams)

This B-47B-50-BW (51-2327) from the 381st BS, 310th BMW, was equipped with Phase III ECM as denoted by the blister on the aft fuselage. Note the squadron color resplendently applied to the tail and fuel tank. It also appears as if the canopy frame was painted in yellow. (Nils S. Ohlson via MSgt. D. W. Menard)

This B-47E-30-DT (52-0178) was assigned to the 546th BS, 384th BMW, Little Rock AFB, Arkansas. The last four digits of the tail number were applied to the nose in red. Rescue placards had been installed on the forward fuselage. The large last three digits on the tail had been painted out with silver paint. (Gary Baker)

This EB-47E(TT), from the 55th SRW, reveals a tail number that equates to s/n 53-3235. This was a spurious number. Note the Phase III ECM wingtip extensions. The aircraft was equipped with a pair of towel rack antennas on the nose that were used for detection of Soviet missile launch telemetry. The electronics bay access door was painted white, most being a replacement from a B-47 with the full white anti-radiation paint scheme. (Via Bruce M. Bailey)

This B-47E-65-DT (53-2167) reveals only the SAC Milky Way band and red diagonal squadron stripe. This aircraft was equipped with the clamshell canopy. (Major B. Gordon via MSgt. D. W. Menard)

This RB-47E-16-BW (51-15841) sat alert with two-thirds of its RATO rack loaded. The aircraft was assigned to the 91st SRW. Note the open camera bay doors. (Gordon S. Williams)

This B-47E-75-BW (51-7069) is spectacularly marked with red and white stripes on the nose, waist, wingtips, and vertical tail. Note the theodolite pattern aft and to the right of the canopy. A camera was mounted in the fairing along the spine. (Via Gordon S. Williams)

This RB-47E was undergoing flight tests at Edwards AFB. The interior of the gear doors and wheel well, and bomb bay were painted Chromate Yellow for corrosion resistance. A red bomb bay door actuator lock was installed for safety reasons. (Gordon S. Williams)

This WB-47E-60-BW (51-2417) of Air Weather Service's (MATS) 55th WRS, McClellan AFB, California, was captured in flight circa 1967. A 55th WRS insignia was placed below the tail number, while a MATS insignia was applied to the waist. Note the U-1 foil inlet/exhaust mounted on the bomb bay door. (USAF Weather Agency)

The first YDB-47E-60-BW (51-5219) taking off from Boeing Field, with a GAM-63 RASCAL missile. (Via Gordon S. Williams)

This QRB-47E (53-4250) was photographed at Eglin AFB. Test antennas were installed in the nose and in pods suspended beneath the wings. The Day-Glo Red paint afforded enhanced visibility during the tests. (Via OCAMA Historian)

The sole WB-47B-30-BW (51-2115) was operated by the 55th WRS, McClellan AFB, California. In 1956 the aircraft was modified at General Precision Laboratories for its specialized mission and first flew in support of the U.S. Weather Bureau during the 1956 hurricane season. This photograph was taken in 1962 at Scott AFB, Illinois, then headquarters for the Air Weather Service in 1960. (A. T. Lloyd)

This RB-47H-BW (53-4291) was equipped for the Operation IRON LUNG mission during the early days of the war in Southeast Asia. (Via SAC Combat Crew Magazine)

A DB-47B-50-BW (51-2328) formated with another DB-47 that was carrying a GAM-67 Crossbow missile on its No. 4 pylon. The aircraft in the background reveals the size of the pylons that were required for the missile. (Edward King)

This 301st BMW crew was inspecting the 33-bottle RATO installation on one of their EB-47Es. The igniter wires may be seen attached to the forward ends of the bottles. Each bottle generated 1,000-lbf thrust. Note the rack's articulating rod that translated the rack down and away to prevent thermally induced skin damage to the fuselage. (Augustine "Gus" Letto)

# PRODUCTION NUMBERS

## BOEING PRODUCED B-47s

| Series | USAF S/N(s) | Boeing S/N(s) | Model No. | Contract No. | Remarks |
|---|---|---|---|---|---|
| XB-47-BO | 46-065 – 46-066 | 15972 – 15973 | 450-3-3 | W33(038) AC-8429 | |
| B-47A-BW | 49-1900 – 49-1909 | 450001 – 450010 | 450-10-9 | W33(038) AC-22413 | |
| B-47B-1-BW | 49-2642 – 49-2645 | 450011 – 45014 | 450-11-10 | W33(038) AC-22413 | |
| B-47B-5-BW | 49-2646 | 450015 | 450-11-10 | W33(038) AC-22413 | |
| B-47B-5-BW | 50-001 – 50-012 | 450016 – 450027 | 450-11-10 | W33(038) AC-22413 | |
| B-47B-10-BW | 50-013 – 50-025 | 450028 – 450040 | 450-11-10 | W33(038) AC-22413 | |
| B-47B-15-BW | 50-026 – 50-050 | 450041 – 450065 | 450-11-10 | W33(038) AC-22413 | |
| B-47B-20-BW | 50-051 – 50-082 | 450066 – 450097 | 450-11-10 | W33(038) AC-22413 | |
| B-47B-25-BW | 51-2045 – 51-2081 | 450098 – 450134 | 450-67-27 | AF33(038)-21407 | 19 aircraft assembled at Douglas and Lockheed |
| B-47B-30-BW | 51-2082 – 51-2136 | 450135 – 450189 | 450-67-27 | AF33(038)-21407 | |
| B-47B-35-BW | 51-2137 – 51-2191 | 450191 – 450244 | 450-67-27 | AF33(038)-21407 | |
| B-47B-40-BW | 51-2192 – 51-2446 | 450245 – 450299 | 450-67-27 | AF33(038)-21407 | |
| B-47B-45-BW | 51-2247 – 51-2301 | 450300 – 450354 | 450-157-27 | AF33(038)-21407 | |
| B-47B-50-BW | 51-2302 – 51-2356 | 450355 – 450489 | 450-157-27 | AF33(038)-21407 | |
| B-47E-55-BW | 51-2357 – 51-2411 | 450410 – 450464 | 450-157-27 | AF33(038)-21407 | |
| B-47E-60-BW | 51-2412 – 51-2445 | 450465 – 450498 | 450-157-27 | AF33(038)-21407 | |
| B-47E-60-BW | 51-5214 – 51-5234 | 450499 – 450519 | 450-157-27 | AF33(038)-21407 | |
| B-47E-65-BW | 51-5235 – 51-5257 | 450520 – 450542 | 450-157-27 | AF33(038)-21407 | |
| B-47E-65-BW | 51-7019 – 51-7050 | 450562 – 450593 | 450-157-35 | AF33(038)-21407 | |
| B-47E-70-BW | 51-7051 – 51-7064 | 450594 – 450607 | 450-157-35 | AF33(038)-21407 | |
| B-47E-75-BW | 51-7065 – 51-7083 | 450608 – 450626 | 450-157-35 | AF33(038)-21407 | |
| B-47E-75-BW | 51-17368 – 51-17386 | 450650 – 450678 | 450-157-35 | AF33(038)-21407 | |
| B-47E-80-BW | 52-394 – 52-431 | 450679 – 450716 | 450-157-35 | AF33(600)-22284 | |
| B-47E-85-BW | 52-432 – 52-469 | 450717 – 450754 | 450-157-35 | AF33(600)-22284 | |
| B-47E-90-BW | 52-470 – 52-507 | 450755 – 450792 | 450-157-35 | AF33(600)-22284 | |
| B-47E-95-BW | 52-508 – 52-545 | 450793 – 450830 | 450-157-35 | AF33(600)-22284 | |
| B-47E-100-BW | 52-546 – 52-583 | 450831 – 450868 | 450-157-35 | AF33(600)-22284 | |
| B-47E-105-BW | 52-584 – 52-620 | 450869 – 450905 | 450-157-35 | AF33(600)-22284 | |
| B-47E-110-BW | 53-2171 – 53-2296 | 4501074 – 450109 | 450-157-35 | AF33(600)-22284 | 53-2171 through 53-2260 cancelled |
| B-47E-115-BW | 53-2297 – 53-2331 | 450110 – 4501144 | 450-157-35 | AF33(600)-22284 | |
| B-47E-120-BW | 53-2332 – 53-2367 | 4501145 – 4501180 | 450-157-35 | AF33(600)-22284 | |
| B-47E-125-BW | 53-2368 – 53-2402 | 4501181 – 4501215 | 450-157-35 | AF33(600)-22284 | |
| B-47E-130-BW | 53-2403 – 53-2417 | 4501216 – 4501230 | 450-157-35 | AF33(600)-22284 | |
| B-47E-130-BW | 53-4207 – 53-4244 | 4501231 – 4501268 | 450-157-35 | AF33(600)-22284 | |
| B-47E-135-BW | 53-6193 – 53-6244 | 4501346 – 4501402 | 450-157-35 | AF33(600)-22284 | |
| RB-47E-1-BW | 51-5258 – 51-5264 | 450543 – 450549 | 450-126-29 | AF33(038)-21407 | |
| RB-47E-5-BW | 51-5265 – 51-5270 | 450530 – 450555 | 450-126-29 | AF33(038)-21407 | |
| RB-47E-10-BW | 51-5271 – 51-5276 | 450556 – 450561 | 450-126-29 | AF33(038)-21407 | |
| RB-47E-15-BW | 51-15821 – 51-15853 | 450643 – 450659 | 450-126-29 | AF33(038)-21407 | |
| RB-47E-20-BW | 52-685 – 52-719 | 450906 – 450940 | 450-158-36 | AF33(600)-5148 | |
| RB-47E-25-BW | 52-720 – 52-754 | 450941 – 450975 | 450-158-36 | AF33(600)-5148 | |
| RB-47E-30-BW | 52-755 – 52-789 | 450976 – 4501010 | 450-158-36 | AF33(600)-5148 | |
| RB-37E-35-BW | 52-790 – 52-825 | 4501011 – 4501046 | 450-158-36 | AF33(600)-5148 | |
| RB-37E-40-BW | 52-3374 – 52-3400 | 4501047 – 4501073 | 450-158-36 | AF33(600)-5148 | |
| RB-47E-45-BW | 53-4245 – 53-4264 | 4501269 – 4501288 | 450-158-36 | AF33(600)-5148 | |

## BOEING PRODUCED B-47s (CONTINUED)

| Series | USAF S/N(s) | Boeing S/N(s) | Model No. | Contract No. | Remarks |
|--------|-------------|---------------|-----------|--------------|---------|
| RB-47H-1-BW | 53-4280 – 53-4321 | 4501304 – 4501333 | 450-171-51 | AF33(600)-22284 | 52-4310 through 53-4321 cancelled |
| RB-47H-1-BW | 53-6245 – 53-6249 | 4501398 – 4501402 | 450-171-51 | AF33(600)-22284 | |
| RB-47K-1-BW | 53-4265 – 53-4279 | 4501289 – 4501303 | 450-171-51 | AF33(600)-22284 | |

## DOUGLAS-TULSA PRODUCED B-47s

| Series | USAF S/N(s) | Douglas S/N(s) | Model No. | Contract No. | Remarks |
|--------|-------------|----------------|-----------|--------------|---------|
| B-47B-35-DT | 51-2141 | 43624 | 450-67-27 | AF33(038)-18564 | Assembled from components built at Boeing-Wichita |
| B-47B-35-DT | 51-2150 | 43625 | 450-67-27 | AF33(038)-18564 | Assembled from components built at Boeing-Wichita |
| B-47B-35-DT | 51-2155 | 43626 | 450-67-27 | AF33(038)-18564 | Assembled from components built at Boeing-Wichita |
| B-47B-35-DT | 51-2160 | 43627 | 450-67-27 | AF33(038)-18564 | Assembled from components built at Boeing-Wichita |
| B-47B-35-DT | 51-2165 | 43628 | 450-67-27 | AF33(038)-18564 | Assembled from components built at Boeing-Wichita |
| B-47B-35-DT | 51-2170 | 43629 | 450-67-27 | AF33(038)-18564 | Assembled from components built at Boeing-Wichita |
| B-47B-35-DT | 51-2175 | 43630 | 450-67-27 | AF33(038)-18564 | Assembled from components built at Boeing-Wichita |
| B-47B-35-DT | 51-2180 | 43631 | 450-67-27 | AF33(038)-18564 | Assembled from components built at Boeing-Wichita |
| B-47B-35-DT | 51-2185 | 43632 | 450-67-27 | AF33(038)-18564 | Assembled from components built at Boeing-Wichita |
| B-47B-35-DT | 51-2190 | 43633 | 450-67-27 | AF33(038)-18564 | Assembled from components built at Boeing-Wichita |
| B-47E-1-DT | 52-019 – 52-028 | 43634 – 43643 | 450-157-35 | AF33(038)-18564 | |
| B-47E-5-DT | 52-029 – 52-041 | 43644 – 43656 | 450-157-35 | AF33(038)-18564 | |
| B-47E-10-DT | 52-042 – 52-054 | 43657 – 43669 | 450-157-35 | AF33(038)-18564 | |
| B-47E-10-DT | 52-055 – 52-058 | 43751 – 43754 | 450-157-35 | AF33(038)-18564 | |
| B-47E-15-DT | 52-059 – 51-081 | 43744 – 43777 | 450-157-35 | AF33(038)-18564 | |
| B-47E-20-DT | 52-082 – 52-111 | 43778 – 43807 | 450-157-35 | AF33(038)-18564 | |
| B-47E-25-DT | 52-112 – 52-120 | 43808 – 43816 | 450-157-35 | AF33(038)-18564 | |
| B-47E-25-DT | 52-146 – 52-176 | 44000 – 44030 | 450-157-35 | AF33(038)-18564 | |
| B-47E-30-DT | 52-177 – 52-201 | 44031 – 44055 | 450-157-35 | AF33(038)-18564 | |
| B-47E-30-DT | 52-1406 – 52-1417 | 44090 – 44101 | 450-157-35 | AF33(038)-18564 | |
| B-47E-35-DT | 53-2028 – 53-2040 | 44149 – 44161 | 450-157-35 | AF33(038)-18564 | |
| B-47E-40-DT | 53-2090 – 53-2103 | 44436 – 4449 | 450-157-35 | AF33(038)-18564 | |
| B-47E-45-DT | 54-2104 – 53-2117 | 44450 – 44463 | 450-157-35 | AF33(038)-18564 | |
| B-47E-50-DT | 53-2118 – 53-2131 | 44464 – 44477 | 450-157-35 | AF33(038)-18564 | |
| B-47E-55-DT | 53-2132 – 53-2144 | 44478 – 44490 | 450-157-35 | AF33(038)-18564 | |
| B-47E-60-DT | 53-2145 – 53-2157 | 44491 – 44503 | 450-157-35 | AF33(038)-18564 | |
| B-47B-65-DT | 53-2158 – 53-2170 | 44504 – 44516 | 450-157-35 | AF33(038)-18564 | |

## LOCKHEED-MARIETTA PRODUCED B-47s

| Series | USAF S/N(s) | Lockheed S/N(s) | Model No. | Contract No. | Remarks |
|--------|-------------|-----------------|-----------|--------------|---------|
| B-47B-30-LM | 51-2145 | None assigned | 450-67-27 | AF33(038)-21030 | Assembled from components built at Boeing-Wichita |
| B-47B-30-LM | 51-2197 | 1 | 450-67-27 | AF33(038)-21030 | Assembled from components built at Boeing-Wichita |
| B-47B-40-LM | 51-2204 | 2 | 450-67-27 | AF33(038)-21030 | Assembled from components built at Boeing-Wichita |
| B-47B-40-LM | 51-2210 | 3 | 450-67-27 | AF33(038)-21030 | Assembled from components built at Boeing-Wichita |
| B-47B-40-LM | 51-2217 | 4 | 450-67-27 | AF33(038)-21030 | Assembled from components built at Boeing-Wichita |
| B-47B-40-LM | 51-2224 | 5 | 450-67-27 | AF33(038)-21030 | Assembled from components built at Boeing-Wichita |
| B-47B-40-LM | 51-2231 | 6 | 450-67-27 | AF33(038)-21030 | Assembled from components built at Boeing-Wichita |
| B-47B-40-LM | 51-2237 | 7 | 450-67-27 | AF33(038)-21030 | Assembled from components built at Boeing-Wichita |
| B-47B-40-LM | 51-2243 | 8 | 450-67-27 | AF33(038)-21030 | Assembled from components built at Boeing-Wichita |
| B-47E-5-LM | 51-15804 – 51-15810 | 9 – 15 | 450-157-35 | AF33(038)-21030 | |
| B-47E-10-LM | 51-15811 – 51-15812 | 16 – 17 | 450-157-35 | AF33(038)-21030 | |
| B-47E-10-LM | 52-202 – 52-207 | 18 – 23 | 450-157-35 | AF33(038)-21030 | |
| B-47E-15-LM | 52-208 – 52-220 | 24 – 36 | 450-157-35 | AF33(038)-21030 | |
| B-47E-20-LM | 52-221 – 52-235 | 37 – 51 | 450-157-35 | AF33(038)-21030 | |
| B-47E-30-LM | 52-236 – 53-260 | 52 – 76 | 450-157-35 | AF33(038)-21030 | |
| B-47E-35-LM | 52-261 – 52-292 | 77 – 108 | 450-157-35 | AF33(038)-21030 | |
| B-47E-40-LM | 52-293 – 52-330 | 109 – 146 | 450-157-35 | AF33(038)-21030 | |
| B-47E-45-LM | 52-331 – 52-362 | 147 – 178 | 450-157-35 | AF33(038)-21030 | |
| B-47E-50-LM | 52-363 – 53-393 | 179 – 209 | 450-157-35 | AF33(038)-21030 | |
| B-47E-50-LM | 52-3343 – 52-3373 | 210 – 240 | 450-157-35 | AF33(038)-21030 | |
| B-47E-55-LM | 53-1819 – 53-1849 | 241 – 271 | 450-157-35 | AF33(600)-22278 | |
| B-47E-60-LM | 53-1850 – 53-1880 | 272 – 302 | 450-157-35 | AF33(600)-22278 | |
| B-47E-65-LM | 53-1881 – 53-1911 | 303 – 333 | 450-157-35 | AF33(600)-22278 | |
| B-47E-70-LM | 53-1912 – 53-1942 | 334 – 364 | 450-157-35 | AF33(600)-22278 | |
| B-47E-75-LM | 53-1943 – 53-1972 | 365 – 394 | 450-157-35 | AF33(600)-22278 | 53-1973 through 53-2027 cancelled |

## B-47 CONVERSIONS

| Series | USAF S/N(s) | Model No. | Contract No. | Remarks |
|---|---|---|---|---|
| B-47B-II | 51-2045 – 51-2246 | 450-67-27 | AF33(38)-21407 | Production change |
| | | | | |
| DB-47B-BW | 51-2160 | 450-173-53 | AF24(601)-1560 | GAM-63 RASCAL carrier. Boeing modification |
| DB-47B-BW | 51-2162 – 51-2174 | 450-173-53 | AF24(601)-1560 | GAM-63 RASCAL carrier. Boeing modification |
| DB-47B-BW | 51-2176 – 51-2291 | 450-173-53 | AF24(601)-1560 | GAM-63 RASCAL carrier. Boeing modification |
| DB-47B-BW | 51-2328 | 450-174-54 | AF33(600)-33370 | GAM-67 Crossbow missile carrier. Boeing modification |
| DB-47B-BW | 51-2350 | 450-174-54 | AF33(600)-33370 | GAM-67 Crossbow missile carrier. Boeing modification |
| | | | | |
| EB-47B | 51-2279 | | | |
| | | | | |
| ERB-47B | 50-005 | | | |
| | | | | |
| RB-47B-BW | 51-5258 – 51-5276 | 450-126-29 | AF33(038)-21407 | Delivered as RB-47E. |
| RB-47B-BW | 51-15821 – 51-15853 | 450-126-29 | AF33(038)-21407 | Delivered as RB-47E. |
| | | | | |
| TB-47B-BW | 49-2642 – 49-2646 | 450-11-10 | | Project FIELD GOAL Douglas modification |
| TB-47B-BW | 50-001 – 50-082 | 450-11-10 | | Project FIELD GOAL Douglas modification |
| | | | | |
| WB-47B | 51-2115 | | | General Precision Laboratories modification |
| | | | | |
| YB-47C-BW | 50-082 | 450-155-33 | AF33(038)-12883 | Production change to B-47B |
| | | | | |
| XB-47D-BW | 51-2103 | 450-162-48 | | Boeing modification |
| XB-47D-BW | 51-2046 | 450-162-49 | | Boeing modification |
| | | | | |
| JB-47E | 51-2359 | | | Temporary test aircraft. |
| | | | | |
| YB-47E | 51-2186 | | | |
| | | | | |
| YDB-47E | 51-5219 – 51-5220 | 450-167-50 | AF33(600)-22108 | GAM-63 RASCAL carrier. Boeing modification |
| DB-47E-BW | 53-2345 – 53-2346 | 450-172-52 | AF33(600)-22108 | GAM-63 RASCAL carrier. Boeing modification |
| DB-47E-BW | | 450-174-54 | | GAM-67 Crossbow missile carrier. Boeing modification |
| DB-47E-BW | 52-538 | 450-177-58 | AF33(600)-3290 | GAM-72 Quail carrier. Boeing modification |
| DB-47E-BW | 53-2104 | 450-177-58 | AF33(600)-3290 | GAM-72 Quail carrier. Boeing modification |
| | | | | |
| EB-47E | 52-394 – 52-403 | | | |
| EB-47E | 52-405 – 52-431 | | | |
| EB-47E | 52-437 | | | |
| EB-47E | 52-429 – 52-441 | | | |
| EB-47E | 52-446 – 52-447 | | | |
| EB-47E | 52-454 | | | |
| EB-47E | 52-467 – 52-471 | | | |
| | | | | |
| EB-47E (TT) | 53-2315 – 53-2316 | | | |
| EB-47E (TT) | 53-2320 | | | |
| | | | | |
| JQB-47E | 53-4256 | | | Lockheed modification |
| JQB-47E | 53-4264 | | | Lockheed modification |
| | | | | |
| QB-47E | 52-0823 | | | Lockheed modification |
| QB-47E | 53-4243 | | | Lockheed modification |
| QB-47E | 53-4250 | | | Lockheed modification |
| QB-47E | 53-4253 – 53-4254 | | | Lockheed modification |
| QB-47E | 53-4256 | | | Lockheed modification |
| QB-47E | 53-4263 | | | Lockheed modification |
| | | | | |
| ETB-47E | 50-040 | | | Lockheed modification |
| | | | | |
| WB-47E | 51-2358 | | | Lockheed modification |
| WB-47E | 51-2360 | | | Lockheed modification |
| WB-47E | 51-2362 – 51-2363 | | | Lockheed modification |
| WB-47E | 51-2366 | | | Lockheed modification |
| WB-47E | 51-2369 | | | Lockheed modification |
| WB-47E | 51-2373 | | | Lockheed modification |

## B-47 CONVERSIONS (CONTINUED)

| Series | USAF S/N(s) | Model No. | Contract No. | Remarks |
|--------|-------------|-----------|--------------|---------|
| WB-47E | 51-2375 | | | Lockheed modification |
| WB-47E | 51-2380 | | | Lockheed modification |
| WB-47E | 51-2383 | | | Lockheed modification |
| WB-47E | 51-2385 | | | Lockheed modification |
| WB-47E | 51-2387 | | | Lockheed modification |
| WB-47E | 51-2390 | | | Lockheed modification |
| WB-47E | 51-2396 – 51-2397 | | | Lockheed modification |
| WB-47E | 51-2402 | | | Lockheed modification |
| WB-47E | 51-2406 | | | Lockheed modification |
| WB-47E | 51-2408 | | | Lockheed modification |
| WB-47E | 51-2412 – 51-2415 | | | Lockheed modification |
| WB-47E | 51-2417 | | | Lockheed modification |
| WB-47E | 51-2420 | | | Lockheed modification |
| WB-47E | 51-2427 | | | Lockheed modification |
| WB-47E | 51-2435 | | | Lockheed modification |
| WB-47E | 51-5218 | | | Lockheed modification |
| WB-47E | 51-5257 | | | Lockheed modification |
| WB-47E | 51-7021 | | | Lockheed modification |
| WB-47E | 51-7046 | | | Lockheed modification |
| WB-47E | 51-7049 | | | Lockheed modification |
| WB-47E | 51-7058 | | | Lockheed modification |
| WB-47E | 51-7063 | | | Lockheed modification |
| WB-47E | 51-7066 | | | Lockheed modification |
| YB-47F | 50-069 | | | Probe receiver. Boeing modification |
| KB-47G | 50-040 | 450-176-57 | AF34(601)-2841 | Hose & Drogue tanker. Boeing modification |
| ERB-47H | 53-6245 – 53-6246 | 450-171-55 | AF33(600)-2284 | ALD-4 system. Boeing modification |
| ERB-47H | 53-6249 | 450-171-55 | AF33(600)-2284 | ALD-4 system. Boeing modification |
| YB-47J | | | | MA-2 bomb-nav test bed. Boeing modification |
| EB-47L | 52-031 | | | Project PIPECLEANER. Tempco modification |
| EB-47L | 51-033 – 51-035 | | | Project PIPECLEANER. Tempco modification |
| EB-47L | 51-038 | | | Project PIPECLEANER. Tempco modification |
| EB-47L | 51-041 | | | Project PIPECLEANER. Tempco modification |
| EB-47L | 51-059 | | | Project PIPECLEANER. Tempco modification |
| EB-47L | 51-061 | | | Project PIPECLEANER. Tempco modification |
| EB-47L | 51-066 – 51-067 | | | Project PIPECLEANER. Tempco modification |
| EB-47L | 51-069 | | | Project PIPECLEANER. Tempco modification |
| EB-47L | 51-071 | | | Project PIPECLEANER. Tempco modification |
| EB-47L | 51-078 | | | Project PIPECLEANER. Tempco modification |
| EB-47L | 51-081 – 51-082 | | | Project PIPECLEANER. Tempco modification |
| EB-47L | 51-086 | | | Project PIPECLEANER. Tempco modification |
| EB-47L | 51-099 | | | Project PIPECLEANER. Tempco modification |
| EB-47L | 51-105 | | | Project PIPECLEANER. Tempco modification |
| EB-47L | 51-154 | | | Project PIPECLEANER. Tempco modification |
| EB-47L | 51-204 | | | Project PIPECLEANER. Tempco modification |
| EB-47L | 51-211 | | | Project PIPECLEANER. Tempco modification |
| EB-47L | 51-214 | | | Project PIPECLEANER. Tempco modification |
| EB-47L | 51-217 | | | Project PIPECLEANER. Tempco modification |
| EB-47L | 51-220 | | | Project PIPECLEANER. Tempco modification |
| EB-47L | 51-224 | | | Project PIPECLEANER. Tempco modification |
| EB-47L | 51-291 | | | Project PIPECLEANER. Tempco modification |
| EB-47L | 51-298 | | | Project PIPECLEANER. Tempco modification |
| EB-47L | 51-303 | | | Project PIPECLEANER. Tempco modification |
| EB-47L | 51-305 | | | Project PIPECLEANER. Tempco modification |
| EB-47L | 51-308 – 51-309 | | | Project PIPECLEANER. Tempco modification |
| EB-47L | 51-510 | | | Project PIPECLEANER. Tempco modification |
| EB-47L | 51-513 | | | Project PIPECLEANER. Tempco modification |
| EB-47L | 53-2329 | | | Project PIPECLEANER. Tempco modification |
| CL-52 | 51-2059 | | | Canadair modification |

## MONTHLY PRODUCTION SUMMARY

| Year/Month | BW | LM | DT | TOTAL |
|---|---|---|---|---|
| **1950** | | | | |
| Dec | 1 | - | - | 1 |
| **1951** | | | | |
| Jan | 1 | - | - | 1 |
| Feb | 0 | - | - | 0 |
| Mar | 1 | - | - | 1 |
| Apr | 5 | - | - | 5 |
| May | 3 | - | - | 3 |
| June | 0 | - | - | 0 |
| July | 5 | - | - | 5 |
| Aug | 8 | - | - | 8 |
| Sept | 1 | - | - | 1 |
| Oct | 8 | - | - | 8 |
| Nov | 16 | - | - | 16 |
| Dec | 11 | - | - | 11 |
| **1952** | | | | |
| Jan | 12 | - | - | 12 |
| Feb | 16 | - | - | 16 |
| Mar | 27 | - | - | 27 |
| Apr | 30 | - | - | 30 |
| May | 32 | - | - | 32 |
| June | 39 | - | - | 39 |
| July | 36 | - | - | 36 |
| Aug | 41 | - | - | 41 |
| Sept | 30 | - | - | 30 |
| Oct | 17 | - | - | 17 |
| Nov | 8 | - | - | 8 |
| Dec | 11 | - | - | 11 |
| **1953** | | | | |
| Jan | 25 | - | - | 25 |
| Feb | 26 | - | 1 | 27 |
| Mar | 26 | 1 | 1 | 28 |
| Apr | 27 | 1 | 3 | 31 |
| May | 28 | 2 | 3 | 33 |
| June | 27 | 3 | 2 | 32 |
| July | 22 | 3 | 3 | 38 |
| Aug | 30 | 2 | 3 | 35 |
| Sept | 36 | 5 | 4 | 45 |
| Oct | 35 | 6 | 5 | 46 |
| Nov | 22 | 7 | 7 | 36 |
| Dec | 20 | 8 | 9 | 37 |
| **1954** | | | | |
| Jan | 26 | 9 | 9 | 34 |
| Feb | 28 | 10 | 10 | 48 |
| Mar | 31 | 11 | 11 | 53 |
| Apr | 20 | 12 | 12 | 44 |
| May | 15 | 13 | 10 | 38 |
| June | 25 | 13 | 14 | 52 |
| July | 30 | 15 | 7 | 52 |
| Aug | 31 | 11 | 9 | 51 |
| Sept | 31 | 13 | 5 | 49 |
| Oct | 29 | 13 | 6 | 48 |
| Nov | 31 | 12 | 8 | 51 |
| Dec | 27 | 11 | 6 | 44 |
| **1955** | | | | |
| Jan | 27 | 11 | 8 | 46 |
| Feb | 26 | 1 | 6 | 33 |
| Mar | 23 | 11 | 7 | 41 |
| Apr | 20 | 11 | 8 | 39 |
| May | 19 | 11 | 6 | 36 |
| June | 26 | 11 | 8 | 45 |
| July | 25 | 10 | 5 | 30 |
| Aug | 14 | 9 | 5 | 28 |
| Sept | 13 | 9 | 5 | 27 |

## MONTHLY PRODUCTION SUMMARY (CONTINUED)

| Year/Month | BW | LM | DT | TOTAL |
|---|---|---|---|---|
| **1955 (continued)** | | | | |
| Oct | 14 | 9 | 7 | 30 |
| Nov | 16 | 9 | 3 | 28 |
| Dec | 12 | 8 | 5 | 25 |
| **1956** | | | | |
| Jan | 13 | 7 | 5 | 25 |
| Feb | 13 | 7 | 5 | 25 |
| Mar | 13 | 7 | 5 | 25 |
| Apr | 13 | 7 | 5 | 25 |
| May | 13 | 7 | 5 | 25 |
| June | 13 | 7 | 5 | 25 |
| July | 13 | 7 | 5 | 25 |
| Aug | 13 | 7 | 5 | 25 |
| Sept | 15 | 7 | 3 | 25 |
| Oct | 8 | 7 | 3 | 18 |
| Nov | - | 7 | 3 | 10 |
| Dec | - | 7 | 0 | 7 |
| **1957** | | | | |
| Jan | 2 | 7 | 0 | 9 |
| Feb | 0 | 2 | 0 | 2 |
| Mar | 0 | 0 | 0 | 0 |
| Apr | 0 | 0 | 0 | 0 |
| May | 0 | 0 | 0 | 0 |
| June | 0 | 0 | 0 | 0 |
| July | 0 | 0 | 0 | 0 |
| Aug | 5 | 0 | 0 | 5 |

## PRODUCTION SUMMARY

| Type | No. Built | Plant |
|---|---|---|
| XB-47-BO | 2 | Boeing-Seattle |
| B-47A-BW | 10 | Boeing-Wichita |
| B-47B-BW | 399 | Boeing-Wichita |
| B-47E-BW | 931 | Boeing-Wichita |
| B-47E-DT | 274 | Douglas-Tulsa |
| B-47E-LM | 386 | Lockheed-Marietta |
| RB-47H-BW | 32 | Boeing-Wichita |
| RB-47K-BW | 15 | Boeing-Wichita |

## CONVERSION SUMMARY

| Type | No. Built | Plant |
|---|---|---|
| B-47B-II | 200 | Boeing-Seattle, Douglas-Tulsa, Lockheed-Marietta |
| DB-47B | 74 | Boeing-Wichita |
| RB-47B | 24 | Boeing-Wichita |
| TB-47B | 66 | Douglas-Tulsa, Oklahoma City Air Materiel Area |
| YB-47C | 1 | Boeing-Wichita |
| WB-47B | 1 | General Precisions Laboratory |
| XB-47D | 2 | Boeing-Wichita |
| YDB-47E | 2 | Boeing-Wichita |
| DB-47E | 2 | Boeing-Wichita |
| QB-47E | 14 | Lockheed-Marietta |
| RB-47E | 240 | Boeing-Wichita |
| ETB-47E | | |
| WB-47E | 34 | Lockheed-Marietta |
| YB-47F | 1 | Boeing-Wichita |
| KB-47G | 1 | Boeing-Wichita |
| ERB-47H | 3 | Boeing-Wichita |
| YB-47J | 1 | Boeing-Wichita |
| EB-47L | 35 | Tempco |
| CL-52 | 1 | Orenda – Canada |

# Appendix C

# *UNITS AND MARKINGS*

Tracking the unit assignments and unit markings is very difficult to do after the fact because Strategic Air Command operated under a high level of security. Such determinations may only be made by studying photographs from the period, finding often-obscure official records, and pulsing fading memories of those who were there at the time. After 1951 SAC markings were extremely sparse and with the advent of the organizational maintenance squadrons in late 1958, no tactical markings were displayed. While the dates for which the various units were assigned to the combat wings may well have been beyond those dates cited in these tables, the dates shown are close to the actual dates that the B-47s were assigned.

## STRATEGIC AIR COMMAND UNITS

**2nd BMW**     Hunter AFB, Ga.     *25 Nov 53 – 1 Apr 63*

Assigned to Eighth Air Force

12"-wide diagonal stripe sloped 45° downward & aft

| | | |
|---|---|---|
| 20th BS | Yellow | 25 Nov 53 -1 Apr 63 |
| 49th BS | Blue | 25 Nov 53 -1 Apr 63 |
| 96th BS | Red | 25 Nov 53 -1 Apr 63 |
| 429th BS | Black | 10 Oct 58 – 1 Jan 62 |

Transferred without personnel & equipment to Barksdale AFB, La. & transitioned into B-52s from the 4238th SRW

**9th BMW**     Mountain Home AFB, Idaho   10 May 54 – 25 June 66

Assigned to Fifteenth Air Force

Colored fin cap

| | | |
|---|---|---|
| 5th BS | Red | 10 May 54 – 25 June 66 |
| 5th BS | Blue | 10 May 54 – 25 June 66 |
| 99th BS | Yellow | 10 May 54 – 25 June 66 |
| 658th BS | None | 1 Oct 58 – 1 Jan 62 |

**19th BMW**     Pinecastle AFB, Fla.     *11 June 54 – 1 June 56*
                        Homestead AFB, Fla.     *1 June 56 – 1 Jan 61*

Assigned to Eighth Air Force

12"-wide stripe below fin cap

| | | |
|---|---|---|
| 28th BS | Green | 11 June 53 – 1 June 56 |
| 30th BS | Blue | 11 June 53 – 1 June 56 |
| 93rd BS | Red | 11 June 53 – 1 June 56 |
| 659th BS | None | 1 Nov 58 – 1 July 61 |

Transitioned into B-52s.

## STRATEGIC AIR COMMAND UNITS (CONTINUED)

**22nd BMW**     March AFB, Calif.     *1 Nov 52 – 15 Mar 63*

Assigned to Fifteenth Air Force

18"-wide band below fin cap – Later, Arrow below fin cap

| | | |
|---|---|---|
| 2nd BS | Red | 1 Nov 52 – 15 Mar 63 |
| 19th BS | Blue | 1 Nov 52 – 15 Mar 63 |
| 33rd BS | Yellow | 1 Nov 52 – 15 Mar 63 |
| 408th BS | Green | 1 Jan 59 – 1 Jan 62 |

Transitioned into B-52s.

**40th BMW**     Smoky Hill AFB, Kans.     *28 May 52 – 20 June 60*
                        Forbes AFB, Kans.     *20 June 60 – 1 Sept 64*

Assigned to Eighth Air Force

18"-wide band below fin cap

| | | |
|---|---|---|
| 25th BS | Blue | 1 Feb 59 – 1 Jan 62 |
| 44th BS | Red | 8 July 52 – 1 June 60 |
| 45th BS | Yellow | 20 June 60 – 15 June 62 |
| 660th BS | Green | 1 Feb 59 – 1 Jan 62 |

**43rd BMW**     Davis-Monthan AFB, Ariz.     *25 Sept 53 – 15 Mar 60*

Assigned to Fifteenth Air Force

Two 18"-wide stripes evenly spaced between fin cap & tail number

| | | |
|---|---|---|
| 63rd BS | Yellow | 25 Sept 53 – 15 Mar 60 |
| 64th BS | Green | 25 Sept 53 – 15 Mar 60 |
| 65th BS | Red | 25 Sept 53 – 15 Mar 60 |
| 403rd BS | None | 1 Dec 58 – 15 Mar 60 |

Transferred to Carswell AFB, Texas, and transitioned to B-58s.

## STRATEGIC AIR COMMAND UNITS (CONTINUED)

**44th BMW**  *Lake Charles AFB. La.*  25 Apr 63 – 15 June 60

Assigned to Second Air Force

18"-wide diagonal stripe on fin. Bull's eye on drop tanks

| 66th BS | Blue | 25 Sept 53- 15 June 60 |
| 67th BS | Yellow | 25 Sept 53- 15 June 60 |
| 68th BS | Red | 25 Sept 53- 15 June 60 |
| 506th BS | None | 1 Dec 58 – 15 Mar 60 |

**68th BMW**  *Lake Charles AFB, La.*  25 Oct 53 – 15 June 63

Assigned to Second Air Force

18"-wide band on rudder only

| 51st BS | Yellow | 25 Oct 53 – 15 June 63 |
| 52nd BS | Red | 25 Oct 53 – 15 June 63 |
| 656th BS | Green | 25 Oct 53 – 15 June 63 |
| 657th BS | None | 1 Dec 58 -1 Jan 62 |

**70th BMW**  *Little Rock AFB, Ark.*  25 June 61 – 25 June 62

Assigned to Second Air Force

No markings.

| 6th BS | None | 25 June 61 – 25 June 62 |
| 26th BS | None | 25 June 61 – 25 June 62 |
| 61st BS | None | 25 June 61 – 25 June 62 |

Assumed personnel & assets of 70th SRW.
Replaced by the 4123rd SW at Clinton-Sherman AFB, Okla. & transitioned into B-52s.

**93rd BMW**  *Castle AFB, Calif.*  15 Apr 54 – 1 Apr 55

Assigned to Fifteenth Air Force

18"-wide band 6" below fin cap

| 328th BS | Blue | 15 Apr 54 – 1 Apr 55 |
| 329th BS | Red | 15 Apr 54 – 1 Apr 55 |
| 330th BS | Yellow | 15 Apr 54 – 1 Apr 55 |

Transitioned into B-52s.

**96th BMW**  *Altus AFB, Okla.*  18 Nov 53 – 3 Sept 57

Assigned to Second Air Force

12"-wide band beneath fin cap

| 337th BS | Blue | 18 Nov 53 – 3 Sept 57 |
| 338th BS | Red | 18 Nov 53 – 3 Sept 57 |
| 339th BS | Yellow | 18 Nov 53 – 3 Sept 57 |
| 413th BS | None | 1 Dec 58 – 1 Jan 62 |

Not operational 18 Nov 53 – 13 Mar 55.
Transitioned into B-52s.

## STRATEGIC AIR COMMAND UNITS (CONTINUED)

**97th BMW**  *Biggs AFB, Tex*  1 Apr 55 – 1 Oct 59

Assigned to Fifteenth Air Force

Colored fin cap

| 340th BS | Red | 1 Apr 55 -1 Oct 59 |
| 341st BS | Blue | 1 Apr 55 -1 Oct 59 |
| 342nd BS | Yellow | 1 Apr 55 -1 Oct 59 |

Not operational 15 Jan – 30 Sept 59
Transferred to Blytheville AFB, Ark. and transitioned into B-52s.

**98th BMW**  *Lincoln AFB, Neb.*  15 Oct 54 – 25 June 66

Assigned to Eighth Air Force 15 Oct 54 – 31 Dec 58
Assigned to Second Air Force 31 Dec 58 – 25 June 66

Two 12"-wide diagonal tail stripes

| 343rd BS | Orange | 15 Oct 54 – 25 June 66 |
| 344th BS | Green | 15 Oct 54 – 25 June 66 |
| 345th BS | White | 15 Oct 54 – 25 June 66 |
| 415th BS | None | 16 June 52 – 1 Jan 62 |

Not operational 8 Dec 65 – 25 June 66.
Transferred without personnel & equipment to Torrejon AB, Spain & redesignated 98th SW, gaining tanker assets from the 3970th SW.

**100th BMW**  *Portsmouth AFB, N.H.*  1 Jan 56 – 25 June 66

Assigned to Eighth Air Force

12"-wide diagonal tail stripe

| 349th BS | Blue | 1 Jan 56 – 25 June 66 |
| 350th BS | Red | 1 Jan 56 – 25 June 66 |
| 351st BS | Yellow | 1 Jan 56 – 25 June 66 |
| 418th BS | None | 1 Mar 59 – 1 Jan 62 |

Not operational 12 Feb – 24 June 66
418th not operational 31 Oct 61 – 1 Jan 62.
Transferred to to Beale AFB, Calif. transitioned into U-2s and DC-130s.

**301st BMW**  *Barksdale AFB, La.*  20 June 53 – 15 Apr 58
*Lockbourne AFB, Ohio*  15 Apr 58 – 15 June 64

Assigned to Second Air Force (XFR without personnel & equipment)
Assigned to Eighth Air Force (gained personnel & assets of 26th SRW)

18"-wide horizontal band below fin cap & fwd gear doors

| 32nd BS | Red | 20 June 53 – 8 June 64 |
| 352nd BS | Yellow | 20 June 53 – 8 June 64 |
| 353rd BS | Blue | 20 June 53 – 8 June 64 |
| 419th BS | None | 1 Dec 58 – 1 Jan 62 |

NOTE: Squadron colors were applied to the aircraft while at Barksdale AFB. When the unit moved to Lockbourne AFB, they came under the organizational maintenance plan and only carried a red band on the upper portion of the fin beneath the fin cap. Many aircraft adopted the SAC Milky Way scheme for their engine inlet cones. At Lockbourne, the crews had red, yellow, or blue hats and scarves to differentiate the 32nd, 352nd, and 353rd squadrons, respectively.

Transitioned into KC-135s.

## STRATEGIC AIR COMMAND UNITS (CONTINUED)

**303rd BMW**     *Davis-Monthan AFB, Ariz.*     *20 Jan 53 – 15 June 64*

Assigned to Eighth Air Force

24"- wide band at fin cap

| | | |
|---|---|---|
| 358th BS | Black | 20 Jan 53 – 15 June 64 |
| 359th BS | Blue | 20 Jan 53 – 15 June 64 |
| 360th BS | Red | 20 Jan 53 – 15 June 64 |
| 427th BS | None | 1 Dec 58 – 1 Jan 62 |

Deactivated.

**305th BMW**     *MacDill AFB, Fla.*     *5 Apr 52 – 15 Feb 61*
              *Bunker Hill AFB, Ind.*     *16 Feb 61 – 1 Apr 63*

Assigned to Eighth Air Force 5 Apr 52 – 15 Feb 61
Assigned to Second Air Force 16 Feb 61 – 1 Apr 63

Square G – later 12"-wide band below fin cap

| | | |
|---|---|---|
| 364th BS | | 16 June 52 – 1 Apr 63 |
| 365th BS | | 16 June 52 – 1 Apr 63 |
| 366th BS | | 16 June 52 – 1 Apr 63 |
| 422nd BS | | 1 Jan 59 – 1 Oct 59 |

Transitioned into B-58s.

**306th BMW**     *MacDill AFB, Fla.*     *10 Feb 51 – 1 Apr 63*

Assigned to Second Air Force 10 Feb 51 – 1 Jan 59
Assigned to Eighth Air Force 1 Jan 59 – 1 Apr 63

Square P – later 24"-wide band below fin cap

| | | |
|---|---|---|
| 367th BS | Red | 16 June 52 – 1 Apr 63 |
| 368th BS | Yellow | 16 June 52 – 1 Apr 63 |
| 369th BS | Blue | 16 June 52 – 1 Apr 63 |
| 423rd BS | None | 1 Jan 59 – 1 Jan 62 |

Squadrons were attached 10 Feb 51 – 15 June 52.
Transitioned into B-52s.

**307th BMW**     *Lincoln AFB, Neb.*     *11 Jan 55 – 25 June 65*

Assigned to Eighth Air Force 11 Jan 55 – 15 June 59
Assigned to Second Air Force 15 June 59 – 25 June 65

18"-wide horizontal band below fin cap with forward lower taper

| | | |
|---|---|---|
| 370th BS | Red | 11 Jan 55 – 25 Mar 65 |
| 371st BS | Yellow | 11 Jan 55 – 25 Mar 65 |
| 372nd BS | Blue | 11 Jan 55 – 25 Mar 65 |
| 424th BS | White (not used) | 1 Sept 58 – 1 Jan 62 |
| 4362nd PACCS | Green | 20 July 62 – 24 Dec 64 |

Transitioned into KC-135s.

## STRATEGIC AIR COMMAND UNITS (CONTINUED)

**308th BMW**     *Hunter AFB, Ga.*     *25 Sept 53 – 14 July 59*
              *Plattsburgh AFB, N.Y*     *15 July 59 – 25 June 61*

Assigned to Eighth Air Force

12"-wide horizontal stripe below fin cap

| | | |
|---|---|---|
| 373rd BS | Blue | 25 Sept 53 – 25 June 61 |
| 374th BS | Red | 25 Sept 53 – 25 June 61 |
| 375th BS | Yellow | 25 Sept 53 – 25 June 61 |
| 425th BS | None | 1 Oct 58 – 25 June 61 |

Not operational 15 July – 25 June 61.
Inactivated.

**310th BMW**     *Smoky Hill AFB, Kans.*     *10 May 54 – 25 June 65*

Assigned to Eighth Air Force 10 May 54 – 25 Jan 57
Assigned to Fifteenth Air Force 25 Jan 57 – 25 June 65

12"-wide diagonal stripe below fin cap sloping down & aft. Bull's eye or scalloped stripe on OUTBD side of drop tanks

| | | |
|---|---|---|
| 379th BS | Red | 10 May 55 – 25 Mar 65 |
| 380th BS | Blue | 10 May 55 – 25 Mar 65 |
| 381st BS | Yellow | 10 May 55 – 25 Mar 65 |
| 428th BS | None | 1 Feb 59 – 1 June 62 |

Not operational 25 Feb – 25 Mar 65.
Inactivated.

**320th BMW**     *March AFB, Calif.*     *23 July 53 – 15 Sept 60*

Assigned to Fifteenth Air Force

Two 12"-wide diagonal stripes

| | | |
|---|---|---|
| 441st BS | Red | 23 July 53 – 15 Sept 60 |
| 442nd BS | Yellow | 23 July 53 – 15 Sept 60 |
| 443rd BS | Blue | 23 July 53 – 15 Sept 60 |
| 444th BS | None | 1 Dec 52 – 15 Sept 60 |

Not operational 1 July – 15 Sept 60.
Transferred to Mather AFB, Calif. and transitioned into B-52s.

**321st BMW**     *Pinecastle AFB, Fla.*     *15 Dec 53 – 25 Oct 61*

Assigned to Second Air Force 15 Dec 53 – 1 Jan 59
Assigned to Eighth Air Force 1 Jan 59 – 25 Oct 61

Two 12"-wide diagonal stripes

| | | |
|---|---|---|
| 445th BS | Red | 15 Dec 53 – 25 Oct 61 |
| 446th BS | Yellow | 15 Dec 53 – 25 Oct 61 |
| 447th BS | Blue | 15 Dec 53 – 25 Oct 61 |
| 448th BS | None | 1 Feb 54 – 25 Oct 61 |

Not operational 15 Dec 53 – 31 May 54

## STRATEGIC AIR COMMAND UNITS (CONTINUED)

| | | |
|---|---|---|
| *340th BMW* | *Whiteman AFB, Mo.* | *8 Aug 53 – 1 Sept 63* |

Assigned to Eighth Air Force 8 Aug 53 – 31 Dec 58
Assigned to Second Air Force 1 Jan 59 – 1 Sept 63

18"-wide band below fin cap

| | | |
|---|---|---|
| 486th BS | | 8 Aug 53 – 1 Sept 63 |
| 487th BS | | 8 Aug 53 – 1 Sept 63 |
| 488th BS | | 8 Aug 53 – 1 Sept 63 |
| 489th BS | | 1 Oct 58 – 1 Jan 62 |

Not operational 8 Aug 53 – Feb 54.
Transferred to Bergstrom AFB, Tex. and transitioned into B-52s.

| | | |
|---|---|---|
| *376th BMW* | *Barksdale AFB, La.* | *23 Feb 54 – 15 Mar 65* |
| | *Lockbourne AFB, Ohio* | |

Assigned to Second Air Force 23 Feb 54 – 1 Dec 57
Assigned to Eighth Air Force 1 Dec 57 – 15 Mar 65

| | | |
|---|---|---|
| 512th BS | Red | 23 Feb 54 – 15 Mar 65 |
| 513th BS | Yellow | 23 Feb 54 – 15 Mar 65 |
| 514th BS | Blue | 23 Feb 54 – 15 Mar 65 |
| 515th BS | None | 1 Dec 58 – 1 Jan 62 |
| 4363rd PACCS | None | 20 July 62 – 15 Feb 65 |

NOTE: Squadron colors were applied to the aircraft while at Barksdale AFB. When the unit moved to Lockbourne AFB, they came under SAC's organizational MX plan and no tactical markings were applied.

Deactivated.

| | | |
|---|---|---|
| *379th BMW* | *Homestead AFB, Fla.* | *1 Nov 55 – 1 Dec 60* |

Assigned to Second Air Force

12"-wide diagonal band sloping down & aft on vertical tail, & colored engine inlet cones

| | | |
|---|---|---|
| 524th BS | Red | 1 Nov 55 – 1 Dec 60 |
| 525th BS | Yellow | 1 Nov 55 – 1 Dec 60 |
| 526th BS | Blue | 1 Nov 55 – 1 Dec 60 |
| 527th BS | None | 1 Nov 55 – 1 Dec 60 |

Transferred to Wurtsmith AFB, Mich. and transitioned into B-52s.

| | | |
|---|---|---|
| 380th BMW | Plattsburgh AFB, N.Y. | 1 July 55 – 25 June 65 |

Assigned to Eighth Air Force

Horizontal band dropped below fin cap

| | | |
|---|---|---|
| 528th BS | Yellow | 1 July 55 – 25 June 65 |
| 529th BS | Blue | 1 July 55 – 25 June 65 |
| 530th BS | Red | 1 July 55 – 25 June 65 |
| 531st BS | None | 1 May 50 – 1 Jan 62 |
| 4365th PACCS | None | 20 July 62 – 24 Dec 64 |

Not operational 11 – 31 July 55.
Transitioned into B-52s.

## STRATEGIC AIR COMMAND UNITS (CONTINUED)

| | | |
|---|---|---|
| *384th BMW* | *Little Rock AFB, Ark.* | *1 Aug 55 – 2 Apr 66* |

Assigned to Second Air Force

18"-wide band below fin cap

| | | |
|---|---|---|
| 544th BS | Blue | 1 Aug 55 – 1 Sept 64 |
| 545th BS | Yellow | 1 Aug 55 – 1 Sept 64 |
| 546th BS | Red | 1 Aug 55 – 1 Sept 64 |
| 547th BS | Black/White Checkerboard | 1 Sept 58 – 1 Jan 62 |

Deactivated.

| | | |
|---|---|---|
| *509th BMW* | *Pease AFB, N.H.* | *1 July 58 – 2 Apr 66* |

Assigned to Eighth Air Force

Arrow head midway between base of fin cap & tail number

| | | |
|---|---|---|
| 393rd BS | Yellow | 11 Aug 58 – 2 Apr 66 |
| 661st BS | None | 11 Mar 59 – 1 Jan 62 |
| 715th BS | Blue | 11 Aug 58 – 2 Apr 66 |
| 830th BS | Red | 11 Aug 58 – 2 Apr 66 |

Not operational 23 Nov 65 – 22 Mar 66.
Transitioned into B-52s.

| | | |
|---|---|---|
| 4347th CCTW | Wichita AFB, Kans. | 1 July 58 – 15 June 63 |

36"-wide band below fin cap

| | | |
|---|---|---|
| 4347th CCTS | | 1 July 58 – 15 June 63 |
| 4348th CCTS | | 1 July 58 – 15 June 63 |
| 4349th CCTS | | 1 July 58 – 15 June 63 |
| 4350th CCTS | | 1 July 58 – 15 June 63 |

Deactivated.

### YRB/RB-47 UNITS

| | | |
|---|---|---|
| *26th SRW (M)* | *Lockbourne AFB, Ohio* | *28 May 52 – 1 July 58* |

Assigned to Eighth Air Force

12" Stripe 6" below fin cap & fwd gear doors

| | | |
|---|---|---|
| 3rd SRS | Red | 28 May 52 – 1 July 58 |
| 4th SRS | Blue | 28 May 52 – 1 July 58 |
| 10th SRS | Yellow | 28 May 52 – 1 July 58 |

Not operational 28 May 52 – 2 Sept 53 & 15 Apr 58 – 1 July 58.
Inactivated & replaced by 301st BMW.

| | | |
|---|---|---|
| *55th SRW (M)* | *Forbes AFB, Kans.* | *Sept 54 -16 Aug 66* |

Assigned to Eighth Air Force

18"-wide horizontal stripe 24" below fin cap, colored engine inlets, & fwd gear doors

| | | |
|---|---|---|
| 38th SRS | Blue | Sept 54 – 16 Aug 66 |
| 338th SRS | Yellow | Sept 54 – 16 June 63 |
| 343rd SRS | Red | Sept 54 – 16 June 66 |

NOTE: Squadron colors were deleted for overseas deployments.

## YRB/RB-47 UNITS (CONTINUED)

**70th SRW (M)**     *Little Rock AFB, Ark.*     *24 Jan 55 – 25 Oct 61*

Assigned to Second Air Force

Horizontal fin stripe, colored fwd gear doors, & sometimes colored engine inlets

| | | |
|---|---|---|
| 6th SRS | Blue | 24 Jan 55 – 25 Oct 61 |
| 26th SRS | Yellow | 24 Jan 55 – 25 Oct 61 |
| 10th SRS | Red | 24 Jan 55 – 25 Oct 61 |

Replaced by 70th BMW.

**90th SRW (M)**     *Forbes AFB, Kans.*     *8 Jan 54 – 20 June 60*

Assigned to Eighth Air Force

Lightning bolt on vertical fin

| | | |
|---|---|---|
| 319th SRS | Blue | 8 Jan 54 – 20 June 60 |
| 320th SRS | Red | 8 Jan 54 – 20 June 60 |
| 321st SRS | Green | 8 Jan 54 – 20 June 60 |

Inactivated.

**91st SRW (M)**     *Barksdale AFB, La.*     *6 July 50 – 11 Sept 51*
                     *Lockbourne AFB, Ohio*   *11 Sept 51 – 8 Nov 57*

Assigned to Second Air Force

18"-wide diagonal fin stripe

| | | |
|---|---|---|
| 322nd SRS | Yellow | 28 May 52 – 8 Nov 57 |
| 323rd SRS | Red | 28 May 52 – 8 Nov 57 |
| 324th SRS | Blue | 28 May 52 – 8 Nov 57 |
| 338th SRS | | Attached 1 – 24 Nov 50 |
| 343rd SRS | | Attached 1 Nov 50 – 3 Jan 52 |

NOTE: 322nd, 323rd, and 324th were attached 10 Feb 51 – 27 May 52.

**305th BW**     *MacDill AFB, Fla.*     *1952 – 1958-*

RB-47Bs for Project 52 AFR-18

## E/ERB-47 UNITS

**9th SAW**     *Mountain Home AFB, Idaho*     *20 July 62 -25 Mar 65*

Assigned to Fifteenth Air Force

4364th SS (PACCS)     20 July 62 – 25 Mar 65

Not operational 20 July – 1 Dec 62.

**55th SRW**     *Forbes AFB, Kans.*     *1954 – 1967*

**307th BW (M)**     *Lincoln AFB, Neb.*     *20 July 62 – 24 Dec 64*

4362nd SS (PACCS)     20 July 62 – 24 Dec 64

Assigned to Second Air Force.

## E/ERB-47 UNITS (CONTINUED)

**376th BW (M)**     *Forbes AFB, Kans.*     *20 July 62 -15 Feb 65*

Assigned to Second Air Force

4363rd SS (PACCS)     20 July 62 – 15 Feb 65

Not operational July – Nov 62.

**380th BW (M)**     *Plattsburgh AFB, N.Y.*     *20 July 62 – 24 Sept 64*

Assigned to Eighth Air Force

4365th SS (PACCS)     20 July 62 – 24 Sept 64

Not operational 12 Sept – 24 Dec 64.

## MILITARY AIR TRANSPORT SERVICE UNITS

| | | |
|---|---|---|
| 53rd WRS | Hunter AFB, Ga. | 1963-1966 |
| 53rd WRS, Det. 2 | Ramey AFB, P.R. | 1966-1969 |
| 54th WRS | Andersen AFB, Guam | 1966-1965 |
| 55th WRS | McClellan AFB, Calif. | 1957-1969 |
| 55th WRS, Det. 1 | Eielson AFB, Alaska | 1960-1968 |
| | Clark AB, Philippines | 1960-1968 |
| 56th WRS | Yokota AB, Japan | 1962-1966 |
| 57th WRS | Hickam AFB, Hawaii | |
| 57th WRS, Det. 2 | Clark AB, Philippines | 1969 |
| 9th WRS, Det. 2 | Clark AB, Philippines | 1969 |
| AACS | Tinker AFB, Okla. | 1955-1961 |

# Appendix D

# *BOEING MODEL NUMBERS*

During the late 1940s and early 1950s the USAF was extremely interested in turboprop aircraft. Of the 205 design studies conducted by Boeing with the B-47 Stratojet, 65 were for turboprops – of which only two were actually produced and flown. In addition, nine afterburning configurations were considered. Because of the newness of the turbojet engine, numerous combinations were studied, not only for the B-47 program, but also for use on future jet aircraft.

| Model No. | Designation | Data Date | No. Built | Remarks |
|---|---|---|---|---|
| 450-1-1 | XB-47 | 16 Apr 46 | 0 | 1,300 sq. ft. wing area. 125,000-lb. design gross weight. |
| 450-2-2 | XB-47 | | 0 | Extended wingspan. |
| 450-3-3 | XB-47 | 11 Apr 47 | 2 | 1,427 sq. ft. wing area. 105,000-lb. design gross weight. 6 TG-180 engines. First flight on 17 December 1947. |
| 450-4-4 | XB-47 | 14 Sept 47 | 0 | As 450-3-3 for photo-recon. Moved radome 75 inches aft. Removed tail guns. Installed 6 TG-190 engines in lieu of TG-180s. |
| 450-5-5 | XB-47 | 28 Jan 48 | 0 | 189,000-lb. design gross weight. |
| 450-6-6 | XB-47 | Aug 48 | 0 | |
| 450-3-7 | XB-47 | 4 Mar 48 | 0 | As 450-3-3, but modified for photo-recon with redesigned fuselage mid-section interior. Engine options: 6 TG-180s, 6 TG-190A (without afterburner), or 6 J40, for a cruise speed of 464 mph, 521 mph, or 521 mph; and tactical operating radius of 1,310, 1,660, or 2,100 miles, respectively. |
| 450-3-8 | XB-47 | 15 Mar 48 | 0 | As 450-3-3, but modified for photo-recon with redesigned nose section interior. |
| 450-7-3 | XB-47 | 13 Apr 48 | 0 | As 450-3-3 with JT7A engines and revised outrigger landing gear at wingtips. 6 separate nacelles. |
| 450-8-3 | XB-47 | 20 Apr 48 | 0 | As 450-3-3 with revised wing section. |
| 450-9-3 | XB-47 | 5 May 48 | 0 | As 450-3-3 with 4 Allison Model 500 turboprops. 157,000-lb. design gross weight. |
| 450-10-9 | B-47A | 18 May 48 | 10 | 1,428 sq. ft. wing area. 6 J47-GE-11 engines. 125,000-lb. design gross weight. First flight on 25 February 1950. |
| 450-11-10 | B-47B | 18 May 49 | 87 | 1,428 sq. ft. wing area. 6 J47-GE-11 engines. 125,000-lb. design gross weight. 185,000-lb. alternate gross weight. First flight in April 1951. |
| 450-12-11 | B-47B | 17 Jan 48 | 0 | As 450-11-10 with 4 J40-WE-10 afterburning engines in paired inboard pods. Eliminated outboard nacelles. |
| 450-13-12 | B-47B | 3 Feb 49 | 0 | As 450-12-11 except eliminated 1 fuel tank and afterburners. 148,000-lb. design gross weight. |
| 450-11-13 | RB-47B | 3 Feb 49 | 0 | As 450-1-10 modified for photo-recon. |
| 450-14-13 | RB-47B | 2 Mar 49 | 0 | As 450-13-12 except increased wing area to 1,800 sq. ft. by constant percentage chord increase along trailing edge. |
| 450-15-14 | B-47 | 2 Mar 49 | 0 | A revised airfoil section and increased wing area to 1,575 sq. ft. 4 J40-WE-12 engines. Revised wing-body intersection cutout in fuselage to accommodate new wing. Changed FWD fuel tank. |
| 450-16-10 | B-47B | 2 Mar 49 | 0 | As 450-11-10 with 4 J35-A-23 engines on the 1,428 sq. ft. wing. 180,000-lb. gross weight. 4,350-mile range at 450 mph at 43,300 ft. |
| 450-17-10 | B-47B | 2 Mar 49 | 0 | As 450-11-10 with 4 J40-WE-12 engines. |
| 450-11-15 | B-47B | 28 Apr 49 | 0 | As 450-11-10 modified for photo-recon with camera and ECM in compartment aft of rear MLG. |
| 450-11-16 | B-47B | 28 Apr 49 | 0 | As 450-11-15 except with camera and ECM compartment located aft of bomb bay. |
| 450-11-17 | RB-47 | 28 Apr 49 | 0 | As 450-11-10 with 6 GE TG190B5A (J47) engines. 185,000-lb. gross weight. |
| 450-16-17 | RB-47 | 28 Apr 49 | 0 | As 450-11-17 with 4 J40-WE-6 engines. 184,220-lb. gross weight. Combat radius 2,130 miles. |
| 450-11-18 | B-47B | 2 May 49 | 0 | As 450-11-15 except cameras and ECM in FWD end of bomb bay, ECM below copilot. |
| 450-11-19 | B-47B | 2 May 49 | 0 | As 450-11-15 except ECM in aft end of bomb bay, camera below copilot. |
| 450-11-20 | B-47B | 2 May 49 | 0 | As 450-11-15 except with cameras below copilot and ECM operators along left side of control cabin. |
| 450-11-21 | B-47B | 2 May 49 | 0 | As 450-11-15 except cameras and ECM below pilots' floor. |
| 450-16-21 | B-47B | 19 May 49 | 0 | As 450-11-21 except 4 J40-WE-6 engines. |
| 450-11-22 | RB-47 | 18 May 49 | 0 | As 450-11-10 except with 6 GE TG-190B5A (J47) engines. |
| 450-16-22 | RB-47 | 18 May 49 | 0 | As 450-11-22 except with 4 J40-WE-6 engines. |
| 450-18-14 | B-47B | 18 May 49 | 0 | As 450-11-10 except with 4 J40-WE-6 engines and new wing design. |

| | | | | |
|---|---|---|---|---|
| 450-11-23 | B-47B | 21 June 49 | 0 | As 450-11-17 except with ECM deleted. For night operations all cameras removed except radar recording camera and K-37 camera installed in vertical station. |
| 450-16-23 | B-47B | 21 June 49 | 0 | As 450-16-17 except with ECM deleted. For night operations all cameras removed except radar recording camera and K-37 camera installed in vertical station. |
| 450-19-10 | B-47C | 2 Mar 49 | 0 | As 450-11-10 except with 4 J35-A-23 axial-flow turbojets. |
| 450-19-11 | RB-47C | 15 Nov 49 | 0 | As 450-19-10 but modified for photo recce with FWD oblique camera located aft of photo-navigator, and trimetrogon and 2 vertical cameras under copilot. |
| 450-20-24 | | | 0 | As 450-11-10 except with 4 J40-WE-6 engines and wing modified for integral fuel tanks. |
| 450-21-24 | | | 0 | As 450-20-24 except with 4 J35-A-13 engines. |
| 450-22-25 | | | 0 | Fuselage as 450-20-24. New tapered wing configuration with integral fuel tanks, and 4 J40-WE-6 engines. |
| 450-23-25 | | | 0 | As 450-22-25 except with 4 J35-A-25 engines. |
| 450-24-26 | RB-47C | 2 Feb 40 | 0 | Ass 450-11-10 except with 4 J35-A-23 engines. |
| 450-25-10 | | 14 Feb 50 | 0 | Similar to 450-19-10 with 6 TG-190x3 engines. 180,000-lb. gross weight. 3,880 NM combat range. |
| 450-26-10 | | 14 Feb 50 | 0 | Similar to 450-19-10 with 4 XJ57-PW engines. 180,000-lb. gross weight. 4,874 NM combat range. |
| 450-27-10 | | 14 Feb 50 | 0 | Similar to 450-19-10 with 2 GT-18 turboprop engines driving a 15' dia. prop. 208,000-lb. gross weight. 8,140 NM combat range. |
| 450-28-10 | | 14 Feb 50 | 0 | Similar to 450-19-10 with 4 TJ14 engines. 180,000-lb. gross weight. 4,730 NM combat range. |
| 450-29-10 | | 14 Feb 50 | 0 | Similar to 450-19-10 with 4 J40-14 engines. 180,000-lb. gross weight. 4,326 NM combat range. |
| 450-30-10 | | 14 Feb 50 | 0 | Similar to 450-19-10 with 4 T40-A-8 turboprop engines driving 11' dia. props. 180,000-lb. gross weight. 5,280 NM combat range. |
| 450-31-10 | | 14 Feb 50 | 0 | Similar to 450-19-10 with 4 T40-A-8 turboprop engines driving 11' dia. props. 180,000-lb. gross weight. 5,960 NM combat range. |
| 450-32-10 | | 14 Feb 50 | 0 | Similar to 450-19-10 with 2 JT-3A turboprop engines driving 15' dia. props. 180,000-lb. gross weight. 6,040 NM combat range. |
| 450-33-10 | | 14 Feb 50 | 0 | Similar to 450-19-10 with 2 JT-3A turboprop engines driving 15' dia. props. 180,000-lb. gross weight. |
| 450-34-10 | | 14 Feb 50 | 0 | Similar to 450-19-10 with 2 Turbodyne V engines. 180,000-lb. gross weight. 5,240 NM combat range. |
| 450-35-10 | | 14 Feb 50 | 0 | Similar to 450-19-10 with 2 JGT-18 turboprop engines. 220,000-lb. gross weight. 5,640 NM combat range. |
| 450-36-10 | | 14 Feb 50 | 0 | Similar to 450-19-10 with 4 J35-A-23 engines. 208,000-lb. gross weight. 5,880 NM combat range. |
| 450-37-10 | | 14 Feb 50 | 0 | Similar to 450-19-10 with 2 JGT-18 turboprop engines. 180,000-lb. gross weight. 5,760 NM combat range. |
| 450-38-10 | | 14 Feb 50 | 0 | Similar to 450-19-10 with 4 T40-A-8 turboprop engines driving 11' dia. props. 208,000-lb. gross weight. 7,836 NM combat range. |
| 450-39-10 | | 8 Mar 50 | 0 | Similar to 450-19-10 with 4 J57-P-1 engines. 250,000-lb. gross weight. 7,070 NM combat range. |
| 450-40-10 | | 8 Mar 50 | 0 | Similar to 450-19-10 with 4 J35-A-23 engines. 250,000-lb. gross weight. 6,200 NM combat range. |
| 450-41-10 | | 8 Mar 50 | 0 | Similar to 450-26-10 with 4 XJ57 engines. 208,000-lb. gross weight. 6,720 NM combat range. |
| 450-42-10 | | 8 Mar 50 | 0 | Similar to 450-31-10 with 4 T40-A-8 turboprop engines driving 11' dia. props. 250,000-lb. gross weight. |
| 450-43-10 | | 8 Mar 50 | 0 | Similar to 450-39-10 with 4 J57-P-1 engines. 250,000-lb. gross weight. 9,180 NM combat range. |
| 450-44-10 | | 8 Mar 50 | 0 | Similar to 450-40-10 with 4 J35-A-23 engines. 250,000-lb. gross weight. |
| 450-45-10 | | 8 Mar 50 | | Similar to 450-42-10 with 4 T40-A-8 turboprop engines driving 11' dia. props. 208,000-lb. gross weight. 8,340 NM combat range. |
| 450-46-10 | | 8 Mar 50 | 0 | Similar to 450-32-10 with 4 JT-3A turboprop engines driving 15' dia. props. 290,000-lb. gross weight. |
| 450-47-10 | | 8 Mar 50 | 0 | Similar to 450-32-10 with 2 JT-3A turboprop engines driving 15' dia. props. 208,000-lb. gross weight. 7,780 NM combat range. |
| 450-48-10 | | 8 Mar 50 | 0 | Similar to 450-46-10 with 4 JT-3A turboprop engines driving 15' dia. props. 290,000-lb. gross weight. |
| 450-49-10 | | 22 Apr 50 | 0 | Similar to 450-26-10 with 4 XJ57 engines. 180,000-lb. gross weight. 4,940 NM combat range. |
| 450-50-10 | | 22 Apr 50 | 0 | Similar to 450-26-10 with 4 XJ57 engines. 180,000-lb. gross weight. 4,940 NM combat range. |
| 450-51-10 | | 22 Apr 50 | 0 | Similar to 450-41-10 with 4 XJ57 engines. 216,130-lb. gross weight. 9,180 NM combat range. |
| 450-52-10 | | 22 Apr 50 | 0 | Similar to 450-31-10 with 4 T40-A-8 turboprop engines driving 11' dia. props. 180,000-lb. gross weight. 4,940 NM combat range. |
| 450-53-01 | | 22 Apr 50 | 0 | Similar to 450-19-10 with 4 PT-2E turboprop engines driving 15' dia. props. 180,000-lb. gross weight. |
| 450-54-10 | | 22 Apr 50 | 0 | Similar to 450-19-10 with 2 PT-2E & 2 PT-22 turboprop engines. 180,000-lb. gross weight. |
| 450-55-10 | | 22 Apr 50 | 0 | Similar to 450-19-10 with 4 PT-22 turboprop engines. 180,000-lb. gross weight. |
| 450-56-10 | | 21 Apr 50 | 0 | Similar to 450-19-10 with 4 J35-A-23 engines. 195,000-lb. gross weight. 104,604 NM combat range. |
| 450-57-10 | B-47 | 26 Apr 50 | 0 | Similar to 450-19-10. 220,000-lb. gross weight. |
| 450-58-10 | | 23 May 50 | 0 | Similar to 450-19-10 with 4 T40-A-6 turboprop engines. 180,000-lb. gross weight. 6,312 NM combat range. |
| 450-59-10 | | 23 May 50 | 0 | Similar to 450-19-10 with 4 T40-A-8 turboprop engines driving 15' dia. props. 180,000-lb. gross weight. 5,986 NM combat range. |
| 450-60-10 | | 23 May 50 | 0 | Similar to 450-19-10 with 4 PT-2E turboprop engines driving 15' dia. props. 180,000-lb. gross weight. 6,100 NM combat range. |
| 450-61-10 | | 23 May 50 | 0 | Similar to 450-19-10 with 4 JT-3A turboprop engines. 180,000-lb. gross weight. 7,510 NM combat range. |
| 450-62-10 | | 23 May 50 | 0 | Similar to 450-19-10 with 4 JT-3A turboprop engines. 180,000-lb. gross weight. 7,134 NM combat range. |
| 450-63-10 | | 23 May 50 | 0 | Similar to 450-19-10 with 4 JT-3A turboprop engines. 220,000-lb. gross weight. 7,704 NM combat range. |
| 450-64-10 | | 23 May 50 | 0 | Similar to 450-19-10 with 4 JT-3A turboprop engines. 180,000-lb. gross weight. 5,750 NM combat range. |
| 450-11-26 | YRB-47B | | 0 | Proposed as the YRB-47B, cancelled, and replaced by 450-126-29, the RB-47B. |
| 450-65-10 | | 5 July 50 | 0 | Fuselage as 450-11-10 with 484-405B wing, empennage, and powerplant. Span 87' 6". Wing area 2,190 sq. ft. 47° sweep back at quarter chord. Powered by 4 J57-P-5 with afterburner. 200,000-lb. gross weight. 4,360 nautical mile combat range. |
| 450-66-10 | | | 0 | A study of wing extension for the B-47C (450-19-10) in conjunction with the 450-51-10 design study. Span 167'. |
| 450-67-27 | B-47B | 16 Oct 50 | 282 | As 450-11-10 except powered by 6 J47-GE-23 engines. 125,000-lb. design gross weight. 3,460 NM combat range. |
| 450-68-10 | | | 0 | As 450-19-10 except with 6 Sapphire engines. |
| 450-69-10 | | | 0 | As 450-19-10 except with 4 J57 (WAC Olympus B) engines. |
| 450-70-10 | | | 0 | As 450-19-10 except with 4 J47-21 engines. |
| 450-71-10 | | | 0 | As 450-19-10 except with 4 J57-P-5 advanced engines. |
| 450-72-10 | | | 0 | As 450-19-10 except with 4 GE (?)-22A turboprop engines. |
| 450-73-10 | | | 0 | Ass 450-57-10 except with 4 J57-P-1 engines. |
| 450-74-10 | | | 0 | As 450-57-10 except with 4 Sapphire engines. |
| 450-75-10 | | | 0 | As 450-57-10 except with 4 J67 (TJ-32B) engines. |
| 450-76-10 | | | 0 | As 450-57-10 except with 4 J40-14 engines. |
| 450-77-10 | | | 0 | As 450-57-10 except with 4 J47-21 engines. |

| Model | Designation | Date | Qty | Description |
|---|---|---|---|---|
| 450-78-10 | | | 0 | As 450-57-10 except with 4 T40-A-6 turboprop engines. |
| 450-79-10 | | | 0 | As 450-57-10 except with 4 T40-A-8 turboprop engines. |
| 450-80-10 | | | 0 | As 450-57-10 except with 4 PT2E turboprop engines. |
| 450-81-10 | | | 0 | As 450-57-10 except with 4 J57-P-5 advanced engines. |
| 450-82-10 | | | 0 | As 450-57-10 except with 4 GE (?)-22 turboprop engines. |
| 450-83-10 | | | 0 | As 450-19-10 except with 4 T34 turboprop engines. |
| 450-84-10 | | | 0 | As 450-57-10 except with 4 T34 turboprop engines. |
| 450-85-10 | | | 0 | As 450-60-10 except with 2 J47-23 engines added to outboard positions. |
| 450-86-10 | | | 0 | As 450-19-10 except with 6 J57-P-1 engines. |
| 450-87-10 | | | 0 | As 450-19-10 except with 6 J47-P-21 engines. |
| 450-88-10 | | | 0 | As 450-19-10 except with 6 J67 engines. |
| 450-89-10 | | | 0 | As 450-19-10 except with 6 J35A-23 engines. |
| 450-90-10 | | | 0 | As 450-57-10 except with 6 J57-P-1 engines. |
| 450-91-10 | | | 0 | As 450-57-10 except with 6 J47-P-21 engines. |
| 450-92-10 | | | 0 | As 450-57-10 except with 6 J67 engines. |
| 450-93-10 | | | 0 | As 450-57-10 except with 6 J35A-23 engines. |
| 450-94-10 | | | 0 | As 450-19-10 except with 4 PT2E turboprop engines. |
| 450-95-10 | | | 0 | As 450-19-10 except with 4 J67 engines, a wing span of 133' 4", and a drop tank at approximately 90% of semi-span. |
| 450-96-10 | | | 0 | As 450-19-10 except with 4 J67 engines, a wing span of 140'. |
| 450-97-10 | | | 0 | As 450-19-10 except with 2 T47 (TP51B) inboard turboprops and 2 J47-23 outboard engines. |
| 450-98-10 | | | 0 | As 450-97-10 with 4 TP51B turboprop engines installed at inboard locations. |
| 450-99-10 | | | 0 | As 450-97-10 with 4 J35-A-23 engines, increased gross weight to utilize static test wing strength, added wing chord extension, installed ejection seats, and B-47C equipment, fuel systems, etc. |
| 450-100-10 | | | 0 | As 450-99-28 with 6 J40-WE-6 engines. |
| 450-101-10 | | | 0 | As 450-99-28 with 4 J40-WE-12 engines. |
| 450-102-10 | | | 0 | As 450-99-28 with 4 J47-GE-21 engines. |
| 450-103-10 | | | 0 | As 450-99-28 with 6 J47-GE-23 engines. |
| 450-104-10 | | | 0 | As 450-99-28 with 4 J57-P-1 engines. |
| 450-105-10 | | | 0 | As 450-99-28 with 6 J65-W-1 (TJ-31A) engines. |
| 450-106-10 | | | 0 | As 450-99-28 with 4 J67-W (TJ32B) engines. |
| 450-107-10 | | | 0 | As 450-99-28 with 4 T34 turboprop engines and tip tanks. |
| 450-108-10 | | | 0 | As 450-99-28 with 4 T34 turboprop engines. |
| 450-109-10 | | | 0 | As 450-99-28 with 4 T47 (TP51B) turboprop engines. |
| 450-110-10 | | | 0 | As 450-99-28 with 4 T40-A-6 turboprop engines |
| 450-111-10 | | | 0 | As 450-99-28 with 2 T47 (TP51B) turboprop engines and tip tanks. |
| 450-112-10 | | | 0 | As 450-99-28 with 4 T34 turboprop engines and 2 J47-GE-21 engines. |
| 450-113-10 | | | 0 | As 450-99-28 with 4 T34 turboprop engines and 2 J47-GE-23 engines. |
| 450-114-10 | | | 0 | As 450-99-28 with 4 T34 turboprop engines and 2 J57-P-1 engines. |
| 450-115-10 | | | 0 | As 450-99-28 with 4 T34 turboprop engines and 2 J65-W-1 engines. |
| 450-116-10 | | | 0 | As 450-99-28 with 4 T34 turboprop engines and 2 J67-W (TJ32B) engines. |
| 450-117-10 | | | 0 | As 450-99-28 with 4 T34 turboprop engines and 2 J47-GE-21 engines. |
| 450-118-10 | | | 0 | As 450-99-28 with 4 T34 turboprop engines and 2 J57-P-1 engines. |
| 450-119-10 | | | 0 | As 450-99-28 with 4 T34 turboprop engines and 2 J65-W-1 engines. |
| 450-120-10 | | | 0 | As 450-99-28 with 4 T34 turboprop engines and 2 J67-W (TJ32B) engines. |
| 450-121-10 | | | 0 | As 450-99-28 with 2 T47 (TP51B) turboprop engines and 2 J47-GE-21 engines. |
| 450-122-10 | | | 0 | As 450-99-28 with 2 T47 (TP51B) turboprop engines and 3 J47-GE-23 engines. |
| 450-123-10 | | | 0 | As 450-99-28 with 2 T47 (TP51B) turboprop engines and 2 J47-P-1 engines. |
| 450-124-10 | | | 0 | As 450-99-28 with 2 T47 (TP51B) turboprop engines and 2 J65-W-1 engines. |
| 450-125-10 | | | 0 | As 450-99-28 with 2 T47 (TP51B) turboprop engines and 2 J67-W (TJ32B) engines. |
| 450-126-29 | | | 0 | 52 RB-47Bs with s/n 51-5258/51-5276 and 51-15821/51-15853 were to be produced under Letter Contract AF33 (038)-21407; however, the USAF stated that the aircraft be redesignated RB-47Es (450-158-36) and retained the same serial numbers and contract number. |
| 450-127-10 | B-47 | 28 Feb 51 | 0 | As 450-19-10 except with 4 P&W PT-2 turboprops driving 15' dia. props. 125,000-lb. gross weight. 45,850 NM range. |
| 450-128-10 | | 28 Feb 51 | 0 | As 450-127-10 with 4 T40A-8 turboprop engines. |
| 450-129-10 | | 28 Feb 51 | 0 | As 450-127-10 with 4 T34-P-6 turboprop engines and 2 J47-GE-23 engines. 15' dia. prop. 125,000-lb. gross weight. 4,880 NM range. |
| 450-130-10 | | 28 Feb 51 | 0 | As 450-127-10 with 4 T34-P-10 turboprop and 2 J47-GE-23 engines driving a 15' dia. prop. 125,000-lb. gross weight. 6,520 NM range. |
| 450-131-10 | | 28 Feb 51 | 0 | As 450-127-10 with 2 T47A turboprops and 2 J47-GE-23 engines. |
| 450-132-10 | | 28 Feb 51 | 0 | As 450-127-10 with 2 T47A turboprops and 2 65-W-1 engines. |
| 450-133-10 | | 28 Feb 51 | 0 | As 450-127-10 with 2 T40A-8 turboprops and 2 J47-GE-23 engines. |
| 450-134-10 | | 28 Feb 51 | 0 | As 450-127-10 with 2 J57-P-1 and 2 J47-GE-23 engines driving 15' dia. props. 125,000-lb. gross weight. 4,690 NM range. |
| 450-135-10 | | 28 Feb 51 | 0 | As 450-127-10 with 2 J57-P-1 and 2 J47-GE-23 engines driving 15' dia. props. 125,000-lb. gross weight. 5,580 NM range. |
| 450-136-10 | | 28 Feb 51 | 0 | As 450-127-10 with 2 T47C turboprops and 2 J47-GE-23 engines. |
| 450-137-10 | | 13 Mar 51 | 0 | As 450-11-10 with 4 T34-P-6 turboprop and 2 J47-GE-11 engines driving 15' dia. props. 125,000-lb. gross weight. 4,710 NM range. |
| 450-138-10 | | 26 Mar 51 | 0 | As 450-127-10 with 4 Allison 509 and 2 J47-GE-23 engines. 125,000-lb. gross weight. 4,070 NM range. |

| Model | Desig. | Date | Qty | Description |
|---|---|---|---|---|
| 450-139-10 | | 26 Mar 51 | 0 | As 450-127-10 with 6 Allison 509 engines. 125,000-lb. gross weight. 3,940 NM range. |
| 450-140-10 | | 28 Mar 51 | 0 | As 450-11-10 with 2 T34-P-6 turboprop and 2 J47-GE-11 engines driving 15' dia. props. 125,000-lb. gross weight. 5,860 NM range. |
| 450-141-10 | | 30 Mar 51 | 0 | As 450-57-10 with 4 J35-A-23 engines. 125,000-lb. gross weight. |
| 450-142-10 | | 2 Apr 51 | 0 | As 450-127-10 with 2 T47A turboprops and 2 J47-GE-23-11 engines. 15' dia. prop. 125,000-lb. gross weight. |
| 450-143-10 | | | 0 | As 450-127-10 with 4 Rolls-Royce Conway fanjets. |
| 450-144-10 | | 19 Apr 51 | 0 | As 450-127-10 with 4 J57-P-5 engines. 125,000-lb. gross weight. |
| 450-145-10 | | 24 Apr 51 | 0 | As 450-19-10 with 4 Allison 509 engines. 125,000-lb. gross weight. |
| 450-146-10 | | 2 May 51 | 0 | As 450-141-10 with 6 J47-GE-23 water injected engines. 185,000-lb. gross weight. |
| 450-147-10 | | 17 Aug 51 | 0 | As 450-141-10 with 6 J47-GE-23 engines. 125,000-lb. gross weight. |
| 450-148-30 | USN | 20 Nov 51 | 0 | USN aerial minelayer. Powered by 2 T49-WI turboprops and 2 J67-WI engines. 145,000-lb. gross weight. |
| 450-149-30 | USN | 5 Dec 51 | 0 | As 450-148-30 except with 4 J67-W-1 non-afterburning engines. |
| 450-150-30 | USN | 27 Dec 51 | 0 | USN aerial minelayer with 4 J57-P-1 afterburning engines. 145,000-lb. gross weight. 2,400 NM max range with mines. 3,320 NM max endurance for photo-recce. |
| 450-151-31 | | 2 Feb 52 | 0 | Similar to Model 701-238-1 with J57-P-1 afterburning engines. 2,190 sq. ft. wing area. 200,000-lb. gross weight. |
| 450-152-27 | | 25 Feb 52 | 0 | Similar to Model 701-243-1 with 4 J57-P-1 afterburning engines. 2,178 sq. ft. wing area. 180,000-lb. gross weight. |
| 450-153-27 | | 3 Mar 52 | 0 | Similar to Model 701-243-1 with J57-P-1 afterburning engines. 2,100 sq. ft. wing area. 180,000-lb. gross weight. |
| 450-154-32 | | 4 Mar 52 | 0 | Similar to Model 701-243-1 with 4 J57-P-1 afterburning engines. 180,000-lb. gross weight. |
| 450-155-33 | YB-47C | 12 Mar 52 | 0 | Powered by 4 J57-P-1 afterburning engines. 1,570 sq. ft. wing area. Added spoilers. 125,000-lb. gross weight. |
| 450-156-34 | | 29 May 52 | 0 | Similar to Model 701-249-36 with J67-W-1 afterburning engines. 2,190 sq. ft. wing area. 200,000-lb. gross weight. |
| 450-157-27 | B-47B | 23 Sept 53 | 110 | As 450-67-27 with 6 J47-GE-25 engines. 1,428 sq. ft. wing area. 125,000-lb. gross weight. |
| 450-158-36 | RB-47E | 23 Sept 52 | 297 | As 450-11-10 with 6 J47-GE-25 engines. 1,428 sq. ft. wing area. Overall length increased from 107' 1.5" to 109' 6.7". 125,000-lb. gross weight. 3,670 NM combat radius. (Includes the redesignated 52 450-126-29 aircraft.) |
| 450-157-35 | B-47E | 23 Sept 52 | 586 | As 450-157-27 with 6 J47-GE-25 engines. 125,000-lb. gross weight. 3,460 NM combat radius. |
| 450-159-27 | | 10 Oct 52 | 0 | As 450-67-27 except with 2 X-24A afterburning engines inboard and 2 X-24A non-afterburning engines outboard. 122,000-lb. gross weight. |
| 450-160-27 | | 10 Oct 52 | 0 | As 450-159-27 plus a wing chord extension. 185,000-lb. gross weight. |
| 450-161-27 | | 10 Oct 52 | 0 | As 450-160-27 except that takeoff gross weight increased to 230,000 lbs. |
| 450-162-48 | XB-47D | Feb 51 | 1 | As 450-11-10 except with 2 YT49-W-1 turboprops inboard and 2 J47-GE-23 engines outboard driving 15' dia. Curtiss C-86S-A props. 125,000-lb. gross weight. 5,434 NM range. |
| 450-165-49 | XB-47D | Feb 51 | 1 | As 450-162-48 except with 2 YT49-W-1 turboprops inboard and 2 J47-GE-23 engines outboard driving 15' dia. Curtiss C-86S-A props. |
| 450-167-50 | YDB-47E | 6 Jan 53 | 0 | Design objective was to permit the YDB-47E to be used as a prototype carrier for the B-63 RASCAL pilotless parasite bomber, yet retain the capability of being reconverted into a B-47E bomber. |
| 450-157-37 | | 26 May 53 | 0 | As 450-157-35 except for mission differences. Powered by 6 J47-GE-25 engines. |
| 450-163-38 | | 28 May 53 | 0 | To have been powered by J57-P-1W engines. While the max taxi gross weight was to have been 230,000-lb., the design capacity was limited to 221,450-lb. |
| 450-164-38 | | 28 May 53 | 0 | As 450-163-38, but with 6 J65-W engines. Wing had a 33.5% chord extension and the horizontal stabilizer was redesigned to increase the area from 199.5 to 402 sq. ft. While the max taxi gross weight was to have been 230,000-lb., the design capacity was limited to 221,090-lb. |
| 450-166-38 | | 28 May 53 | 0 | As 450-163-38, but with 6 J57 engines. Wing had a 33.5% chord extension and the horizontal stabilizer was redesigned to increase the area from 199.5 to 402 sq. ft. While the max taxi gross weight was to have been 230,000-lb., the design capacity was limited to 221,090-lb. |
| 450-167-39 | | 28 May 53 | 0 | Hose and drogue B-47E tanker with 6 J47-GE-25 engines. |
| 450-168-40 | | 28 May 53 | 0 | As 450-167-39 except stripped for tanker use only. Non-tactical aircraft. |
| 450-169-39 | | 28 May 53 | 0 | As 450-167-39 except stripped for tanker use only. Non-tactical aircraft. Powered by 6 J57-P-1 engines. While the max taxi gross weight was to have been 230,000-lb., the design capacity was limited to 206,460-lb. |
| 450-170-40 | | 28 May 53 | 0 | As 450-167-39 except stripped for tanker use only. Non-tactical aircraft. Powered by 6 J57-P-1 engines. While the max taxi gross weight was to have been 230,000-lb., the design capacity was limited to 205,290-lb. |
| 450-166-41 | | 5 June 53 | 0 | As 450-166-38 except a J57-powered tanker. While the max taxi gross weight was to have been 230,000-lb., the design capacity was limited to 211,230-lb. |
| 450-157-42 | B-47E | 25 June 53 | 0 | As 450-157-35 with 6 J47-GE-25 engines. 200,000-lb. gross weight. |
| 450-157-43 | B-47E | 25 June 53 | 0 | As 450-157-42 except a tactical B-47E bomber, convertible bomber-tanker, and bomber configuration provisions. |
| 450-157-44 | B-47E | 25 June 53 | 0 | As 450-157-42 except a tactical B-47E bomber, convertible bomber-tanker, and tanker configuration provisions. |
| 450-157-45 | | 25 June 53 | 0 | As 450-157-35 except reinforced for 230,000-lb. max taxi weight. Capacity limited to 220,820-lbs. |
| 450-157-46 | | 25 June 53 | 0 | As 450-157-45 heavy bomber, convertible bomber-tanker, and bomber configuration provisions. Capacity and max taxi weights limited to 219,950-lbs. |
| 450-157-47 | | 25 June 53 | 0 | As 450-157-45 heavy bomber, convertible bomber-tanker, and tanker configuration provisions. Capacity and max taxi weights limited to 217,720-lbs. |
| 450-171-51 | RB-47H | 10 Dec 53 | 35 | Similar to 450-157-35 and 450-158-36 with 6 J47-GE-25 or -25A engines. Design gross weight 125,000-lbs. Alternate gross weight 195,160-lbs. with external fuel tanks. With RATO, gross weight increased to 218,546 lbs. |
| 450-172-52 | DB-47E | 27 Sept 54 | 2 | Similar to 450-157-35 with 6 J47-GE-25 or -25A engines. Design began as 450-1676-50. Bell GAM-63 RASCAL launch platform. |
| 450-173-53 | DB-47B | | 30 | Similar to 450-11-10 with 6 J47-GE-25 or -25A engines. Bell GAM-63 RASCAL launch platform. |
| 450-174-54 | DB-47B | | 2 | B-47B s/n 51-2328 and 51-2350 modified to launch up to 4 Radioplane GAM-67 Crossbow missiles. Powered by 6 J47-GE-25 or -25A engines. |
| 450-171-55 | ERB-47H | 20 Feb 56 | 3 | Similar to 450-171-51. Also had AN/ALT-4 pod installed and 1 less Raven. |

# Appendix E

# *B-47 ACCIDENT RATES*

The data displayed in this table illustrates the various accident rates for the B-47 over its entire service life by calendar year (CY). It may be easily seen that there was an initial learning curve during which there were a significant number of accidents. With the advent of the toss bombing maneuver for weapon delivery came another upsurge in losses. Six of the 32 Class A accidents were attributed to wing failures, resulting in Project MILK BOTTLE. The increase in both Class A and B accidents during 1962 were a result of the Cuban Missile Crisis when three RB-47s were lost, claiming the lives of all 12 crewmembers.

| Year | Class A Accidents # | Rate | Class B Accidents # | Rate | Destroyed Aircraft | Destroy Rate | Fatal Accidents Pilot | All | Flight Hours |
|---|---|---|---|---|---|---|---|---|---|
| CY50 | 0 | 0.00 | 0 | 0.00 | 0 | 0.00 | N/R | 0 | 70 |
| CY51 | 8 | 217.21 | 2 | 54.30 | 2 | 54.30 | N/R | 3 | 3,683 |
| CY52 | 16 | 80.98 | 8 | 40.49 | 5 | 25.31 | N/R | 13 | 19,758 |
| CY53 | 29 | 27.43 | 20 | 18.92 | 9 | 8.51 | N/R | 18 | 105,734 |
| CY54 | 30 | 9.58 | 20 | 6.39 | 13 | 4.15 | N/R | 27 | 313,012 |
| CY55 | 32 | 7.03 | 14 | 3.08 | 21 | 4.61 | N/R | 42 | 455,070 |
| CY56 | 25 | 4.40 | 13 | 2.29 | 22 | 3.88 | N/R | 59 | 567,543 |
| CY57 | 28 | 4.48 | 7 | 1.20 | 24 | 4.11 | 31 | 63 | 583,718 |
| CY58 | 32 | 5.56 | 1 | 0.18 | 25 | 4.42 | 38 | 58 | 565,313 |
| CY59 | 24 | 15.97 | 1 | 0.67 | 22 | 14.64 | 30 | 45 | 150,238 |
| CY60 | 14 | 11.00 | 0 | 0.00 | 12 | 9.51 | 12 | 23 | 126,159 |
| CY61 | 13 | 13.21 | 0 | 0.00 | 13 | 13.21 | 19 | 30 | 98,406 |
| CY62 | 15 | 17.59 | 12 | 14.07 | 14 | 16.412 | 19 | 38 | 85,290 |
| CY63 | 9 | 2.86 | 8 | 2.54 | 9 | 2.86 | 9 | 14 | 314,771 |
| CY64 | 9 | 3.59 | 2 | 0.80 | 8 | 3.19 | 10 | 22 | 251,015 |
| CY65 | 3 | 9.96 | 1 | 3.32 | 3 | 11.30 | 5 | 8 | 30,132 |
| CY66 | 1 | 11.30 | 1 | 11.30 | 1 | 0.00 | 1 | 1 | 8,851 |
| CY67 | 0 | 0.00 | 1 | 5.30 | 0 | 0.00 | 0 | 0 | 18,884 |
| CY68 | 0 | 0.00 | 0 | 0.00 | 0 | 0.00 | 0 | 0 | 16,315 |
| CY69 | 0 | 0.00 | 0 | 0.00 | 0 | 0.00 | 0 | 0 | 11,168 |
| CY70 | 0 | 0.00 | 0 | 0.00 | 0 | 0.00 | 0 | 0 | 62 |
| CY71 | 0 | 0.00 | 0 | 0.00 | 0 | 0.00 | 0 | 0 | 65 |
| CY72 | 0 | 0.00 | 0 | 0.00 | 0 | 0.00 | 0 | 0 | 43 |
| CY73 | 0 | 0.00 | 0 | 0.00 | 0 | 0.00 | 0 | 0 | 88 |
| CY74 | 0 | 0.00 | 0 | 0.00 | 0 | 0.00 | 0 | 0 | 106 |
| CY75 | 0 | 0.00 | 0 | 0.00 | 0 | 0.00 | 0 | 0 | 65 |
| CY76 | 0 | 0.00 | 0 | 0.00 | 0 | 0.00 | 0 | 0 | 26 |
| Lifetime | 288 | 7.73 | 111 | 2.98 | 203 | 5.45 | 174 | 464 | 3,725,585 |

# INDEX

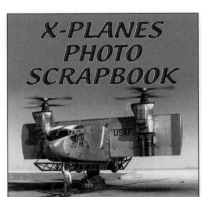
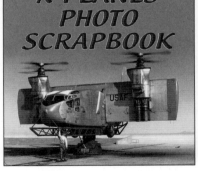